The Films of

Hopalong Cassidy

by

Francis M. Nevins, Jr.

The World of Yesterday
Waynesville, North Carolina
1988

ISBN : 0-936505-09-5

Library of Congress Catalog Card Number: 88-40500

Published by
The World of Yesterday
Route 3, Box 263-H
Waynesville, NC 28786
(704) 648-5647

First Printing 1988 9 8 7 6 5 4 3

Printed and Manufactured in the United States of America

Contents

A publicity photo of Harry Sherman and William Boyd used for **Border Patrol** (1943, United Artists).

For Spencer Bennet (1893-1987),
who wasn't a part of the Hoppy saga.
And for Rand Brooks,
who was.
And for Boyd Magers,
who helped more than anyone.

William Boyd as Hopalong Cassidy and Jimmy Ellison as Johnny Nelson relax on location for **The Eagle's Brood** (1935, Paramount).

Introduction

Hopalong Cassidy.

If you were interested in Westerns, either in print or on film, at any time from about 1905 till the middle 1950s, that name meant something. Between the early years of the century and the mid-1930s it meant the red-thatched, tobacco-spitting, limping Arthurian knight who was the main character in a long interconnected series of novels and short stories. From 1935 through the late Forties it meant the silver-haired, black-garbed hero of the saddle who galloped across the nation's movie screens on his white horse Topper. From 1949 until the middle-to-late Fifties it meant the premier cowboy star of the dawn years of television. Since then the name has been almost completely forgotten.

Unfairly forgotten too. For the best of the Hopalong Cassidy movies are among the finest series Westerns ever made. When seen complete and uncut, in good prints on a decent-sized screen, they're as compulsively watchable as they were forty to fifty years ago. But the chances that they'll ever be seen again by sizable audiences the way they were meant to be seen are slim to nil. This book celebrates and remembers (though not uncritically) a part of our past which has gone and will never return.

I came along too late to see the Hoppy pictures in theaters but in time to catch all of them---not once but over and over again---on the 12 1/2-inch TV set my parents bought in the early Fifties. More than twenty years later, seeing some of these pictures again at various Western film fairs, I found that the good ones were even better than I had remembered them. During the past dozen years I've met and chatted with several of the actors and actresses from the series---Jimmy Ellison, Russell Hayden, Jimmy Rogers, Victor Jory, Louise Currie, Pierce Lyden and Edgar Buchanan among others---and, by one of those wild coincidences that are common in real life but taboo in fiction, I wound up being related by marriage to Rand Brooks, the last man to portray Hoppy's young sidekick. Although I never met William Boyd, the unforgettable star of the series, or Harry Sherman, the producer of the pictures during their prime years, I've been privileged to meet Boyd's widow and Sherman's daughter. And, not long before his death, I had an all too short telephone conversation with the finest and most prolific of the directors who worked on the series, Lesley Selander. All of these men and women helped me put this book together, but most of their contributions were indirect: their reminiscences gave me a feel for what working on those pictures must have been like. The vast bulk of what I have to say about the films comes simply from having watched them.

Some of Hoppy's screen adventures I have no desire to see again. But the best of them I can still watch with pleasure over and over just as I did in my boyhood on that 12 1/2-inch set. If this book does what I set out for it to do, you'll want to see them again too.

A publicity still of Jimmy Ellison used for **Heart of the West** (1936, Paramount).

Chapter One

The saga of Hopalong Cassidy began in the waking dreams of a meek and scholarly-looking young man, a Brooklyn marriage-license clerk who visualized a frontier world he had never seen and then put words to his imaginings at the end of each day's drudgery. At the center of that vast domain in the young man's mind was a Texas ranch he called the Bar-20, and at the center of the Bar-20 was Hopalong Cassidy.

The only child of German-American parents, Clarence Edward Mulford was born on February 3, 1883 in Streator, Illinois, a town 98 miles southwest of Chicago. Mulford's father designed and manufactured low pressure boilers for hot-water heating plants, and was operating his own steam heater factory in Streator at the time of Clarence's birth. Business kept the family on the move throughout the boy's childhood, first to Galva, Illinois, then to Chicago, then southwest to St. Louis, then back to Streator where Clarence completed his third year of high school. He was a quiet introverted boy who kept his desk so crowded with five-cent Wild West paperbacks that there was scarcely room for anything else. Every Sunday afternoon he'd visit his grandparents' home just outside of Streator, borrow one of their bound volumes of Harper's Weekly and retire to the barn to read all the cowboy tales in the magazine.

In 1899 the Mulfords made their last move as a family, to Utica, New York where Clarence's father obtained a job with the International Heater Company which he kept until his death in 1910. By this time Clarence was sixteen, a solitary youth whose main pleasures in life were reading and working out with a punching bag. After graduating from Utica Academy in 1900, young Mulford left the family home and moved to Brooklyn. He quickly found a job writing technical articles for an engineering magazine, but in his off hours he began first to imagine and then to put on paper a universe all his own which he much preferred to the teeming streets of New York. Between April of 1904 and June of 1905 he wrote the first seven short stories about the men of the Bar-20, and they were published in Caspar Whitney's Outing Magazine between December 1905 and December 1906, many with illustrations by N.C. Wyeth, the father of the great American artist Andrew Wyeth.

Mulford had no taste for the insecurity of self-employed life. Even though his first stories sold almost at once, he needed a regular job and a guaranteed paycheck. In 1906 he took and scored well in the New York civil service examination, and by late 1907 he was a marriage license clerk in Brooklyn, earning $1500 a year. He hung onto that or another place on the public payroll for almost twenty years, using his nights, weekends and vacation time during those two decades to write the Bar-20 novels and stories that made him famous.

Mulford's writing style was a somewhat vivid but still rather stiff and bureaucratic Victorian English. His plots are almost never unified but sprawl every-which-way over the terrain. His skills at drawing character and relationship were primitive, especially when a situation involved a woman. His notions of cowboy and ethnic dialect grate on the nerves. But in grasp of detail and breadth of vision he was one of the most remarkable Western novelists ever.

The key to his grasp of detail was research, not on the ground but in books. Early in his literary career he began to assemble a huge library of materials on the history and development of the West, from Manuel Liza's expedition up the Missouri River to the death of the great cattle trails. He kept three secondhand book dealers supplying him with histories and military reports and maps and pioneers' diaries and would read them for hours at a time. Then he cross-indexed all this material in a system of handwritten 4x6 file cards that at their peak filled 34 drawers, probably the largest organized collection of data ever put together about the West. The system consisted of

William Boyd in silent film days was a big star but his career declined until Hopalong Cassidy made him an even bigger star.

about two dozen major headings---The Santa Fe Trail, The Oregon Trail, Western Towns, The Cattle Trade, Firearms, Military Posts, Indians--- and each of these was broken down into major categories and narrower subcategories. Thanks to these more than 17,000 file cards, Mulford was able to describe all the events in the background of his books, the ranch life and cattle drives and poker games and trail lore and firearms details, with meticulous accuracy even though he had never been west of the Mississippi in his life.

Like thousands of intelligent young men and women in the late nineteenth century, Mulford was profoundly affected by Darwin's theory of evolution through natural selection, and found the Darwinian vision of nature as a vast and violent panorama hopelessly at odds with traditional Christian teaching. However intense the battle of ideas and values may have been, naturalism won an early victory, and for the rest of his life Mulford considered himself a pagan and an unbeliever. His youthful obsession with muscle-building may have been rooted in a Darwinian desire to make himself a stronger animal, more fit for the struggle of living. And as a writer he found ways to integrate his views on philosophy and religion into the fabric of his fiction.

It was Darwin, and the social Darwinian thinkers like Herbert Spencer, and the documents of nineteenth-century paganism like the Fitzgerald translation of Omar Khayyam, that shaped Mulford's vision of the Western hero. Although the background and the interstitial events of his novels come from history, the people of this world are not at all like the workaday cowboys who actually lived in the West. Their ancestors are the brawling, larger-than-life heroes of the Greek epics and the Arthurian legends and Dumas. Their spiritual home, the Bar-20---a place so real to Mulford that he drew a detailed map of it which he kept among his most prized posses- sions---is a sort of Camelot West, an idealized government-that-governs-least, the focus of free men's loyalty to the death. Its men are good

10

SHERMAN S. KRELLBERG *Presents*
CLARENCE E. MULFORD'S

"*Hopalong* CASSIDY ENTERS"

WITH WILLIAM BOYD · JIMMY ELLISON
GEORGE "*Gabby*" HAYES · PAULA STONE
A GOODWILL PICTURE

A lobby card for the reissue of the first Hopalong Cassidy film.

pagans one and all, uncorrupted by formal religion but imbued with natural piety, invested with the qualities of Achilles and Lancelot and d'Artagnan, standing together in good times and bad, one for all and all for one, through days of backbreaking labor in burning sun and seething storm, through hours of roughhousing and practical jokes and the exchange of elaborate insults. Like the epic heroes from whom they descend, they have an incredible capacity for suffering multiple wounds in battle, and ignoring them to fight on. They are wild, boyish, undisciplined, full of sass and vinegar, Nature's Noblemen to the core. They make the reader want to be among them, playing squire to these knights of the frontier.

Besides the accuracy of his backgrounds and the wild energy of his community of protagonists, Mulford offers the crowning gift of scope. His fictional universe is a vast saga of more than two dozen interlocking books, written over a third of a century, in which the main characters go adventuring, marry, procreate, grow old and see their

natural or symbolic children enter the saga as adults and have their own adventures; in which a bit player in an early exploit can become a key figure fifteen or twenty years later and fade back into a minor role ten years after that; in which the ambience of the West evolves from the stink of cattle and horses and unwashed men in squalid little trail towns to the comfort of clean beds in hotels where one can order fine meals and whiskeys. The saga of the Bar-20 is a bit like Galsworthy's Forsyte Saga played out in a less polite and far more violent society. But if the reader cares for none of these finer points and craves nothing but action, he'll find that at his best Mulford was one of the best action-scene writers that ever turned out a Western.

By 1926 Mulford had published seventeen books of fiction, dozens of short stories and countless nonfiction pieces about the West. He was making well over $10,000 a year from his writing, plus an additional $2,000 from the civil service job which he'd clung to since 1906. That

11

William Boyd as Hopalong Cassidy points to evidence as Jimmy Ellison as Johnny Nelson listens in this scene from **Hop-A-Long Cassidy** (1935, Paramount).

year, he and his wife Eva decided to uproot themselves from the noise and congestion of Brooklyn and make a permanent move to Fryeburg, a southwestern Maine village which they had visited on fishing vacations and had come to love. From then on, Mulford lived on his literary income alone.

As a Western writer he probably ranked third in the nation, somewhere behind Zane Grey and Max Brand but well ahead of the pack. Readers of outdoor fiction loved his books, but the people in Hollywood who made Western movies almost unanimously passed him by. Only two silent films were ever adapted from Mulford properties: **The Orphan** (Fox, 1920), starring Dustin Farnum and based on the 1908 novel of the same name which had no connection at all with the Bar-20 saga, and **The Deadwood Coach** (Fox, 1925), starring Tom Mix, a streamlined-for-action remake of the earlier picture. Mulford didn't care for either movie, and no one in Hollywood seemed to care for Mulford's Bar-20 novels.

Until the early 1930s when an imaginative independent producer came along who didn't care for Mulford's books either but did see in them all sorts of cinimatic possibilites.

Mulford was the originator of Hopalong Cassidy, but the man ultimately responsible for Hoppy's transformation into a screen hero, a household name and the role model for youthful millions was a tall, prematurely white-haired, scholarly-looking Jewish entrepreneur who loved the legend of the American West as Mulford loved what he took to be the reality. Harry Sherman was born in Boston on November 5, 1882 and gravitated into the movie business early in the twentieth century, beginning as a theater operator in Minneapolis. It was as a distributor however that he brought off his first coup. The great director D.W. Griffith desperately needed additional money to complete his epic of the post-Civil War South, **The Birth of a Nation** (1915), and Sherman put up $100,000 in return for several

12

William Boyd and Jimmy Ellison have the **bad guys** covered in this scene from **Hop-A-Long Cassidy** (1935, Paramount). That is Ted Adams on the floor.

years' worth of exclusive distribution rights to the film in Minnesota, North and South Dakota, and thirteen other states west of the Mississippi.

In 1916 Sherman moved to Hollywood and gradually drifted from the distribution end of the business into production. It was in this capacity that he worked on **The Light of Western Stars** (Sherman-United, 1918), directed by Charles Swickard and starring Dustin Farnum, the earliest of the four movies more or less based on Zane Grey's 1914 novel of the same name. Sherman had nothing to do with the second version (Paramount, 1925), directed by action specialist William K. Howard and starring Jack Holt, nor with the early talkie remake (Paramount, 1930), which starred Richard Arlen, was co-directed by Otto Brower and Edwin H. Knopf, and recycled several of the big action sequences from the 1925 version so as to cut costs. As we'll see, however, Sherman's company was

responsible for the fourth and final adaptation, released in 1940, when he had become the premier independent Western producer in the business.

In 1930 Sherman and fellow entrepreneur Jack D. Trop (1901-) formed their own small studio, Majestic Pictures, with Sherman as president and Trop as executive vice-president. Their first venture was **Today** (Majestic, 1930), directed by low-budget workhorse William Nigh from a screenplay by Seton I. Miller based on a stage play well known in the Yiddish theatre. The radically de-ethnicized film version, starring Conrad Nagel and Catherine Dale Owen, was a garish melodrama of less than blockbuster dimensions. The company's only stab at making Westerns came in 1932-33 with a six-picture series starring one of the most ridiculous-looking cowboys ever to face a camera, Jack Hoxie. Majestic soon folded but Sherman and Trop continued separately in the picture business and talked

13

William Boyd as Hoppy is greeted by George Hayes as Uncle Ben in this scene from **Hop-A-Long Cassidy** (1935, Paramount).

every so often about working together again.

In the late summer or early fall of 1934, Trop and a promoter named Herman Garfield invited Sherman to a meeting at Trop's office in the Paramount Building. Paramount, it seems, was interested in contracting with Trop and Garfield to produce independently a series of six Westerns for the studio to release, and the two men remembered Sherman's **Light of Western Stars** experience and asked him to join them. There were several discussions about the subject matter of the proposed half-dozen films. Paramount wanted them to do pictures based on the *Death Valley Days* radio series, which had been broadcast on the NBC Blue Network since 1930. Sherman at first was more interested in adapting for the screen Western novelist W.C. Tuttle's tales of cowboy adventurer Hashknife Hartley. Eventually they agreed that they would produce a half-dozen cinematic exploits of Mulford's famous character Hopalong Cassidy.

Harry Sherman's daughter Teddi was a very young child in the early 1930s but grew up to become a writer of Western scripts for movies and television. According to the account which Teddi gave to Jon Tuska, who retold it in his book *The Filming of the West* (1976), Sherman traveled east by transcontinental train and negotiated a rights contract with Mulford in a Brooklyn saloon. Mulford sported puttees, plus-fours and a rakish cap during the bargaining. Lacking ready cash, Sherman offered Mulford no "up front" money but a flat 5% of the gross receipts on whatever Mulford-based films he might produce. When Mulford agreed, the two drew up a contract on a piece of toilet paper from the saloon men's room. Sherman lost the paper on the train ride back to California. "I probably blew my nose in it," he guessed. So runs the Teddi-Tuska version of events, which for all its vividness has scarcely a word of truth in it. In 1934 Mulford was unshakably ensconced in Fryeburg and would not have left Maine for any reason on earth. After the problems over the two Fox Studios movies based

Jimmy Ellison acts unhappy with the greeting William Boyd is getting from George Hayes and Frank McGlynn, Jr. in this scene from **Hop-A-Long Cassidy** (1935, Paramount).

on *The Orphan* it's unlikely that he would have negotiated personally with a Hollywood producer, and certainly Sherman was too sharp a business-man to write a crucially important contract on a scrap of toilet paper. The documents signed by the parties, and the survivors' testimony in legal proceedings years later, combine to tell a story that is less dramatic but far more plausible.

Sherman, Garfield and Trop were frightened that Paramount might buy the necessary rights directly from Mulford if word leaked out about their plan to produce Hopalong Cassidy movies. To prevent that from happening, the three partners subtly misled Paramount into believing they were still planning a **Death Valley Days** series, while in fact they went ahead negotiating an option for movie rights to the works of Mulford. After some preliminary soundings by long-distance telephone, around September of 1934 Sherman and Trop went to New York and met with Daniel Nye of Doubleday Doran. Although Mulford's publica-tion contracts with Doubleday made it clear that

the author retained all movie rights to his novels, Nye was acting on a commission basis as Mulford's agent. The Sherman-Trop proposition satisfied Nye provided the producers paid $2500 for the rights to each story they filmed. Ultimately it was agreed that Sherman and his partners would pay $250 on the signing of the option contract, $2250 when the first Cassidy movie went into production, and $2500 for each subsequent picture.

The contract, drafted by Doubleday lawyers and dated February 27, 1935, was between Double-day, acting as Mulford's agent, and Prudential Studios Corporation, an entity the three partners had recently formed for the purpose of producing the Cassidy films. Prudential was granted an option, vis-a-vis 21 specified Mulford books, to "acquire...all motion picture rights and the rights to produce, transmit, reproduce, distribute, exhibit and exploit [the movies made under the option] in any manner or by any method or device (except as hereinafter specified) now or hereafter known or

15

George Hayes as Uncle Ben and Frank McGlynn, Jr. as Red Connors greet Hoppy in this scene from **Hop-A-Long Cassidy** (1935, Paramount).

used...." A later paragraph provided that: "Prudential may (within the limits of this agreement) make, exhibit and market everywhere, motion pictures...based upon or adopted from any of the above books in respect to which Prudential has exercised its option using any methods or devices for such purpose which are now or hereafter known or used." The only limitations on Prudential's rights were encompassed in the following two sentences:

"All rights of production and use upon the spoken stage with living actors appearing and speaking in person in the actual and immediate presence of the audience are specifically reserved to Mr. Mulford.

All television, broadcasting and radio rights are specifically reserved to Mr. Mulford."

The reason behind these reservations is that Daniel Nye wasn't terribly happy with the amount of money Sherman and his partners were paying Mulford and wanted to make sure that the author kept control over something. The unanswered question was: *over what?* In what works were all "television...rights" reserved to Mulford? In light of the broad language in the granting clauses of the contract, most readers would interpret the reservation to mean simply that Mulford kept the right to license "live" TV dramas based on his stories, analogously with his right under the language of the first indented sentence to license live stage dramas. But if that was what the parties agreed in 1935, the words they chose to express themselves were hideously inept and in fact constituted a time bomb ticking away in a file cabinet. And in the late 1940s, when the fortunes to be made from television exhibition of old movies dominated the minds of media people, Mulford and Doubleday, as we shall see, came up with a reading of the TV reservation clause which would keep businessmen, lawyers and judges yapping at each other for decades.

When everyone including Mulford up in Fryeburg had signed the option contract, Sherman and his partners entered into a financing arrange-

16

William Boyd as Hopalong Cassidy seems upset about the reward poster in his hand in this scene from **The Eagle's Brood** (1935, Paramount).

ment for the first six Cassidys with Western Pictures Corporation, an entity consisting of Jack Curtis, William Fisk and tire manufacturer Nicholas Ludington. The contract between Prudential and Western was dated June 5, 1935 and called for the sum of $85,000 to finance the initial Cassidy picture. It was only after this agreement had been signed that Sherman and his partners went back to Paramount and revealed that they were going to make not a *Death Valley Days* series but a group of Cassidy adventures. Paramount consented to release the first six films, and the stage was set for pre-production work to begin.

A publicity photo of Jimmy Ellison used for **Hop-A-Long Cassidy** (1935, Paramount).

Chapter Two

Once the rights deal with Mulford was made, Harry Sherman began putting together the team that would make Hopalong Cassidy pictures for him. He had worked out a personal formula for Westerns and was looking for writers, directors and actors who had roots in silent films but, like Sherman himself, with minimal experience in Western talkies---in other words, people who were unlikely to have too many fixed ideas of their own about how such pictures should be made. He wound up with a gang of maverick individualists anyway, but that's another story.

To direct the first season's output of six films he picked Howard Bretherton (1896-1969), who for the past ten years had been a contract director at Warner Brothers, specializing in low-budget melodrama. As chief screenwriters he hired two people who had never done a script for a talking picture: Doris Schroeder, credited with 28 silent scenarios (only two of them Westerns), and Harrison Jacobs, author of several Art Acord and Jack Hoxie quickies for Universal in the 1920s. As film editor Sherman chose Edward Schroeder, whose relation to Doris Schroeder is unknown but who was likewise a newcomer to talking Westerns. When it came to cinematography, however, Sherman broke his own rule and brought in the veteran Archie Stout, who had photographed most of the John Wayne B Westerns at Monogram during the past two seasons and would later work on big-budget Wayne films like John Ford's **Fort Apache** (1948).

In choosing actors Sherman returned to the new-faces approach. Nondescript utility player Frank McGlynn Jr. was cast as Bar 20 ranch hand Red Connors. That quintessential menace of cliff-hanger serials, Charles Middleton, who would become famous as the Emperor Ming in Universal's three Flash Gordon chapterplays later in the 1930s, was picked for the part of the Bar 20's owner, Buck Peters. A brash and fresh-faced young beginner, James Ellison (1910-   ), landed the role of Cassidy's sidekick Johnny Nelson, whom Sherman and his collaborators transformed from a mature and independent friend, as Mulford had created the character, into a naive and hot-tempered braggart who was constantly getting himself and Cassidy into trouble. Finally, as if he felt a need to have one seasoned talking-picture Westerner in front of the cameras to match Archie Stout's experience behind them, Sherman offered a series contract without any continuing character part to George Hayes (1885-1969). Born in Wellsville, New York on May 7, 1885, Hayes had played in burlesque and vaudeville since his teens, and migrated to Hollywood and a film acting career near the end of the silent era. He had appeared in dozens of low-budget Westerns in the early Thirties, including most of the Wayne pictures at Monogram, but had not yet earned his peculiar immortality and was not yet known as Gabby.

The most important casting decision Sherman had to make was on the role of Hopalong Cassidy himself. Apparently his first choice was comic actor James Gleason, who, according to some in Sherman's entourage, looked like the Cassidy of Mulford's novels. But when Gleason learned that the Cassidy series was going to be released by Paramount and not one of the independents, he demanded a higher salary than Sherman was willing to pay. According to some sources, Sherman then approached David Niven, but the idea of that suave and dapper Scotsman as Hoppy is so ridiculous that surely he would have mentioned the incident in one of his autobiographical books if he'd really been offered the part. (In a 1958 interview with the Saturday Evening Post, Niven did claim to have played unbilled bits in some of the early Cassidys.) In any event, Sherman finally settled on a mature-looking actor in his late thirties, with fifteen years of Hollywood experience and a career that seemed to have gone down the tubes.

William Lawrence Boyd was born in Cambridge, Ohio on June 5, 1898, one of five

Charles Middleton played Buck Peters instead of his usual villainous role, here with William Boyd in a scene from **Hop-A-Long Cassidy** (1935, Paramount).

children of a laborer. When he was quite young his family moved to Oklahoma, but both of his parents died when he was in his teens, and he had to quit the Tulsa school where he was enrolled and scrounge for work as a surveyor and tool dresser in the oil fields. When the United States entered World War I he was rejected for military service because of a problem with his heart. He moved to Arizona, got a job managing a hotel, met a young heiress named Ruth Miller and before long was married to her. They had a son but the marriage quickly fell apart. Boyd headed west to California, worked at a variety of jobs (including night watchman and PX manager), and began hunting for movie parts, hoping that his cool blue eyes and silver-blond hair were just what directors were looking for. His luck was good, for the flamboyant Cecil B. DeMille hired him as an extra in his sex comedy **Why Change Your Wife?** (1920). DeMille saw great potential in Boyd and gave him increasingly meatier parts in pictures like **The Road to Yesterday** (1925), which starred

Joseph Schildkraut and Jetta Goudal. Boyd starred in DeMille's **The Volga Boatman** (1926) and married the picture's female lead, Elinor Fair, who went on to play opposite Boyd in **Jim the Conqueror** (1926) and **The Yankee Clipper** (1927). Boyd's first and only role in a silent Western was as star of **The Last Frontier** (1926). DeMille cast him as Simon of Cyrene in the Biblical spectacle **King of Kings** (1927), Lewis Milestone gave him the lead in **Two Arabian Knights** (1927), and the great D.W. Griffith starred him with Lupe Velez in his last silent feature, **Lady of the Pavements** (1929). That same year, Boyd and Elinor Fair were divorced.

Most of Boyd's work in the late Twenties and early Thirties was for Pathé Studios, where he starred in action flicks like **The Night Flyer** (1928), **The Cop** (1928), **The Leatherneck** (1929), **The Flying Fool** (1929), **Officer O'Brien** (1930), and **His First Command** (1930). Dorothy Sebastian, the leading lady in the

Jimmy Ellison and William Boyd along with the Bar 20 hands fight the outlaws in this scene from **Hop-A-Long Cassidy** (1935, Paramount).

last of these films, became Boyd's next wife. His only experience in a talking Western before meeting Harry Sherman was as the star of RKO-Pathé's **The Painted Desert** (1931), in which the chief bad guy was played by a young beginner named Clark Gable. But Boyd's career took a nosedive a year or two later when several newspapers mistakenly published photographs of him in connection with a liquor-and-gambling scandal involving another actor who happened to be named William Boyd. By early 1935 the only studios that would hire him were bottom-of-the-barrel independents like Invincible and Winchester that starred him in super-el-cheapo fodder like **Port of Lost Dreams** (1934).

At this point Boyd was still married to Dorothy Sebastian (they were divorced in 1936) and living mainly on her earnings in pictures. Like many men who had prospered during Prohibition, he had developed a serious drinking problem. According to Jon Tuska's <u>The Filming of the West</u>, Harry Sherman tried to phone Boyd at Sebastian's beach house, was told by her 12-year-old daughter that Boyd wasn't available at the moment, and made an appointment to come out and see the child's stepfather about a part in a movie. Sebastian and her daughter then went out on the beach where Boyd was sleeping off a two-day drunk and sobered him up with two pots of black coffee.

Apparently Boyd made a strong impression on the producer. Sherman became convinced that this man of almost forty, with light blond hair that photographed as white, with piercing blue eyes and minimal athletic ability and (despite having starred in two Westerns) a deathly fear of horses, would be a sensation as Hopalong Cassidy. As Sherman conceived the part, Cassidy would need to project both great tenderness and great strength, and he thought Boyd could do the job. He offered the actor $30,000 for starring in the first six Cassidy pictures, but made it a condition of the deal that Boyd had to quit drinking for as long as he was in the series. Boyd agreed, and kept his

21

William Boyd vows vengeance at the death of George Hayes in this scene from **Hop-A-Long Cassidy** (1935, Paramount).

word: for the next nine years, throughout the period he worked for Sherman, he drank nothing stronger than white wine spritzers. In time he even got to like horses, a little.

Sherman's notion of a Western was worlds apart from Clarence Mulford's. He considered Mulford an extremely old-fashioned and pedestrian writer and believed that the Hopalong Cassidy novels were impossible to film without radical restructuring of plot, characterization, action and event. What he wanted from Mulford and paid to obtain were the exploitation value of the author's name and the names of his famous characters, and an occasional idea or incident that might be adaptable to the screen. Everything else was to be supplied by Sherman himself, his directors, screenwriters and actors. The early Cassidy movies share a common structure that was Sherman's creation. They begin very slowly, build deliberately and with action subordinated to story and characterization, until about ten minutes from the end when all hell breaks loose, riders charge across the screen,

guns bark, stuntmen tumble in the dust, and the sound track comes alive with a reorchestrated version of the Dance of the Furies from Christoph Willibald Gluck's Orfeo ed Eurydice to match the sudden visual excitement of pit shots and running inserts. It's been suggested that Sherman's concept of a Western climax was inspired by the stunning ride of the Ku Klux Klan in the Griffith **Birth of a Nation** for which Sherman had served as a regional distributor back in the Nineteen Teens.

Sherman put his personal stamp not only on the structure of the first Cassidy films but on the portrayal of their hero. As far back as Broncho Billy Anderson and William S. Hart, and throughout the films of the great screen cowboys of the Twenties and Thirties---Tom Mix, Buck Jones, Hoot Gibson, Ken Maynard, Tim McCoy, Bob Steele and John Wayne---the Western star had been a man alone. Sherman's innovation was to make the star part of a trio, in which each member would have a clearly defined personality and

Wiliam Boyd and Jimmy Ellison finally join forces to fight the villains in this ending scene from **Hop-A-Long Cassidy** (1935, Paramount).

function: the father or older brother figure, the callow young hothead-protegé, and the grizzled old comic. Where the men of Mulford's Bar-20 were literally incapable of serious internal conflict, much of the storyline in the early Cassidy films stemmed precisely from such disputes, particularly between Boyd's Cassidy and Ellison's brash and mercurial Johnny Nelson. It was a masterful device, a neat way of adding character conflict to the elements of the traditional action Western, and an approach that was to prove hugely influential as other studios put out their own "trio Western" series like The Three Mesquiteers, The Range Busters and The Rough Riders in competition with the Cassidy pictures.

As distinctive as the Cassidy films' structure and hero was the hero's costume. Accounts differ as to who first thought of outfitting Boyd in hat, shirt and trousers of such a dark shade of blue that they photographed as black and strikingly set off Boyd's pale hair and white stallion. Apparently it wasn't Sherman, who hated the costume and

ridiculed it as a monkey suit but didn't dare to get rid of it once the pictures started to make money. We can be sure that Mulford with his vast knowledge of workaday cowhand garb was not amused at the way Cassidy looked on screen, and that the unforgettable visual magnificence of Boyd's image wouldn't have meant a damn to the authenticity-fixated Fryeburger.

The first film in the series was **Hop-A-Long Cassidy** (1935), later retitled **Hopalong Cassidy Enters**, which was based on Mulford's 1910 novel *Hopalong Cassidy* at least to a certain extent. Book and film follow the same general storyline in which Shaw and his rustlers, headquartered on impregnable Thunder Mesa, form an alliance with a crooked employee of the H 2 ranch for the purpose of fomenting a range war between Jim Meeker's H 2 and the Bar 20 as a screen for the gang's cattle stealing activities under cover of their own brand the HQQ. For obvious reasons the film-makers eliminated Mulford's version of the traitor, the cowardly greaser Antonio, and

23

Handsome Jimmy Ellison played the young callow Johnny Nelson to perfection is shown here in a publicity still for **Hop-A-Long Cassidy** (1935, Paramount).

substituted a corrupt Anglo, Pecos Jack Anthony, played hissably by Kenneth Thomson. Also dropped were literally dozens of the characters in Mulford's sprawling novel, and most of those retained were altered out of all semblance to their originals. For example Salem, the H 2 cook, described by Mulford as a former New England whalingman who might have sailed on the Pequod with Captain Ahab, was turned into the worst sort of hatchet-waving gibberish-spouting Chinaman stereotype and portrayed by Willie Fung (who was the meal caterer for the company while on location) but was still given the now ludicrously unsuitable name Salem!

The film starts slowly with scenes of ranch life and insult humor, sanitized of course but still somewhat in the Mulford vein. But while it was Cassidy himself who fell in love with Mary Meeker in the book, the Romeo function in the movie is assigned to young Johnny Nelson (Jimmy Ellison), who meets Mary (Paula Stone) along the trail while he's herding some H 2 cattle

off Bar 20 range and instantly begins to fall for her. Unfortunately she's accompanied by H 2 foreman Pecos Jack Anthony (Kenneth Thomson), who shoots Johnny's horse and is about to do likewise to its rider when the gun is skillfully shot out of his hand. Into the scene rides Bill Cassidy (William Boyd), a former Bar 20 hand returning after a long absence. (In the book of course he never left the ranch at all.) The scene ends with glares of hatred all around as Cassidy and Johnny ride double back to the ranch house.

Cassidy is warmly welcomed home by his old friends Buck Peters (Charles Middleton), Red Connors (Frank McGlynn Jr.) and the warm-heartedly cantankerous Uncle Ben (George Hayes). Johnny, who has heard of Cassidy's reputation but never before met the man, is determined in his hotheaded way to prove himself Cassidy's equal---an attitude unthinkable in a Mulford book but employed as a major storyline in this and several other films in the series.

Meanwhile Pecos Jack conspires with the

George Hayes chides young Jimmy Ellison in this scene from **Hop-A-Long Cassidy** (1935, Paramount).

Thunder Mesa rustlers to take advantage of the Bar 20-H 2 dispute by stealing cattle from both ranches and letting each blame the other. The rustling and shooting incidents push the spreads closer to range war but this in no way dampens Johnny's ardor for Mary Meeker. One night Johnny slips away from the Bar 20 and crashes a party at the H 2, not just to see Mary but to prove his manhood to Cassidy. Luckily Cassidy and Red follow him and, after a fight breaks out between Johnny and Pecos Jack, save the young fool from being lynched.

During the film's first week of production Boyd had fallen off his white stallion and broken a leg. For several days Howard Bretherton had to film the picture around its star, and when Boyd returned to work he was walking with a pronounced limp. Bretherton and Doris Schroeder turned accident into advantage by inserting a new scene in which Cassidy is shot in the leg while rescuing Johnny from the H 2. Afterwards, asked whether he can walk on the injured leg, Cassidy

replies: "I can hop along with the best of them," and limps for the rest of the picture in order to justify his famous nickname. The game leg of Mulford's Cassidy had had nothing to do with the 1910 source novel and the origins of the limp had not been explained until the 1912 short story "Hopalong's Hop" which under their initial contract with Mulford the film-makers were not licensed to use.

The film's next major incident, in which to avoid bloodshed Mary Meeker acts as bait to help her father's men capture a strategically located Bar 20 line cabin, follows Mulford fairly closely, although in the movie it's Johnny who's tricked out of the cabin and there is no gunbattle in which Jim Meeker (Robert Warwick) is crippled. Twice humiliated and twice saved by Cassidy, Johnny apologizes profusely for his hot-blooded foolishness and recognizes that he has a lot of growing up to do.

While recovering from his leg wound, Cassidy comes to suspect that both ranches are being

25

Jimmy Ellison sneaks off to attend Paula Stone's birthday party. Also pictured are Robert Warwick and Willie Fung in this scene from **Hop-A-Long Cassidy** (1935, Paramount).

victimized by rustlers, and when Uncle Ben reports that railroad crews are being sold cattle wearing the brand HQQ, Cassidy demonstrates that it's the perfect brand to hide stock stolen from both the H 2 and the Bar 20. He then brings the evidence to Buck Peters and Jim Meeker and unites them against their common enemy. On the way to warn the gang that the game's up, Pecos Jack Anthony is intercepted on the trail by Uncle Ben and shoots the old man in the back. With his last few breaths Ben manages to write the beginning of the words "Thunder Mesa" in the sand. Cassidy finds his friend's body and swears revenge.

Now comes the long-awaited moment when all hell breaks loose. There is a rapid montage of action as the men of the two ranches prepare for battle, checking guns, saddling up, racing across the terrain with the Gluck "Dance of the Furies" on the soundtrack accompanying the running insert shots of charging riders. The scene ends all too quickly as the siege of the outlaw fortress begins---a siege that lasted for weeks in the book but consumes only a few minutes of screen time. Finally, somewhat as in Mulford's version, Cassidy and Johnny and some others manage to use ropes to climb above the rustlers' near-impregnable position and attack them from behind. Almost at once the battle is over. A captured rustler, on his knees begging for mercy, confesses that the murderer of Uncle Ben is Pecos Jack. Bretherton then cuts to Anthony's body at the foot of a cliff and a frayed rope dangling above him: cowardly like his prototype Antonio, he'd tried to escape down the rope Cassidy and his men had used to scale the cliffs, but poetic justice had intervened. "The way it says in the Book," Cassidy says over the broken body, "whatever measure you give out, the same measure will be given out to you." One can imagine how Mulford must have reacted to the Biblical overtones after all the trouble he'd taken to portray his Cassidy as the good pagan. With the ranches now at peace, romance blooms between Johnny and Mary---until

Led by Kenneth Thomson and Robert Warwick the H2 hands turn on Jimmy Ellison as Paula Stone tries to stop them. John Merton is also pictured in this scene from **Hop-A-Long Cassidy** (1935, Paramount).

the young man decides to follow the trail to adventure with his new friend and mentor Hopalong Cassidy.

William Boyd was physically inept, disliked horses and could hardly stay in the saddle even when his white stallion was standing still. For years most of his riding and fighting sequences were performed for him by veteran stuntman Cliff Lyons, and his directors concealed the doubling with extreme long shots and unusual camera angles. It was no wonder then that **Hop-A-Long Cassidy** and the later films in the series were relatively light on riproaring action. But in terms of strong storylines, dramatic values and powerful performances these were among the finest Westerns of their time. William Boyd's permanent contribution to the art of the Western film was not as an action star but as an actor. Projecting great forcefulness and great tenderness with equal credibility, chilled-steel deadly one moment and laughing uproariously the next, with a capacity to command obedience, to forgive and to sacrifice

himself totally for others, he was the ideal and ultimate father figure for millions of Western fans over a period of more than twenty years. Harry Sherman's hunch about Boyd had paid off.

By the time shooting began on the next Cassidy film, **The Eagle's Brood** (1935), Boyd was no longer limping and gave viewers unfamiliar with the earlier movie no way of knowing why he was called Hopalong or Hoppy. Bretherton directed from a screenplay by Doris Schroeder and Harrison Jacobs nominally based on Mulford's 1931 novel *Hopalong Cassidy and the Eagle's Brood*, Archie Stout once again manned the cameras and Edward Schroeder edited. Boyd and Ellison were back as Cassidy and Johnny, George Hayes played Spike the bartender, that scenery-chewing old ham William Farnum was cast as the elderly Mexican bandit El Toro, and the four major villains were mainstream actor Addison Richards, Paul Fix (best known in later years as the marshal on TV's **The Rifleman**), Frank Shannon (Dr. Zarkov in Universal's Flash Gordon serials) and

27

Robert Warwick watches as his hands get ready to lynch Jimmy Ellison in this tense scene from **Hop-A-Long Cassidy** (1935, Paramount).

veteran Western badman John Merton.

The first scene of the movie depicts the offstage event that precipitated the plot of Mulford's book: Big Henry (Addison Richards) and his gang, whose base is a saloon in the town of Hell's Center, attack a young married couple in order to steal their gold. In the book the victims were childless Caucasians who in fact had no gold, and the husband survived the attack, while in the film they are Mexican and both are killed but are survived by their small son Pablo (George Mari) who doesn't exist in the novel. Dolores (Joan Woodbury), a dancer at Henry's saloon, happens to witness the murders and Pablo's escape, and takes the boy to her cabin. She soon learns that he's the grandson of El Toro (William Farnum) and writes a note to the old bandit in Mexico. Meanwhile Big Henry and his men discover that the man they killed was El Toro's son and that the murdered couple had a little boy with them who can identify the killers. Henry orders his men to find and kill the boy.

When word reaches Texas that El Toro is about to cross the border into the States, deputy sheriff Bill Cassidy is sent out to find the bandit. Cassidy spots El Toro on the trail and gives chase but his horse (for obvious reasons not his white stallion) stumbles into a quicksand bog. Cassidy is about to be buried alive in the bog when El Toro returns and pulls him out, after which Cassidy reluctantly arrests the old man. El Toro begs to be released so that he can rescue his grandson and tells the story of his son's murder as Dolores' letter told it to him. Cassidy promises to rescue the boy himself if El Toro will go back to Mexico, and the bandit consents. Returning to town and turning in the badge he feels he had no choice but to betray, Cassidy sets out with his pal Johnny Nelson for Hell's Center in search of Dolores.

They reach the town and Cassidy contrives to meet the dancer in Big Henry's saloon. But before he can ask her where Pablo is, she is summoned to Henry's office and brutally murdered. Henry then claims she committed suicide, but Johnny

28

William Boyd and Jimmy Ellison share a friendly moment in this publicity still for **The Eagle's Brood** (1935, Paramount).

Nelson witnessed the murder while spying on Henry through his office window. Cassidy doesn't call Henry a liar but pretends to be a gunman. Hotheaded Johnny, outraged that Henry is getting away with murder, picks a fight with gang member Ed (John Merton), whom Cassidy then has to kill in order to save his young protegé. After this display of gunmanship Henry invites the newcomer to join his gang.

Eventually Cassidy goes off to Dolores' isolated cabin to look for Pablo but is unable to find the boy, who's hiding in the woods. While searching for Pablo, Cassidy is surprised and disarmed by Henry's henchman Mike (Frank Shannon), who distrusts and has been following the new recruit. Cassidy turns the tables and Mike is dragged to his death behind his horse. Then Cassidy returns to Hell's Center and reports Mike's death as an accident. Big Henry soon becomes convinced that Cassidy is a spy and must be killed.

Meanwhile Johnny Nelson has found little Pablo in the woods but the two are ambushed by Henry's man Steve (Paul Fix), who wounds Johnny and is wounded by him in turn. Steve reports back to Big Henry, who sends out Cassidy and Steve on a pretext, planning to ambush Cassidy along the trail. When the two have left town Henry rounds up all his men, including old Spike (George Hayes), the half-witted bartender forever trying to roll a cigarette one-handed, whom Cassidy has befriended. Henry plans first to ambush Cassidy and then to kill Johnny and Pablo where they are holed up on a mountainside. Knowing he's about to be bushwhacked, Cassidy changes positions on the trail with Steve so that Henry kills his own man instead of Hoppy. A gunfight breaks out between Cassidy and Henry's gang. Remotely as in Mulford's novel, Spike crawls across to Cassidy's side, warning that Big Henry has left his men and gone off alone to kill Johnny and Pablo. The old bartender is mortally wounded by Henry's men and dies the moment after he finally succeeds in rolling a cigarette one-handed.

29

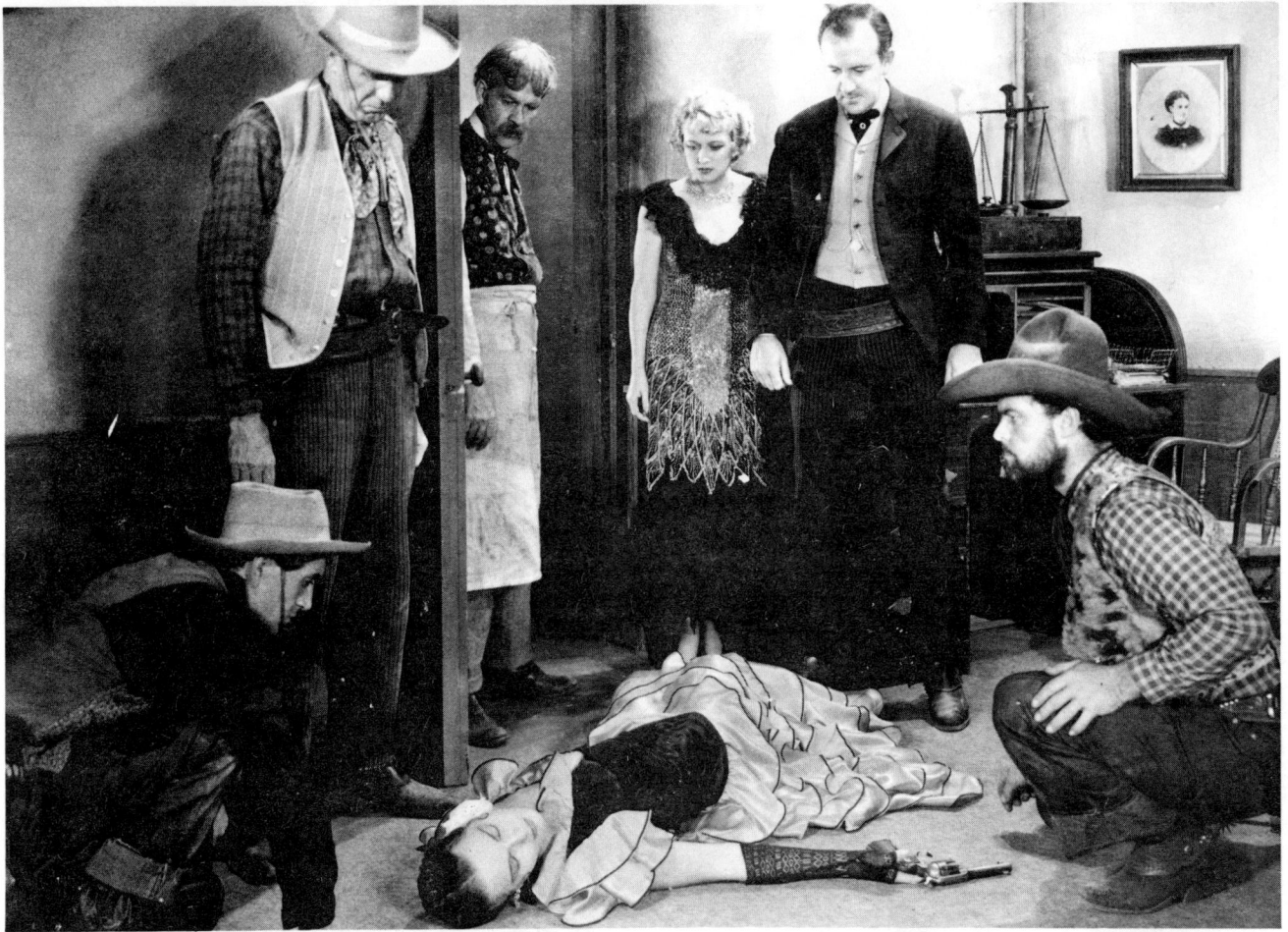

Paul Fix, Frank Shannon, George Hayes, Dorothy Revier, Addison Richards and John Merton all stare at the body of Joan Woodbury in this tense scene from **The Eagle's Brood** (1935, Paramount).

Cassidy kills all of Henry's men, then races after Henry and catches him on the mountainside just in time to save Johnny and Pablo. In the climactic fistfight between the men Henry like Pecos Jack Anthony before him falls over the cliff to his death. Cassidy and Johnny return Pablo to his jubilant grandfather and the film ends with a fiesta.

The Eagle's Brood is a spare, harsh, taut film memorable for the beauty of its mountain and woodland scenery and for its villains' unusual brutality (rare indeed is the Western whose bad guys murder two women and try several times to kill a child). Sherman, Bretherton and the screen-writers took one of Mulford's most loosely constructed, heavily populated, incident-crammed books, jettisoned all but one general thread of story and a few casual incidents, and substituted their own creations so as to turn the movie into an autonomous entity. Mulford needless to say was not impressed. He had written his novel, he said, "with the aid of thirty years of accumulation of

data. I put in hard work on it to make it real. The picture did not touch the story in any one detail." This as we've seen was an exaggeration, but only a slight one. What disturbed Mulford even more was that it was ridiculous for Boyd to play Hopalong Cassidy without displaying the limp that justified the character's name. "In the first movie Bill Boyd limped a little," he explained to a reporter, "but the Hollywood producers thought that that would hurt box office---and so Bill plays the role their way." But complain as Mulford would, the Cassidy films would utilize his characterizations and storylines less and less until within a few years the only surviving link would be the famous character and place names from the Mulford canon.

The third film in the series and perhaps the finest in the first set of six was **Bar 20 Rides Again** (1925), directed by Bretherton from a screenplay by Doris Schroeder and newcomer Gerald Geraghty nominally adapted from Mulford's 1926 novel of the same name, with photography by

30

George Hayes as Spike seems unhappy with William Boyd in this publicity still for **The Eagle's Brood** (1935, Paramount).

Archie Stout and editing by Edward Schroeder as before. Finally realizing what a mistake they'd made killing off George Hayes in the earlier pictures, the film-makers this time let his lovable-old-grouch character not only survive but integrate himself into the developing trio concept of the series. Boyd, McGlynn and Ellison were back as Hoppy, Red and Johnny, but Charles Middleton was unavailable to play Buck Peters again and the role went to old-time silent serial director J.P. McGowan, who had often given himself acting jobs in his own productions.

The broad outline of the screenplay comes from Mulford: the SV Ranch is raided by cattle rustlers led by a man known variously as Perdue and Nevada, whose headquarters is an isolated stronghold in the Snake Buttes, and Cassidy comes in to clean up the gang. Although a few incidents in the outlaws' camp and a few characters like Jim and Margaret Arnold and the rustlers Carp and Concho and Elbows are based on roughly analogous material in the Mulford novel, the majority of the film's elements comes directly from its makers. The most striking change they made was in their concept of the gang leader. Mulford's Perdue/Nevada was an unwashed, unshaven, fairly run-of-the-mill tough guy; his counterpart in the film is one of the most striking characters in any Western. Harry Worth plays the part to perfection as a meticulously dressed fop, savoring snuff and fine brandy, devoted to chess, so obsessed by the life and victories of Napoleon that he wears an N on his belt buckle and models his rustling raids on Bonaparte's tactics, so cold and emotionless that he can look down on one of his dying men (played by former Keystone Kop Al St. John who would later win fame as the bearded sidekick Fuzzy in dozens of B Westerns for PRC) and sneer: "Did you expect to live forever?" Combining aspects of the conventional effete snob from the East and the ruthless Boss figure of socially conscious 1930s drama, Worth's Perdue is one of the all-time unforgettable villains of the Western film.

31

Dorothy Revier looks lovingly at Jimmy Ellison as he tries to figure out the clue he has stumbled across in this publicity still for **The Eagle's Brood** (1935, Paramount).

Like **Hop-A-Long Cassidy** this movie begins slowly with scenes of life and horseplay on the Bar 20 as the hands prepare for the arrival of Buck Peters' fussy old-maid sister Clarissa (Ethel Wales). Then Cassidy's old friend Jim Arnold (Howard Lang) writes to ask Hoppy's aid in the fight the ranchers of his area are waging against the mystery man Nevada and his rustlers. Arnold asks Hoppy not to bring Johnny Nelson along with him, so that the once fervent romance between Johnny and Arnold's daughter Margaret (Jean Rouverol) will not be rekindled. (In Mulford's novel Johnny had been married to Margaret for some time and was running the SV for his father-in-law, and it was he who had sent to Hoppy for help.) Hoppy and Red Connors decide to leave for the SV at once, but when Johnny is told why he can't accompany them he storms off in a characteristic fit of pique and heads for the SV on his own. At the ranch Johnny is introduced to neighboring cattleman George Perdue (Harry Worth), a man of considerable charm and culture, and quickly learns that this newcomer from the East has turned Margaret's head with his veneer of breeding. At this point only the audience knows that Perdue is in fact the mysterious Nevada. The rustlers attack the SV but are driven off in a scene in which Cinco (Al St. John) suffers his mortal wound.

While Johnny and Perdue compete for Margaret's favors, Cassidy waits in the hills for a secret meeting with Jim Arnold. Then, more or less following the strategy of Tex Ewalt in Mulford's novel, Hoppy dresses up like a tail-coated dude, assumes the identity of gambler Tex Riley, and rides into the Snake Buttes, hoping to locate Nevada's hideout and then send up a smoke signal for the ranchers to close in and attack. On the trail Hoppy encounters a cantankerous old grouch named Windy (George Hayes), who constantly boasts that he's the best friend and mentor of the famous Hopalong Cassidy. Without revealing who he is, an amused Hoppy takes Windy along with him as cover. They locate Nevada's

William Boyd assures George Mari that he will return him to his grandfather as soon as they fix up Jimmy Ellison's arm in this scene from **The Eagle's Brood** (1935, Paramount).

stronghold and simply ride in, pretending to be lost, and "Riley" claims that he's in the area to settle an old grudge by killing a young skunk named Johnny Nelson. After demonstrating his skill with cards and guns Hoppy is invited to join the gang, with Windy being drafted as the rustlers' cook. During the next several days Cassidy manipulates men, cards and events so as to pit various gang members against each other somewhat as Tex Ewalt had in Mulford's version. Finally Hoppy is ordered by Nevada to prove himself by shooting Johnny from ambush under the eyes of others in the gang, but he manages to control the situation so that Johnny, who still has no idea Cassidy is around, escapes with only a slight wound.

After several of the gang have killed each other or been killed by Hoppy in gunfights over card games he has rigged, Cassidy sets his prearranged smoke signal and, with Windy in tow, races away from the hideout. This is the all-hell-breaks-loose moment to which the film has been building, and

now the army of ranchers and cowhands led by Jim Arnold and Johnny prepares for battle in a montage scene underscored as in **Hop-A-Long Cassidy** by Gluck's "Dance of the Furies." The cattlemen join up with Hoppy and Windy and charge hell-for-leather into Nevada's sanctuary where a pitched battle breaks out between them and the rustlers. Perdue is trapped in his luxurious private quarters and, while trying in Napoleonic manner to arrange favorable terms for his own surrender, is shot down by one of his dying gunmen who throws back in his boss' face the question Perdue had asked earlier: "Did you expect to live forever?". Having cleaned out the gang in a sequence more exciting than the rather tame finale of Mulford's novel, Hoppy and Johnny and Red head home amid signs that Windy is about to become a new member of the Bar 20 family.

But apparently no firm decision had been made about continuing the Windy character, for in the next Cassidy film, the slow and disappointing

Jimmy Ellison and William Boyd return George Mari to his grandfather William Farnum as Juan Torena looks on in this scene from **The Eagle's Brood** (1935, Paramount).

Call of the Prairie (1936), Hayes---who had had some experience playing bad guys opposite John Wayne at Monogram---appeared not as Windy but as the outlaw leader Shanghai McHenry. The bandit's name but nothing else about him was taken from the wily old reprobate in Mulford's 1926 novel *Hopalong Cassidy's Protegé* which was the nominal source of the Doris Schroeder-Vernon Smith screenplay. Bretherton directed, Stout photographed and Edward Schroeder edited as usual, but this time the background music for the climax was not the Dance of the Furies but some themes composed by Lee Zahler earlier in the 1930s for Mascot Pictures' cliffhanger serials. Frank McGlynn Jr. and his Red Connors character were absent from this picture and never again returned to the series, but hatchet-waving Willie Fung was back, this time in the role of Wong the Bar 20 cook, and the Buck Peters part was assigned to Howard Lang (Jim Arnold in **Bar 20 Rides Again**), the third man to play this character in four films. The most

familiar evil face in the picture was veteran Alan Bridge, portraying Apache-raised sadist Sam Porter, whose last name and nothing more came from Pecos Slim Porter in the Mulford novel. Venerable silent movie comic Chester Conklin as Sheriff Sandy McQueen had not one moment nearly as funny as the scene where a "dead" outlaw starts to rise to his feet while the cameras are still rolling. That this gaffe was kept in the final prints of the movie indicates all too well the attitude of the people who made it.

Hopalong Cassidy returns from a cattle-selling trip and finds that Johnny Nelson has been drinking and gambling with an unsavory bunch including Sam Porter (Alan Bridge) and an old man known as Shanghai (George Hayes). When Buck Peters (Howard Lang) refuses Johnny a loan, the hotheaded youth goes off on a bender with Shanghai's gang, whose real aim is to rob the Bar 20 of the cattle sale money Hoppy has brought back. The gang drug Johnny's drinks, leave him unconscious in a back room of the

34

William Boyd reads a note which is a call for help as Jimmy Ellison looks on in this scene from **Bar 20 Rides Again** (1935, Paramount).

saloon, and ride out to the Bar 20 after dark, taking Johnny's distinctive neckerchief with them. The thieves overpower Buck and order him to open the safe and wrap the money in the neckerchief. Peters reaches for his gun and is seriously wounded. The thieves get away without the money but leave the neckerchief behind, so that Johnny appears to have been involved in the crime. When Hoppy finds Buck badly wounded and Johnny seemingly implicated, he vows to bring his former friend to justice.

Meanwhile Shanghai has taken Johnny as his prisoner out into the wilderness. While forcing Johnny at gunpoint to dig his own grave, Shanghai explains to the young man how he's been framed. Johnny flings a shovelful of dirt into the old bandit's face and escapes, determined to clear his own name by tracking down Porter and the rest of the gang. Subsequently, while on their trail, he meets lovely Linda McHenry (Muriel Evans), who tells him that she lives on a small remote ranch with her father, an old prospector

known as Shanghai.

Back at the Bar 20, Hoppy decides that the cattle sale money will be safer in the town bank than at the ranch. He has Wong the cook (Willie Fung) quietly take the money into town, then so as to trick the thieves into thinking the money's with him, he conspicuously heads for town himself. On the trail Cassidy is ambushed and wounded by Porter's gang, but with the unlikely help of Wong he turns the tables and captures one of the outlaws alive. (It's here that the embarrassing moment with the not-quite-dead-enough gunman takes place.) When the outlaws realize how Cassidy has tricked them, Shanghai devises a scheme for them to break their comrade out of jail and rob the bank at the same time. Porter meanwhile has become tired of taking orders from Shanghai and is planning to make himself leader of the gang after the robbery. Both the jailbreak and the bank holdup go off as expected---hardly surprising since the town has an idiot (Chester Conklin) for a sheriff---and afterwards Hoppy sets out once again on the

35

William Boyd tells Paul Fix to leave George Hayes alone in this scene from **Bar 20 Rides Again** (1935, Paramount).

bandits' trail.

Meanwhile Johnny has managed to hang around the McHenry ranch, helping Linda with chores, falling a bit in love with her as he does with every attractive woman he meets, and waiting for her father and his gang to return. When they do, however, they recognize and overpower Johnny and prepare him for a bizarre death dreamed up by Sam Porter. In the film's only sequence rooted in Mulford's novel, the outlaws tie Johnny to a supporting beam inside a deserted cabin, fasten a rawhide noose around the trigger of a gun, and leave a candle burning so that after a period of agonized waiting the flame will sever the rope and the gun will go off and kill Johnny. Porter uses this opportunity to oust Shanghai as gang leader, and while the rest of the thieves are preparing the death trap, Shanghai sneaks off with the stolen money, planning to return to his ranch, take Linda away with him and give the loot back to the bank.

Hoppy reaches the deserted cabin just in time to disarm the booby trap and save Johnny's life, and the two reunited friends then shoot down every member of the gang except Porter, who races away to the accompaniment of Lee Zahler's music, pursuing Shanghai back to the McHenry ranch and pursued himself all the while by Hoppy and Johnny. At the ranch Porter gets the drop on Shanghai and Linda while they're packing to leave. By keeping his gun on the old man, Porter forces Linda to step outside when Hoppy and Johnny approach and to insist that nothing is wrong, so that Porter can shoot them down in the open while they're off guard. Shanghai shouts out a warning and struggles with Porter over the gun. Porter shoots the old man but then Hoppy races into the ranch house and guns down Porter. Luckily Shanghai's wound is not fatal, and the film ends happily as he clears Johnny of complicity in all the gang's crimes.

In number five of the first half-dozen, **Three on the Trail** (1936), Boyd and Ellison returned as Hoppy and Johnny, Hayes as Windy was fully integrated into the trio for the first time, Muriel

36

William Boyd disguised as gambler Tex Riley coldly stares down two outlaws in this scene from **Bar 20 Rides Again** (1935, Paramount).

Evans had the female lead for the second Cassidy picture in a row, old silent-serial leading man William Duncan became the fourth actor in less than a year to play Buck Peters, and expert villainy was provided by Onslow Stevens as saloonkeeper Pecos Kane. Bretherton was at the megaphone, Stout behind the cameras and Edward Schroeder in the cutting room. The Doris Schroeder-Vernon Smith screenplay allegedly adapted Mulford's excellent 1921 novel *The Bar-20 Three*, but took only a few character and place names and some highly abstract ideas like the hideout on the far side of the desert and a frame-up for robbery. Perhaps the moviemakers should have borrowed more, because the movie isn't one-tenth as exciting as Mulford's book.

While in the town of Mesquite, Hoppy, Johnny and Windy see several beautiful young women getting off the stagecoach and are told that they've come to work in Pecos Kane's Paradise Saloon. Johnny instantly falls for one of the women, Mary Stevens (Muriel Evans), but quickly learns that she's not a dancer but a schoolteacher who came to town by mistake and is now broke. Although Mesquite has no need for a teacher, Kane (Onslow Stevens) suavely offers Mary a job as bookkeeper (heh, heh) at the Paradise. Hoppy saves her from Kane's clutches by stepping in and claiming that Buck Peters had sent him into town to pick her up and take her to the Bar 20. He gives Johnny the job of driving her to the ranch, and love blooms as usual in the young Romeo's fickle heart.

While on the way to the Bar 20 with Mary, Johnny comes upon the robbery of a stagecoach which is carrying a bundle of money belonging to wealthy J.P. Ridley (Claude King) of the Question Mark ranch. Johnny is wounded while trying to stop the robbery, and only Hoppy's intervention in the gun battle saves the young man's life. Kane, who is behind the robbery, attempts to get even with Johnny for stealing Mary from him and interfering with the stagecoach holdup by framing Johnny for the robbery and the shooting of the stage driver. When Ridley posts a large reward for

37

William Boyd coldly tricks several outlaws into gunfights over cards enabling him to cut down the gang in this scene from **Bar 20 Rides Again** (1935, Paramount).

the capture of the holdup men, Kane orders the corrupt Sheriff Corwin (John St. Polis) to arrest Johnny for the crime. Hopalong interferes, faces the sheriff down, and keeps Johnny out of jail. Later at Kane's saloon Johnny identifies gunman Jim Trask (Ted Adams) as one of the stage robbers, and in the resulting gunfight Trask is killed.

The presence of Mary Stevens at the Bar 20 creates a rift between Hoppy and Johnny, who's infatuated with the girl and jealous that she seems to prefer the more mature Cassidy. During a party at the ranch in Mary's honor, Kane's men kidnap both Hoppy and Johnny and take them to the gang's hideout on the far side of the desert. Then Kane tries to persuade the wealthy Ridley that Cassidy and Johnny themselves robbed the stagecoach. While left alone at the desert hideout with only the outlaw Lewis (John Rutherford) to guard them, Hoppy and Johnny get free, overpower Lewis and force him to trek back across the sands with them without water. At the point where all three are near collapse from thirst, Hoppy and

Johnny come upon Sheriff Corwin and the posse searching for them, get the drop on them, relieve them of their horses and canteens, and ride the rest of the way back to civilization with their prisoner.

When Lewis confesses the truth, Ridley puts a price on Pecos Kane's head, and in the by now traditional all-hell-breaks-loose montage, the men of the Bar 20 and the Question Mark prepare for action as agitato music fills the soundtrack. Mary happens to be in town shopping when Kane learns that the attack force is approaching. He takes her hostage and barricades himself and his men in the Paradise. Hoppy and his comrades besiege the building in a manner vaguely reminiscent of the siege near the end of Mulford's novel, and cowhand Idaho (played by that sublime weasel-face of 1930s Westerns, Ernie Adams) gives his life while setting the saloon afire. Only then does Hoppy realize that Mary is trapped inside with the gang. He races into the flaming saloon to rescue her and is wounded by Kane while trying to pull her out of the blaze but kills the bandit leader in

Paul Fix watches Alan Sears disarm Jimmy Ellison in this scene from **Bar 20 Rides Again** (1935, Paramount).

turn. With the destruction of the gang and the return of friendship between Hoppy and Johnny the picture ends.

The first season came to a finish with **Heart of the West** (1936), in which the usual people did the usual chores---Bretherton directing, Doris Schroeder scripting, Stout lensing, Edward Schroeder cutting---and turned out the slowest and dullest Cassidy film yet. Mainstream actor Sidney Blackmer looked uncomfortable in cowboy togs as the lead villain, but his henchmen included such reliable screen outlaws as John Rutherford, Warner Richmond, Walter Miller, Ted Adams and Fred Kohler. Even though Cassidy never appeared in Mulford's 1931 novel *Mesquite Jenkins, Tumbleweed,* that was the source of the screenplay's broad outline which had the hero helping tenderfoot Jordan of the Three J protect both his land and his sister from neighboring rancher Trumbull, although as usual most of the details were original with the film-makers.

Hoppy and Johnny are on their way to the Tumbling T ranch whose owner, John Trumbull (Sidney Blackmer), has hired them as hands. Along the trail they save the life of a bullwhip-cracking old cowboy named Windy (George Hayes), who was shot at from ambush and almost drowned in a raging river while taking a valuable stud bull to the depot. Either Bretherton and Schroeder forgot that the old grouch had already been with Cassidy in two films or this is supposed to be a brand new old grouch named Windy---or else no one cared. Windy explains that he works for young Jim Jordan (Charles Martin), whose Three J ranch borders on the Tumbling T, and that Jordan is constantly being harassed by John Trumbull. When Cassidy and Johnny reach town and meet Trumbull they refuse to go to work for him and instead take jobs with the Three J---a decision especially pleasing to love-prone Johnny when he meets Jordan's beautiful sister Sally (Lynn Gabriel).

Trumbull is in league with a gang of rustlers who drive large herds of stolen cattle across the

William Boyd introduces George Hayes to Jimmy Ellison in this scene from **Bar 20 Rides Again** (1935, Paramount).

back trails of the Tumbling T and Three J ranches. When Jim and Sally Jordan took over the previously deserted Three J the rustlers' scheme was jeopardized, and Trumbull's harassment campaign has been designed to scare the Jordans off their property so that the stolen herds can continue to pass through undetected. One of Trumbull's tactics has been to have his own herds invade and trample down the best Three J grazing land, and, like Mesquite Jenkins in Mulford's novel, Hoppy advises Jordan to fence in his property in order to keep Trumbull's cattle out. When Trumbull learns of the fencing activity he is furious, especially since he knows that a stolen herd will shortly be coming through the very pass that's being fenced. In a sequence taken fairly directly from Mulford, Trumbull rides to the Three J to demand that the fence building stop, finds Sally Jordan alone at the ranch and baking in the kitchen, and makes advances to her. Terrified, Sally repulses Trumbull and scratches his face with her flour-stained fingers. When Trumbull

rides out to the fence site for a showdown, Hoppy notices the flour streaks on his face and fears he may have injured Sally. At gunpoint Hoppy and Jordan force Trumbull to ride back with them to the Three J, where they find Sally frightened but unhurt. They reluctantly and rather stupidly let Trumbull go but warn him not to interfere with the fencing again.

The trail boss of the stolen herd (Fred Kohler) comes to the Tumbling T to warn Trumbull that the cattle are about to enter the fenced pass. They decide that the only way to get through is to stampede the herd right into the fence, which is our signal that the film has reached its hell-let-loose, Dance-of-the-Furies moment. Hearing the sounds of the approaching stampede, Hoppy and the Jordan hands place dynamite charges along the fence line and set off explosions in the face of the raging herd, forcing the cattle to wheel around and charge madly in the opposite direction. The rustlers are routed and Trumbull is trampled to death in the stampede. With the Jordans peacefully

40

William Boyd tames a wild horse in this scene from **Bar 20 Rides Again** (1935, Paramount).

in possession of the ranch, Hoppy and Johnny return to the Bar 20.

At this point "Pop" Sherman seems to have realized how much vigor the Cassidy films had lost since the first few entries, for he decided that it was time to clean house. George Green the associate producer was fired, both Doris and Edward Schroeder were let go, and Bretherton was dropped too (although he returned several years later to direct a few more mediocre Cassidys). The only member left from the original team was cinematographer Archie Stout, and he left the company three films later. Boyd, Ellison and Hayes, who had established themselves solidly in the leads, were of course kept on. But Sherman made it his business to put together a new production team before work began on the second season of exploits of Hopalong Cassidy.

A publicity photo of William Boyd for **Hop-A-Long Cassidy** (1935, Paramount).

Jimmy Ellison in a publicity photo for **Hop-A-Long Cassidy** (1935, Paramount).

William Boyd and Addison Richards fight for the possession of Hoppy's gun in this scene from **The Eagle's Brood** (1935, Paramount).

William Boyd holds Joan Woodbury's hand in this scene from **The Eagle's Brood** (1935, Paramount).

A publicity photo of William Boyd from **The Eagle's Brood** (1935, Paramount).

A moody publicity photo of Jimmy Ellison from **The Eagle's Brood** (1935, Paramount).

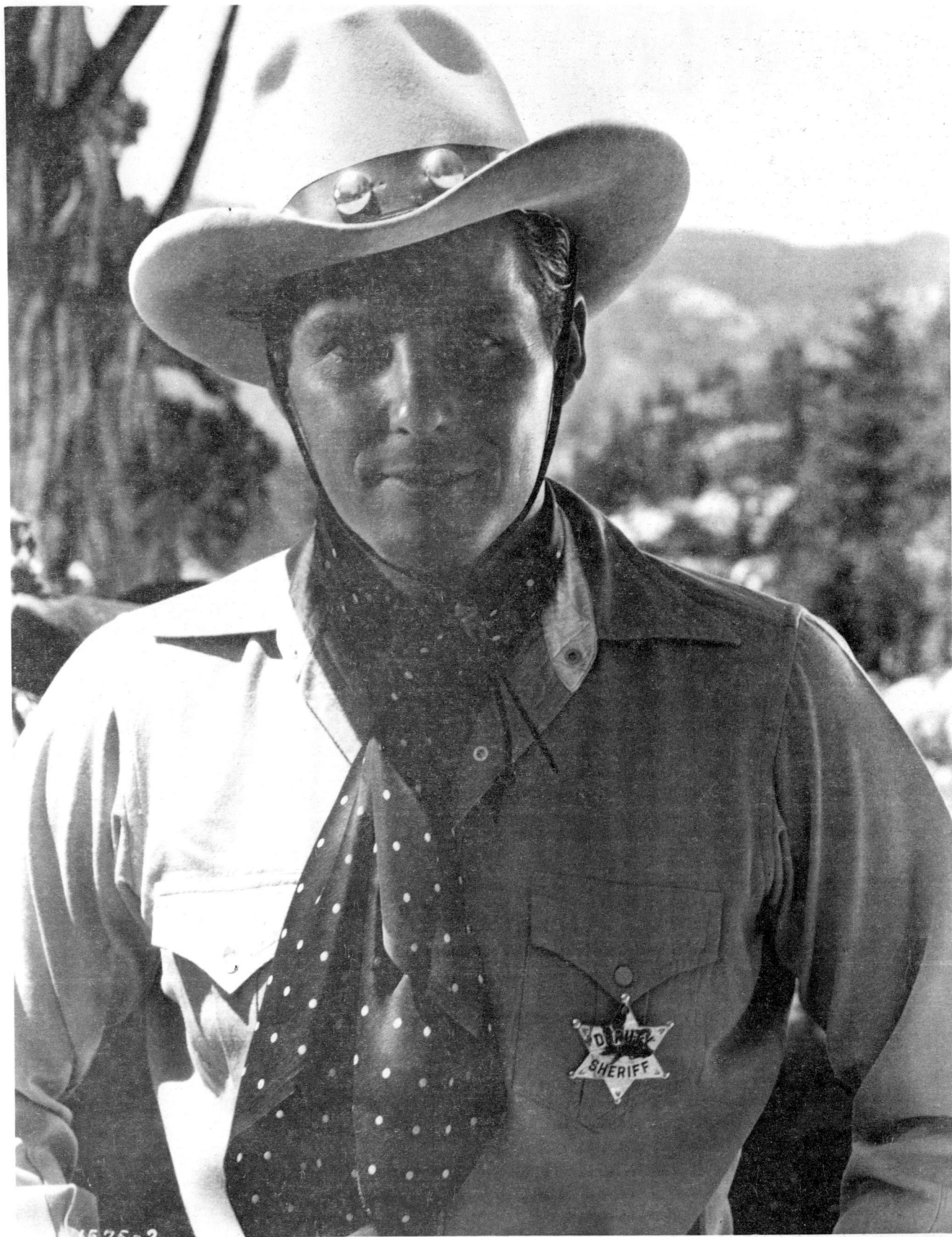

Another publicity of Jimmy Ellison from **The Eagle's Brood** (1935, Paramount).

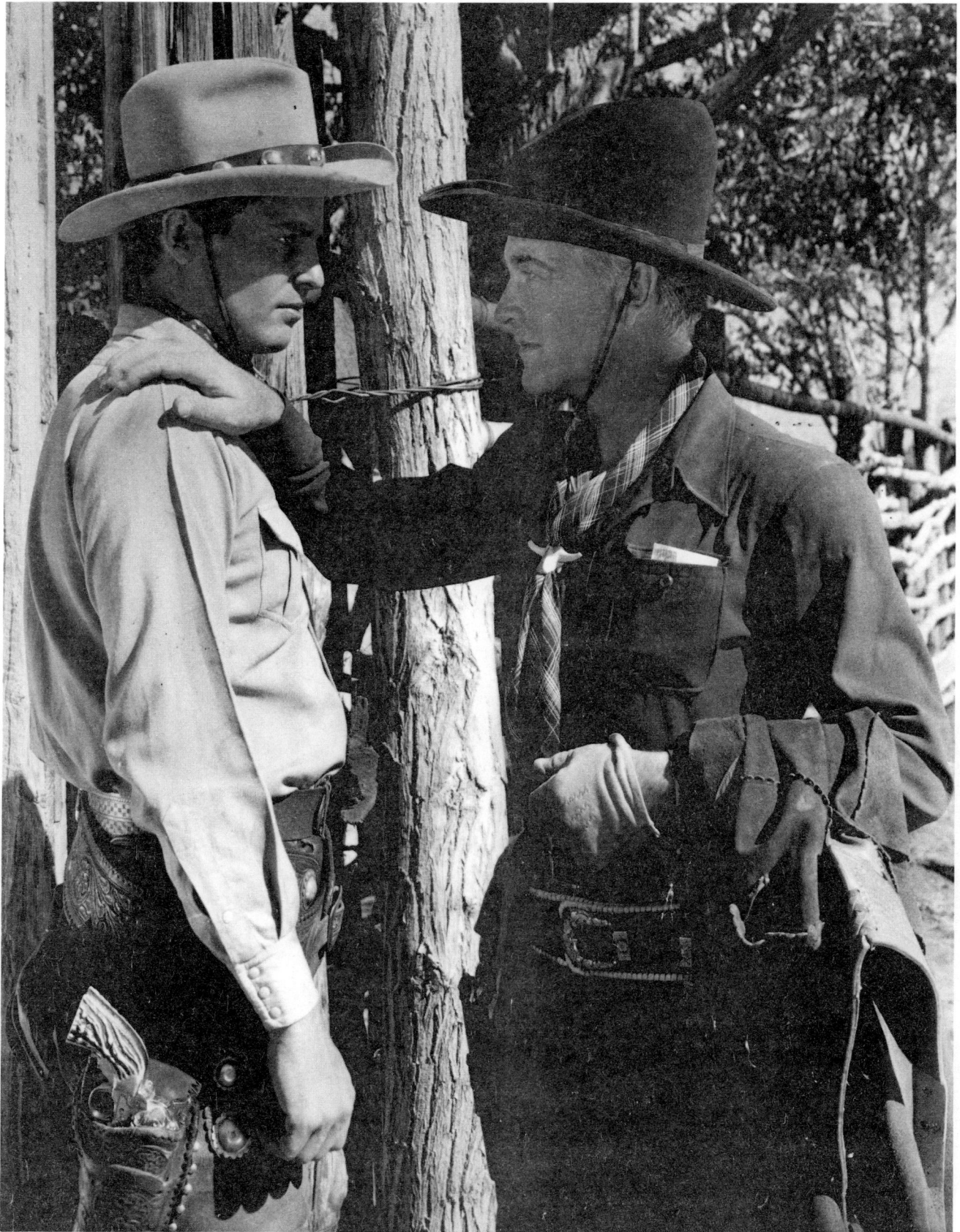

William Boyd breaks the news that Jimmy Ellison can't come in this scene from **Bar 20 Rides Again** (1935, Paramount).

George Hayes has knife ready and William Boyd has both guns ready in this scene from **Bar 20 Rides Again** (1935, Paramount).

William Boyd dressed up as dude in this publicity photo for **Bar 20 Rides Again** (1935, Paramount).

Howard Lang and William Boyd in a publicity still for **Bar 20 Rides Again** (1935, Paramount).

William Boyd in another publicity photo for **Bar 20 Rides Again** (1935, Paramount).

Jimmy Ellison is ready for action in this scene from **Bar 20 Rides Again** (1935, Paramount).

Another action publicity still of Jimmy Ellison for **Bar 20 Rides Again** (1935, Paramount).

Ethel Wales gets ready to belt Jimmy Ellison in this publicity still for **Bar 20 Rides Again** (1935, Paramount).

Howard Lang, Jimmy Ellison and Frank McGlynn, Jr. in a publicity still for **Bar 20 Rides Again** (1935, Paramount).

Jimmy Ellison and Jean Rouverol in a publicity still for **Bar 20 Rides Again** (1935, Paramount).

58

William Boyd gleefully holds back George Hayes in this publicity photo for **Bar 20 Rides Again** (1935, Paramount).

William Boyd has his fancy scrollwork guns drawn in this publicity photo for **Call of the Prairie** (1936, Paramount).

Chapter Three

The first half-dozen Cassidys were successful enough so that Paramount, which had released them, agreed to do the financing on the entries for the 1936-37 season. The budgets were increased to $125,000 per picture and Boyd's salary went up to $10,000 for each film. But the fresh team Sherman fielded was just as new to Westerns as his original group had been. Associate producer Eugene Strong and film editor Robert Warwick were newcomers to the genre, and the scriptwriters engaged for the season had penned few if any previous shoot-em-ups. The director of the second half-dozen Cassidys was Nate Watt (1897-1963), who had made a few quickie Westerns in the early 1920s but had spent most of his career as an assistant director, notably under Lewis Milestone on pictures like **Two Arabian Knights** (1927) starring none other than William Boyd. Watt's set of six Hoppy pictures proved that his forte was neither pace nor fast action but emotionally charged dramas, most of them from 70 to 85 minutes long, with exceptionally strong key scenes, and featuring a compelling new villain named Stephen Morris who became better known as a mainstream actor under the name of Morris Ankrum.

Watt's debut as a Cassidy director was slow and unexciting but clearly showed where his strength lay. The few high points of **Hopalong Cassidy Returns** (1936) are drenched with emotion as no picture in the series had been before, and for the first time an older woman was provided as romantic interest for Hoppy himself. The only similarity between Mulford's 1924 novel of the same name and the Harrison Jacobs screenplay was that Cassidy had a young protegé who got into a peck of trouble. From this point on, with only two or three exceptions, no Cassidy film depended on a Mulford plot even slightly.

Although Boyd and Hayes were in their usual roles as Hoppy and Windy, Jimmy Ellison had been borrowed by Cecil B. DeMille for the role of Buffalo Bill in **The Plainsman** (Paramount,

1936) with Gary Cooper and Jean Arthur and so was unavailable to play Johnny Nelson. He was replaced by a virtual clone of his immature, hotheaded Johnny character in the person of William Janney, ineptly portraying Hoppy's kid brother Buddy. The role of the woman outlaw leader who develops an unrequited passion for Cassidy went to Evelyn Brent, who had been the female lead in such silent Josef von Sternberg classics as **Underworld** (Paramount, 1927) and **The Drag Net** (Paramount, 1928). Stephen Morris turned in his first mad-gunman performance as Brent's psychotically jealous henchman, and among the gang members could be seen the familiar faces of Ernie Adams, Al St. John, and young Western musician Ray Whitley.

An outlaw band led by Lilli Marsh (Evelyn Brent), mature but still attractive owner of Mesa Grande's Crystal Slipper saloon, is routinely murdering any prospectors who discover gold in the area before they can stake their claims. After the death of Peg Leg Holden (Irving Bacon), who had just struck gold, and the subsequent registration of a new mine in Lilli's name, Robert Saunders (John Beck), the wheelchair-bound crusading editor of the town newspaper, sends for his old friend Hopalong Cassidy to bring law and order to the community. While Hoppy and his impetuous younger brother Buddy (William Janney) are on their way to Mesa Grande, Hoppy saves Lilli's life when her horse is frightened by a snake and runs away with her. It's made clear that Lilli finds her rescuer a most attractive man. Just before the Cassidys reach town, Lilli's top gunman Blackie Felton (Stephen Morris) lassos Saunders' wheelchair and drags the crippled editor through the streets to his death. Cassidy accepts the marshal's badge from his dying friend's hands and vows to find the killers.

After some time-wasting scenes of loveplay between Buddy and Saunders' daughter Mary (Gail Sheridan), the first break in the case comes when Hoppy catches Dugan (Claude Smith), one

William Boyd cautions George Hayes to keep quiet in this scene from **Bar 20 Rides Again** (1935, Paramount).

of Lilli's gunmen, who was about to ambush Windy as that cantankerous old grouch was riding near Lilli's mine. Hoppy takes Dugan to town and locks him in jail, but Blackie shoots him through the cell window before he can be questioned. That lead gone, Hoppy pays an official visit to the Crystal Slipper to announce that law and order have come to Mesa Grande. Lilli offers him her friendship (with all that that implies) if he will be "reasonable," but Hoppy is not moved by her wiles, and Lilli finds herself torn between her growing attraction to Cassidy and her knowledge that she must kill him to save herself.

The impulsive Buddy Cassidy, desperate to get out from under the shadow of his older brother, becomes a regular customer at the Crystal Slipper. One day when Hoppy comes into the saloon and orders him to stop gambling, Buddy openly defies his brother. Blackie Felton tries to capitalize on the situation by shooting Hoppy in the back, but Hoppy beats Blackie to the draw, wounds him and kicks him out of town. Then he drags Buddy

to jail to cool off. Thanks to Windy's remonstrances Buddy eventually realizes the error of his ways and apologizes to Hoppy, whose response as it was so many times before with Jimmy Ellison is a generous "Aww, forget it."

During a conversation in the Crystal Slipper office, Lilli offers to make Hoppy her partner (with all that that implies). Cassidy refuses and deftly pockets an ore sample lying on her desk. An assay test proves the ore identical to the sample Peg Leg Holden deposited for assay before his death. Hoppy then arrests Bob Claiborne (Grant Richards), Lilli's gambling house manager, and forces him to confess that it was Blackie who killed both Peg Leg and Saunders. Forming a posse of the town's decent citizens, Hoppy rides out to round up the gang at Lilli's mine. During the ensuing gun battle, Buddy foolishly gets himself captured by the outlaws, who threaten to kill him if the posse doesn't withdraw. Hoppy and Windy sneak up from behind, get the drop on the gang and save Buddy's life.

The sound of shots bring Jimmy Ellison, William Boyd and Bob McKenzie to the street in this scene from **Heart of the West** (1936, Paramount).

That night Blackie comes back into town, challenges Cassidy to an open gunfight, then hides in Lilli's upstairs office over the saloon, planning to shoot Hoppy from above without giving him a chance. Lilli struggles with Blackie to keep him from shooting and in the scuffle is fatally wounded herself, whereupon Hoppy shoots Blackie. In the most emotional scene in the series to date, Lilli dies in Hoppy's arms, having repaid Cassidy with her own life for his earlier having saved her. A saddened Hoppy returns to his home range.

Watt's second Cassidy picture was infinitely better, skillfully blending action, incident, emotion, comedy, suspense, and overtones of the world beyond the screen; so well made in fact that the director's personality was lost in the shuffle. Westerns have always revealed more about the period in which they were made than about the period in which they were set, and all the great American crises of the past fifty years---Depression, world war, cold war, the struggle against racism, Viet Nam---have been reflected in countlesss ways in the theatrical and television Western films of their time. Such excellent Westerns of the Thirties as Lambert Hillyer's **One Man Law** (Columbia, 1931) with Buck Jones and Alan James' **Trail Drive** (Universal, 1933) with Ken Maynard had been deeply rooted in the milieu of the Great Depression even though nominally set generations earlier. Harry Sherman desired not to remind audiences of the desperation outside the movie house but to help them escape for an hour or so into a cleaner and less ambiguous fantasy world where one's destiny seemed to be in one's own hands. He made an exception however with the next Cassidy film, **Trail Dust** (1936). Although the script by veteran silent-film title writer Al Martin was far more faithful than usual to the episodic nature, the overall thrust and specific incidents in Mulford's 1934 novel of the same name, the film is set in an atmosphere of hunger, despair and economic exploitation clearly mirroring the real world of the

Assorted townspeople including bartender Bob McKenzie watch William Boyd and Jimmy Ellison deal with a bad guy in this scene from **Heart of the West** (1936, Paramount).

1930s---something the fiercely anti-New Deal Mulford had not done even though *his Trail Dust* had been written during those same lean years.

This very long film begins with an evocation of famine that is threatening huge areas of the United States. A relief committee is formed and its members come to the Southwest to buy cattle to feed the starving millions. Certain profiteers demand outrageous prices for their herds, but Hopalong Cassidy and his friends Johnny and Windy offer their small herd at a fair price, and persuade several other ranchers to pool their herds for a large collective trail drive to the railhead at Plainsville. (The drive in Mulford's version had been inspired totally by the profit motive.) The profiteers determine to sabotage Cassidy's drive in order to force the relief committee to deal with them, and send gunmen Tex Anderson (Stephen Morris) and Joe Wilson (Ted Adams) to join Cassidy's group and slow down his progress so that the profiteers' herd will reach the railhead first.

As Hoppy's herd is driven to market the profiteers throw all sorts of obstacles in his way, starting with Lewis (Harold Daniels), who poses as an official trail cutter and claims half of Cassidy's herd as strays much like the rustlers in Mulford's novel. Hoppy defies Lewis' authority---the first but hardly the last anti-establishment action he takes in Nate Watt's Cassidy films---and pushes the herd onward.

Later Hoppy and Johnny find a young woman (Gwynne Shipman) unconscious along the trail and take her back to their camp. When she recovers she says that she's Beth Clark, the daughter of the genuine trail cutter, who has disappeared. Susceptible Johnny instantly falls in love with Beth and his clumsy attempts to woo her provide the film with some comic relief.

One evening after the trail herders have made camp, the profiteers raid the herd, and while Hoppy and his men are pursuing the thieves, another group of the profiteers' gunmen raid Hoppy's camp, set fire to the supply wagon and

Jimmy Ellison and William Boyd protect Muriel Evans in this publicity still for **Call of the Prairie** (1936, Paramount).

douse the food with coal oil. The next day Hoppy and Windy set out for Waggoner's trail store to buy more food, an incident quite close to one segment of Mulford's novel. Because Hoppy and Waggoner (Dick Dickinson) had had a run-in before, Cassidy tells Windy to drive up to the store by himself and purchase the supplies without revealing he's with the Bar 20. Windy however inadvertently betrays himself, and Hoppy has to break in on the scene with drawn guns and rescue his sidekick. Meanwhile Johnny and some other hands follow the trail of the rustled cattle, encounter some of the thieves and shoot it out with them. A dying rustler (Al St. John) tells Johnny that John Clark, Beth's father, is a prisoner in Lewis' camp.

Further along the trail, two of Hoppy's men are mysteriously murdered while on sentry duty. Hoppy suspects Tex Anderson but has no definite proof. Nevertheless he orders Tex to leave camp. The next morning Cassidy puts out word that the herd is to be driven the rest of the way at top speed. But the profiteers, whose herd is behind Cassidy's, try to pass him on the trail in violation of cattlemen's ethics. Johnny suggests that Hoppy take a short cut through Black Canyon Gorge to the railhead, and Beth rides ahead to Plainsville to get help from the townspeople. Hoppy sets fire to the brush behind his herd in order to keep the profiteers from passing him. In the fire and confusion John Clark (John Elliott) makes his escape from Lewis' camp and joins Hoppy, who kills Lewis during a scuffle. Meanwhile Tex Anderson and Joe Wilson, learning of Hoppy's plan to race the herd through Black Canyon Gorge, steal all the dynamite from Windy's supply wagon and ride off to mine the gorge's mouth. Hoppy discovers what has happened, races after the two saboteurs, and succeeds in killing them and extinguishing the fuses just in time to save the herd from being blown up in the canyon.

The cattle reach Plainsville without further incident and Beth Clark is reunited with her father.

Jimmy Ellison and Muriel Evans show an interest in each other in this publicity still for **Call of the Prairie** (1936, Paramount).

Hoppy heads for home, alone and wretched, for Johnny is apparently staying behind with Beth and Windy feels he's too old to continue herding cattle. For a brief moment as Watt shows us Cassidy riding with a look of utter loneliness and despair on his face, one believes this film will end on a downbeat note like **Hopalong Cassidy Returns**. But suddenly Hoppy's two companions come galloping over the crest of a hill to catch up with him, and as they ride on together we hear over the end titles the hauntingly appropriate lyrics: " 'Mid the sage and the clover/Let me live my life over once again/Where a friend is a friend/ And where a pal is a pal all along."

The season's third Cassidy picture was quintessential Nate Watt: 82 minutes long, deathly slow and actionless but building to a climax of almost hysterical emotional intensity, with screenplay and direction transforming Cassidy into an all-but-overt Jesus figure confronting a near-Satanic adversary who yet in many respects is the mirror image of the hero himself. Except that parts of both book and film take place in territory belonging to Mexico, there is not the least similarity between the Harrison Jacobs script and Mulford's 1922 non-series novel *Bring Me His Ears* which was its nominal source, and one can only imagine Mulford's reaction when he saw his good pagan suffering symbolic crucifixion on the screen.

Jimmy Ellison as Johnny rejoined Boyd and Hayes to make up the lead trio, but it was his last hurrah in a Cassidy film, for "Pop" Sherman was about to cast him in a new series of movies he was producing, "based on" Rex Beach's Alaskan adventure novels, and when that project flopped Ellison would sign on as a contract player with RKO. Lovely Nora Lane appeared as the female lead, Trevor Bardette had a good role as a disguised officer of the Mexican Secret Service, and that perennial snake-oil huckster of Western films, Earle Hodgins, was given the uncharacteristically serious part of a major in the Texas Rangers. Prominent among the gunmen were

William Boyd tries to calm down Willie Fung in this publicity still from **Call of the Prairie** (1936, Paramount).

distinctive-voiced George Chesebro (The Whine) and Al Bridge (The Rasp). But by far the most memorable performance in the film, indeed the most stunning enactment of a villain in any of the 66 pictures in the series, was that of Stephen Morris as Cassidy's diabolical adversary. The bizarre, hypnotically repetitive agitato score at the film's protracted climax, although uncredited in the movie itself, is by Lee Zahler.

What precipitates the plot is a situation suggestive of President Roosevelt's "Good Neighbor" policy towards Mexico: a mysterious bandit known as The Fox has been leading raids that have caused havoc on both sides of the border, and U.S. and Mexican officials team up to run down the gang. But the plan devised by Colonel Gonzales (Trevor Bardette) and Texas Ranger Major Stafford (Earle Hodgins) is strange indeed. They ask Hopalong Cassidy to sacrifice his reputation as an honest man and agree to be disgraced and despised in order to set a trap for The Fox. With the altruism of a Jesus taking on the sins of

the world, Hoppy consents. In the presence of Ranger Johnny Nelson, Major Stafford accuses Cassidy of being in league with rustlers, and Hoppy refuses to deny the charge even though he knows it means he has destroyed himself in the eyes of his young protegé. Ordered out of the territory, Hoppy leaves for the border town of El Rio without a word of explanation either to Johnny or to cantankerous old Windy. In due course both of his former sidekicks follow Cassidy to El Rio, where he treats them with brutal contempt.

Hoppy rents a room at an El Rio boardinghouse run by young widow Grace Rand (Nora Lane), who lives there with her little daughter Molly (Charlene Wyatt). In order to maintain his image as a badman Hoppy continues to abuse everyone he sees, Molly included. At the saloon where he hangs out, Cassidy encounters a halfwit called Loco who cadges drinks and is mistreated by all the customers, and who has a unique method of tearing cigarette papers into symmetrical patterns.

67

George Hayes makes Jimmy Ellison dig his own grave in this scene from **Call of the Prairie** (1936, Paramount).

Hoppy arranges to meet most of the local tough guys and tries to wangle an invitation to join their gang. Meanwhile Colonel Gonzales has drifted into El Rio, disguised as a Mexican street singer, and slips Hoppy the message that a band of his troops will be ready to ride whenever Cassidy gives the word.

One day, soon after The Fox and his gang raid a gold-laden mule train, Hoppy goes reconnoitering in the desert and comes upon the outlaw chief's headquarters cabin. There he finds some distinctively torn cigarette papers that tell him what those viewers who recognized Stephen Morris beneath his derelict make-up have already learned, namely that The Fox and Loco are the same man. Like Cassidy, he has made himself despised among the people, although for diametrically opposite reasons. On the way back to town Hoppy witnesses a Fox gunman ambushing Johnny Nelson, who has also been out trying to pick up the trail of the mule train raiders. Johnny is seriously wounded but Hoppy kills the gunman

and carries his estranged quasi-son back to town, leaving him unconscious at the boardinghouse door. When Johnny recovers he has no idea that it was Cassidy who saved his life.

As expected, Hoppy is eventually asked to join The Fox's gang. He agrees and slips a note to Colonel Gonzales to fetch his troops. But before the trap can be sprung, disaster strikes. In his Loco persona, The Fox overhears Windy telling little Molly Rand that Hoppy is not really evil but is just playing a game. Windy of course doesn't know that he's speaking the absolute truth, but his well-meaning words tip off the listening Fox that Cassidy is a spy. Loco tells Windy and Molly that Hoppy wants to meet them on the desert road and the three set out in a buckboard. Grace, seeing them drive away and then seeing Hoppy still in town, worriedly reports the incident to Cassidy. Knowing as he does that Loco is The Fox, Hoppy races to the rescue as Lee Zahler's weirdly effective agitato score fills the soundtrack. No sooner is Cassidy gone than The Fox's henchmen in

68

William Boyd with Topper and Jimmy Ellison are ready for action in this publicity still for **Call of the Prairie** (1936, Paramount).

town ride off in pursuit of him. Colonel Gonzales and his troops roar into El Rio, learn what is happening and dash off again, adding a fourth element to the chase. And when Johnny learns the news from Grace and leaves his sickbed to race after the others, the fifth and final component enters the bizarre climax.

Meanwhile at the head of the procession, Loco forces Molly and Windy into his headquarters cabin just before Cassidy overtakes the buckboard. The cabin is stocked with dynamite, and Loco threatens to blow up himself and his hostages unless Cassidy surrenders to him. Christlike, Hoppy turns himself over to Loco, who keeps his word by letting Windy and Molly go free, although not before a last tearful goodbye between Cassidy and his ancient friend. Before Loco can take his revenge Hoppy leaps for his adversary's gun and gets the drop on him but is shot in the leg during the struggle. Now the film rises to a peak of frenzy as Watt intercuts from the blood oozing out of Cassidy's leg to the maniacal

eyes of Loco to the running insert of the approaching gang to the running insert of the Mexican troops behind them to Johnny at the tail of the parade, while Zahler's score hypnotically repeats itself again and again. Hoppy desperately tries to stay conscious and keep Loco covered as the gang nears the cabin. Just as the outlaws are about to attack, Gonzales' troops come up from behind and draw them into a pitched battle. The colonel's soldiers drive off the gang and Gonzales bursts into the cabin and takes Loco prisoner just as Cassidy is losing consciousness. Johnny finally arrives, is told the truth about Hoppy's deception, and the two are joyously reunited as this long, slow but cumulatively powerful film comes to a close.

Watt's fourth Cassidy marked the end of the trail for Archie Stout, who was going on to photograph much higher-budgeted films elsewhere, and the start of a new career for a forceful-looking young fellow with the curious name of Pate Lucid (1910-1981), who had started out in the picture

William Boyd and George Hayes watch Muriel Evans and Jimmy Ellison make eyes at each other in this scene from **Call of the Prairie** (1936, Paramount).

business as a film cutter at Paramount. Lucid and Jimmy Ellison had been rooming together at the Los Angeles YMCA in 1935 when Harry Sherman hired Ellison to play Johnny Nelson and Lucid to work without credit as a production manager on the Cassidy series. Over the next two years Sherman noticed that Lucid seemed to have the makings of an actor, and offered him the slot as Hoppy's new protegé when he decided to move Ellison to the Rex Beach films. They agreed that Lucid's screen name would be Russell Hayden, a variant of the name of Russell Harlan (1903-1974), Archie Stout's assistant cinematographer and Sherman's choice to replace Stout after one more picture.

Hayden came across as tougher, more gunwise and mature than Ellison, and rather than force the new actor into his predecessor's rebellious-adolescent characterization, Sherman and his associates decided that he would play a new sidekick completely, a cowhand named Lucky Jenkins, whose only similarity to anyone in the Mulford

canon is that he has the same last name as Mesquite Jenkins. Hayden took to the part like a bird to the open air and continued to play Lucky for a total of 27 consecutive films over a four-year period. Almost all aficionados of the Western would agree that he was the best of the many actors who were to portray Cassidy's young sidekick over the years.

Hayden's first film as Lucky was **Hills of Old Wyoming** (1937), another excellent picture featuring a very slow buildup to a rousing climax. Having stressed the plight of the starving in **Trail Dust** and positive images of Mexicans in **Borderland**, Nate Watt took the opportunity to include in his fourth Cassidy film a highly sympathetic look at Indians, and not just painted white men but a real tribe, speaking its own language and performing its own rites throughout the picture. Stephen Morris was back as another mad-eyed villain, Earle Hodgins had a second serious part as a naive Indian agent and whiny-voiced George Chesebro was prominent among

70

Jimmy Ellison or William Boyd has shot Al Bridge as Muriel Evans tends to a wounded George Hayes in this scene from **Call of the Prairie** (1936, Paramount).

the gunslingers. Although the nominal basis of the script was Mulford's 1933 novel *The Round-Up*, at most only one minuscule incident from that book was used, and the true starting point of the screenplay by Maurice Geraghty (a Mascot serials veteran and the brother of Cassidy scenarist Gerald Geraghty) was his having once been unjustly imprisoned on an Arizona reservation by a tyrannical Indian agent.

The film is set on tribal land in Wyoming. All the nearby ranchers including Hopalong Cassidy have been plagued for some time by cattle rustlers. Hoppy's pals Lucky and Windy chase a few of the rustlers onto the reservation and are convinced that the thieves are Indians. In fact however the head cattle thief is Andrews (Stephen Morris), the deputy agent, who with the connivance of several other deputies and the half-breed Lone Eagle (Steve Clemente) has been trying to pin the crimes on the tribe he represents.

Lucky and Windy decide to hang around the reservation trading post run by Ma Hutchins

(Clara Kimball Young) and her daughter Alice (Gail Sheridan), looking for clues to the guilty parties, although Lucky takes time off to romance with Alice and Windy indulges in some interminable implement-swapping deals with her mother and tall tales of his prowess as a tracker. Andrews becomes worried Lucky and Windy will learn the truth and has them arrested, but in his most anti-authoritarian scene yet, Hoppy enters the picture, faces Andrews down and forces him to let his pals go free. Before long Cassidy suspects that Andrews is up to no good.

Panic-stricken by Hoppy's arrival, Andrews sends out Lone Eagle to kill him. In a scene vaguely echoing an incident in Mulford's novel, Lone Eagle kills one of Hoppy's cattle and leaves a clear trail away from the steer for him to follow, hoping to lure him into an ambush. Hoppy turns the tables and captures Lone Eagle alive, but while the half-breed is being held prisoner at Hoppy's camp Andrews quietly rescues him and later kills him so as to foment trouble between the Indians

71

William Boyd looks down at the slain body of Al Bridge in this climactic scene from **Call of the Prairie** (1936, Paramount).

and the ranchers. Understandably believing that Hoppy and his pals are the murderers, the Indians take them prisoner. In a memorable scene Cassidy tries to explain to Chief Big Tree (Chief John Big Tree) the root of Lone Eagle's evil. "Lone Eagle half white. That half bad," he says---words heard rarely indeed in Westerns dealing with race relations. Eventually Cassidy persuades the chief to release him so he can prove his innocence, but Big Tree keeps Lucky and Windy as hostages to insure Hoppy's return.

Cassidy sneaks up to the Indian Agent's office, steals Andrews' rifle from its saddle scabbard and brings it back to the tribal camp, where he performs a simple ballistics test proving that the deputy agent's rifle murdered Lone Eagle. The hell-breaks-loose moment has arrived, and the Indians join Hoppy and the ranchers in a bi-racial attack on their white overseers as the Lee Zahler score used in **Borderland** once again heightens the tempo with its frenzied repetitions. Andrews and his gang bludgeon Thompson (Earle

Hodgins), the inept head agent who's been duped all along by his subordinates, and race off the reservation, pursued by Cassidy and the ranchers and Indians. Hoppy captures Andrews after a bizarre one-on-one near the edge of a cliff. With the rustlers brought to justice, Lucky says goodbye to lovely Alice, Windy makes an idiot of himself in some last-minute swapping with Ma Hutchins, and Cassidy takes them back with him to their ranch.

Those who wonder how much the director contributes to the storylines of the movies he makes should take a close look at Nate Watt's fifth Cassidy exploit, **North of the Rio Grande** (1937). Although the script is credited to new-comer Jack O'Donnell (who as Joseph O'Donnell became a prolific B Western scenarist for PRC Pictures in the 1940s) and its nominal source was Mulford's 1924 novel *Cottonwood Gulch* (in fact the use of Cottonwood in the name of the town is the only similarity between the two), the key elements are strikingly familiar for another reason.

William Boyd warns the bartender in this scene from **Call of the Prairie** (1936, Paramount).

A mysterious outlaw leader with a fearsome *nom de guerre* and a daylight identity inside the town, a distinctive attribute of both the villain's personalities which tips Hoppy off to his respectable persona, a multi-component hell-for-leather chase at the climax with a fillip of extra-heavy emotion---it's all quite evidently a replay of Watt's **Borderland** in a minor key. Russell Harlan took over as cinematographer, Robert Warwick carried on in the cutting room as he had throughout Watt's tenure, Stephen Morris was back once again as the dual-identity bandit, and in the small role of the railroad president Mr. Wooden (an apt name in view of his performance) was a balding, gruff-voiced young nobody acting on the sly in films under the pseudonym of Lee Colt but better known to patrons of New York's left-wing Group Theater as Lee J. Cobb.

Before the picture begins, Hopalong Cassidy's kid brother Buddy, who had added so little to **Hopalong Cassidy Returns**, has been "accidentally" shot and killed by Deputy Jim Plunkett (Al Ferguson) while in a sheriff's posse during a running gun battle with the mysterious Lone Wolf and his gang. So much, Watt seems to be saying, for William Janney's future in this series! Even though a later inquest vindicates the deputy, Lucky Jenkins is not satisfied with Plunkett's version of events and prevails upon Hoppy to come to Cottonwood Gulch and avenge his brother by tracking down the Lone Wolf gang. (No real reason for Buddy's murder is ever provided.)

Hoppy's cantankerous old sidekick Windy drifts into town, wangles a job as piano player in the saloon of Ace Crowder (John Rutherford) so as to be on hand for the showdown, and kills time by boasting to one and all of his awesome skill as a railroad engineer. In due course Cassidy rides into town posing as a gunman, starts hanging around the saloon, strikes up a friendship with the hostess Faro Annie (Bernadene Hayes), and acts tough as he did in **Borderland**, and for the same reason: to bait the gang into contacting him. Deputy

73

Al Bridge asks George Hayes what to do with Jimmy Ellison who is being held by John Merton in this scene from **Call of the Prairie** (1936, Paramount).

Plunkett becomes suspicious of the newcomer and follows him one night to the house Buddy Cassidy had shared with his wife Mary (Lorraine Randall). In a gun duel in the darkness Hoppy shoots down the deputy and evens the score for his kid brother. Then Cassidy pulls a one-man train holdup and waits for an invitation to join the Lone Wolf gang. Sure enough Ace Crowder, who is also the bandit leader's chief henchman, soon sets up a secret meeting so that Cassidy and the disguised mystery man can size each other up. The Lone Wolf asks Hoppy to join the gang in a raid on a gold shipment the next day. Cassidy notices a distinctive ring on the other's finger.

Hoppy and Lucky work out a plan to trap the gang during the gold raid and Hoppy rides into town to visit its leading citizen, Mr. Henry Stoneham, and get his help. He identifies himself and explains his plan to Stoneham before he notices the distinctive ring on Stoneham's finger and realizes (as those viewers already have who recognize the face of Stephen Morris) that he's

talking to The Lone Wolf. Hoppy is wounded and left bound and gagged in Stoneham's office while the outlaw leader prepares to leave town in a hurry and take all the gang's loot with him.

Stoneham forces Windy out of the saloon at gunpoint and, remembering the old man's claims of prowess as an engineer, makes him climb aboard the locomotive of a train that has stopped at the town depot and steam out of Cottonwood Gulch at top speed. Realizing that their chief has doublecrossed them, Ace Crowder and the rest of the gang race out of town in pursuit of the train, but before long they are in turn pursued by a posse led by Lucky and Hoppy, who has managed to free himself and escape Stoneham's office. In the running gun battle between the two groups of horsemen Lucky is wounded and falls onto the railroad tracks, directly in the path of the oncoming train. After the posse has rounded up Crowder and the others, Hoppy notices for the first time that Lucky isn't with them, doubles back along the route of the chase, sees his protegé lying

The outlaws have really set up a diabolical death for Jimmy Ellison in this scene from **Call of the Prairie** (1936, Paramount).

unconscious on the track with the train only yards away (shades of the old silent serials!), and throws a switch that sends the entire train plummeting over a cliff. It's only then that Lucky gets around to telling Hoppy that Windy was on that train, and for a moment of unspeakable grief both men are convinced that their ancient friend was killed in the wreck with Stoneham. But their tears turn to instant joy when that familiar cantankerous voice calls out to them from a cactus patch that he was thrown clear and, except for several hundred needles in his hide, is unhurt. Faro Annie, the second woman in the series to lose her heart to Hoppy but the first to survive the experience, waves a sad farewell as the three comrades leave Cottonwood Gulch.

Nate Watt seems to have learned one unfortunate lesson from Howard Bretherton: he too began the season with strong films and ended with leaden-footed bores. The last, shortest and weakest Cassidy of the half-dozen, **Rustlers' Valley** (1937), is notable mainly for its unconventional

casting. Having made Stephen Morris the chief heavy in each of his prior Cassidys, Watt gave him this time the sympathetic role of the female lead's father and assigned the villainy to none other than Lee Colt/Lee J. Cobb. The screenplay---by Harry O. Hoyt, who had directed or scripted forty silent features of which the best known is the early special-effects classic **The Lost World** (1925)---actually did incorporate a few elements from its advertised source, Mulford's 1924 novel of the same name. At the start of both works a man framed for a bank robbery is chased by a posse and has to make a leap for life, a kindly old rancher and his daughter figure prominently in later developments, and the villain Cal Howard's insane jealousy causes the female lead to break her engagement to him which in turn motivates him to try to take over her family's ranch. Also both works feature a gang of rustlers who hide stolen cattle in a secret valley where the climax is played out. Not a huge number of similarities, and certainly not enough to placate Mulford, but it was

75

A large group of extras give this scene a rich look you would find in later entries in the Cassidy series, here with William Boyd from **Call of the Prairie** (1936, Paramount).

the last time a Cassidy picture would follow a Mulford plot to any extent at all. The film was photographed by Russell Harlan and edited by newcomer Sherman Rose. The background music at the climax was lifted, with the studio's permission, from the tracks used in Paramount's current series of Zane Grey-based Westerns---an arrangement Sherman continued well into the next season of Cassidy films.

At the opening Lucky Jenkins is more or less in the situation of Jed Hollister in Mulford's novel: pursued by a sheriff's posse, he escapes by plunging with his horse over a cliff into the river below. Meanwhile grouchmaster Windy breaks the news to Hoppy that the town bank has been robbed and that Lucky is on the run after being accused of the crime by an alleged witness named Taggart (Ted Adams). In fact the men behind the robbery are bank president Clem Crawford (Oscar Apfel) and shady lawyer Cal Howard (Lee Colt/ Lee J. Cobb). Howard's ultimate aims are to take over a ranch with valuable water rights owned by

Glenn Randall (Stephen Morris) and to force himself on Randall's daughter Agnes (Muriel Evans).

Sheriff Boulton (John Beach) returns to town with his posse and tells Cassidy that Lucky is dead, a scene which permits Boyd once more to project unspeakable grief. That evening during a party at the Randall ranch, Cal Howard announces his engagement to Agnes. Meanwhile, just as Hoppy is breaking the news of Lucky's death to Windy (another moment Watt milks for its full measure of pathos), who should turn up but Lucky himself, shaken by his leap over the cliff but alive and well, so that his pals' grief is instantly transformed into radiant joy. Lucky explains rather unconvincingly that he went on the run to avoid being lynched, and Hoppy, anti-authoritarian as he consistently is in Watt's pictures, advises him not to turn himself in but to stay in hiding. Then Cassidy visits the Randalls' party and is introduced to Agnes, whose obvious liking for Hoppy infuriates Cal Howard. The next day, after Hoppy and Agnes are seen riding

William Boyd's looks says that somebody is going to pay for what has been done to Howard Lang in this scene from **Call of the Prairie** (1936, Paramount).

together, Howard bullies Agnes and orders her to stop seeing Cassidy. To keep his fiancée under his thumb, Howard tells banker Crawford not to renew the mortgage note on the Randall ranch.

With Sheriff Boulton's approval Cassidy begins his own investigation of the bank robbery, and soon becomes suspicious both of Cal Howard and of Taggart the self-proclaimed witness. Meanwhile Howard orders Taggart to rustle Randall's cattle, so that he can't sell them and pay the mortgage note, and to hide the herd in Lost Canyon. Agnes breaks her engagement to the domineering Howard, while Hoppy and Windy go to work for Glenn Randall and try to save his cattle. When he learns that Crawford has refused to renew Randall's mortgage note, Cassidy accuses Howard of being behind the scheme and stupidly reveals to him that Lucky is still alive and can identify the real bank robber. Later Howard dispatches Taggart to rustle every head of cattle left on Randall's ranch and to kill Cassidy.

Lucky, who has spent the film's arid middle

reaches hiding in a Randall line shack, witnesses the rustling and rides to the ranch for help. When Hoppy and Agnes ride out to investigate, Cassidy foolishly lets the young woman ride his white stallion, with the result that when she's alone on the trail she's shot at from long range and wounded by Taggart, who mistakes her for Cassidy. Eventually Hoppy and his pals track the stolen cattle into Lost Canyon. While Lucky and Windy ride for help, Cassidy takes over the gang's cabin at gunpoint and holds Howard and a few of his men prisoners. In a watered-down variant of the climax in Watt's **Borderland**, the rest of the gang besiege the cabin and are about to overrun it when Lucky, Windy and the ranchers ride in to the rescue. By climbing the cliff above the cabin and rolling down huge boulders through its roof, Lucky and Windy help Hoppy subdue the gang. With the rustlers jailed, peace returns to the community.

On this unmemorable note the 1936-37 season of Cassidy films ended and Nate Watt went back

A publicity still from **Call of the Prairie** (1936, Paramount) which shows William Boyd and Topper against some of the outdoor scenery which made the early Cassidy's special westerns.

to work for Lewis Milestone as second unit director. He sold one Cassidy script to Harry Sherman in 1938 and returned to direct a final Hoppy picture in 1939, but his major contributions to the Western film were now behind him. Let him be fondly remembered. He kept the series going through heavy personnel changes, left his personal stamp on the half-dozen in a row he directed, and batted .500 during his single season in the sun. It was not his fault that his successor turned out to be one of the all-time great action-masters, whose best films would rank among the finest and most rousing Westerns ever.

Chapter Four

Lesley Selander (1900-1979) was that rare bird, a native Californian. He was born in Los Angeles and entered the motion picture industry at age sixteen as handyman for a film laboratory. After stints as assistant cameraman and $5-a-day extra on various cheap silent movies of the early 1920s he was promoted to cinematographer. Then director W.S. Van Dyke brought Selander to Fox Studios as his assistant on a series of Westerns starring Buck Jones. Selander stayed on at Fox when Van Dyke left to direct high-budget pictures at MGM, but several years later, in the early 1930s, Van Dyke again hired Selander as his assistant director, a capacity in which Selander worked on such pictures as **The Thin Man** (MGM, 1934), the classic mystery-comedy with William Powell and Myrna Loy. Two years later, when a director was needed for the Buck Jones Westerns at Universal, Van Dyke recommended his assistant to his old star. Selander directed all eight of Jones' films during the 1936-37 season, six completely on his own and the other two in some sort of collaboration so that the direction was credited to Jones himself. The director and the star became good friends, and when Jones' pal William Boyd happened to mention that Harry Sherman was looking for a director, it was once again Selander who was recommended for and was given the job. Over the next eight years (1937-1944) he made a total of twenty-eight Hopalong Cassidy films, far more than anyone else who worked on the series, plus eight higher-budgeted outdoor features also produced by Sherman.

Selander's contributions to the series took a number of forms. He tightened the pictures' structure, sped up their pace, reduced their average length by almost ten minutes. He added slickness and action to the emotional intensity of the earlier directors---a move in which he was aided by Sherman's having just acquired the right to use in Cassidy soundtracks the music scores from other Paramount-released outdoor films including the Zane Grey series and the Henry Hathaway Technicolor epic **The Trail of the Lonesome Pine** (Paramount, 1936). As a former cinematographer Selander had a keen eye for visually striking locations, and found scenic splendors to replace the drab settings too often favored by Bretherton and Watt. He excelled at staging exuberant fight and chase scenes even though hampered by having to make the stunts look as though they were being performed by the athletically indifferent Boyd. He loved to spice scripts with reversals of Western-film convention like having the villain shoot the gun out of the hero's hand---or giving traditionally masculine action scenes to his female characters. Selander's women are among the strongest and most independent in the history of the Western film. Several years before the role of American women in World War II defense industries inspired other directors to give their women a piece of the action, Selander was pursuing his private experiments in the destruction of sex-based stereotypes. And whatever one thinks of today's feminism, it must be conceded that Selander's innovations make his films more memorable than the Westerns helmed by others of his time.

He debuted as a Cassidy director with the first film of the third season, **Hopalong Rides Again** (1937). Russell Harlan remained as cinematographer, Robert Warwick was film editor, and "Pop" Sherman of course carried on as producer. The screenplay was by unit novice Norman Houston, who had earned more than fifteen writing credits in the silents and early talkies including one as a dialogue scripter for **The Broadway Melody** (MGM, 1929). Although the nominal source of the film was Mulford's 1923 novel *Black Buttes*, the only similarities between the two are that they both deal with rustlers holed up in that location and that the chief villain's last name is Hepburn. Boyd, Hayden and Hayes were in their accustomed roles as Hoppy, Lucky and Windy, and Buck Peters was back

Jimmy Ellison and an outlaw have a rough-and-tumble fight in this scene from **Bar 20 Rides Again** (1935, Paramount).

after an absence of several films in the person of former silent star William Duncan. In a bid to give teen-age viewers a character to identify with, Sherman hired young Billy King to come into the series as Buck's adolescent nephew Artie beginning with this picture. The female lead, a quite conventional lady compared to Selander's later action women, was given to Nora Lane from **Borderland**, who eventually killed herself over a failed marriage. As the main villain Selander cast Harry Worth who had made such a memorable Perdue/Nevada in **Bar 20 Rides Again**. Indeed Worth once again played the gang leader as half a ruthless Boss figure and half an effete fop who's killed at the climax by an abused henchman, and the recycling of his earlier part worked almost as well the second time around. John Rutherford and weasel-puss Ernie Adams had prominent roles as bad guys. Although the film has no more fast action than those of Bretherton or Watt, its strong story helps make it one of the better Cassidys.

Unlike many recent entries in the series,

Hopalong Rides Again begins at the Bar 20. Buck Peters orders Cassidy to drive a cattle herd to the railhead at once. Because time is of the essence Hoppy is told to use the short cut through the Black Buttes, even though a year ago rustlers stampeded a herd there and stole more than 200 cattle. While Cassidy is receiving his instructions a visitor drives his wagon into the Bar 20 yard. It is Horace Hepburn (Harry Worth), a paleontologist and the brother of widowed neighboring rancher Nora Blake (Nora Lane), of whom Hoppy is very fond. During the chat between Hepburn and Cassidy, nosey old Windy peeks under the tarpaulin covering the back of Hepburn's wagon. Beneath the cloth he discovers several boxes of dynamite.

Thanks to Keno (Ernie Adams), their spy at the Bar 20, the rustlers know about the coming drive. Before hitting the trail Hoppy becomes suspicious of Keno and fires him, and soon afterwards the luckless little weasel is shot in the back by Hepburn after telling his boss in effect to go to

Jean Rouverol and Jimmy Ellison enjoy a intimate moment in this publicity still for **Bar 20 Rides Again** (1935, Paramount).

hell. The drive starts out from the Bar 20 and is soon joined by Buck Peters' visiting teen-age nephew Artie (Billy King), who rides with Windy in the chuckwagon. At the mouth of the Black Buttes the herd is stampeded by a dynamite-caused avalanche. Windy and Artie are buried under the falling rocks but rescued by Cassidy. Artie however is too seriously injured to be moved, and Hoppy sets up a makeshift shelter in the rocks for Windy and the boy while the rest of the herd moves on. In rescuing Artie, Hoppy comes across fragments of the box that contained the rustlers' dynamite. And when Windy remembers the dynamite he saw in Hepburn's wagon, Hoppy jumps to the conclusion that both Nora and her brother are in league with the gang.

Cassidy sets a trap by paying a social call at the Blake ranch and telling Nora that Lucky will be returning with the cattle sale money on a particular date and by a specified route---a conversation overheard by Hepburn. Then during a chat between Nora's brother and Hoppy, the foppish

paleontologist shows Cassidy what he claims is the skull of the Missing Link. Hoppy demonstrates that it's the skull of Pecos Jack Anthony from the first picture in the series, an object lesson in the fate of those who steal cattle from the Bar 20. For the next week he stays at the ranch, and is soon satisfied that Nora herself is innocent. What he doesn't know is that his trap has gone haywire. He had ordered Windy to ride back to the Bar 20 and round up some men to lie in wait for the gang where they were to ambush Lucky, but later Artie had developed a fever and Windy didn't dare leave him alone. When time has almost run out, Artie himself rides back to the ranch, arrives weak and exhausted, and summons the help Hoppy needs.

Hepburn pretends to go off to deliver some paleontological specimens but pulls up near his sister's ranch house and takes a rifle shot at Cassidy as he crosses the yard. The shot misses but not by much, and nets Hoppy a kiss from Nora before he rides out to meet Lucky. As Cassidy approaches their rendezvous site, Lucky

Paul Fix watches over William Boyd's shoulder as he warns George Hayes in this scene from **Bar 20 Rides Again** (1935, Paramount).

comes through with the money as instructed and is ambushed as Hoppy expected, but since the Bar 20 men aren't there to capture the gang, Hoppy has to ride into the ambush alone and rescue his protegé. As Cassidy and Lucky are racing for cover in the rocks where Windy has been waiting, Hepburn's chief gunman Blackie (John Rutherford) defies an order, saying "Cassidy's too much of a man to shoot in the back," and is himself coldly shot down by his boss. The stage is set for Selander's favorite climactic gambit, the siege and rescue. Hepburn orders his gang to make a frontal assault on the stronghold in the rocks. But no sooner has the battle begun than Buck Peters and his men storm onto the scene and rout the rustlers. Hepburn takes a box of dynamite and starts to climb a nearby cliff, apparently planning to blow up Cassidy and all his allies. When he is a dot in the upper distance, the dying Blackie raises his pistol and fires a bullet that seems to have a range of miles. The dynamite is hit and Hepburn blown to bits. (One can imagine the fit firearms buff

Mulford must have had when and if he saw that scene!) As the film ends Hoppy makes sure that Nora will never learn her brother's true nature.

Shortly after **Hopalong Rides Again** was in the can, shooting was slated to begin on **The Barrier** (Paramount, 1937), the first of what "Pop" Sherman hoped would be a series nominally based on the high adventure novels of Rex Beach, starring Leo Carrillo, Jean Parker and Jimmy Ellison. Sherman had engaged Edward Ludwig to direct but decided at the last minute to substitute Selander, who suddenly found himself on location in Washington's Mount Baker National Forest.

Even a Selander couldn't make movies in two places at once. As his replacement on the next Cassidy Sherman hired David Selman (19??-1957), a Columbia veteran who had made seven out of eight of that studio's final season of Tim McCoy Westerns (1934-35) and four of its first complement of eight (1935-36) with Charles Starrett. **Texas Trail** (1937) was Selman's only

Harry Worth seems unimpressed with William Boyd's marksmanship in this scene from **Bar 20 Rides Again** (1935, Paramount).

Cassidy picture, a straightforward unemotional action flick with magnificent scenery and brisk pace. Russell Harlan photographed, Sherman Rose edited. The Jack O'Donnell screenplay with additional dialogue credited to Jack Mersereau was nominally based on Mulford's 1922 novel *Tex* but in fact had not the least similarity to the book, in that sense setting a precedent for almost every remaining film in the series. Along with Boyd and Hayden and Hayes young Billy King was back, this time playing not Artie Peters but the teen-age son of an army officer, and that quintessential medicine-show huckster Earle Hodgins was cast against type in a bit part as a general. The film was enlivened by B Western stalwarts like Karl Hackett, Bob Kortman, Jack Rockwell and Raphael Bennett. But Selman's most vital contribution was that he took the cameras to some visually stunning locations that were new to this series and rarely if ever used in other Westerns.

The story is set in 1898, just after the outbreak of the Spanish-American War, and the U.S. Army finds itself desperately in need of cavalry horses. Black Jack Carson (Alexander Cross), crooked owner of the Triple X ranch, capitalizes on the situation by having his gang steal the horse herds as the soldiers are driving them to Fort Boone. Post commandant Major McCreedy (Karl Hackett) prevails upon Hopalong Cassidy to forego his current patriotic endeavor (military drills with his ranch hands prior to their all going off to join Teddy Roosevelt's Rough Riders!) and round up and deliver five hundred horses within a week. Cassidy organizes a party to capture a huge herd of wild horses and pen them in Ghost Canyon while those most suitable for the military are chosen. His preparations however are spied on by Carson's men Hawks and Shorty (Bob Kortman and Jack Rockwell). The roundup is launched, perhaps the most visually magnificent sequence in any Cassidy thus far, and Hoppy and his men corral vast numbers of wild horses while secretly observed by Carson and his gunmen.

Carson has some Triple X horses planted among

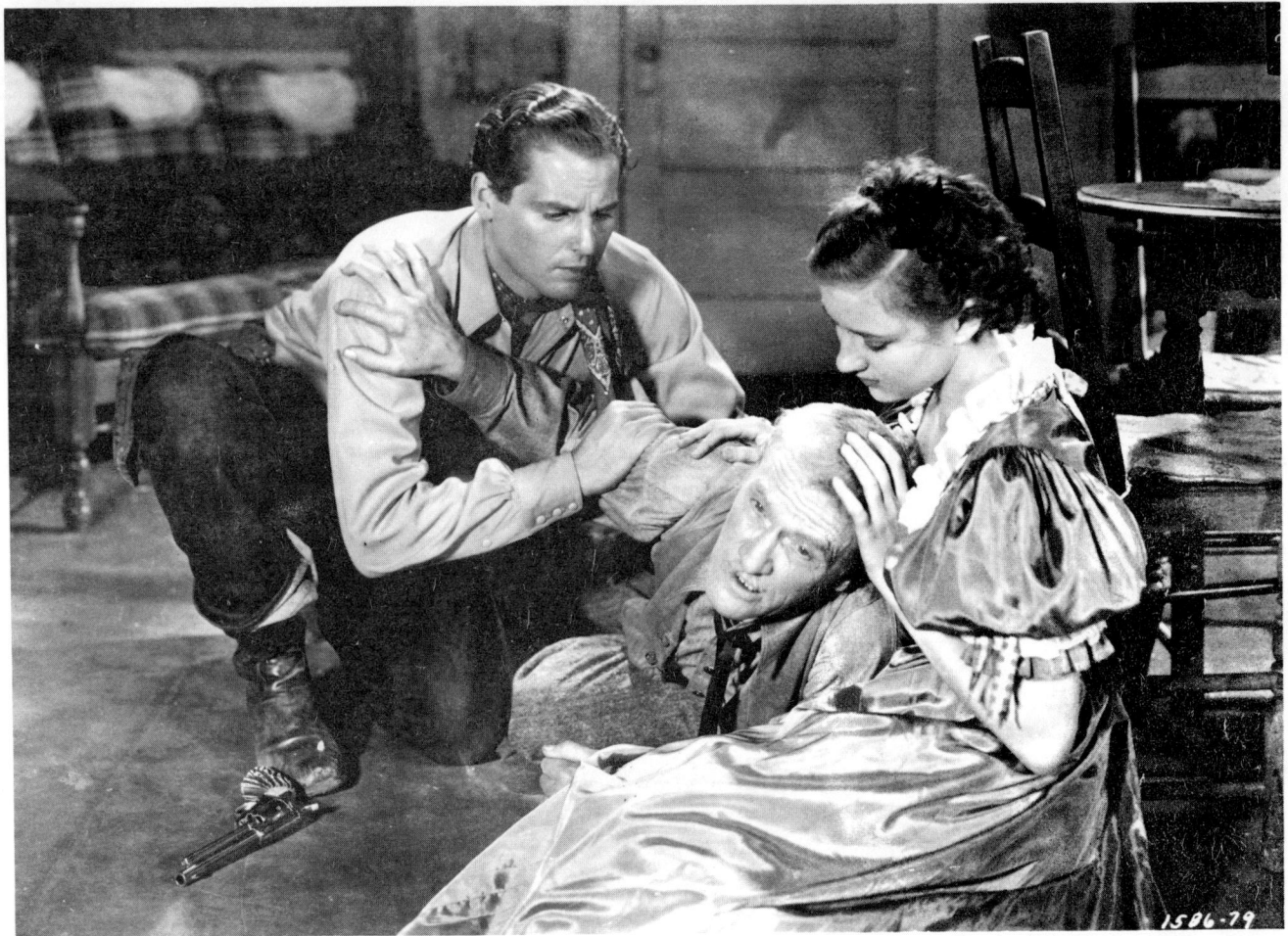

Jimmy Ellison and Jean Rouverol comfort a wounded Howard Lang in this scene from **Bar 20 Rides Again** (1935, Paramount).

the Ghost Canyon herd, then rides onto the scene, "finds" his own animals and accuses Cassidy of theft. After his men surround and overpower Hoppy's crew, Carson rides back to the Triple X, leaving to his gang the pleasure of hanging Cassidy as a horse thief. The day is saved by Major McCreedy's spunky young son Boots (Billy King), who rides out to Ghost Canyon without his father's permission to watch his idol Hoppy in action and witnesses Carson's capture of the horse wranglers. Boots sneaks down the cliffside to where the prisoners are being held and quietly unties them. Hoppy and his men pretend they're still securely bound and wait to catch their captors off guard. When the fighting breaks out the sentries are subdued and Hawks is killed falling on his own knife.

Hoppy has his men start a fire in the canyon in order to stampede the horses out at a dead run, planning to gain control of the herd at the canyon's narrow mouth and then drive the animals straight to the fort. In a stunning set-piece of action, Cassidy and his men chase off the gunmen watching the herd and launch the breakneck drive out of the canyon. When he learns what has happened, Carson and the rest of the Triple X gang race to intercept Hoppy before he reaches the fort with the horses. Lovely schoolteacher Barbara Allen (Judith Allen), who for reasons unknown seems to be staying at Carson's ranch, overhears the gang's plan and rides wildly to Fort Boone to alert Major McCreedy. Cassidy leaves the herd, takes up a concealed position and singlehandedly tries to hold back Carson's crew. Outnumbered and low on ammunition, he's saved at the crucial moment by the arrival of Major McCreedy and a troop of cavalry. With the gang captured and the horses delivered to the fort, Hoppy receives a lieutenant's bars, an assignment with Roosevelt's Rough Riders in Cuba, and his grateful country's thanks as the film ends in a burst of patriotic hokum.

When he came back from location work on **The Barrier** (which did so poorly at the box office

The townspeople spokesman asks William Boyd for the story behind the wounded man in this scene from **Call of the Prairie** (1936, Paramount).

that Sherman scrapped his plans for a Rex Beach-based series) Selander plunged into the season's third Cassidy, a draggy but intriguing little item which seems anything but the work of an action connoisseur and admirer of strong capable women. **Partners of the Plains** (1938) was directed by Selander from a Harrison Jacobs script supposedly based on Mulford's 1918 novel *The Man From Bar-20* but in fact having not a blessed thing in common with its putative source. Harlan photographed as usual and Warwick was back in the cutting room. Al Bridge was featured as the main villain and Earle Hodgins' part as a lame-brained sheriff fit him like a glove, but for reasons built into the story most of the cast were strangers to the Western screen. A contract dispute with Sherman had led to George Hayes' temporary absence from the series and Selander had to substitute chunky, balding Harvey Clark, whom he'd used in some of the Buck Jones pictures at Universal. Clark's lumbering efforts at a Hayes imitation served only to prove what a natural

comic genius Hayes was.

As the film opens Lucky Jenkins and Baldy Morton (Harvey Clark), two cowhands on the L-D ranch, are in town to meet the ranch's absentee owner who's arriving by stagecoach on an inspection trip. The owner turns out to be a frigid, imperious and lovely Englishwoman named Lorna Drake (Gwen Gaze), and accompanying her are her fusspot Aunt Martha (Hilda Plowright) and her stuffy British fiance Ronald Harwood (John Warburton). Arriving in town on the same stage-coach is Scar Lewis (Al Bridge), just out of prison and bent on revenge against the man who sent him up---Hopalong Cassidy.

On the way back to the ranch Lorna impatiently grabs the reins of the wagon team and whips up the horses into a fast run. Hoppy sees this and races to overtake and bring under control what he thinks is a runaway wagon. This is how he meets the boss he has never before seen, and the battle of the sexes is on. After a series of beautifully staged run-ins with Lorna, Hoppy quits the ranch

85

George Hayes doesn't seem to trust Jimmy Ellison even though he is tied-up in this publicity still for **Call of the Prairie** (1936, Paramount).

in disgust. Lorna however claims that the white stallion he rode away on belongs not to him but to the ranch, and forces the sheriff (Earle Hodgins) to arrest Cassidy. After he's jailed Lorna inveigles the sheriff into paroling Hoppy in her custody so that he'll be compelled to remain on the ranch and obey her every command. When he learns of this condition, Cassidy at first refuses to leave his cell, then good-naturedly consents.

Throughout the clash of wills between Lorna and Hoppy, Ronald Harwood has become increasingly jealous of Lorna's obvious if unacknowledged attraction to Cassidy. Scar Lewis observes the conflict and sees a chance to use Harwood in a scheme of revenge against Hoppy. At Scar's instigation, Harwood attempts to "accidentally" shoot Cassidy, but the plan misfires and Hoppy becomes permanently suspicious of the Englishman from then on. Despite being legally under Lorna's thumb, Cassidy still refuses to knuckle under to her. In a rage she threatens to get even by turning the L-D into a sheep ranch,

and a furious Hoppy warns her that any such crazy idea will lead only to a range war.

Scar Lewis and Harwood plot to get rid of Hoppy by luring him to a deserted cabin near the dam on the L-D property and then blowing up the dam so that the cabin and Hoppy will be submerged. But Cassidy, already suspicious of Harwood, remains ready for trouble. After one more fight with Lorna, Hoppy rides away from the ranch. Baldy, learning that Lorna really loves Cassidy, devises a plan to bring them together. He has Lorna ride out to the dam near the cabin (where by a curious coincidence Scar Lewis and his gang are waiting) and promises to bring Hoppy there so that the two can kiss and make up.

Scar's henchman Doc Galer (Al Hill) is waiting at the dam for Hoppy to ride into the trap. But expecting an ambush as he is, Cassidy gets the drop on Doc and shoots him, and a repentant Harwood pulls the lit fuse out of Galer's dynamite before it can go off. Like an idiot he throws the burning fuse into dry brush where it starts a

Jimmy Ellison literally stumbles into a meeting with Muriel Evans in this scene from **Call of the Prairie** (1936, Paramount).

raging forest fire. Baldy arrives and tells Hoppy that Lorna is trapped in the cabin which is directly in the path of the flames. Cassidy sends Lucky to the L-D for help, then braves both the fire and the guns of Scar and his gang in a desperate attempt to reach the burning cabin and rescue Lorna. He gets her out of the fire but the two of them and Baldy are trapped among the rocks by Scar's gunmen until in Selander's usual siege-and-rescue gambit Lucky and the ranch hands arrive to rout the gang and kill Scar Lewis. A chastened Lorna submits to Cassidy's orders for the first but clearly not the last time, and when she leaves the territory to return to England it is hinted unsubtly that she's not through trying to win Hoppy's heart. A feminist Selander might have been; an uncritical feminist he was not.

The fourth Cassidy of the season and the only irredeemably weak entry in the half-dozen was **Cassidy of Bar 20** (1938). Boyd and Hayden carried on in their by now time-honored roles but the unsatisfactory Harvey Clark was replaced by the even less pleasing Frank Darien, who was billed as "Pappy" but was obviously bending over backwards to do a Windy imitation. The screenplay by Norman Houston pretended to be based on Mulford's 1929 novel *Me An' Shorty* but was actually a sort of sequel to his own script for **Hopalong Rides Again**, in the sense that the female lead was rancher Nora Blake from that film, who again was portrayed by Nora Lane. Suave, shifty-eyed Robert Fiske played the chief villain, Carleton Young (who would later play the romantic sidekick in several quickie Westerns at PRC Pictures) had a good role as a weak-willed youth under the outlaw leader's thumb, and the boy's mother was played by indomitable Gertrude Hoffmann, later famous as sprightly old Mrs. Odetts in the 1950s TV sitcom *My Little Margie.* Russell Harlan photographed and Sherman Rose was back for his third stint in the editor's chair.

After the death of her brother in **Hopalong Rides Again**, Nora Blake apparently moved

Jimmy Ellison seems to be causing some amusement for George Hayes and his gang in this scene from **Call of the Prairie** (1936, Paramount).

away and bought another ranch. As the film opens she is being harassed by her ruthless neighbor Clay Allison (Robert Fiske), who wants her property for himself and is trying to force her out by cutting her fences and stealing her cattle. Finally Nora writes Cassidy for help and Hoppy along with sidekicks Lucky and Pappy ride to her rescue. On the way to Nora's ranch the three have a run-in with young Jeff Caffrey (Carleton Young), Allison's foreman, who orders them to leave the territory. Hoppy takes Jeff's gun away from him and the trio ride on. They reach the ranch and are talking with Nora and her foreman Tom Dillon (John Elliott) when Allison appears with the sheriff (Edward Cassidy), who arrests Hoppy and his pals on charges of trespass and damage to Allison's property and assault on Caffrey. After the three are jailed, Allison makes another attempt to buy Nora's ranch and is turned down.

At their trial Hoppy, Lucky and Pappy offer to work at Allison's ranch until their fines are paid off. Allison agrees and the three are put to work. In due course they find exactly what they expected and hoped for, some of Nora's rustled cattle commingled with the Allison herd. Hoppy makes a break for freedom and safely reaches Nora's ranch. Expecting trouble now, Allison summons a small army of gunmen from Texas.

While Cassidy and Nora are making plans at the ranch house, Allison gets into a dispute with Tom Dillon at the boundary line between the two spreads. In the presence of a horrified Jeff Caffrey, Allison coolly shoots Dillon in the back. Just as Pappy tells Cassidy about the army of gunmen drifting into town, Dillon's horse trots into the ranch yard with its master's body on its back. Vowing revenge, Cassidy first sends for help from the Bar 20, then rides into town and accuses Allison of the murder. But the showdown between them is aborted, ostensibly so that indomitable old Ma Caffrey (Gertrude Hoffmann) can find out whether her son was involved in Dillon's murder, actually for the simple reason

The bartender looks worried as Jimmy Ellison and George Hayes face off in this scene from **Call of the Prairie** (1936, Paramount).

that the film would be much too short if the climax came here.

Ma Caffrey learns that her son knows who killed Dillon and forces the sheriff to lock him up until he talks. That night Jeff discovers a secret tunnel running under the jail, makes his escape and goes to Allison for getaway money. Allison shoots him in cold blood to keep his mouth shut. Dying, Jeff crawls back through the tunnel to the cell and calls for his mother, who finds him dead on the jail floor, clutching the ejected shell of the bullet that killed him. It's a .44-40, an unusual caliber favored only by Clay Allison, and it convinces Ma Caffrey that Allison murdered her son.

Allison and his Texas gunmen attempt to get rid of Hoppy and his sidekicks by attacking Nora's ranch, and we are treated to another Selander siege, which is broken when the Bar 20 men summoned by Hoppy storm into the picture. Cassidy and his allies chase the gang into town where they barricade themselves in the jailhouse, which is also Ma Caffrey's general store. Ma accuses

Allison of Jeff's murder, and Allison is about to kill her too when Hoppy gets into the building by the same secret tunnel Jeff used earlier in the film and kills Allison. With the gang disposed of, Hoppy and his friends head back to the Bar 20.

Under Bretherton and Watt the Cassidy seasons had tended to open with the strong pictures and close with the weak, but the films of 1937-38 broke the tradition, and this time the mediocrities were in the middle and the powerhouses at both ends. Indeed the third season's final pair of pictures rank among the best of all the Cassidys and among the finest movies of any sort in Selander's long career. With **Heart of Arizona** (1938) Mulford's old business buddy J.D. Trop came aboard as associate producer, while Sherman Rose carried on with the editing and Russell Harlan with the cinematography. The best news in the casting department was that George Hayes had settled his salary dispute with Sherman and was back supporting Boyd and Hayden. Although Billy King once again played Buck Peters' teen-

89

George Hayes and his gang (which includes John Merton and Al Bridge) get Jimmy Ellison drunk in this publicity still for **Call of the Prairie** (1936, Paramount).

age nephew, the role of Peters himself was temporarily taken over by John Elliott, who had had kindly-old-man parts in several earlier Cassidys. The two exceptionally vital female roles went to Natalie Moorhead and Dorothy Short and the biggest black hats to Lane Chandler (star of several super-el-cheapo B Westerns in the early Thirties) and Alden Chase. This time Mulford was not credited as the author of any source novel but only for having created the main characters, an honest statement of the limit of his involvement which was followed in the credits of almost all the later Cassidys. Working from a strong screenplay by Norman Houston, Selander directed one of his best and most personal films, using the two powerfully drawn women characters to reverse the sex-role conventions of the traditional Western.

The picture opens with Belle Starr (Natalie Moorhead) returning by stagecoach to her Arizona ranch after serving five years in prison for her late husband's rustling activities. Sheriff Hawley (John Beach) halts the coach along the trail and tries to stop Belle from going back to the ranch and her daughter Jacqueline (Dorothy Short). Hopalong Cassidy happens by and helps Belle escape by lending her his horse. Belle is deeply in love with Hoppy but, as an ex-convict, is too ashamed to reveal her feelings, and Cassidy is too much a stranger to his own emotions to tell Belle that her prison term doesn't affect his fondness for her. The tragedy of their inability to communicate is not passed on to their children, so that when Hoppy's quasi-son Lucky meets Jacqueline Starr, love seems to bloom quickly and naturally. What this film really deals with is not good guys and bad guys but the emotional entanglements of these four people---and a fifth.

During Belle's prison term her ranch has been run by foreman Dan Ringo (Alden Chase), who has his own designs on Belle and becomes insanely jealous of her obvious attraction to Cassidy. Ringo has been rustling from all the ranches in the area, including Belle's, and selling the herds to crooked cattle buyer Trimmer Winkler

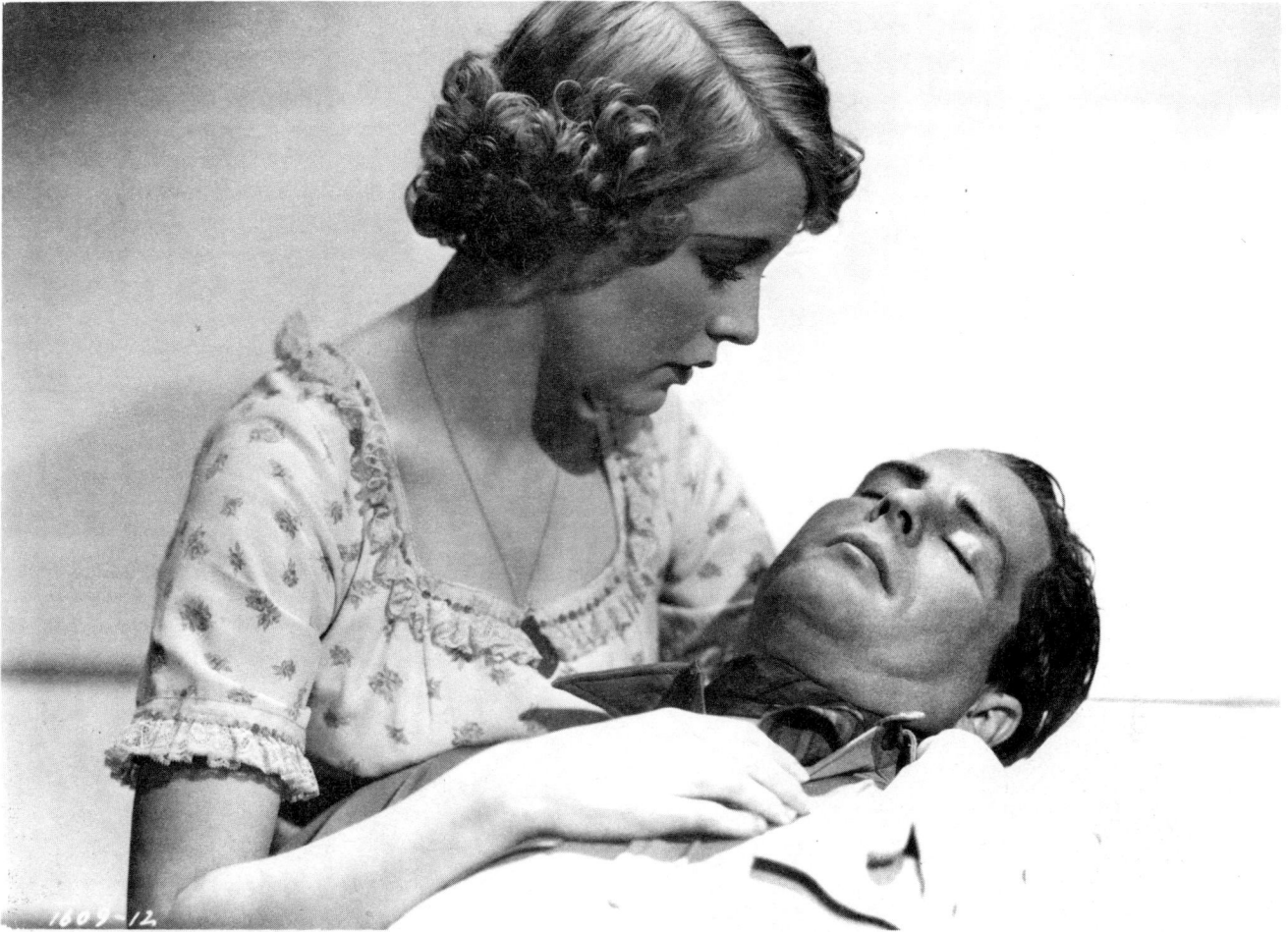

Lovely Muriel Evans looks at an unconscious Jimmy Ellison in this publicity still for **Three on the Trail** (1936, Paramount).

(Lane Chandler). Ringo's "mole" on the Bar 20 is a cowhand aptly named Twister (Leo McMahon), whom Hoppy eventually comes to suspect and kicks off the ranch much as he did the rustler spy Keno in Houston's script for **Hopalong Rides Again**. Later Twister tries to shoot Cassidy from ambush, but teen-age Artie Peters (Billy King) spots Twister in the nick of time and kills him, saving Hoppy's life.

Ringo plots to remove Cassidy from Belle's life by framing him and his pals for the rustling. After several sequences of confrontation with Sheriff Hawley, who is all too ready to believe the worst of Hoppy, Cassidy persuades the lawman of his innocence and devises a plan to trap the rustlers. They visit Belle's ranch, where Hoppy ropes one of her steers and inserts a small Mexican coin in its hoof. Then they arrange to leave the herd unguarded so that it's sure to be stolen, and as expected the rustlers quickly scoop up the cattle. Sheriff Hawley happens to be keeping watch on Trimmer Winkler's corral when the stolen herd is

delivered there by Ringo. When the sheriff rides up and retrieves the Mexican coin from the marked steer's hoof, Winkler murders him. Then Ringo and his men race back to the Starr ranch to get rid of Cassidy. Winkler stays behind and is caught and killed by Windy, who then races to the Bar 20 to get help for Hoppy.

Ringo and his gang follow the standard Selander siege gambit by trapping Cassidy, Belle and Jacqueline in the rocks near the ranch house. They offer to let the women live if Cassidy will come out in the open and let himself be killed. Hoppy is ready to emerge from the shelter of the rocks but Belle refuses to let him go. Then comes the magic moment of role-reversal: Belle herself steps out from the rocks, marching inexorably towards Ringo and his men with two guns blazing until she's shot down. Hoppy runs out into no man's land to save her, but too late. Lucky, Windy and the Bar 20 men complete the by now traditional Selander climax by roaring onto the scene in time to kill or capture all of the gang. In one of the

In this publicity still for **Three on the Trail** (1936, Paramount) it is Jimmy Ellison who is looking lovingly at Muriel Evans.

most touching final sequences in any Western, Hoppy sadly lays Belle to rest beneath the Arizona rocks she loved so dearly, knowing by the way she died how desperately she cared for him.

The season's last film emphasized suspense and intrigue rather than straight action but ended with one of the most rousing chase-and-fight scenes in the 66-picture series. **Bar 20 Justice** (1938) was directed by Selander from an excellent script by newcomer Arnold Belgard, with "additional sequences and dialogue" by our old friend Harrison Jacobs. William Duncan reclaimed the Buck Peters part, Gwen Gaze came back as another strong-minded woman---although a sweeter one than her imperious bitch from **Partners of the Plains**---and the chief villains were Pat O'Brien (no, not *that* Pat O'Brien) and a tall, slender, hypnotically deep-voiced young man named Paul Sutton who is best known for his long stint on radio as Sergeant Preston of the Yukon. The excellent uncredited score of mysterioso and agitato themes came as usual from other Para-

mount features of a few seasons back. Russell Harlan and Robert Warwick did their accustomed work of cinematography and cutting.

Early in the film Denny Dennis (John Beach) is killed by an apparently fallen support timber in a tunnel of his gold mine, the Freeze Out, which has a reputation as a jinx. Frazier (Pat O'Brien), owner of the nearby Devil May Care mine, later offers to buy the Freeze Out from Dennis' widow Ann (Gwen Gaze), but she refuses. Suspecting that her husband's death was murder and that the Freeze Out miners are being deliberately frightened by a sabotage campaign into quitting their jobs, Ann seeks help from her old friend Hopalong Cassidy, who postpones a long-awaited trip to New York in order to aid her.

The truth of the matter is that Frazier has dug a secret tunnel connecting his own played-out Devil May Care with the still prosperous Freeze Out. With the connivance of Slade (Paul Sutton), the Freeze Out foreman, a team of Frazier's miners has been using the tunnel every night to enter the

92

The "trio westerns" started with these three film buddies William Boyd, George Hayes and Jimmy Ellison, seen here in a publicity still for **Three on the Trail** (1936, Paramount).

Freeze Out, mine its ore and take it back through the passage to the Devil May Care. When Dennis had become suspicious Frazier had had him killed. Naturally Frazier is far from overjoyed when Hoppy arrives on the scene.

Cassidy confers with Ann and they decide that despite the series of continuing "accidents" the Freeze Out will remain open. Soon Hoppy begins to suspect the truth. He pressures Slade to hire a night watchman for the Freeze Out, and when as expected Slade employs one of his own henchmen, Hoppy kidnaps the man his first night on the job and has Lucky take him out to the Bar 20. The next morning, in the best comedy sequence in any Cassidy film, Windy casually visits the mine site, pretending to be stone deaf, all but senile and in need of work. This is just the kind of idiot Slade needs as a guard, and he hires Windy to take over as night watchman just as Cassidy knew he would. Before many nights on the job are behind him Windy has observed Frazier's men secretly mining the Freeze Out tunnels. Cassidy explores

the Freeze Out, hunting for the moles' entrance from the Devil May Care, and captures Pierce (Walter Long), the malevolent-faced keeper of the secret tunnel.

Hoping to expose Slade by pretending still to trust him, Hoppy brings his prisoner to the foreman, and the next morning the two of them take Pierce to a deserted shack where they can question him about Dennis' murder. Slade gives himself away but Cassidy's plan literally goes up in smoke, for Frazier has trailed them to the shack and he and Slade overpower Hoppy and set fire to the building after leaving him securely bound inside. Fortunately Windy has also followed the men to the shack and pulls Hoppy out of the blaze. Cassidy decides to play dead for a while so that Frazier will be off guard.

That night Hoppy and his pals set a trap. When the Devil May Care gang has started its work in the Freeze Out, watchman Windy is to light his pipe in the mine's entranceway, the signal will be passed along from hilltop to hilltop by the Bar 20

93

The most familiar publicity photo from the Cassidy series shows Jimmy Ellison, George Hayes and William Boyd. Used for **Three on the Trail** (1936, Paramount).

men and their main force will invade the Devil May Care, storm the secret passage and get the drop on the gang from behind. But Windy has picked this of all evenings to go to work without matches, and his frantic attempts to give the signal without them produce a wonderful scene of comedy and suspense, capped with neat irony when Slade graciously hands a match to the deaf old watchman. Hoppy and the Bar 20 men follow through with their plan and a furious gun battle breaks out in the Freeze Out tunnels, ending with the death of Slade and the capture of the gang. Meanwhile Frazier, who was caught in his office earlier and was being guarded by Buck Peters, breaks away and races for freedom. Cassidy chases him into the mountains and captures him after a fantastically imaginative fight. Ann Dennis adds a touch of social conscience to the final moments by arranging to share the Freeze Out profits with her workers.

Chapter Five

The 1938-39 season of Cassidy films saw no radical personnel changes on either side of the cameras. Boyd, Hayden and Hayes carried on nobly as Hoppy, Lucky and Windy, insulting and enjoying each other on screen as only the best of friends can. Boris Morros, who is less famous for his creative work than for his infiltration of the American Communist Party as an FBI counterspy, joined the unit as music director, with responsibility for heightening the films' key scenes with a blend of new themes and music recycled from other Paramount features. Lesley Selander directed five of the season's six Cassidys, Russell Harlan photographed the entire half-dozen, and the cutting-room work was shared by unit veterans Robert Warwick and Sherman Rose. Yet it turned out to be a disappointing brace of pictures: one or two gems, two mixed bags, two dogs.

Perhaps the fault rests primarily with Harry Sherman. It was at this time, having dropped his plan for a series "based on" the tales of Rex Beach, that Sherman took over as producer of Paramount's other great contribution to 1930s action films, the quasi-series "based on" the classic Western novels of Zane Grey. These films had been a tradition at the studio since the early Twenties; indeed the screenplay of the first entry, **To the Last Man** (Paramount, 1923), had been by the earliest Cassidy scriptwriter, Doris Schroeder. For the past fifteen years Paramount had been releasing new cinematic versions of each of the small number of Grey books to which it held rights. The silents had been directed by such aces as Victor Fleming and William A. Howard and had starred top names like Richard Dix, Jack Holt and the young Gary Cooper. In the early 1930s the elaborate action scenes from these silents had been supplemented with sound effects and spliced into talking-picture remakes, many directed by an energetic novice named Henry Hathaway and starring the lean, taciturn and youthful Randolph Scott. Paramount had turned

out at least three so-called Zane Grey Westerns every year from 1933 through 1937. For the 1938-39 season it cut back to two pictures and turned over a generous budget and full responsibility for making the films to Sherman's organization. As his director "Pop" naturally chose Selander. His workload may just have been too heavy, the temptation too strong to concentrate on the more prestigious and expensive films--- **The Mysterious Rider** (Paramount, 1938) starring Douglass Dumbrille and Russell Hayden, and **Heritage of the Desert** (Paramount, 1939) in which Hayden appeared with Donald Woods--- and to slough off the Cassidys. Whatever the explanation, that season proved by and large rather tepid.

And the most disastrous of the lot, the most yawnful Cassidy in the entire series to that date, was the first of the six. Selander directed **Pride of the West** (1938) from an original screenplay by his immediate predecessor at the Cassidy helm, Nate Watt, but the film is actionless, emotionless, lacking any hint of reversals of convention---in short it has neither the Selander hallmarks nor those of Watt and might as well have been filmed on an indoor set and directed by a robot. Besides Boyd and Hayden and Hayes there were several old friends in the cast including Earle Hodgins as another nincompoop sheriff, Billy King as another spunky adolescent and Willie Fung once again ridiculing his race as a gibberish-spouting Chink. Among the bad guys were James Craig, soon to work his way up to B-picture leading man, and Glenn Strange, a fine Western villain better known in his old age as the bartender in TV's *Gunsmoke*. Russell Harlan photographed, Sherman Rose edited, but the trouble with **Pride of the West** is that no one seemed to take any pride in it at all.

Several ranchers have mortgaged their property to land dealer Nixon (James Craig) but have fallen behind in their payments and face foreclosure. The town banker Caldwell (Kenneth Harlan) agrees to

William Boyd has a big smile for his protegé Jimmy Ellison in this publicity still for **Three on the Trail** (1936, Paramount).

loan the ranchers the $30,000 necessary to keep Nixon from foreclosing and sends for the funds in gold from a distant bank. But the stagecoach bringing the gold to town is held up and Lucky, who happens to be a passenger, is wounded. Mary Martin (Charlotte Field), the sheriff's daughter, is also on board and takes Lucky to a doctor, while Windy rides to town for the sheriff (Earle Hodgins). The posse that combs the countryside for the thieves comes back emptyhanded. Actually the robbery has been engineered by Nixon and Caldwell in a plot to take over the mortgaged ranches, and their gunmen led by Saunders (Glenn Strange) have hidden the sacks of gold in a deserted shack outside of town. Hoping to oust Sheriff Martin from office, Caldwell accuses him of being in with the thieves.

Mary and her teen-age brother Dick (Billy King) ride to enlist the aid of Hopalong Cassidy. On their way to the Bar 20 they encounter some tough-looking men hanging around the old shack, and when they report this incident Hoppy begins to suspect that the gunmen's presence near the long-deserted cabin may be connected with the stagecoach robbery. He keeps the shack under observation and finds the toughs still there. Later, while Hoppy is elsewhere, young Dick Martin keeps an eye on the shack. He observes two gang members taking some of the sacks away, follows the men into town and is amazed to see them secretly deliver the gold to the bank. This news convinces Hoppy that Caldwell was behind the robbery and he devises a scheme to prove it.

While Cassidy himself starts a diversionary fistfight with Caldwell and Nixon in Sing Loo's cafe (one of the most inept fight scenes in any B Western of the late Thirties), Lucky and Windy stage a bold daylight bank robbery. Although Hoppy is subdued during the fight, he manages to get away in the confusion following the announcement that the bank has been robbed. Caldwell, Nixon, several gang members and a sheriff's posse pursue Lucky and Windy to the deserted shack where Hoppy's pals make a stand. While

96

Another publicity photo of Jimmy Ellison and Muriel Evans from **Three on the Trail** (1936, Paramount).

the posse is besieging the cabin Cassidy rides up, negotiates a cease fire and "persuades" his friends to surrender peacefully. At the jail, when the stolen bank loot is turned over to the sheriff, it proves to consist of the same sacks of gold that had been stolen from the stagecoach. The evidence squarely against them, Caldwell and Nixon and their gang are locked up without a scintilla of resistance and this impossibly boring excuse for a Western crawls to an end.

The shooting schedule for **The Mysterious Rider**, which Selander was directing, conflicted with that of the next Cassidy, and to helm the latter Sherman hired Edward D. Venturini, an Argentinian of Italian descent whose specialty was making Spanish-speaking versions of Hollywood films. Venturini's only other English-language talking picture was **The Llano Kid** (Paramount, 1939), an unsuccessful attempt, produced by Sherman and starring Tito Guizar and Gale Sondergaard, to compete with 20th Century-Fox's popular Cisco Kid series. **In Old Mexico** (1938)

however was one of the season's better Cassidys, with powerful emotional currents and deep empathy for the people and culture below the border. The Harrison Jacobs screenplay brings back from his script for the 1937 **Borderland** both Colonel Gonzales of the Mexican Secret Service and that master of malevolence The Fox. Although the colonel was once again played by Trevor Bardette, Stephen Morris apparently wasn't available to repeat his role as the villain, and lean young baritone Paul Sutton's performance in the part owed nothing to Morris and everything to the dashing romantic tradition of the Zorro films. (Zorro of course is Spanish for fox, and ironically it was a Sutton look-alike named Reed Hadley who starred a year later in Republic's fantastically exciting 12-chapter serial **Zorro's Fighting Legion**.) Jane Clayton, who played Colonel Gonzales' fiery sister Elena, later entered a brief marriage with Russell Hayden, then changed her professional name to Jan Clayton and won fame on Broadway in Rodgers

Both William Boyd and Jimmy Ellison are not wearing their normal costumes in this scene with John Rutherford from **Three on the Trail** (1936, Paramount).

and Hammerstein's *Carousel* and on TV as the Mom figure in the long-running *Lassie* series. Russell Harlan photographed, Robert Warwick edited, the original music for the film was by Gregory Stone and the music director was Boris Morros.

The Fox (Paul Sutton) has escaped from prison and is after the men who put him there, Colonel Gonzales (Trevor Bardette) and Hopalong Cassidy. Hoppy receives a letter signed with the colonel's name, requesting that they meet at the Gonzales rancho below the border, and the colonel gets a similar letter apparently from Cassidy. Both of course have been sent by The Fox. On the way with Lucky and Windy to the hacienda, Hoppy asks directions from an old peasant who is actually The Fox in disguise. At the rancho the three are cordially welcomed by the colonel's father Don Carlos Gonzales (Allen Garcia), even though the visit is completely unexpected. Don Carlos introduces the new-comers to his daughter Anita (Jane Clayton) and to

Janet Leeds (Betty Amann), a house guest and friend of Anita's---and in reality The Fox's sister. As Colonel Gonzales rides toward the rancho he's captured by The Fox's gang and shot down in cold blood, dying with supreme dignity. That night, during a party at the hacienda, a gang member throws a rock through a window. Tied to the rock is a note advising where the now long overdue colonel can be found. Hoppy, Lucky and Windy ride to the indicated spot with Don Carlos' vaqueros and find young Gonzales' body. Beside the corpse is a three-letter message, ZOR, written in the sand. Cassidy deduces that in his last moments alive the colonel was trying to write *zorro*, the Spanish for fox, and realizes that both Gonzales and he himself were tricked into coming to Mexico so that The Fox could kill them. Strangely however he doesn't go chasing The Fox but is content to hang around Gonzales' hacienda, playing up to Janet Leeds. This course of inaction convinces the fiery Elena that Cassidy is a coward, but in fact Hoppy has come to suspect

98

Onslow Stevens watches as John Rutherford ties up William Boyd in this scene from **Three on the Trail** (1936, Paramount).

that Janet is allied with The Fox and is setting a trap of his own.

Finally one day Janet invites Cassidy for a horseback ride into the desert, and knowing that she'll lead him to The Fox, Hoppy consents. When they're alone on the trail she pulls a gun on him. Hoppy takes it away from her and tells her to go back to the States and start life over without her brother. The Fox comes out from behind a nearby rock and covers Cassidy, but Hoppy jumps him, and while they're fighting Janet takes Cassidy's advice and rides pell-mell out of the picture. Cassidy subdues The Fox, and Windy who's been hiding just out of sight joins them. But meanwhile, not far away, Lucky and Anita have been hunting for clues to The Fox and stumble upon his gang's hideout. A gunfight breaks out, and Hoppy sends Windy back to the hacienda for help while he himself and his prisoner join Anita and Lucky in an attempt to hold back the gang. Windy is badly wounded as he races towards the Gonzales ranch but arrives and summons help.

There are elements taken from the climax of **Borderland** but even more from the usual Selander end-game as Hoppy, Lucky and Anita make their stand in the rocks with The Fox held at gunpoint among them. At the darkest moment Don Carlos and his vaqueros storm onto the scene to rout the gang, and The Fox meets his long-deserved death when he tries to stab Cassidy in the back with a concealed knife. The final scene is as genuinely emotional as any Watt close, with Hoppy and Lucky tenderly insulting the wounded Windy in his sickbed.

Selander was back at the helm for **The Frontiersman** (1938), which at 74 minutes was the longest Cassidy since the Nate Watt season. Its last ten minutes feature one of Selander's best chase-and-fight climaxes but until then the film is all too slow and dull, with no action, some interesting relationships, and far too much footage of the Bar 20 men rounding up and subjecting to compulsory education a passel of hooligan children. William Duncan carried on as Buck

Jimmy Ellison, George Hayes and William Boyd are all angrily ready for action in this scene from **Three on the Trail** (1936, Paramount).

Peters but Billy King had apparently outgrown the role of Artie, which was played this time by the much younger child actor Dick Jones (whose main claim to Western fame came in the early 1950s when he was Jock Mahoney's sidekick in that action-crammed TV series *The Range Rider*). We may pass over in silence the performance of Charles A. Hughes as the chief villain, but his top gunman was portrayed by Roy Barcroft who was then at the start of a long and honored career as perhaps the most famous badman in B Westerns. The screenplay was by Norman Houston, photography by Russell Harlan, editing by Sherman Rose.

A band of cattle rustlers led by a mystery man named Dan Rawley has been plaguing the Bar 20 and neighboring spreads, while at the same time Buck Peters' wild 10-year-old nephew Artie (Dickie Jones) has been unleashing minor plagues of his own on Hoppy and the other adults. When the unruly behavior of all the local children causes the town schoolteacher to quit in mid-term, Mayor

Judson Thorpe (Charles A. Hughes) hires a replacement teacher by mail, expecting the person to be a man who can keep order in the classroom. In a typical Selander role reversal the teacher who arrives turns out to be a beautiful woman, June Lake (Evelyn Venable). At first the male chauvinist Thorpe refuses to give her the job, but after pressure from Cassidy---and from the parents whose kids have been running wild for several weeks---the mayor relents. All the single men for miles around begin to compete for June's favors, all that is except Cassidy, the man to whom she's most attracted. On the rebound she becomes involved with Mayor Thorpe, having no idea of course that on top of his official function Thorpe is also the notorious rustler Dan Rawley.

While the Rawley gang continues raiding cattle, Cassidy and the Bar 20 hands become self-appointed truant officers, rounding up Artie and all the wild children in the area and forcing them to attend classes. Day by day under June's tutelage the undisciplined brats are transformed into

William Duncan listens as William Boyd tries to make a point with Claude King in this scene from **Three on the Trail** (1936, Paramount).

scrubbed, combed, shiny-faced and patriotic little citizens.

Shortly before graduation day June tells Hoppy that she and Thorpe are going to be married and move to Boston at term's end. Cassidy, who by now suspects that Thorpe is Rawley but has no evidence, opposes June's marriage on various pretexts, and June angrily accuses him of being jealous. The graduation ceremony takes place, featuring several songs by the St. Brendan Boys Choir, and without a word of liberal philoso-phizing Selander shows the way things ought to be by filming black and white children sitting and singing together.

The only action in the movie follows the cere-mony. As Thorpe and June are about to elope, his top gunman Sutton (Roy Barcroft) slips into the schoolhouse and confronts his boss. Overheard by June in the next room, Sutton refers to the mayor as Rawley and accuses him of planning to run out on his men. Thorpe kills Sutton and makes a frantic getaway. Understanding at last

why Hoppy opposed her marriage, June runs to tell him what has happened, and Cassidy and the Bar 20 men ride off in pursuit. Thorpe joins his gang and they decide to make one last cattle raid before leaving the territory. While the raid is in progress Hoppy and his men catch up with the gang and a large-scale, superbly directed battle breaks out. Thorpe manages to shoot the gun out of Cassidy's hand---another of those marvelous little reversals of expectation Selander loved---and flees from the battle, but in a great chase-and-fight sequence Hoppy overtakes and overpowers him. As the film ends a sadder but wiser June Lake returns east but promises Hoppy that someday she'll come back to teach school there again.

Throughout the four seasons of the Cassidy series Harry Sherman had been bombarded with complaints about the films from Mulford, and quite legitimate complaints from the author's point of view. After all, Mulford had spent a third of a century making himself an authority on the history and development of the West. He'd built his

101

A wounded Ernie Adams is surrounded by William Boyd, George Hayes and Jimmy Ellison in this scene from **Three on the Trail** (1936, Paramount).

literary reputation on investing novels and stories with painstakingly accurate detail. Now he saw his rough-hewn knight of the frontier sanitized and prettified with that fancy black outfit and the white circus horse, and even worse, he saw his own name on the screen as in some sense the author of these wildly inaccurate action fantasies. A disgusted and outraged Mulford not only wrote nasty letters to "Pop" Sherman but gave countless newspaper interviews in which he blasted the Cassidy films all over the map. "I wish I had never sold the screen rights to my books," he told one reporter, "and if I had them back, Hollywood would never get them while I lived." At first Sherman tried to placate Mulford, mailing him boxes of his favorite cigars. By early 1939 however either "Pop" or Selander or someone decided that it was time to put the old crank in his place. The vehicle chosen was the next Cassidy film.

Sunset Trail (1939) was by far the best of the season, with swift action, a well-crafted Norman Houston screenplay---including like his **Heart of**

Arizona script a widowed mother and her lively daughter---and many opportunites for Selander's reversals of convention. Robert Fiske from **Cassidy of Bar 20** was back as the lead villain and Glenn Strange as his chief heavy, and Jane Clayton from **In Old Mexico** played the younger of the two women. Boyd's role is gleefully written and directed so as to poke fun at his aversion to horses and stunting, but the major butt of the film's satire is a pompous little comic Easterner named E. Prescott Furbush, on his first trip West after years of writing the wild-and-woolly adventures of Deadeye Dan, whom he insists on describing as a "real" person. This delicious mock-Mulford is portrayed with zest by Maurice Cass, who specialized in playing eccentric scientists and other kinds of stuck-up oldsters. If he's remembered today at all, it's for his role as the Dr. Zarkov-inspired comic genius of the future in that Grade Z science-fiction series of early 1950s TV, *Rocky Jones, Space Ranger*. Russell Harlan photographed, Robert

102

Claude King, George Hayes, William Duncan, Jimmy Ellison and Muriel Evans gather round a wounded William Boyd in this scene from **Three on the Trail** (1936, Paramount).

Warwick edited.

As the film opens, rancher John Marsh (Kenneth Harlan) has decided to move to Sacramento with his wife Ann (Charlotte Wynters) and their daughter Dorrie (Jane Clayton) so that Dorrie can have a better education. Saloonkeeper Monte Keller (Robert Fiske) buys Marsh's cattle for $30,000 and then sends out gunmen to recover the money. Keller's men attack the stagecoach taking the Marshes to California, killing John Marsh and stealing the $30,000.

Ann reports her husband's murder to the stage line superintendent (Alphonse Ethier) and gives him the serial numbers on some of the stolen bills. The superintendent suggests that she support herself and Dorrie by turning their spread into a dude ranch and promises to send her some paying guests, among them his friend William H. Cassidy. Later the superintendent tells Hoppy that a band of Trail Patrolmen will be at his disposal to help him round up the killers. Cassidy sends Lucky and Windy into Silver City to hunt for

information. Meanwhile Ann and Dorrie Marsh are hard at work converting their home into a dude ranch, assisted by Steve Dorman (Anthony Nace), a gunman on loan from Keller to help the women out.

Windy and Lucky try to get jobs at Keller's casino and are kicked out of town. Then they try for jobs at the Marsh ranch and are almost kicked out by Steve Dorman, but Ann Marsh overrules Dorman and hires them. When their first guests arrive from the East they include one William H. Cassidy, who is dressed like a fop and acts like a nervous wreck. It was Boyd's first fling at comedy during the series, and his imitation of a helpless milquetoast is an absolute delight. Also among the guests is the film-makers' mock Mulford figure E. Prescott Furbush (Maurice Cass).

Cassidy baits Keller by flashing a large roll of bills and claiming he likes to gamble. At the ranch he plays the total fool, pretending he can't even mount a horse, sporting an outlandish pair of sheepskin chaps that Boyd borrowed from his

103

John St. Polis intervenes between William Boyd and Onslow Stevens as Muriel Evans watches in this scene from **Three on the Trail** (1936, Paramount). John Rutherford is one of the crowd.

friend Buck Jones for this picture. But he succeeds in stopping a fight between Steve Dorman and Lucky, who are rivals for Dorrie Marsh's favors. When not acting like an incompetent lily-liver Hoppy plays poker as much as possible, hoping he'll encounter some of the stolen money with the serial numbers he's looking for. Eventually he catches Steve Dorman playing with just those bills. Drawing his gun like a pro and dropping his meek facade, Cassidy demands the rest of the money. Steve upsets the poker table and flees the ranch with Cassidy in pursuit. Ann Marsh inadvertently rides into the middle of the chase and Steve is about to shoot her when Hoppy kills him.

Cassidy reveals his identity to Ann, then sends Lucky to fetch the Trail Patrol and has Ann ride to town and set a trap for Keller. She's to tell him that Cassidy is about to return East and to suggest that Keller try to clean out the dude in a high-stakes poker game before his stagecoach leaves. Hoppy arrives in town, pretends to be reluctant to play but lets himself be enticed into a game with

Keller---a suspenseful game indeed, and so well directed that even the non-pokerphile can follow the turns of fortune. During the game Cassidy abandons all of his dude mannerisms and wins all the stolen money from the now terrified Keller. Then he covers Keller's gunmen and backs out of the saloon to the waiting stagecoach. At this point one of Keller's men rides in to report what has just been blurted out to him by E. Prescott Furbush: that Steve Dorman is dead and the man who killed him is Hopalong Cassidy. Keller and his gang mount up and chase the coach. The men of the Trail Patrol break into the pursuit and round up most of the gang but Selander twists the tail of the customary B Western climax of the good guy on horseback pursuing the bad guys in the coach by having Keller alone continue to chase the stage. Finally Hoppy leaps from the stagecoach roof, drags Keller from his horse, and finishes him off in a one-on-one.

With the Marsh women's money returned and his own cowboy clothes on his back again,

104

Muriel Evans doesn't seemed pleased with Jimmy Ellison's note on the blackboard in this scene from **Three on the Trail** (1936, Paramount).

Hoppy sets off with his pals for the Bar 20.

Clarence Mulford had been fascinated since his late teens with the idea of the Western detective story, but his stabs at merging the two genres had always been weak and half-hearted. Whether by chance or intentionally the next Cassidy film, **Silver on the Sage** (1939), was likewise at bottom a mediocre rangeland detective yarn, centering on that most ancient of whodunit clichés, the twins who give each other alibis. Selander directed from an original screenplay by Maurice Geraghty. Jack Rockwell and Roy Barcroft were back in good subsidiary parts, with the dual role of the twins going to mainstream actor Stanley Ridges. Harlan and Warwick did the usual honors in the cinematographer's seat and the editing booth. It's a competent watchable picture, with nothing much to complain about but nothing to get excited over either---a description which would also apply to far too many Cassidys of the next few years.

While Hoppy is away, Lucky and Windy deliver a herd of cattle to Tom Hamilton (Frederick Burton) of the Lazy J ranch. That night, while Windy is guarding the cattle, rustlers overpower him and escape with the herd. Hamilton insists that since he hadn't yet officially taken delivery, the herd was still Bar 20 property at the time it was stolen, and therefore he's entitled to another herd. Lucky and Windy accuse Hamilton and his foreman Dave Talbot (Stanley Ridges) of being in league with the rustlers. In order to prove it, Windy poses as a gunman (as if anyone could take that wonderful old grouch seriously as a tough guy) and begins to mix with the hardboiled types who hang out in town at Earl Brennan's gambling hall, looking for clues to the rustlers. When Hoppy returns and learns the herd was stolen he decides to do his own detective work and, posing as a gambler, is hired as a dealer by Brennan (Stanley Ridges).

In fact Brennan and Talbot are twin brothers and partners in crime. Whenever Talbot is out doing something illegal, Brennan dresses in his cowboy

William Boyd is cutting in on Muriel Evans and Jimmy Ellison in this scene from **Three on the Trail** (1936, Paramount).

clothes and makes himself conspicuous in a public place, providing his brother with a perfect alibi. One day, at the same time that Cassidy and the town marshal (Jack Rockwell) are playing poker with Brennan in his Talbot outfit, the real Talbot murders Tom Hamilton on the trail. Lucky happens to all but witness the killing and recognizes Talbot as the murderer, but when the body is discovered it's Lucky himself thanks to his earlier accusations against Hamilton who's arrested for the crime, and his claim that Talbot did it is ridiculed in view of Talbot's apparent perfect alibi. Lucky swears he's innocent but breaks jail and rejoins Hoppy and Windy out on the desert.

Hoppy, still calling himself Bill Thompson and dealing poker in Brennan's saloon, plays at different times with both the real Talbot and with Brennan in Talbot's clothes. Observing how the other player's poker mannerisms change from game to game, Cassidy eventually realizes that "he" is two men. Then a gunman named Pierce (Edward Cassidy) happens to see "Thompson"

making a fast draw, recognizes the poker dealer as Hopalong Cassidy and tips off Brennan. The gambler invites "Thompson" to join his rustling gang, planning to kill Hoppy during a forthcoming raid on the Lazy J herd, and Cassidy readily agrees. Meanwhile Lucky and Windy have set up camp at a desert waterhole. Two riders stop there for a drink and Hoppy's pals overhear them talking about the impending raid. Lucky rides to the ranch with a warning but is taken prisoner by Hamilton's daughter Barbara (Ruth Rogers), who still believes that Lucky murdered her father.

While Brennan again dresses as Talbot and plays poker in the saloon, Pierce and the real Talbot lay an ambush on the trail for Hoppy. Cassidy outwits the two and brings them back to town, where in front of the marshal he confronts the real Talbot with his twin at the gambling hall. Brennan and his gang shoot their way out of town and escape to their desert hideout, pursued by Hoppy, who leaves trail signs for the posse to follow. The posse attacks Brennan's gang, killing or capturing

106

George Hayes and William Boyd are ready for action in the blazing end of **Three on the Trail** (1936, Paramount).

all of them, and with the stolen cattle recovered this mildly entertaining picture comes to an end.

The curtain came down on the season with **The Renegade Trail** (1939), one of the shortest in running time and lightest on action of all the Cassidy films to date, but brim-full of character interplay and emotion and the most unsubtle attempts in the entire series to present Hoppy as a role model for the young. Selander directed from an original screenplay by unit newcomer John Rathmell, with Harrison Jacobs once again credited for additional dialogue and Mulford merely for having created the series characters (or more precisely the characters' names). In addition to Boyd and Hayden and Hayes, the cast boasted several veterans of previous Cassidys, including Charlotte Wynters from **Sunset Trail** as another widow with her cap set for Hoppy and Roy Barcroft and John Merton as middle-management personnel in the outlaw gang. Joining the unit for the first of several small roles was a golden-voiced young singer named Eddie Dean, who a few years

later would become a Western star in his own right at PRC Pictures. Russell Harlan again served as photographer, Sherman Rose as editor, Boris Morros as music director.

Hoppy and Lucky are on their way to the town of Cactus Springs, where their old pal Windy has somehow gotten himself elected marshal, although most of his duty hours are spent regaling little Joey Joyce (Sonny Bupp), child of widowed Mary Joyce (Charlotte Wynters), with the exploits of the famous Cassidy. Approaching the territory simultaneously is escaped convict Smoky Joslin (Russell Hopton), who in fact is Mary's husband and Joey's father. Joslin links up with former associates Stiff Hat Bailey (Roy Barcroft) and Tex Traynor (John Merton) and plans a series of cattle raids. But first he pays a secret night visit to Mary's Circle J ranch and learns that she has always told Joey that his father died a hero's death. By threatening to reveal the truth to Joey unless he gets co-operation, Joslin forces his wife to pass him off as her visiting brother, Dan Bennett.

Jimmy Ellison seems to have saved George Hayes and William Boyd looks mad in this scene from **Heart of the West** (1936, Paramount).

Stiff Hat Bailey and Hopalong Cassidy happen to reach town from opposite directions at almost the same moment. Bailey is hardly out of the saddle before he's kicked Joey Joyce's dog (whose name is Hoppy) and slapped the boy to boot. Cassidy steps in and shoots Bailey's gun out of his hand. Somehow Mary misinterprets the incident and berates Cassidy as a bully, and Hoppy meekly plays along, a sure sign that chaste romance will bloom between them later.

While Joslin and his gang plot to rustle the Circle J cattle, Hoppy keeps his identity concealed from the hero-worshipping Joey---until the boy falls into a cattle chute and Cassidy saves his life and sets his broken leg. It's shortly after he reveals his identity that Hoppy becomes suspicious of Mary Joyce's alleged brother, who claims to have spent the last five years in Mexico but can't speak a work of Spanish. He gets the drop on Joslin, but Mary reveals that the man is her husband and begs Cassidy to let him go so that Joey won't learn the truth. Hoppy magnanimously

agrees, thus permitting the picture to reach feature length.

For Joslin, needless to say, is not a man of his word. As soon as Hoppy and Lucky leave to join the Circle J herd, Joslin overpowers Mary and locks her in a shed, ordering Traynor to stay at the ranch to guard her and Joey. Meanwhile with the herd, Lucky is wounded while he and cowhand Red (Eddie Dean) are investigating suspicious hoofprints. Certain that a raid from Joslin's gang is imminent, Hoppy sends Windy to town for reinforcements and tells Lucky to go back to the ranch in the chuck wagon. Driving into the Circle J yard, Lucky quickly sizes up the situation, shoots Traynor and rescues Mary and Joey. The three then make a wild dash in the chuck wagon to rejoin Hoppy and the herd, but in an extemely well directed if all too brief action sequence the gang chases and overtakes the wagon and captures them. Joslin stays behind with them while Bailey and the others move against the herd.

Spotting the outlaws in the distance, Hoppy

Jimmy Ellison and William Boyd confer in this publicity still for **Heart of the West** (1936, Paramount).

slips away, allows Bailey and his men to capture the rest of the wranglers, then gets the drop on the gang from behind and snares them all without a shot being fired. Meanwhile on the trail, Joslin is tormenting his wife by all but coming out and telling Joey he's his father. He is just about to shoot Lucky in cold blood when Windy and the posse from town race onto the scene and kill him. Unfortunately the chuck wagon horses pick this moment to bolt, with Mary and Joey still in the vehicle. Hoppy spots the runaway wagon, races in pursuit and stops the team. At the fadeout Mary demonstrates her status as a Selander take-charge lady by almost asking Hoppy to marry her, but it's quite clear that his answer will be a flattered and polite but unequivocal No Thanks.

The Renegade Trail was not only the last Cassidy film of the season but the last appearance in the series of George Hayes. Early in the picture there's a superb scene of comedy and unabashed male love in which Hoppy and Lucky give Windy a new gun and holster. It doesn't have the least connection with the storyline, but it's a magnificent last hurrah for the trio and a beautiful showcase for Hayes' unique talents. He was never just a stupid buffoon like so many comic sidekicks in Western films. He created a consistent and unforgettable character, a wonderful old grouch with a cornucopia of warmly funny shticks, and each of his routines was perfectly in keeping with that character. When another salary dispute came up between him and Harry Sherman, Hayes signed a contract with Republic Pictures, and for the next dozen years he played the grizzled old sidekick to Roy Rogers and Wild Bill Elliott and even on occasion to John Wayne in films with budgets astronomically higher than at Monogram where he and Wayne had first worked together. When Sherman claimed to own the character name "Windy" and threatened to sue if Republic used that name for Hayes, the studio ducked the issue by coming up with a new monicker for him, and for the rest of his career he was billed as George "Gabby" Hayes. The loss of him was a blow from which the comedy side of the Hopalong Cassidy series never recovered. Other Western sidekicks could make us laugh; Hayes alone made us love him.

A publicity photo of Jimmy Ellison used for **Heart of the West** (1936, Paramount).

Chapter Six

Five years is a long time for any series to stay fresh, and a few strains began to show during the fifth season of Cassidy films, 1939-40. Boyd and Hayden continued of course as Hoppy and Lucky, "Pop" Sherman as producer and Russell Harlan as cinematographer. But most of the season's scripts were written by people new to the unit and to Westerns, although the veteran directors of the series were on hand to whip the screenplays into familiar shape. As in the 1938-39 season, Sherman assigned Lesley Selander to direct the two high-budget Zane Grey features "Pop" was producing for Paramount release ---**Knights of the Range** (Paramount, 1940), starring Russell Hayden and with Victor Jory as the villain, and **The Light of Western Stars** (Paramount, 1940), with Jory in the lead and Hayden in a character role---but this year Sherman wisely cut back Selander's work on the Cassidys from five pictures to four. Replacing George Hayes as Hoppy's comic sidekick (as if anyone could replace that dear curmudgeon) was ex-vaudevillian Britt Wood (1895-1965), who had played a Bar 20 hand in **Trail Dust** back in 1936. Wood's Speedy McGinnis character consisted mainly of a slow Southern drawl and some mournful dirges on the harmonica, and few viewers found him a laugh riot. Paramount's house composer Victor Young scored the background music for the season's first two films, with John Leipold credited for the rest. Early on in the season, newcomers Joseph W. Engel and Carrol Lewis came aboard as associate producer and film editor respectively. Despite all the fresh blood on the team, most of the next six Cassidys turned out rather dull, although usually redeemed by a few off-trail aspects.

First in release and by far the most exciting of the season's output was **Range War** (1939), directed by Selander and utilizing to full advantage the end-of-track set built for Cecil B. DeMille's just-completed epic Western **Union Pacific** (Paramount, 1939). The screenplay was by unit newcomer Sam Robins, based on an original screen story by an unknown named Josef Montiague, with additional dialogue credited to one Walter Roberts and the series characters of course to Mulford. Many of the actors were also new to Cassidy pictures, but Kenneth Harlan from **Pride of the West** and **Sunset Trail** was back, Earle Hodgins performed nobly as an idiot deputy sheriff, and Eddie Dean had a nice bit as one of the outlaws. Other names in the cast--- Francis McDonald, Raphael Bennett, Glenn Strange, George Chesebro---either already were or would soon become familiar to followers of the series.

Naturally enough in view of the standing sets, the film deals with railroad building. Jim Marlow (Matt Moore) is trying desperately to finish the line on time but the work is being sabotaged by rancher Buck Collins (Willard Robertson), whose power to make his neighbors pay him tribute will end if they can ship their cattle to market by rail. When their friend Speedy McGinnis (Britt Wood) is wounded during a stagecoach holdup in which Collins' men stole a railroad payroll, Hoppy and Lucky come down to help Marlow complete the line. They set up headquarters at the mission of Padre José (Pedro de Cordoba), and Lucky true to form falls head-over-spurs in love with Marlow's spunky teen-age daughter Ellen (Betty Moran). Soon afterwards, while Marlow is away raising money for a new payroll, Collins' saboteurs lead the unpaid railroad laborers in an attempt to dynamite the tracks, and Hoppy pulls Ellen away from the explosion.

Lucky takes a job with the construction crew in order to get evidence against the saboteurs. Meanwhile, knowing that Marlow is on his way back to the base camp with the new payroll and expecting that this coach too will be attacked, Hoppy works a scam. Disguised as a padre, he visits town and leaves a note with the halfwit deputy (Earle Hodgins) warning that the coach will be held up. Then he proves himself a true

George Hayes looks unhappy about a wounded Ted Adams as William Boyd and Jimmy Ellison listen in this scene from **Heart of the West** (1936, Paramount).

prophet by meeting the stage on the trail and stealing the payroll from Marlow before the real bandits can. Once the coach is gone Hoppy is jumped by the outlaws, and just as he expected the sheriff (Glenn Strange) then rides up with a posse and arrests them all and throws them in jail together. Having driven into town to meet Marlow, Lucky and Ellen are flabbergasted to learn of the holdup and even more amazed a few seconds later when the posse returns with Cassidy among its prisoners.

While they are all in jail, gang member Staley (Raphael Bennett) invites Cassidy and Speedy to join the bandits when they get out---which is precisely the invitation Hoppy had been hoping for when he planned the scam. In one of the great comic jailbreak scenes in Westerns, Hoppy tricks the idiot deputy and all the prisoners escape. Staley leads them to the gang's hideout and introduces Cassidy, who calls himself Jim Grant, to the rest of the gang. One of the outlaws at the hideout is Dave Morgan (Francis McDonald), who

is almost certain he's seen "Grant" before but can't remember where. Meanwhile back at the railroad camp, Lucky has overheard the saboteurs plotting to blow up a trestle, follows and catches them in the act, but the quick thinking Collins men convince Marlow and the ranchers that Lucky himself is the saboteur, and Hoppy's young pal has to run for his life.

At the outlaw hideout, Speedy eavesdrops on Morgan, Staley and Pete (Eddie Dean) as they plot to keep the original stolen payroll for themselves, but he is caught in the gang's barn. Now suspicious of "Grant" as well, the three demand that he kill Speedy. Cassidy gets the drop on them and wounds Morgan. Pretending to think Morgan is dead, Cassidy invites the other two to join Speedy and himself in a new gang, and loudly announces that all four of them are riding to Padre José's mission. Sure enough, when they've left and Collins returns to the hideout with the rest of his gang, Morgan repeats the planted information and the entire outfit races for the mission, where

112

A publicity still of William Boyd used for **Heart of the West** (1936, Paramount). The scene is actually from the first film in the series **Hop-A-Long Cassidy** (1935, Paramount).

Hoppy hopes to set a trap.

Meanwhile Lucky has also taken refuge at the mission, and Ellen joins him there just before the Cassidy party arrives. The two outlaws are locked in an adobe hut and Hoppy sends Ellen to bring back the railroad workers to help round up the gang. Soon after she sets out, Collins and his men approach the locked mission gates. Hoppy lures Collins and Morgan inside and captures them but the rest of the outlaws lay siege to the mission. Suddenly everything goes wrong for Cassidy: he is accidentally wounded by Padre José's over-zealous servant boy Felipe (Don Latorre), and Collins and Morgan shoot the priest and break free. Thus Selander reactivates his fine old siege gambit, underscored this time by superb Victor Young action music. Ellen explains the truth to the men at the railroad camp, who take the two saboteurs prisoner and then go off hell-for-leather to the mission, leaving behind an angry and frustrated Ellen, who mounts the camp mule and, keeping faith with the Selander ethos, tries gamely to follow the men into battle. The rescuers reach the mission just as the gang is battering down the gates and a pitched battle is joined. Collins tries to escape but Hoppy nails him in a quick but effective fistfight in which his wound hampers him not at all. As the gang surrenders we are treated to a shot of Ellen miles from the mission, vainly trying to make the stubborn mule move, proving that Selander's admiration for action women didn't inhibit him from throwing in a joke at their expense when the scene called for it. The railroad is completed and Collins and his men are given one-way tickets to the penitentiary as the movie comes to an end.

Next on the schedule was **Law of the Pampas** (1939), directed by Nate Watt of the 1936-37 season and displaying all of the Watt hallmarks---excessive length, slow pace, and deep love for the people and cultures south of the Rio Grande---plus a surprising skill and slickness in the action sequences. The screenplay was by Harrison Jacobs, several of whose earlier scripts (**The**

113

William Boyd followed by Sidney Blackmer and Jimmy Ellison lead a posse out of town in this scene from **Heart of the West** (1936, Paramount).

Eagle's Brood, Borderland, In Old Mexico) had stressed sympathetic Latino elements. The most unusual bit of casting in the picture was that Britt Wood was dropped as the comic sidekick and replaced by none other than Sidney Toler, who took a few weeks off from starring in 20th Century-Fox's Charlie Chan movies and tried on the role of a laughable morose Argentinian. Harry Sherman had been impressed with Toler's comic parts in **The Mysterious Rider** and **The Heritage of the Desert** and let him have a crack at the comedy role in the Cassidys, although Toler seemed more at home playing Oriental sleuths than in range garb. William Duncan returned for his fifth and final appearance as Buck Peters. Hungarian-born Steffi Duna played a cantina dancer, while **Range War**'s Pedro de Cordoba and **In Old Mexico**'s Anna Demetrio were back respectively as a dignified hidalgo and an obese peasant woman. Sidney Blackmer as the chief bad guy looked just as ill at ease this time as he had several years

before in **Heart of the West**. Subsidiary villainy was in the capable hands of Glenn Strange and Eddie Dean. Russell Harlan photographed, Carrol Lewis edited and Victor Young again did the music score.

While on a cattle buying trip to the States, Argentine patriarch Don José Valdez (Pedro de Cordoba) and his party are the house guests of Buck Peters (William Duncan), who takes them to a rodeo. A bull escapes from its pen and almost gores Valdez' small grandson Ernesto (Jojo La Sadio), but Hoppy wrestles the animal to the ground in the nick of time. A grateful Valdez buys half the Bar 20 herd and invites Hoppy and Lucky to deliver the cattle to Argentina and stay at his estancia afterwards. Before they set out, Valdez' foreman Fernando (Sidney Toler), whose nickname is El Melancholio, The Worrier, tells Cassidy that Valdez' son and daughter both died recently in suspicious accidents. Realizing how close Ernesto came to being a third accident victim, Cassidy begins to suspect Valdez' American

George Hayes, Jimmy Ellison, William Boyd and Charles Martin are all transfixed by something off camera in this scene from **Heart of the West** (1936, Paramount).

son-in-law, Ralph Merritt (Sidney Blackmer), who will inherit the estancia on Don José's death if anything happens to the boy first. He agrees to take the herd to Argentina so he'll have a chance to learn the truth.

The cattle cross the pampas to a medley of Anglo and Latino songs. Hoppy rides ahead to let Valdez know the herd is approaching, but on entering the courtyard of the estancia he overhears an intimate conversation between Merritt and Chiquita (Steffi Duna), who is a dancer at Las Boleadoras cafe and also the niece of Fernando's pudgy wife Dolores (Anna Demetrio). It's made clear that Merritt has a habit of abusing Chiquita and that little Ernesto loves her dearly.

Next morning Valdez shows Hoppy his late son's collection of guns, including the pistol that "accidentally" went off and killed him. Cassidy observes that the bullet taken from the young man's body was fired from a Colt .44-40, not from the victim's own gun, and concludes that Valdez' son was murdered, but warns Don José

not to tell Merritt. He and Lucky continue to relax as Valdez' guests, teaching Ernesto to play baseball while Fernando tries in vain to roll cigarettes Anglo style. In due course Cassidy and Fernando ride out to the cliff edge where Valdez' daughter Rosita was thrown to her death from her horse, but they are seen by the dead woman's far from grieving widower, Ralph Merritt.

Cassidy drops in at Las Boleadoras café, buys drinks for the house and learns the use of the bolas, the deadly Argentine weapon for which the cantina is named. Merritt orders his henchman Slim (Glenn Strange) to arrange an accident for Hoppy as he did for Valdez' son and daughter. Then he sweet-talks Chiquita into playing up to Cassidy and finding out how much he knows. The dancer fakes a runaway horse incident on the trail so that Hoppy will rescue her, and he does, but when she starts flirting he drops her abruptly into the creek where, drenched and fuming, she is found by Lucky and starts flirting with him instead.

115

William Boyd teases George Hayes in this publicity still for **Heart of the West** (1936, Paramount).

That night at the estancia, Hoppy sees a messenger deliver a note to Merritt and follows him to Las Boleadoras, where Chiquita is dancing for a roomful of patrons including Lucky. In the back room, overheard by Cassidy outside, Merritt and Slim hatch a plot to kill Lucky. Hoppy enters the café to help his pal, and when Merritt's man Curly (Eddie Dean) throws a knife at Lucky, Hoppy knocks him to the floor. Then Slim takes a poke at Cassidy and suddenly it's a free-for-all, the only one in a Nate Watt picture. With a little help from his friends Lucky and Fernando, Hoppy demolishes the gang.

Next day Merritt invites Hoppy on a hunting trip, hoping for another fatal accident, but Cassidy begs off on the excuse that he hasn't enough shells for his gun---a Colt .44-40. Just as Merritt is about to hang himself by offering shells of that caliber, Lucky blunders in and ruins Cassidy's game. Later in the day Chiquita tries once more to entice Hoppy, boasting that she'll soon be the lady of the estancia. Hoppy warns her against Merritt,

and Chiquita tries to set Cassidy and Lucky against each other. Hoppy asks her to keep her eyes open for a Colt .44-40 and she stupidly tells Merritt, who decides it's time for a showdown. He has a note sent to Cassidy in which Chiquita claims she's found the gun and sets up a rendezvous at a haystack. There he plans first to kill Hoppy and then to launch an all-out raid on the estancia in which both Valdez and Ernesto will die.

Hoppy suspects a trap, goes to the rendezvous ahead of time and captures Merritt, Slim and Curly. But Chiquita, who has followed Merritt to the haystack, misunderstands the situation and gets the drop on Cassidy. Hoppy tells Chiquita that it was Merritt who killed Valdez' son and daughter, and the two break free just as Merritt is about to shoot them both. Hoppy rides to get help from Don José's gauchos while Chiquita races to warn the estancia of the raid. A large wagon carrying Lucky, Fernando, Chiquita, Valdez, Ernesto and a supply of dynamite roars away from

116

Lynn Gabriel and Charles Martin have William Boyd's attention in this scene from **Heart of the West** (1936, Paramount).

the ranch just as the raiders approach. The ensuing chase is the most exciting sustained action sequence in any of Nate Watt's Cassidys, with explosions, running inserts, pit shots and spills aplenty as the gang pursuing the wagon is in turn pursued by Cassidy and a small army of gauchos, with Victor Young's agitato music underscoring the thrills. Finally a battle royal is joined around the overturned wagon and the gang is wiped out in noble fashion, Hoppy personally disposing of Merritt with a bolas. Now that Ernesto's inheritance is secure, Cassidy and Lucky say adios to their Argentine amigos and head back home.

It was not only the end of Nate Watt's tenure on the Cassidy series but almost the end of his directorial career. He returned to the comfortable niche as an assistant director on big-budget pictures that he'd held in the 1920s when he'd first worked with Boyd. The only subsequent features he directed were **Oklahoma Renegades** (Republic, 1940), a Three Mesquiteers adventure with Bob Livingston, Duncan Renaldo and Raymond Hatton, and **Frontier Vengeance** (Republic, 1940), starring Don "Red" Barry, which Watt took over after Barry's regular director George Sherman came down with appendicitis while shooting. Watt continued as an assistant director for many years before his death in 1963, but the high points of his career were the long, slow, cumulatively powerful and emotion-charged Cassidys of the 1930s.

Lesley Selander returned to the megaphone, William Boyd to his **Sunset Trail** dude costume and Britt Wood to the comic sidekick role in the next Cassidy exploit, **Santa Fe Marshal** (1940). The screenplay by Harrison Jacobs recycled several motifs from his 1937 script for **Borderland**, and at least one sequence comes straight out of Selander's 1938 **Bar 20 Justice**, the first instance of what would grow into an epidemic of self-borrowings in the Cassidys. Its most interesting feature is Selander's treatment of the complex and even affectionate relationship between Hoppy and his adversary, a loving but

117

Lynn Gabriel and Charles Martin look on as William Boyd and Jimmy Ellison confront Sidney Blackmer in this scene from **Heart of the West** (1936, Paramount).

ruthless old woman played to the hilt by veteran character actress Marjorie Rambeau. Bernadene Hayes from **North of the Rio Grande** was back as another female entertainer, Earle Hodgins was given more footage for his snake-oil huckster routine than in any other film, and unit stalwarts Kenneth Harlan, Jack Rockwell and Eddie Dean turned in their usual performances. Russell Harlan photographed, Sherman Rose edited, and John Leipold earned his first series credit for the music score.

As the picture opens, silver mine owner John Gardner (Jack Rockwell) rides into the New Mexico town of Del Oro to report to the newly elected marshal (Eddie Dean) that the messenger carrying his mine's payroll, who was also his best friend, has been killed by robbers. It's only the latest in a series of violent crimes around Del Oro, and the new marshal's ineptitude has led to talk of forming a vigilante group. Gardner tells both the marshal and boardinghouse keeper Ma Burton (Marjorie Rambeau) that he's asked the U.S.

Marshal's office in Santa Fe for help. Ma appears to be an extremely kind and generous woman, but inside her boardinghouse we learn that she's also the head of the gang as she helps her henchmen Blake (Kenneth Harlan) and Flint (William Pagan) divide the loot from the payroll robbery.

In due time Cassidy, wearing his tailcoated dude outfit from earlier adventures like **Bar 20 Rides Again**, visits Gardner's mine and identifies himself as the marshal from Santa Fe. Gardner tells Hoppy that the mine office contains $15,000 in silver bullion that he's afraid to ship. Cassidy sets out for Del Oro.

Cut to a colorful medicine show wagon on the road to town. Its proprietor is Dr. Rufus Tate (Earle Hodgins), inventor of Zerbo, "the greatest combination of roots, herbs, barks and bitters that has ever been known to mankind." Its staff consists of Doc's daughter Paula (Bernadene Hayes) and their lugubrious driver Axel (Britt Wood) who is studying the art of hypnotism. The show is a marginal operation at best, thanks to Doc's habit

118

William Boyd warns Sidney Blackmer in this publicity still for **Heart of the West** (1936, Paramount).

of losing at poker whatever he makes hawking Zerbo. When a wheel comes off the wagon and rolls away, the party is stranded, for none of them know how to replace the wheel. Axel is vainly trying to hypnotize it back in place when Cassidy comes by and, in a nice comic scene, helps them fix it.

Further along the road the wagon is stopped by medicine show hating rancher Tex Barnes (George Anderson), who orders the Tate party to turn around. Hoppy prevents a confrontation by agreeing not to play in Del Oro and Tex rides off. Then, seeing the show as an ideal cover for his assignment, Cassidy offers to join as a performer. There follows a wonderful bit of satire on singing cowboys of the Gene Autry type, who dominated the Westerns of the early Forties. Paula asks Hoppy if he can play the guitar. "Me---play a guitar?" he asks incredulously. "All cowboys nowadays play the guitar," she points out. "This is one cowboy," he declares proudly, "that never played a guitar and never will." He agrees instead

to buy a half-interest in the show and to become Paula's partner in a mind-reading act.

As the wagon lumbers into town it is seen by Tex, who threatens trouble. Cassidy gets permission for the show to play in Del Oro from the bumbling marshal. That night the Tate company puts on a performance, which features Doc in mortarboard and academic gown pitching Zerbo ad nauseam and Cassidy in turban and Oriental robes reading minds. Tex and his cronies break up the show and a huge free-for-all ensues. Among the combatants is Lucky, who has just ridden into town, and whom Hoppy signals to pretend they're strangers. During the fight a buckboard runs away with Ma Burton and Cassidy dashes into the street to save her. In gratitude she invites the show troupe to stay at her boardinghouse until their wagon is repaired. Her intuition has convinced her that Cassidy is either the expected marshal from Santa Fe or an outlaw. In a conversation overheard by both Paula and Ma's chief henchman Blake, Hoppy tells Ma that he's an ex-convict just

William Boyd and Jimmy Ellison seem pleased in this publicity still for **Trail Dust** (1936, Paramount).

released from prison. Later Cassidy secretly meets with Lucky and tells him to announce himself as the Santa Fe marshal so that Hoppy can stay under cover.

No sooner has Lucky presented "his" credentials next day than he starts romancing Paula. Meanwhile Axel wastes footage hypnotizing himself. In the saloon Flint confronts Cassidy and warns him not to pull any jobs on the gang's turf. Cassidy invites the gang to join him in a raid on the $15,000 in bullion at Gardner's mine. While they're dickering Lucky comes swaggering idiotically into the saloon, and in a dispute between the young man and Tex Barnes Cassidy saves his pal's life by shooting the gun out of Tex's hand. Later when he justifies his action to the gang on the argument that if a U.S. Marshal is shot the town will soon be aswarm with Federal lawmen, they accept him as a fellow crook and Ma and Blake decide to throw in with him. Cassidy sets up a plan to attack the mine on Sunday when most of Gardner's men will be in town. The raid is meant of course to be a trap.

Sunday morning dawns and the outlaws prepare for the big job. But Cassidy's plan is ruined when Paula, who honestly believes he's an ex-con about to go wrong again, reports the situation to Lucky, and the young fool reveals Cassidy's identity to her and to Ma Burton, who had accompanied her to the marshal's office. Ma races out of town to warn the gang, and when they reach the mine they turn the tables on Hoppy, steal the silver, leave him bound and gagged in the mine office, and---as in a similar sequence in Selander's **Bar 20 Justice**---set the place afire. Lucky reaches the mine just in time to save Cassidy's life. Then the two of them ride to town after the gang.

Back in Del Oro, Doc and Paula and Axel overhear Ma and her men plotting in the boardinghouse. They are captured and held inside the now repaired show wagon, which Blake and Tex drive out to Tex's ranch. Hoppy and Lucky return to town and catch Ma and Flint at the boardinghouse, hiding the stolen silver. In a touching scene

Jimmy Ellison and William Boyd are concerned about an unconscious Gwynne Shipman in this publicity photo for **Trail Dust** (1936, Paramount).

displaying Selander at his emotional best, Cassidy locks Ma in a cell. Then he and Lucky round up Gardner's miners and set out to attack Tex's ranch. The assault unfortunately takes only about five seconds of screen time. As they near the ranch in the show wagon, Blake and Tex see what's happening and lumber off in the opposite direction. Hoppy and Lucky give chase in an excellent action sequence marred only by Boyd's continuing ineptness at close-up fisticuffs. The film ends with Doc and Paula rescued and peace descending on Del Oro.

While Selander was busy with Zane Grey pictures, Harry Sherman recruited another old hand, indeed the earliest director of the series, to helm the season's fourth Cassidy. **The Showdown** (1940) was directed by Howard Bretherton from a screenplay by two obscure brothers, Harold and Daniel Kusell, which in turn was based on an original story by silent scenario veteran Jack Jungmeyer. It turned out to be a typical Bretherton effort, competent enough but the dullest of any

that season, a loose-jointed and largely actionless picture in which Bretherton turned Russell Hayden's Lucky into the same kind of wild, hotheaded, jealous young fool that Jimmy Ellison had enacted when he'd played Johnny Nelson in Bretherton's first films in the series. The number one villain slot went to Morris Ankrum, a superb adversary in Nate Watt's Cassidys of 1936-37 but simply a routine badguy under Bretherton. Jane Clayton from **In Old Mexico** and **Sunset Trail** was back as the ingenue, and the supporting cast was graced by old hands like Roy Barcroft, Eddie Dean and former Western star Kermit Maynard. Russell Harlan handled the photography, Carrol Lewis the editorial work, John Leipold the music.

As the film opens, Colonel Rufus White (Wright Kramer) has sent his foreman Lucky and cowhand Speedy McGinnis (Britt Wood again) to meet the train that is bringing to town Baron Rendor (Morris Ankrum), a foreign nobleman interested in buying the colonel's horses. Speedy dons top

Al St. John cannot believe he has been shot as Frosty Royce, Harold Daniels and friend are under the guns of William Boyd and Jimmy Ellison in this scene from **Trail Dust** (1936, Paramount).

hat and tails for the occasion, and in town the loafers tease him about his attire, leading to a rather inept free-for-all outside the railroad station that is broken up by Hoppy, whom Colonel White has sent for. Just as the Baron steps off the train, the conductor catches a stowaway in the baggage car. Trying to escape arrest, the vagrant clings to a boxcar ladder as the train takes off. Hoppy rides to the rescue, catches the dangling stowaway in the saddle and discovers that the person he's saved isn't a man but an attractive young lady (Jane Clayton) who is also intending to see Colonel White.

All the visitors arrive together in the ranch buckboard. The Baron claims to represent a syndicate of investors who want to establish sulky racing as a European sport. Colonel White offers Hoppy the job of shipping his horses to San Francisco for sale at auction in case the Baron doesn't buy them. The young woman introduces herself as Sue Williard, Colonel White's recently orphaned niece. The Baron witnesses a test run by Warlock,

the colonel's prize racehorse, but postpones making an offer until he's wired to Europe for instructions. When Cassidy visits town a few hours later and discovers that no telegram to Europe has been sent, he concludes what we already know---that Rendor is a phony, casing the ranch as part of a plan to steal the horses. Hoppy drops in at the local saloon and gets into a poker game with the Baron, a tense and well-directed scene in which Cassidy wins against a stacked deck. Afterwards Rendor sends out Bowman (Roy Barcroft) and his gang to steal back the money Hoppy won. They ambush Cassidy and Speedy on the trail and Hoppy turns over the money without a fight---because he's already marked the bills and wants to know where they'll show up next.

Meanwhile, ever since she came to the ranch, Lucky has been romancing Sue. That night he sees Hoppy talking intimately with her and displays pigheaded jealousy in the purest Johnny Nelson manner. The next day Colonel White

A close-up publicity still of William Boyd used for **Trail Dust** (1936, Paramount).

opens a letter addressed to Sue and finds that it's from a lawyer, telling her that she and not the colonel is the rightful owner of the White ranch. Desperate to keep the property, he claims she's an impostor and has the marshal (Eddie Dean) arrest her. Then he suffers a heart attack.

The Baron still hasn't made an offer for the horses, and at Hoppy's suggestion the colonel demands that Rendor put up some good faith money. The Baron offers a $1000 bill complete with Hoppy's marking. Cassidy throws the Baron off the ranch (if he'd had Rendor locked up the picture would have ended half an hour early), but as soon as the fake nobleman is gone Colonel White has another heart seizure and dies. Hoppy finds the letter to Sue that the colonel had pocketed and has her released from jail and installed as owner of the ranch.

Sue decides to go back East and asks Hoppy to take her horses to San Francisco for sale. Miffed because he wasn't put in charge, Lucky throws another Johnny Nelson snit fit and quits in a huff.

He rides into town, where the Baron wheedles out of him the news that the horses are to be moved that night. Rendor is about to offer Lucky a job but is stymied when Cassidy, determined that the boy have a chance to prove himself, asks Lucky to take over the responsibility of shipping the horses. If all this seems slightly similar to an earlier Cassidy picture, it should be remembered that back in 1936 Bretherton had directed **Call of the Prairie** in which Johnny Nelson had also fallen in with low company and seemed to turn bad.

The drive begins, and Lucky and Speedy bed the horses for the night at a barn on the deserted Spring ranch. After dark, the Baron rides up and hints to Lucky that Cassidy gave him the horse-herding job so that he could have Sue for himself. Lucky again races off in a frenzy of Johnny-like jealousy, and the Baron's gang makes short work of seizing the horses---until Hoppy, who's been following the herd, rides onto the scene. Rendor overpowers Cassidy, tells him that Lucky has sold out, ties him in the barn, leaves with the most

123

William Boyd and George Hayes are ready for action in this scene from **Trail Dust** (1936, Paramount).

valuable horses including Warlock and sets the barn on fire with all the other animals trapped in their stalls. In a sequence that should have been much more powerful than Bretherton made it, Hoppy and Speedy free themselves and save the horses. Then he and the White hands set out after the Baron.

Next day along the trail, Lucky comes upon the gang concealing the stolen horses inside a hollow haywagon but is captured by Rendor and forced to drive the clumsy vehicle with a gun at his back. The marshal and a posse overtake the wagon and are riding along beside it, ignorant of the Baron inside, when Hoppy and his men catch up with the rest of the gang a few miles away and engage them in a gun battle. The posse races off to join the fight, catching the outlaws in a crossfire. When the marshal tells Hoppy about the hay-wagon which Lucky was driving, Cassidy and Speedy leave the posse to clean up the gang and tear off in pursuit, still believing that their young pal has sold out. As they approach the wagon

Lucky makes a grab for the Baron's gun and is wounded. The wagon careens wildly around hair-pin turns and cliff edges, pursued by Hoppy, who leaps aboard into the hollow innards and knocks Rendor cold. He and Lucky jump clear just before the wagon---thankfully minus the stolen horses which the thieves had removed earlier---crashes over the cliff. The picture ends with Hoppy and Lucky reconciled and Sue deciding to stay on at the ranch.

For the season's last two Cassidys Selander was back at the helm, enriching the scripts with at least a few personal touches even though neither picture ranks among his best. **Hidden Gold** (1940) wasn't terribly exciting but benefited from some gorgeous scenery, the creative recycling of story elements from Selander's **Bar 20 Justice**, and a unique if frustrating way around William Boyd's problems in action sequences. The screenplay was by Gerald Geraghty, who had co-authored the script for 1935's **Bar 20 Rides Again**, and Jack Mersereau, who had earned a credit for

Gwynne Shipman and Jimmy Ellison cuddle as William Boyd is tickled by George Hayes' sour face in this scene from **Trail Dust** (1936, Paramount).

"additional dialogue" on 1937's **Texas Trail**. Ruth Rogers from **Silver on the Sage** returned for another female lead but seemed sorely out of place with her formal diction and 1930s hairdo. George Anderson on the other hand looked much more convincing as the "brains heavy" than he had in his **Santa Fe Marshal** range garb, and old reliables Roy Barcroft, Eddie Dean and Jack Rockwell did more than their bit for the effort. In the second of her fusspot-spinster roles in a Cassidy film (she'd played Buck Peters' old-maid sister in **Bar 20 Rides Again**), Ethel Wales portrayed the town postmistress. Behind-the-cameras personnel consisted as usual of Russell Harlan for cinematography, Carrol Lewis in the editing booth and Irvin Talbot as music director (although the score itself was by John Leipold).

After a series of stagecoach holdups in which nothing was taken but gold from the mine of Ed Colby (Minor Watson), Hoppy writes his pal Speedy, who's vainly trying to strike it rich on a gold claim, that he and Lucky are about to visit. On the trail to town, Cassidy and Lucky catch a runaway horse and backtrack it to an empty strongbox in the brush---and to Colby's daughter Jane (Ruth Rogers), whose horse had bolted when she discovered the box. The two accompany her to town, where they learn that her father is an old-time outlaw who's suspected by his partner Ward Ackerman (George Anderson) of being behind the gold thefts himself. Hoppy and Lucky join the sheriff's posse to hunt the stagecoach bandits but lose the thieves' tracks in the river.

That night at Speedy's mining camp, Cassidy reveals that he is here to investigate the holdups for the express company. Jane visits the camp and asks Hoppy to take over as foreman of her father's mine. To preserve his undercover status Cassidy turns her down (and off), but on riding back with her to the mine they find Ed Colby seriously wounded in his office. Ackerman claims that Colby shot himself to avert suspicion and demands that his own associate Hendricks (Roy Barcroft) be installed as foreman of the mine.

George Hayes and William Boyd question a tied-up Morris Ankrum in this scene from **Trail Dust** (1936, Paramount).

Suddenly Hoppy announces that he's already accepted the job. When Ackerman and Hendricks have left, he explains why: he had found a button from Hendricks' coat in the mine office near Colby's body.

After a quiet week while Colby recuperates, the action picks up again. First a sniper takes a shot at Hoppy. Then, while Cassidy is inspecting the mine, trying to find out why production has drastically fallen off, Fleming (Raphael Bennett), a miner in the outlaws' pay, weakens a support timber and causes an "accident" in which Hoppy barely escapes being buried alive. Finally the gang raids Speedy's claim and---knowing that Cassidy will drop everything to come help his pal---tears the place apart. Sure enough, Hoppy and Speedy set out on the vandals' trail, accompanied by Buttercup, a poodle belonging to dithering Matilda Purdy (Ethel Wales) whom Selander in one of his little reversals of convention has substituted for any standard breed of tracking dog. The trail leads them to a mine that Hendricks supposedly runs for

Ackerman, but Cassidy can tell that no one has actually dug gold from the site for years. Suddenly realizing that the gang wanted to lure him away from the Colby mine, Cassidy races back.

The long-memoried Hoppy fan who had seen **Bar 20 Justice** might have guessed that as in the earlier picture there's a secret tunnel linking the victim's mine and the villain's, but Selander didn't borrow from himself that closely. While Cassidy is gone, Fleming and another crooked laborer have been removing sacks of gold they've dug from the Colby tunnels but kept hidden pending a chance to carry them away unseen. Lucky goes exploring in the mine, stumbles on the thieves and kills one of them in a gunfight in the dark tunnels, although Fleming escapes. .

The climax is precipitated some time later when Buttercup accidentally discovers gold on Speedy's claim. Hoppy uses the gold to bait a trap, making up a shipment for transportation by stagecoach and riding along as shotgun guard. Sure enough Fleming tips off Hendricks, who attacks the coach

126

William Boyd cradles a wounded Jimmy Ellison in this publicity still for **Borderland** (1937, Paramount).

with his gang, and Cassidy surrenders the gold to them without a peep, knowing they'll take it to the abandoned mine and having arranged in advance for a raid on the place. In town, Sheriff Carson (Lee Phelps), who doubles as the local blacksmith, is organizing a posse which is augmented by the arrival of express company investigator Logan (Eddie Dean) and his men. But the sheriff stupidly mentions the impending raid on the mine to Ackerman, who races out of town to warn the gang. When Hoppy reaches town and the posse prepares for battle, we are treated to a reprise of the grand old Bar 20 montage that goes back to the first Cassidy movie. Lucky meanwhile has organized Colby's mineworkers into a fighting force, and the two groups ride out in a fury of smooth running inserts and agitato music and merge into a visually stunning Y formation. The posse attacks before the gang can escape from the Hendricks mine with the stolen gold and a pitched if rather static gunbattle erupts. Trying to make a getaway, Ackerman is caught by Ed Colby, who

has left his sickbed to follow the miners' posse, but knocks out the old man and runs for cover inside the tunnels. Soon the rest of the gang makes a break for the same place, and the posse traps them by closing off the tunnel mouth. The outlaws surrender except for Hendricks, whom Hoppy shoots down inside the mine. The posse and prisoners are about to leave for town when Colby stumbles onto the scene and reveals that Ackerman is still in the tunnels. Cassidy goes in alone for the showdown, a one-on-one which Selander photographs almost entirely from outside the mine, with only sound effects conveying the fight until we see Ackerman flying backwards out of the tunnel mouth into the creek. Even if viewers may have felt cheated out of a thunderous finale, it was an ingenious solution to the perennial problem of Boyd's lack of athletic grace. With the gold recovered and Buttercup yapping at their heels, the trio leave for new adventures.

Like **The Renegade Trail** which had ended the previous Cassidy sextet, the final picture of the

Morris Ankrum seems disinterested but George Hayes seems concerned as William Boyd gets ready to fight with George Chesebro in this scene from **Borderland** (1937, Paramount).

1939-40 season made up for its minimal action with deep emotional resonance. Selander directed **Stagecoach War** (1940) from a screenplay by unit veteran Norman Houston and prolific B Western scripter Harry F. Olmstead. Although a few bottom-of-the-cast names like Jack Rockwell and Eddie Dean were familiar to series fans, most of the big parts went to players rarely seen in Westerns. But the picture was stolen by Rad Robinson, a member of the King's Men quartet that had appeared in a number of the Cassidys since **The Renegade Trail**, in the role of a jovial, deep-voiced singing cowboy who is not a good guy like every other range warbler in Westerns but the leader of an outlaw gang. And as if one brilliant reversal of convention were not enough, Selander saw to it that the fellow who dressed and acted like the fancy-suited king of bandits in hundreds of earlier Westerns not only turned out to be a good guy but wound up with the leading lady too! As usual Russell Harlan photographed, Sherman A. Rose edited, John

Leipold was credited with the scoring and Irvin Talbot with the direction of the music.

Hoppy, Lucky and Speedy are taking a small herd of mustangs to be used as coach horses on Jeff Chapman's stage line when they run into a Chapman coach that has just been robbed of a silver shipment. Old Jeff Chapman (J. Farrell MacDonald), who had been driving and was wounded in the raid, asks Lucky to take the reins the rest of the way. A cut to the thieves informs us that the gang leader is singing cowboy Smiley (Rad Robinson) and that his spy in town is satan-faced Twister Maxwell (Frank Lackteen), stable foreman for the rival coach line owned by Neal Holt (Harvey Stephens). But Twister has made a fatal blunder: for use in the holdup he borrowed Thunder, one of six black thoroughbreds that make up Holt's prize team, and during the robbery the horse threw an unusually-shaped shoe which Speedy happens to notice and pick up along the trail as he drives the Bar 20 mustangs towards town.

128

Morris Ankrum and Charlene Wyatt are amused at Nora Lane using George Hayes as a manikin in this scene from **Borderland** (1937, Paramount).

Arriving in town with the wounded Chapman and the stage, Hoppy and Lucky encounter Holt, who complains loudly about Chapman's antiquated rolling stock and preference for mustangs over thoroughbreds. After the raid is reported to the sheriff, Lucky drives the coach to Chapman's ranch where he meets and instantly falls for the old man's daughter Shirley (Julie Carter). She however is in love with Neal Holt, whom her father detests as a fortune hunter. Determined to break up Shirley's affair with Holt, Chapman hires Lucky as a stage driver and pressures his daughter to play up to the young man. Lucky's advances are observed by Twister, who returns to Holt's stable on the limping Thunder and alerts his employer to the new man in Shirley's life. Cassidy happens to see Twister enter the stable on that horse.

Later at Chapman's ranch, in one of the most emotionally touching scenes in any Cassidy film, Lucky confesses to Hoppy that he'd rather die than lose Shirley, and Cassidy discreetly sets out

to help his protegé. When mine owner Mart Gunther (Jack Rockwell), whose silver was stolen in the holdup, echoes Holt's complaints about Chapman's use of mustangs to pull coaches, Hoppy angrily defends the breed and suggests a race between a Chapman coach and one of Holt's thoroughbred-pulled stages, with the winner to be awarded a new contract by Wells Fargo agent Quince Cobalt (Eddy Waller). Speedy subsequently shows Cassidy the horseshoe he picked up near the scene of the robbery, and Hoppy remembers seeing Twister ride a limping horse into Holt's stable and erroneously concludes that Holt was behind the raid. That night, while Smiley and his singing bandits are in the saloon regaling most of the town with ballads, Cassidy sneaks into Holt's stable and matches the shoe with Thunder's unshod hoof. He returns to the saloon just in time to break up a fight between Lucky and the wildly jealous Holt. During this sequence Hoppy notices Twister whispering secretly into Smiley's ear and intuits at once who

129

William Boyd doesn't seem happy with Al Bridge's poker hand in this scene from **Borderland** (1937, Paramount).

the coach bandits were. Then he challenges Holt to the race he suggested earlier, and on Holt's acceptance the whole town starts placing bets on the outcome, with Smiley and his men wagering heavily against Chapman.

Lucky begs for and receives the assignment to drive Chapman's coach, and although he's determined to win both the race and Shirley, she is appalled at the stupid machismo of both her suitors and pleads with Holt to call off the dangerous race. When Holt refuses for fear of being thought a coward, Shirley rather foolishly stows away in his coach just before the starting gun sounds. The race is the film's high point emotionally and in terms of action, and Selander stages it for maximum excitement with both coaches flying neck-and-neck along cliff-edge roads full of hairpin turns. At the riskiest point on the route, Lucky sees Shirley inside Holt's coach and reins in his team to protect her from injury. To all the observers it seems that he either "turned yellow" or threw the race, and those who had bet on Chap-

man yank Lucky from the coach and beat him furiously until he's rescued from the mob by Hoppy and Speedy. But he refuses to explain his action even to Cassidy and stalks away, to be befriended by Smiley, who invites the young man to join his gang. Later that day Holt and Shirley tell Hoppy the truth about why Lucky reined in, and Cassidy brings about a reconciliation between Holt and Jeff Chapman.

The next time Mart Gunther ships bullion on a Chapman coach, its driver is Hoppy. Twister as usual tips off Smiley, but by now of course Cassidy has figured out the setup and prepared a trap. Smiley and his gang have been camping in the hills, singing lustily around the cooking fire for all the world as if they were Roy Rogers or Gene Autry and his pals. When Lucky realizes they're about to rob another coach he tries to leave them, but Smiley forces him to come along. With several guns trained on him from hiding, Lucky is ordered to ride into the coach's path and flag Hoppy down. Instead the young man redeems

130

Jimmy Ellison picks a fight with William Boyd as Morris Ankrum, Nora Lane and Al Bridge look on in this scene from **Borderland** (1937, Paramount).

himself by risking his life to warn Cassidy of the ambush ahead. Hoppy leaps down from the coach onto Lucky's horse and the two ride double out of range of the bandits' bullets. The outlaws naturally pursue the runaway coach rather than the men. Not far away Cassidy and Lucky meet the posse that has been trailing the coach at a distance, waiting for the gang to strike. Now they race after Smiley and his men, who have caught the coach down the road and have just discovered it's not carrying silver when the posse roars into sight and the climactic battle begins. The gunfight is over all too soon, with Smiley and Twister shot out of their saddles and the others killed or captured. Chapman and Holt merge their lines into one company as Hoppy, Speedy and a still heartsick Lucky head back for the Bar 20.

It's a shame that Selander didn't let Smiley escape and come back in later pictures, for he was by far the most engaging villain in the history of the series. But even without that fillip, and despite a minimum of action and a preachier than usual script ("Horses and men, that's the backbone of this frontier, working together, both sort of pulling in the same traces"), **Stagecoach War** with its emotional interplay and inspired reversals of Western cliché brought the fifth season of Cassidys to a satisfactory if unspectacular end. If the six films demonstrated anything it was that Britt Wood wasn't terribly effective as a comic sidekick. He was let go, and the rest of his career in Westerns was limited to small character parts, including bits in two of the next season's Cassidys. His departure left Harry Sherman with the job, among many others, of finding a new cactus comic.

131

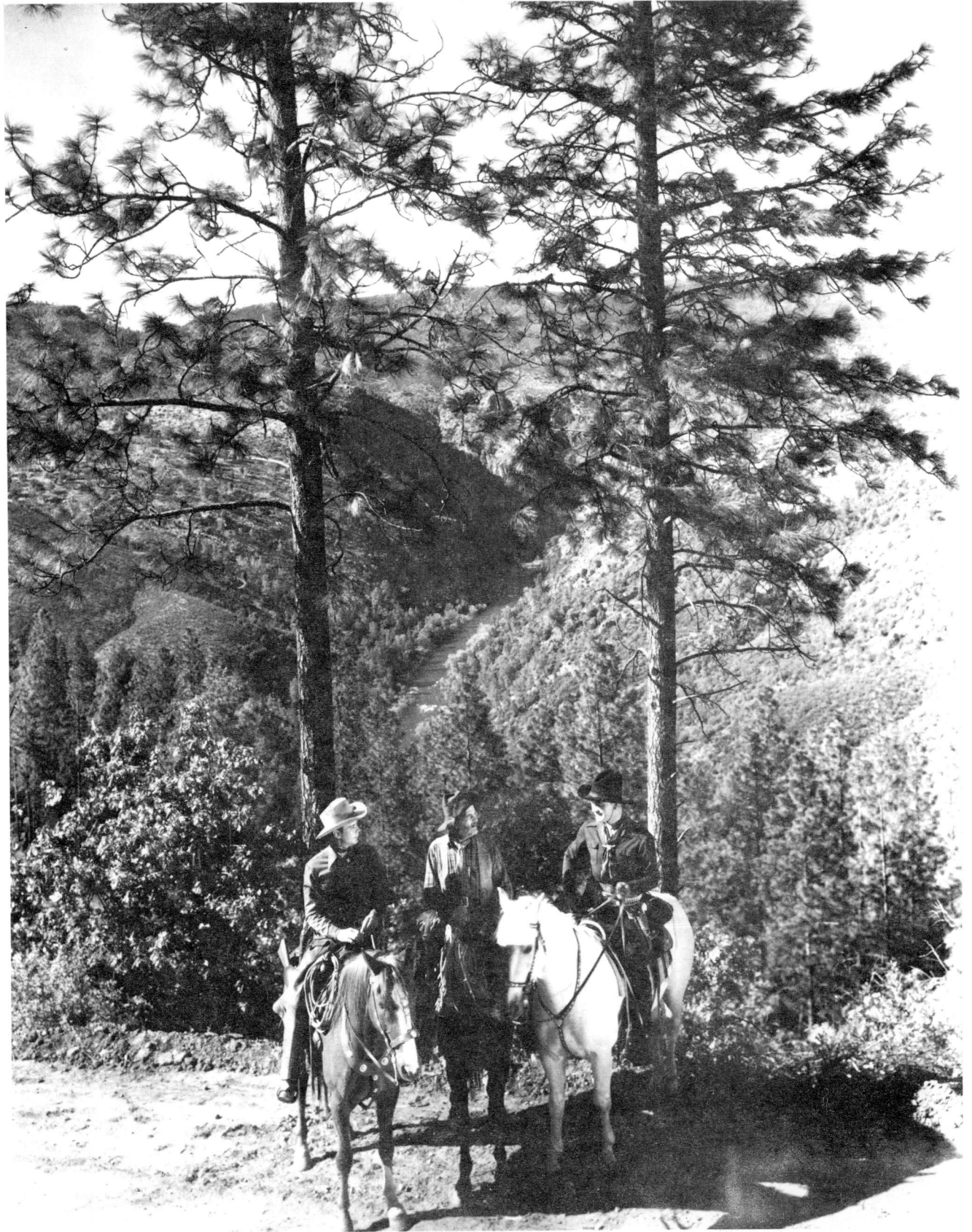

An on location publicity still of Russell Hayden, George Hayes and William Boyd shows some of the fantastic scenery which made the Cassidy westerns exceptional. From **Rustler's Valley** (1937, Paramount).

Chapter Seven

The screen exploits of Hoppy during the 1940-41 season display a symmetry that is no less dazzling for having been accidental. The first and sixth of the season's Cassidys, both directed by Selander, rank among the finest in the 66-film series; the second and fifth, both also by Selander, were quite good if not outstanding; entries number three and four were directed by others and kept in the rut of routine watchability. Although "Pop" Sherman was no longer producing Zane Grey pictures on the side for Paramount, he had contracted to make and the studio to release two reasonably well budgeted 90-minute Westerns starring 1920s screen great Richard Dix. These pictures--- **Cherokee Strip** (Paramount, 1940) in which Dix was supported by Victor Jory and Florence Rice, and **The Round-Up** (Paramount, 1941) with Patricia Morison and Preston Foster backing Dix up---Sherman assigned to Selander. With directorial responsibility not only for the Dix pictures but for four of the season's Cassidys, it was an exceptionally busy period for Selander---and in terms of quality one of his best.

The behind-scenes personnel on the Hoppy films remained largely as before, but Britt Wood's departure required one major change in the cast. For the part of Boyd's and Hayden's new comic sidekick Sherman hired Andy Clyde (1892-1967). Born in Blairgowrie, Scotland and trained in the low comedy of the English music halls and Mack Sennett silent shorts, Clyde was best known prior to 1940 for his role as a buffoonish Scots hotel proprietor in George Stevens' **Annie Oakley** (RKO, 1935). Although he hadn't been in a Western before, his antics had caught the eye of screenwriter Norton S. Parker, who advanced both Clyde's career and his own by writing and selling a Cassidy script that was designed to introduce a new continuing character to the series. As Parker drew him, California Carlson was a distinctive and memorable comic personality, a bragging and scruffy-whiskered buffoon notorious for spinning long-winded whoppers

about his own courageous deeds but a quaking rabbit when trouble strikes---except in cases of really fierce trouble, which transforms him into a laughable lion. For better or worse this conception of the sidekick survived only for one picture, and during the balance of Clyde's eight years on the Cassidys the directors and writers reduced him to a regulation frontier oaf, funny enough at his best but certainly no match for George Hayes when it came to creating a human character.

Clyde's wasn't the only fresh face in that season's output, for many key supporting roles went to players who were new to the unit. But as if to assure continuity with previous Cassidys, Morris Ankrum appeared in all six exploits, although in two of them he was cast on the side of law and order and the traditional Ankrum part went to Victor Jory, a newcomer to the Cassidys but a veteran of the Sherman-Selander Zane Grey pictures and an actor who quickly proved himself a worthy successor to Ankrum in villainy. The 1940-41 season also saw Boyd shedding the Hopalong Cassidy "monkey suit" that Sherman detested and substituting a light-blue or light-gray shirt and trousers, while Russell Hayden as Lucky switched to a checked shirt and dark vest as replacements for the nondescript light shirt he'd worn in the past.

After completing **Cherokee Strip** with Dix, Selander launched the sixth season of Cassidys with **Three Men From Texas** (1940) which he directed from Norton S. Parker's screenplay. It turned out to be the finest Cassidy film in years and perhaps the best ever, a perfect blend of action, strong story and powerful emotion, punctuated by several instances of that Selander hallmark, the reversal of Western-film cliché. "Broke every rule in the book on that one," Parker recalled fondly many years later, referring presumably to both Selander and himself. It's a strange and haunting picture, more than 70 minutes long, and with a storyline that breaks abruptly and deliberately in the middle. The scenery as

Morris Ankrum is ready to ambush William Boyd in this scene from **Hills of Old Wyoming** (1937, Paramount).

photographed by Russell Harlan was magnificent, the music score by Victor Young (his last for a Cassidy film) backed up the action splendidly, and the result was a Western gem that has lost none of its luster after almost fifty years. Joseph W. Engel carried on as associate producer, with Carrol Lewis credited as film editor and Sherman A. Rose as editorial supervisor.

The film begins in Santa Carmen, California, where the ranchers both Anglo and Latino are being terrorized by the local Hitler, Bruce Morgan (Morris Ankrum). Banker Thompson (Davidson Clark), head of the local citizens' committee, asks his old friend Captain Andrews of the Texas Rangers (Morgan Wallace) to send a man who can clean out the rats' nest. Andrews offers the job to his top star-toters, Hopalong Cassidy and Lucky Jenkins. Lucky is eager for the assignment but Hoppy is ready to leave the Rangers and return to the Bar 20. In a scene taut with subtly understated emotion, Lucky decides to break with Cassidy and go it alone. "A man's got to get out on his own

sometime. Any man does." Hoppy rides along for a few miles with his protegé, and their parting, with each man simultaneously full of joy and sadness, is one of the most touching moments in any Western.

The scene shifts to an outlaw hideout where Gardner (Dick Curtis) and his gang are bringing in a stolen herd of horses. Gardner tells his camp cook, a raucous-voiced whopper-spinner named California Carlson (Andy Clyde), that the notorious outlaw Ben Stokes will likely visit the hideout while the gang is driving the horses over the border.

Miles away from the outlaw encampment, Cassidy comes upon one of the hands from whom the Gardner gang stole the herd. The man is an old friend of Hoppy's and dies of his wounds in Cassidy's arms. Cassidy grimly follows the stolen horses' tracks to Gardner's camp, which is deserted except for California who has just challenged a burro to a gunfight. The old blowhard mistakes Hoppy for the expected Ben Stokes and

134

William Boyd dances with Bernadene Hayes in this scene from **North of the Rio Grande** (1937, Paramount).

gives away all the gang's secrets including Gardner's plan to move from Texas to California. After Carlson gleefully boasts about his prowess as a killer, Cassidy flashes his badge and arrests him as a material witness. On their way to the Ranger station the two men are spotted by the real Stokes (Glenn Strange), who goes on to the hideout and warns Gardner and his gang that California is the prisoner of a lawman. The outlaws ride out to shut Carlson's mouth. After a brisk chase sequence Hoppy and California are trapped among some rocks, and Carlson woefully admits that he's never been in a gunfight before in his life. Still they manage to outmaneuver the gang and capture them all except Stokes and Gardner, who escape. Later Cassidy decides to follow Gardner to the west coast, not only to avenge his murdered friend but in hope of seeing Lucky again. Captain Andrews arranges for Cassidy to be appointed a U.S. Marshal and for Carlson, who claims to know the state of California like the back of his hand, to go along as Hoppy's guide. So ends part one of the movie.

The second half returns us to the Santa Carmen setting of the earliest scenes. From a clifftop overlooking the main road to town, Hoppy and California witness a stagecoach robbery. The thieves are Bruce Morgan's gunmen and the only thing they steal is a Spanish land grant that was in the mail pouch, addressed to a U.S. registrar. Morgan has been systematically stealing these grants and then evicting Mexican ranchers for inability to prove title to their property. (This part of the plot was taken by Parker from his own earlier script for **Outlaw Express**, a 1938 Universal Western starring Bob Baker.) As soon as the gunmen have left the scene the coach is robbed again. From the cliff top California recognizes the leader of this band as his old friend Pico Serrano (Thornton Edwards). Carlson and Cassidy ride down the steep cliff and intercept the Mexican gang. Delighted to see his old compadre, Pico explains that he and his vaqueros have had to turn outlaw since Morgan evicted him from the Serrano

135

Al Ferguson (far left) along with Lee J. Cobb and his gang have their hands up as William Boyd, George Hayes and the posse have them covered in this scene from **Rustler's Valley** (1937, Paramount).

hacienda. Pico tries to persuade Carlson and Hoppy to stay with him at his hideout beyond Diablo Pass but they decide to go on to Santa Carmen and visit Lucky.

Meanwhile in town, the young marshal from Texas is about to march into Morgan's Diamond Horseshoe saloon and tackle the gang single-handed. Delighted though he is when Hoppy rides in, Lucky locks up his mentor and Carlson and banker Thompson so that he can prove himself by defeating Morgan without help. As it happens, Morgan's gang has recently been augmented by Gardner and Stokes. Lucky sneaks past the rank-and-file gunmen and gets the drop on Morgan in his saloon office but runs into a blaze of gunfire and is wounded while trying to take Morgan back to jail. He's rescued by Hoppy and California, who by this time have gotten themselves out of their cells. A pitched battle breaks out in the streets of Santa Carmen. Heavily outnumbered, Cassidy and Lucky and California race out of town and take refuge at Pico's hideout, where Lucky

promptly falls in love with the bandit's daughter Paquita (Esther Estrella). After Pico explains how Morgan operates, Hoppy decides to organize all the victimized ranchers and cowhands into a fighting force, a sort of bi-cultural vigilante group legitimized by U.S. deputy marshals' badges. At a secret meeting with the ranchers it's agreed that the signal for the force to assemble will be the blowing of the ram's horn by Pico's sentries.

Don Ricardo Velez (not listed in the credits) rides into Pico's camp for shelter after being evicted from his rancho and seeing his vaqueros slaughtered by Morgan's gang. Cassidy rides to the Velez hacienda with Pico and his bandits. They encounter six Morgan gunmen still on the property and a fight erupts. One outlaw escapes but the other five are taken prisoner. In one of the most haunting scenes in any Selander film, Cassidy argues like a good liberal that these cut-throats are presumed innocent and entitled to a fair trial. Knowing that they are guilty as hell, Pico pulls his gun on Hoppy and orders the five men

136

The townspeople along with the Sheriff (John Beach) wait for Lee J. Cobb to get up after William Boyd has knocked him down in this scene from **Rustler's Valley** (1937, Paramount).

hanged on the spot. When Morgan and his gang reach the rancho from town, all they find is five swinging corpses. Morgan vows that he will have his revenge.

Back at Pico's camp Hoppy admits that he would have lynched the prisoners himself if he had suffered as Pico has, and Serrano in turn apologizes for letting himself be carried away by hate. Hoppy sends Pico's man Juanito (Neyl Marx) into Santa Carmen to arrange a meeting with banker Thompson's citizens' committee. But Morgan and his gang follow the youth back to Serrano's hideout and launch an all-out attack from the surrounding cliffs. The Mexicans are forced to abandon their camp and run a gauntlet of fire to escape. Among those killed is Paquita, who dies in a lovely field amid the singing of birds and is buried by a weeping Lucky and Pico.

The showdown is at hand, and with a barrage of running inserts underscored by a superb Victor Young theme and by the blasts of the ram's horn, an army of Morgan's Anglo and Mexican victims forms out of small groups of horsemen coming together in a series of stunning Y figures. Cassidy and the men invade Santa Carmen and a massive battle begins, culminating with the entire gang being trapped inside the Diamond Horseshoe. Riddled with bullets, Pico stalks into the saloon alone and strangles Morgan to death just before the remnants of the gang including Stokes and Gardner surrender. With the town purged and California installed as the new marshal, Hoppy and Lucky start back for home. But they haven't gone more than a few hundred yards before they are rejoined by California, who will clearly still be with them whenever the next adventure beckons.

And sure enough there he was a few months later in **The Doomed Caravan** (1941), another Cassidy exploit directed by Selander with an abundance of Mexican characters and a plot that splits down the middle. The far from watertight screenplay was a joint effort by Johnston McCulley, creator of the immortal Zorro more than twenty years earlier, and newcomer J.

William Boyd and William Duncan glare at each other as George Hayes, Ernie Adams, Billy King, Russell Hayden, Nora Lane and others look on in this scene from **Hopalong Rides Again** (1937, Paramount).

Benton Cheney, the future author of dozens of Western scripts for movies and television. If **Three Men From Texas** had sympathized with Latinos revolting against the Anglo oppressor, **The Doomed Caravan** with its contempt for phony liberators was of a different political stripe altogether. Apparently Selander preferred to personalize the films he directed not by tinkering with the scripters' social views but in other ways, and Caravan is unmistakably a Selander picture, featuring one of his most aggressive boss-lady figures in the person of Minna Gombell, and recycling all sorts of motifs from the director's earlier Cassidys. Morris Ankrum in his usual role as the king toad was backstopped by Pat O'Brien from **Bar 20 Justice** (now billing himself for obvious reasons Pat J. O'Brien) and unit veterans Trevor Bardette and Raphael Bennett. Engel, Harlan, Lewis and Rose continued respectively as associate producer, photographer, film editor and editorial supervisor, while Irvin Talbot and John Leipold were credited jointly as music directors.

Selander starts this one with a bang or rather a multitude of bangs as Jim Ferber (Pat J. O'Brien) and his gang launch a neatly directed night attack on the headquarters of the Crescent City Freighting Company. The outlaws set fire to some barns and stampede the line's horses and mules but are driven off in a counterattack led by the company's owner, Jane Travers (Minna Gombell). Selander instantly establishes Jane's credentials as an action woman by having her personally kill off more of the raiders than any of her men. Later that night Hoppy and Lucky come to the company's headquarters at the head of a party delivering Jane a gold shipment which she is to take by wagon to the town of El Dorado across the Mexican border. There they are reunited with their old pal California. Jane tells Hoppy that several of her wagon trains have been raided recently and that she has asked for a military detail to escort the next caravan but persuades Cassidy to pitch in as well and help the wagons reach their destination. There's a hint that she might not object to a bit of romance

138

George Hayes lets loose with a big sneeze while William Boyd, Nora Lane and Russell Hayden get a good laugh in this comic scene from **Hopalong Rides Again** (1937, Paramount).

from Hoppy along the way.

The wagons are prepared and loaded for the trail, Jane hefting sacks of goods like a stevedore beside her men. At this point the freight yard is graced by the arrival of lovely Diana Westcott (Georgia Hawkins), who asks to go along with the caravan so she can visit her uncle Stephen Westcott, Jane's business agent in El Dorado. As Lucky true to form begins to make calf eyes at the young lady we are reminded of the double-romance theme from Selander's 1938 **Heart of Arizona**, and once we cut to El Dorado and see Uncle Stephen (Morris Ankrum) we are left in no doubt that he's behind the raids and wants to wipe Jane out and establish his own freight monopoly. On Westcott's orders, Ferber and his gang massacre the soldiers who have been sent to escort the Travers train, put on the dead men's uniforms and ride on to the freight yard posing as the troopers. Cassidy however quickly becomes suspicious: these military men aren't wearing army boots, the uniform of one soldier has a bullet hole over the

heart, and the man calling himself Sergeant Spencer who heads the detail has the initials JF inside his hat. (Don't ask why Ferber didn't take a bit more care with the impersonation, because clearly the scriptwriters didn't.) Hoppy reneges on his commitment to escort the wagons and rides away with his men, leaving Jane terribly hurt and convinced that he's a coward. When the train sets out, Cassidy and his men follow secretly at a distance, waiting for the fake troopers to hold up the caravan. When they make their move, Hoppy and company race pell-mell into the action, dragging brush behind their horses so as to simulate a small army, and drive the gang away after a battle. Diana does her bit in the fighting by bullwhipping Ferber out of his saddle but the outlaw leader manages to get away with the survivors of his gang. After an abject apology from Jane---to which Boyd as Hoppy replies as only he could: "Awww, forget it"---the wagons resume their trek to El Dorado and the first half of the film ends.

Part Two begins with the arrival of the caravan

William Boyd seems disturbed by the news of George Hayes and Russell Hayden in this publicity still for **Hopalong Rides Again** (1937, Paramount).

in El Dorado, which gives rise to several scenes of romance and comedy and general time-wasting to the beat of Mexican music. Hoppy discusses the raider situation with Don Pedro, governor of the province (José Luis Tortosa), who shares the suspicion of the local priest, Fray Sebastian (not listed in the credits), that the outlaws may be linked with Ed Martin (Trevor Bardette), an Anglo rancher described as "one of those reformer fellows" who stir up discontent among the peons. Don Pedro reveals to Cassidy that Mexican troops are secretly on their way to El Dorado to help capture the raiders. It doesn't take long before big-mouth Lucky has spilled the beans to his new girl-friend's Uncle Stephen, who quickly races out of town and thereby arouses Hoppy's suspicion that he's the brains behind the raiders.

Westcott tells his gang about the coming troops and formulates a first-strike plan. On his return to El Dorado he suggests to Don Pedro that a fiesta would help improve relations between the Mexicans and the Anglos. The resulting celebration permits another flurry of romance and comedy scenes and Latin music. But the fiesta is shattered when Martin and his gang ride in and take over the town, declaring that the great proletarian revolution has begun and locking up in the local carcel all the Anglos except Westcott and Diana, who are exempted for no good reason whatsoever. A fat Mexican tamale dispenser, who's been making googoo eyes at California, helps him escape, and Cassidy breaks away separately. Hoppy makes his way under cover of darkness to Westcott's house, where both he and, in her bedroom, Diana happen to overhear Uncle Stephen ordering Martin to have a firing squad execute all the prisoners including Jane Travers the next morning. Both eavesdroppers are caught but escape in a burst of action and happen upon the tamale woman's hut where California is hiding. Hoppy sends the woman to find Fray Sebastian.

At dawn, a man in priest's robes visits the jail to give spiritual comfort to the condemned men and woman. But one needn't have seen Cassidy

140

William Boyd points something out to Russell Hayden, George Hayes and John Beach in this scene from **Texas Trail** (1937, Paramount).

playing padre in Selander's **Range War** to suspect that this is Hoppy again and that what he's giving the prisoners is not the last rites but some weapons. (Could his ability to hide fifteen or twenty pistols inside his robes count as a miracle?) The captives are marched out to be shot, every one of them bravely refusing Martin's offer of blindfolds. And no wonder: when he gives the command to fire, it's his own men that are mowed down, and Martin himself is killed. One firing squad member escapes and tears off to the Martin ranch to warn Westcott and the rest of the gang. Hoppy, Jane and the men go forth to engage the raiders in pitched battle. The two forces converge out on the desert and the final shootout erupts, an adequate but rather perfunctory action scene that ends when Westcott tries to make a getaway and Hoppy lassos him out of his saddle. But, bowing to Selander's penchant for sex-role reversals, Cassidy leaves it to Jane to knock Westcott unconscious with one mighty blow. Now that the revolution has been quelled and El Dorado is at peace,

Hoppy and his pals head back to the Bar 20.

Having committed a large chunk of his annual production budget to the two Richard Dix pictures, Sherman decided to economize on the season's third and fourth Cassidys by arranging for their outdoor sequences to be shot back-to-back at Lone Pine and then having their respective casts return to the studio for the indoor scenes--- all too many of them in both pictures. Selander was busy preparing to make **The Round-Up** with Dix, and to replace him on Hoppy's next adventure Sherman once again brought in the series' first director, Howard Bretherton. **In Old Colorado** (1941) turned out to be a typical Bretherton effort, a garden-variety Western with no emotional resonance, its long dull stretches made even worse by having obviously been shot indoors. Like so many of Selander's Cassidys this one features a mature woman rancher and her attractive daughter, but Bretherton's Ma Woods as routinely portrayed by Sarah Padden was neither boss lady nor action gal but a nondescript

141

Russell Hayden, George Hayes and William Boyd look strange in uniform in this scene from **Texas Trail** (1937, Paramount).

motherly stereotype, forgotten the minute the film is over. The lead villain is portrayed by Morris Ankrum but Bretherton reduces him as he did the year before in **The Showdown** to a standard bad guy without a single memorable characteristic. Indeed, even though the script is credited to Norton S. Parker from **Three Men From Texas** and J. Benton Cheney from **The Doomed Caravan**, many key motifs are derived from the first entry in the series, **Hop-A-Long Cassidy**, which Bretherton had helmed in 1935.

Like Bretherton's **Hop-A-Long Cassidy**, this picture deals with a villainous foreman who's stirring up trouble between two ranches for his own profit. The scene is Cooperstown, Colorado, and as the film opens we see wealthy cattleman George Davidson (Stanley Andrews) and his foreman Joe Weiler (Morris Ankrum) fencing off the waterholes on Davidson's Arrow H ranch so as to keep out Davidson's neighbor Ma Woods (Sarah Padden), whom he blames for recent raids on his herds. Ma, who likewise blames Davidson for her

own cattle losses, penetrates the fence with wire-cutters and takes her herd through. But the water dispute is the least of the troubles faced by Ma and her fellow small ranchers: their notes at the bank are almost due, they can't find buyers for their cattle, and Ma's hands are quitting before a range war with Davidson breaks out. After an interminable scene with their cook Nosey Haskins (Cliff Nazarro), who specializes in rapidfire doubletalk, Ma and her daughter Myra (Margaret Hayes) send a wire to the Bar 20 in Arizona, asking their old friend Buck Peters to buy their cattle. Hoppy, Lucky and California ride from the Bar 20 to the nearest town to dispatch a reply telegram from Buck to the effect that Cassidy and his pals are leaving by train for Colorado with $20,000 in cash. Before climbing on board, California encounters a sharpie (Philip Van Zandt) who entices him into playing the old game of Guess Which Shell The Pea Is Under, and the only point of interest about the sequence is that the gambler is not played by Earle Hodgins! While the

George Hayes' attempt at the bugle has made William Boyd break into a smile in this scene from **Texas Trail** (1937, Paramount).

train is en route, Davidson back in Cooperstown orders the sheriff (not listed in the credits) to serve a writ on Ma Woods, restraining her from using the Arrow H waterholes. Ma decides to drive her cattle out on the open range so that they won't die of thirst before Cassidy arrives with the money to buy them.

When the train from Arizona stops at a water tower fifty miles from Cooperstown, Blackie Reed (Weldon Heyburn) and three henchmen get the drop on Cassidy and steal his monogrammed moneybelt with the $20,000. On reaching town Hoppy confers with the sheriff about the local situation and decides that there's a traitor in Ma Woods' entourage who leaked word to the outlaws about his coming. Davidson interrupts the conference and offers to sell Hoppy twice as many Arrow H cattle as Ma was going to sell him for the $20,000, and Cassidy deduces that Davidson has no idea the money was stolen and therefore can't be the person behind Ma's troubles. Hoppy, Lucky and California ride out to Ma's range camp

and, in the first real action sequence in the picture, manage both to drive off some rustlers attacking the herd and to save Myra from being trampled to death by the stampeding cattle. The three men don't reveal their identities but simply sign on as cowhands so that they can locate the "mole" in the Woods party. Lucky, as usual, starts to romance Myra, while California and Nosey waste time with some labored comic interchanges. Then Davidson pays a visit to the camp and gives away Cassidy's identity. Hoppy explains about the theft of the money and tries to convince both sides in the imminent range war that a third party is responsible for their troubles. The scene ends with Ma and Davidson shaking hands and making peace.

That night the mole shows himself. When Hank Merritt (James Seay) slips out of camp, Hoppy, Lucky and California trail him to a location that looks remarkably like the rustlers' Thunder Mesa hideout from **Hop-A-Long Cassidy**, where Hank reports Cassidy's presence to Weiler and Reed. Hoppy and his pals prowl around the rocks

George Hayes has the attention of Alexander Cross, Russell Hayden and William Boyd in this scene from **Texas Trail** (1937, Paramount).

and dispose of a lookout but are captured by the gang a few minutes later as they're racing away. Weiler keeps out of sight during this sequence but inadvertently drops a few shells from his special long-range rifle. Leaving the three prisoners bound, gagged and under guard at the hideout, the outlaws go off to wipe out the Woods outfit and take the cattle. Hoppy cuts his bonds on Lucky's spurs and overpowers the guards.

Meanwhile Hank returns to the Woods camp with fake orders from Cassidy to move the herd to a spot where the gang is waiting in ambush. Davidson and Weiler accompany Ma and her hands on the drive. As the men and cattle move closer to the cliffs where the rustlers are set to bushwhack them, Hoppy and his pals are racing back to the Woods camp. Cassidy comes upon the rifle shells Weiler dropped but doesn't connect them with Davidson's foreman. The three men happen to be within earshot of the ambush site just when the gang attacks and of course they take hands in the action, Lucky capturing Hank Merritt

while Hoppy and California scale the cliffs as in **Hop-A-Long Cassidy** to get behind the rustlers. From his position down below Weiler spots and snipes at them with his long-range rifle but is wounded in the side by Myra Woods, although he manages to escape without being recognized. Cassidy rounds up the rustlers in the rocks including Blackie Reed, who refuses to squeal on his boss or to tell what happened to the stolen $20,000. Davidson offers to purchase Ma Woods' notes from the bank and hold them until she can sell her cattle, but Weiler unsheaths his long-range rifle again and severely wounds his employer. Hoppy and Lucky inspect the spot from which the shot was fired, find more of those distinctive shells, finally realize who their adversary is and catch the fleeing Weiler between them in a pincers movement. When they search the foreman they find the $20,000 still inside Hoppy's money-belt, which stopped the bullet Myra Woods had earlier fired at Weiler. With Davidson on the mend and the range war aborted, Hoppy and Lucky and

Russell Hayden, William Boyd and George Hayes seem to be happy to be back in their normal clothes after the uniforms in this scene from **Texas Trail** (1937, Paramount).

California board the train that will take them back to the Bar 20.

Sherman hadn't hired a new director for a Cassidy film since Edward D. Venturini had made **In Old Mexico** in 1939. The man he chose to helm Hoppy's next adventure was Derwin Abrahams (1903-1974), who was far from new to the unit, having worked there as an assistant director since 1936, but who made his debut as director in his own right with **Border Vigilantes** (1941), from a screenplay by J. Benton Cheney. Abrahams had no great flair either for action or emotion but proved that he could turn out routine oaters as well as anyone and thereafter spent most of his time directing quickie B Westerns at Monogram and other Poverty Row studios. The truly unusual aspect of his first directorial effort was the offtrail casting. Morris Ankrum was given the role of the female lead Frances Gifford's father instead of his customary outlaw leader part, and all four of the quartet of bad guys were well known for good guy roles earlier in their careers. Victor Jory,

making his debut in a Cassidy after excellent roles in the Sherman-Selander Zane Grey pictures, had starred just the year before in the 15-chapter serial **The Shadow** (Columbia, 1940); Tom Tyler, infamous as the evil Luke Plummer in John Ford's **Stagecoach** (United Artists, 1939), had been the hero of dozens of super-el-cheapo shoot-em-ups since the late 1920s; and Zane Grey veteran Hal Taliaferro before his wise move into character roles had been Wally Wales, star of Grade Z oaters. All three were to return in several more Cassidys over the next few years. But the fourth-ranked villain was the strangest piece of casting in the film, for he was none other than Britt Wood, Hoppy's comic sidekick from the 1939-40 season! Dear old Ethel Wales returned to play another fusspot spinster and Jack Rockwell was back as a mine owner. Joseph W. Engel carried on as associate producer, Russell Harlan behind the cameras, Irvin Talbot and John Leipold as music directors. Credited as film editor was Robert Warwick, who had filled that slot on the

145

William Boyd has both guns ready for action in this scene from **Texas Trail** (1937, Paramount).

first several Cassidys for which Abrahams had been billed as assistant director, while editorial supervision remained in the hands of Sherman A. Rose.

The scene is the town of Silver Center, where the miners have formed for their mutual protection a vigilante organization headed by Henry Logan (Victor Jory). But recently the vigilantes have been ambushed several times by outlaws---which is hardly surprising since, as we learn early on, the head of the outlaws is Logan himself. Mine owner Dan Forbes (Morris Ankrum) has begun to wonder why the bandits have been so successful, and sends for Hopalong Cassidy to ferret out the traitor among the vigilantes. Unfortunately Forbes confides what he's done to Logan, who sends gunman Big Ed Stone (Hal Taliaferro) to ambush Hoppy on the trail and at the same time orders his chief henchman Jim Yager (Tom Tyler) to kill Forbes. Yager shoots Forbes on the main street of town but doesn't kill him, and for the rest of the picture Forbes is confined to a wheelchair.

Stone sets up an ambush for Cassidy at Gunsight Pass. Thanks to California's ineptitude at land navigation, he and Hoppy and Lucky have gotten lost several miles short of the pass, and Cassidy is alone and hunting for the trail when Stone bushwhacks him. Hoppy plays dead, gets the drop on Stone, shoots him and apparently kills him, although he doesn't bother either to make sure the gunman is dead or to bury him. Further along the road to Silver Center Hoppy and his pals are intercepted by Forbes' daughter Helen (Frances Gifford), who tells them about the attack on her father. At the Forbes ranch Hoppy learns that only Henry Logan knew he'd been sent for, and concludes at once that Logan is behind the outlaws. At this juncture Forbes' fusspot sister Jennifer (Ethel Wales) wastes several minutes of screen time by chasing California with matrimony on her mind.

Hoppy, Lucky and California open their campaign against the gang by riding into town and marching into and out of the saloon like a trio of

William Boyd and George Hayes are about to go into action in this publicity still for **Texas Trail** (1937, Paramount).

gunfighters just to see what attention they attract. When Logan approaches and demands to know who they are, they claim to be gunmen out to even an old score with a certain Hopalong Cassidy. Just then a new outlaw raid is reported and most of the vigilantes race out of town, unaware that the raid is a diversion and that the gang's real target is the silver-laden vault of the town bank. The remaining vigilante guards are distracted by a fist-fight on the street while the thieves break into the bank by the back door, loot the vault, come out the front door and start shooting up the town. Hoppy, Lucky and California jump into the action, kill most of the thieves and save the silver.

This adequate but far from pulse-pounding action scene is followed by a quiet interlude *chez* Forbes. While Aunt Jennifer continues running after California, Lucky plucks feebly at a handy guitar and romances Helen, who is unimpressed with the young man's musical talent. "I thought all cowboys played guitars," she teases him. "Not the ones from the Bar 20," he replies heatedly. This

beautiful dig at the Gene Autry type of song-saturated Westerns popular in the early Forties is suddenly ruined when Helen chooses the moment to break into a typical 1940s romantic ballad!

Logan retaliates for the failure of the bank holdup by launching a blitzkrieg. "Hit 'em like a hurricane," he orders his men. Hoppy's counter-move is a plot to set Logan and his top associates against each other. Miner Hank Weaver (Jack Rockwell) announces that he's going to ship a wagonload of silver and asks Logan for a vigilante escort. What is actually in the wagon and is later transferred to a mule train is a load of iron, and California back at Weaver's mine is boxing up the real silver for shipment by another route. Sure enough the gang attacks the mule train and the guards flee. Later Logan visits the hideout and finds his henchmen Yager and Lafe Willis (Britt Wood) at each other's throats over the shipment of iron. Hoppy's plan seems to be working per-fectly, except that it's too soon to end the picture and a new complication is called for. Abrahams

147

Billy King, George Hayes, William Boyd and Russell Hayden seem to be intrigued by something off camera in this scene from **Texas Trail** (1937, Paramount).

and Cheney produce one when word reaches Weaver that what was supposed to have been the real silver shipment has also turned out to be iron. The miners conclude that Hoppy and his pals have stolen the genuine silver and go after Lucky and California in a quite decent chase sequence backed by first-rate action music. As they are capturing and preparing to hang Lucky, a new complication is rearing its head in town when Big Ed Stone re-enters the picture, nursed back to health, as he explains to Logan, by an old desert rat. When Logan points out to him the three gunfighters who supposedly are hunting Cassidy, Big Ed drops the bombshell that the leader of the three is Cassidy himself. Logan sends Stone and several other men to kill Hoppy at once. They corner him in the saloon and are about to ventilate him when California barges in and distracts them long enough for Cassidy to draw and start blazing away, killing Stone and most of the others. Then he and California race off to save Lucky's neck.

They break up the miners' lynching party in the nick of time and Hoppy figures out that the real silver must still be at the Weaver mine. And a search proves him right: California had been so discombobulated by Jennifer's amorous pursuit that he had messed up the shipping instructions beyond belief. Once the silver is found, Hoppy resumes his grand strategy against the gang by sending identical anonymous notes to Logan, Yager and Willis, each note purporting to be from a gang member and claiming that the real silver is hidden in an abandoned mine. Cassidy and the miners take cover near the specified location and wait. Yager and Willis reach the place on each other's heels, accuse one another of treachery and gun each other down. "Double sooeycide," clucks California. Nearing the mine, Logan spots Cassidy and the others huddled over his henchmen's bodies and hightails it for the gang's hideout. He's pursued by a small army of miners, and when Hoppy and his allies reach the hideout they besiege it Thunder Mesa style. The siege is broken when Cassidy drops a bandanna full of bullets

148

Some extras, Russell Hayden, Billy King and John Beach are interested in the dead body, while William Boyd and George Hayes look at something off camera in this scene from **Texas Trail** (1937, Paramount).

from a clifftop into a campfire in front of the shack where the gang is holed up. A machinegun-like bedlam breaks loose and Logan and his men meekly come out with their hands up. With law and order restored to Silver Center, Hoppy and his sidekicks head back for the Bar 20.

If **In Old Colorado** and **Border Vigilantes** were the low points in the 1940-41 season of Cassidys, momentum started to return with number five, **Pirates On Horseback** (1941), directed straightforwardly by Lesley Selander. The screenplay, by free-lancer Ethel LaBlanche and old reliable J. Benton Cheney, was more unusual than most B Western scripts. Morris Ankrum was back in his customary king toad role, and the supporting cast included several actors like Dennis Moore and William Haade who were new to Cassidys but either were at the time or would soon become fixtures in low-budget shoot-em-ups. For the female lead Selander picked up a young actress named Eleanor Stewart, who had little to do in this picture but impressed the director enough so that, as

we'll see, she became his next embodiment of the quintessential action woman. Away from the cameras, Fred Feitshans Jr. joined the unit as film editor, working under Sherman A. Rose's supervision, and John Leipold teamed with someone named Maurice Lawrence on the music for the picture.

Unlike most Cassidy adventures, this one opens with a murder; indeed with the murder of a familiar face. For the part of old Ben Pendleton, who is shot to death in his cabin soon after he apparently rediscovered the fabulous lost El Dorado gold mine, Selander chose none other than Britt Wood, the comic sidekick in the 1939-40 Cassidys. Sheriff John Blake (Henry Hall) sends word to the dead man's only living relatives: his lovely niece Trudy Pendleton (Eleanor Stewart) and a distant cousin going by the handle of California Carlson. Abandoning his new hobby of gardening, California rounds up Hoppy and Lucky and heads for the town of Rimrock to claim his inheritance.

149

William Boyd cautions John Warburton to stay out of the line of fire in this scene from **Partners of the Plains** (1938, Paramount).

Around the time the three reach the area, the stagecoach brings Trudy into town, accompanied by gambler Ace Gibson (Morris Ankrum), who is behind Ben's murder and is playing up to Trudy in order to get the lost mine for himself. Trudy is already in residence at Ben's cabin by the time Hoppy and his pals arrive. Their first order of business after introducing themselves is to pitch in and help clean up the mess the townspeople made hunting for the lost mine. While California prowls around and finds a pile of seed packets in the woodshed behind the cabin, Lucky takes time out from housecleaning to romance Trudy.

Next morning Gibson pays a visit to the cabin. While he's talking to Trudy in the doorway, Hoppy in the main room stumbles upon a note in Ben's handwriting, hidden inside an old catalogue. "Eagle will show way to mine," the note reads, "but only at sundown." Cassidy quickly pockets the note until Gibson leaves, but the gambler senses something amiss and, after saying goodbye, sneaks back to the cabin and

eavesdrops long enough to hear Cassidy read the note aloud to Trudy. Hoppy assumes the note means that the mine's location is known by some Indian named Eagle, but a talk with the sheriff and Chief Flying Cloud (not listed in the credits) convinces him that there's no such Indian in the area. Selander pulls off one of his better cliché reversals when he has California try to communicate in pidgin English and sign language with the Chief, whose cultivated diction would put professors to shame.

While the meeting with Flying Cloud is underway in the sheriff's office, Gibson's henchman Bill Watson (William Haade) leads Cassidy's stallion Topper into the livery stable. Hoppy sees his horse being taken, as he was meant to, and trails Watson. Once he is lured into the stable, Watson and another gunman get the drop on him and try to steal Ben's note, which falls out of Cassidy's pocket during the ensuing fight. The thugs are chased off and Hoppy comes back for the note just in time to frustrate Gibson from picking it up

150

William Boyd points something out to Harvey Clark, Russell Hayden, Gwen Gaze and John Warburton in this scene from **Partners of the Plains** (1938, Paramount).

off the stable floor. Knowing now who was behind the attack, Hoppy and his pals carry on their search for an Indian named Eagle.

At this point the story is interrupted for a lengthy comic interlude. California comes riding into town and blurts out to the livery stable owner (Jack Rockwell) that he's just found a treasure of nuggets in an old mine shaft behind Ben's cabin. Word spreads like wildfire and within minutes there's a mad gold rush, with every man and woman in Rimrock racing out to the mine site to stake claims. Hoppy, Lucky, Trudy and even California himself are fooled by the wild talk and accompany the human stampede. Only after they've all made idiots of themselves blundering through the old mine's tunnels does Hoppy closely question California and discover that the nuggets he found weren't gold but mushrooms!

The film gets serious again when Gibson decides to become Trudy's sole adviser by getting rid of the Bar 20 trio. Meanwhile Hoppy, Lucky and California are combing the desert and moun-

tains, hunting the lost mine. Exhausted, they stop to rest on a mountaintop, where Cassidy begins to wonder whether Eagle might be not a person but a landmark. They look around and suddenly observe an eagle-shaped rock formation on a neighboring mountain. But the gods are playing games: the trio find nothing on the second peak. While they're on their way back to Ben's cabin, Gibson visits Trudy and plants the suggestion that California may not really be a relative of Ben.

A few days later, with the trio off again looking for the mine, Gibson returns with faked evidence that they're confidence men. When Hoppy and his pals return, Trudy demands proof that California is Ben's cousin, and when they can produce none she orders them off the property. Lucky knocks Gibson down as they leave. Cassidy and his buddies go back to the eagle-shaped rock formation and, remembering the exact wording of Ben's note, wait for sundown. Sure enough, the shadow of the eagle at dusk falls square upon Ben's woodshed down below. The trio race down and

151

William Boyd shows Russell Hayden some evidence in this scene from **Partners of the Plains** (1938, Paramount).

tear the shed apart until they find a trapdoor in the floor and beneath it the lost El Dorado tunnel.

Unfortunately Gibson and his men are still at the cabin and get the drop on Hoppy and his pals in the woodshed. Leaving his thugs to tie and guard them, Gibson takes Trudy back to town, ostensibly to get the sheriff but actually to make her sign the mine over to him. Cassidy and his sidekicks manage to untie themselves and overpower their guards. Then Hoppy chases after Gibson, reaching his saloon just as Trudy is about to deed him the mine, and wipes up the floor with the gambler in the season's best fight thus far. Of course with no evidence that Gibson killed Ben he can't be charged with much, but Selander passes over such trivia and closes with a large corporation paying California and Trudy $500,000 for the mine. California, however, is much more excited over word from the Bar 20 that he's just won first prize in a garden show for his petunias.

Pirates On Horseback was acceptable enough, but it was only with the season's last Cassidy film that Selander made a true classic. **Wide Open Town** (1941) ran more than 75 minutes and, according to the credits, was directed by Selander from an original screenplay by unit veterans J. Benton Cheney and Harrison Jacobs. In reality the script was a radical rewrite by Cheney of the Jacobs scenario for **Hopalong Cassidy Returns** (1936), which had been directed by Nate Watt and nominally based on Mulford's episodic novel of the same name. For the first but by no means the last time in the history of the series, the Cassidy people were overtly remaking an earlier exploit of Hoppy. Only rarely does a remake hold up against its source, and **Hopalong Cassidy Returns** had been a slow and dull albeit emotionally powerful picture. One might have expected **Wide Open Town** to be a disaster. Selander, however, transformed it into one of the best Cassidys ever, toning down the excessive emotionalism of the Watt version, tightening the pace, adding action galore. The human core of both versions is the relationship

Nora Lane has the drop on Frank Darien, Russell Hayden and William Boyd in this scene from **Cassidy of Bar 20** (1938, Paramount).

between Cassidy and the woman saloonkeeper-outlaw chief, and silent star Evelyn Brent played the female lead both times, but the differences between the two films and her part in each correspond precisely to the differences in Selander's and Watt's directorial personalities. Morris Ankrum, Brent's top henchman and jealous lover in **Returns**, came back for **Wide Open Town** but in the role of the crusading newspaperman whom Watt killed off early in his version, and the original Ankrum part went to the far more suave and polished Victor Jory. Selander signed on a huge cast of Western regulars for the smaller roles, including Kenneth Harlan, Roy Barcroft, Glenn Strange, Edward Cassidy, Jack Rockwell and Bob Kortman, all of whom had been in the director's earlier Cassidys. The technical personnel consisted of most of the usual names---Russell Harlan on camera, Carrol Lewis editing under Sherman A. Rose, Irvin Talbot directing the John Leipold music score---but Lewis J. Rachmil (1908-1983) was promoted from art director, the

job he'd held since early in the series, to associate producer, the slot he'd keep till the end of the Sherman era.

As was his custom, Selander opens with action: rustlers steal a large cattle herd from the Bar 20. Hoppy, Lucky and California follow the herd's tracks in the direction of the town of Gunsight, which we quickly find to be under the control of the lovely owner of the Paradise Saloon, Belle Langtry (Evelyn Brent). Belle is a diversified lady indeed: one of her sidelines is to have her manager and lover Steve Fraser (Victor Jory) get miners drunk enough to blab about their newly discovered claims. The latest victim of this procedure is old Pete Carter (George Cleveland), who on leaving Belle's saloon is followed and murdered by Ed Stark (Glenn Strange). Stark brings the map of Carter's claim back to Belle, who prepares to ride to the county seat and file in her own name. But she is scrupulous about robbing only the rich, for when her gunmen Red and Blackie (Roy Barcroft and Bob Kortman) steal ten dollars from a

153

William Boyd, Russell Hayden and John Elliott are ready for action in this scene from **Cassidy of Bar 20** (1938, Paramount).

destitute old man, she reimburses him out of her own pocket and rewards the thugs with a tongue-lashing. Belle is a Selander boss lady par excellence, ruthless and imperious yet with great capacity for love, and it's inevitable that the man she'll fall in love with (although in a cooler, less intense way than her counterpart Lilli Marsh in **Returns**) is Hopalong Cassidy.

As Hoppy and his pals are following the stolen herd, he sees what looks to him like a woman's horse running away with her and races to the rescue. In **Returns** Lilli really was in danger but this time around she's simply riding very fast to the county seat to file on Pete Carter's claim. When she sees Hoppy chasing her she reins in and gets the drop on him with her gun, but when she realizes that he meant to help her they become fast friends in record time.

Hoppy, Lucky and California ride into Gunsight just as Fraser and several goons are trashing the local newspaper office as a way of teaching editor Jim Stuart (Morris Ankrum) not to write columns attacking the Paradise gang. Hoppy and his pals hear the commotion, break into the action, knock out Fraser and his men and make them pay for the damage they've caused. Stuart, who is also Gunsight's mayor, tells Cassidy about the grip of terror in which Belle and her thugs are holding the town and offers him the position of sheriff. Meanwhile Lucky helps Stuart's spunky teenage daughter Joan (Bernice Kay, later known as Cara Williams) clean up the newspaper office, and California makes an ass of himself trying to fix the printing press.

When Belle returns from the county seat she learns of Gunsight's new sheriff, but she doesn't identify him with her rescuer on the trail until Cassidy visits the Paradise and announces forcefully that law and order have come to town. In a scene of subtle interplay, Belle tries to win Hoppy over by offering him a glass of her best wine, which Cassidy refuses. Stark draws on Hoppy and forces him to drink, but Cassidy throws a glassful of raw liquor in his face, disarms him and orders

154

Sheriff Edward Cassidy has William Boyd, Russell Hayden and John Elliott covered in this scene from **Cassidy of Bar 20** (1938, Paramount).

him out of town. One of Belle's dance-hall girls remarks to another that Belle doesn't seem to know whether to kiss Hoppy or kill him. In any event she stops Fraser from shooting him in the back, and later gives orders that he is not to be bushwhacked like the town's previous lawmen, saying: "I'm boss here and don't you ever forget it."

That evening, over dinner at the Stuart house, Hoppy meets with leading citizens Tom Wilson and Brad Jackson (Kenneth Harlan and Edward Cassidy) and deputizes them to organize a townsmens' fighting force. Then he launches a scheme to trap the gang by sending a rancher (Jack Rockwell) into town so he can pretend to get drunk in the Paradise and blab about a huge shipment of money being transferred the next day from a train to a coach at the deserted Sandy Junction depot. The gang snaps at the bait as expected, taking over the station before the coach arrives, tying up the driver and guards and staying under cover till the train roars in. But Hoppy and the citizens' force

are on board the train and open fire when the gang goes after the nonexistent money. Hidden inside the depot, Fraser wounds California and escapes, but Lucky captures Stark alive and the rest of the thieves are routed in a brisk gunfight.

Back in town Fraser reports the trap to Belle, who again stops him from shooting Cassidy in the back as he rides in with his posse and prisoner. Later Hoppy visits Belle's office on the second floor of the Paradise and offers her a chance to break with the gang. Like Lilli in the Watt version, Belle makes the counter-suggestion that Cassidy become her partner, although the sexual innuendo is less overt with Selander directing. Hoppy naturally rejects her, and for the third time she forbids Fraser to kill him.

Next the gang try to break Stark out of jail by having a restaurant waiter deliver drugged coffee to California, who's standing guard. Hoppy however has anticipated the plan, and following instructions, California pretends to drink the brew and pass out. Then he follows Stark out of town

155

William Boyd atop Topper is ready for action in this publicity still for **Bar 20 Justice** (1938, Paramount).

and links up with Cassidy and the posse, who pursue the thug across the desert in hopes that he'll lead them to the gang's hideout and the stolen Bar 20 cattle. At the secret encampment a gunfight breaks out between Hoppy's men and the gang. Stark is killed and all the others captured except Red, who races back to town.

For Fraser this incident is the last straw. Believing that Belle has betrayed the gang to save her own skin, he takes over the leadership, holds her prisoner in her own office and has his men spread out all over town to ambush Cassidy and the posse when they ride in. Joan Stuart sees the gang setting the trap and gallops out of town to warn Hoppy but is chased by Fraser and the gang, who capture her on the trail, then launch a frontal attack on the approaching posse. Cassidy and his men beat off the assault and the outlaws head back to town. Hoppy rounds up a huge force of men to raid the Paradise that night, unaware that both Joan and Belle are prisoners inside.

For his climax Selander reworked the saloon siege from his **Three Men From Texas** but added much more action and excitement. The possemen enter town, take up their positions and prepare to hit the building. The first shots are fired and the siege is on, generating one of the finest large-scale action scenes in any Cassidy film. Fraser displays Joan in the saloon's upstairs window and threatens to kill her unless the posse withdraws. Belle pulls a pocket gun on Fraser but is wounded as she and Joan make their way down the saloon's back stairs to the alley outside. With both women safe, Cassidy signals the posse and all hell breaks loose again. Hoppy mounts the back stairs alone for a showdown with Fraser. He's wounded in the doorway just like Pico Serrano in **Three Men From Texas** but comes charging in anyway and takes on Fraser in a furious fight that ends when the outlaw is hurled through the window to his death. Although Belle will have to spend some time in prison, the final scene where she asks Hoppy to send her a hacksaw and he says he just might makes it clear that their friendship is undimmed.

156

Chapter Eight

While preparing for the seventh season of Cassidy films, Harry Sherman had to cope with one crisis after another. First off, he lost the second most valuable actor in the series' permanent cast when Russell Hayden gave up his role as Lucky Jenkins and signed on at Columbia Pictures, where he began by co-starring in Charles Starrett Westerns and then was given a series of his own. Apparently the parting with Sherman was friendly, for although "Pop" had threatened a lawsuit if George Hayes used the nickname Windy at any other studio, he didn't let out a peep when Hayden at Columbia continued to call himself Lucky. To replace Hayden and at the same time to compete head-to-head with other studios' musical Western extravaganzas, Sherman resurrected the character of Johnny Nelson and hired for the part a bland youth named Brad King who, whatever his limitations as an actor, at least could warble soothingly in the Rogers and Autry manner. King quickly showed that he didn't have an ounce of charisma and lasted only the one season.

If the loss of Hayden was beyond Sherman's control, his other problems weren't. The scripts for the seventh season were the weakest in the history of the series, and the dynamic Lesley Selander was given pitifully little to do. Sherman's two big-budget action features that season were **The Parson of Panamint** (Paramount, 1941), starring Charlie Ruggles, Ellen Drew and Philip Terry, and **Tombstone, The Town Too Tough to Die** (Paramount, 1942), with Richard Dix, Kent Taylor, Frances Gifford and Victor Jory. To direct these pictures Sherman brought in Warner Brothers' veteran William McGann (1895-1977) rather than give the jobs to Selander. Indeed Selander was given only two of the season's Cassidys to helm, and it's no wonder that after making them he began looking around for employment elsewhere. But the crowning insult was that, instead of turning out six new Cassidys that season as usual, Sherman's unit limited itself to five. The atmosphere as those five were shot back-to-back during the late summer and early fall of 1941 must have resembled a deathwatch. They were released in haphazard order in the ensuing months and there is no single correct sequence in which to discuss them.

The first of the quintet that was registered with the Copyright Office was **Stick To Your Guns** (1941), an abysmally dull effort directed by Selander from a screenplay by J. Benton Cheney. Although one would never know it from the film's credits, the Cheney script was based on an actual Clarence E. Mulford novel, *The Bar-20 Rides Again* (1926), which had also been the source of the 1935 Cassidy picture of the same name. Paradoxically enough, the former movie, directed by the generally dull Howard Bretherton, had been one of the best early Cassidys even though it had next to nothing in common with Mulford's book, while the 1941 remake, helmed by the usually excellent Selander, was both much closer to Mulford and much more boring than either the novel or the Bretherton version. The Snake Buttes cattle rustling king known as Nevada was portrayed in the new adaptation by Dick Curtis from Selander's **Three Men From Texas**, and Curtis was true to Mulford (and to his own unmemorable performances as the bad guy in dozens of Columbia B Westerns) by playing the part as a run-of-the-mill villain rather than the frontier Napoleon that Bretherton and actor Harry Worth had made him in 1935. The female lead was Jennifer Holt, the daughter of silent star Jack Holt and sister of RKO's resident cowboy Tim Holt, although at this early stage in her career she was calling herself Jacqueline Holt. The members of Nevada's gang included Weldon Heyburn, Jack Rockwell, Ian McDonald (later the chief bad guy in **High Noon**) and former Western star Kermit Maynard, with the role of the crooked gambler Long Ben, who had been left out of the 1935 version, going to Charles Middleton, the first actor to play Buck Peters in the Cassidy films. Behind the scenes, Lewis J. Rachmil served as associate producer,

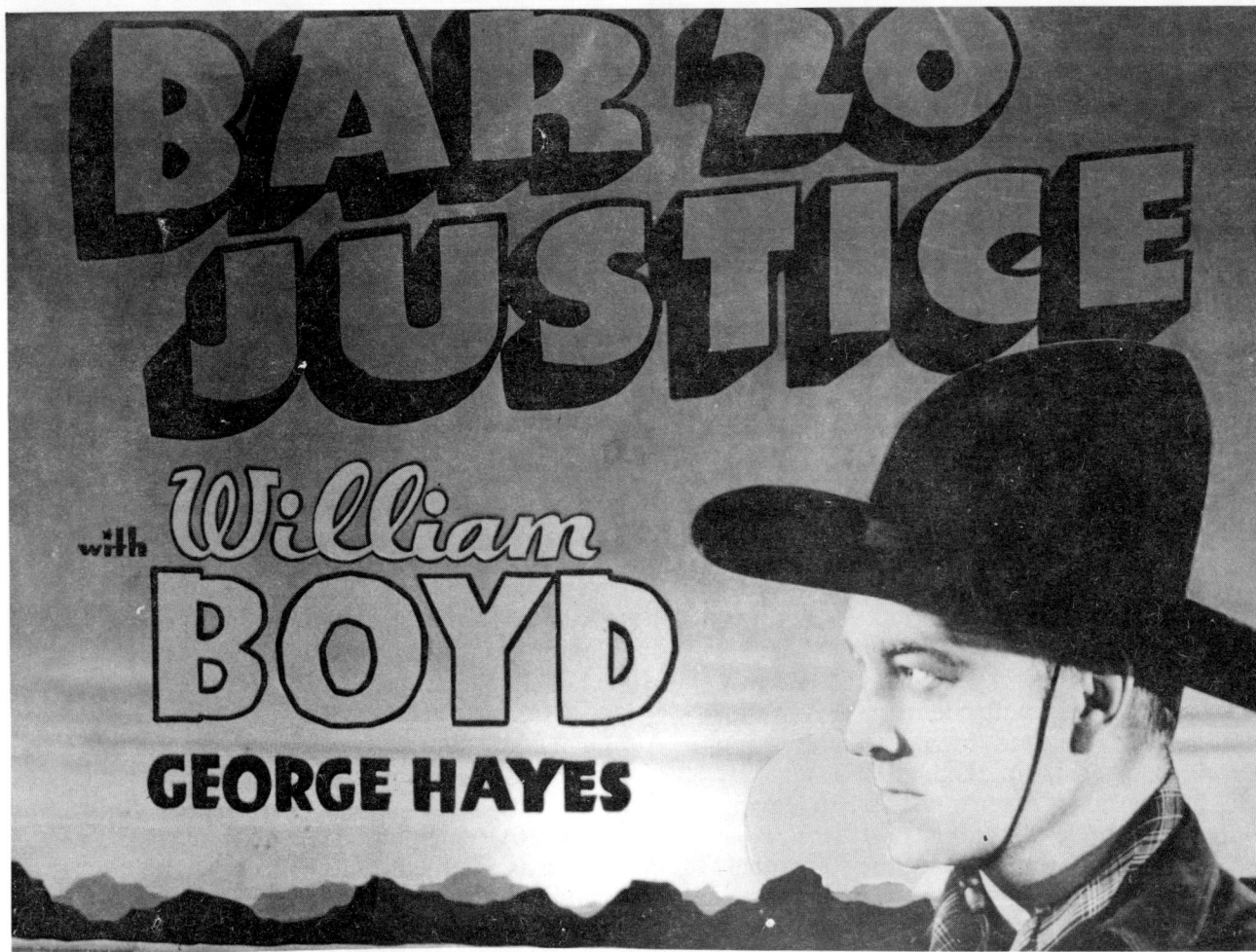

William Boyd is pictured in the Title Card for this 1938 Paramount release.

Russell Harlan as cinematographer, Carrol Lewis (supervised by Sherman A. Rose) in the editing booth, and Irvin Talbot as director of the John Leipold music score. Except for the editing work, all these credits remained the same through the five pictures of the short season.

The best that can be said of **Stick To Your Guns** is that the scenery was easy on the eyes, for of action and excitement there is none. The film begins with Nevada (Dick Curtis) and his gang stealing a herd of cattle from Frenchy Smith (Homer Holcomb) and escaping to their hideout in the near-impenetrable Snake Buttes. Leaving Johnny behind to organize an attack force, Hoppy and California set out after the rustlers. The two stop off in the town of Verde and try to worm the location of Nevada's lair out of shady gambler Long Ben (Charles Middleton), who has his own grudge against the gang (they'd kicked him out of the hideout after he'd trimmed them at poker) and so gives Hoppy and California the information they want. Before leaving Verde, Cassidy goes

shopping for a tailcoated dude outfit like the one he wore in the earlier version of this film, **Bar 20 Rides Again.**

The outlaws are having a meal at their cabin in the Buttes when Hoppy and California ride up. As in the 1935 version, Cassidy claims to be a gambler named Tex Riley. He admits that Long Ben gave him the hideout's location and suggests without actually saying so that he's the sole outlaw to survive the Battle of Cunningham Lake, in which a large number of gunmen were wiped out. As chance would have it, Nevada is the son of Charlie Teal, one of the bandits who died in that battle, and the claimed connection with his father convinces him that "Riley" is a genuine badman. His invitation to the two newcomers to join his gang is quickly accepted.

Next morning, while most of the rustlers are out with the stolen cattle, Hoppy examines one of the poker decks used by the gang, discovers that the cards are marked, and decides to use the deck as a weapon to cut down the gang's size. He goes on

158

William Boyd ties up the guard in this scene from **Bar 20 Justice** (1938, Paramount).

to prepare some brush near the hideout so that when set ablaze it will serve as a signal fire for Johnny and his strike force from the Bar 20 when the time comes to attack.

Meanwhile Johnny and company have arrived in Verde and hire an old frontiersman named Jud Winters (Henry Hall) to draw them a map of the Snake Buttes. Aching for one last hurrah, Jud begs permission to go along on the expedition as a guide, to the consternation of his granddaughter June (Jacqueline Holt). Simultaneously, Hoppy at the hideout helps rebrand some of the gang's stolen cattle and sees that many of the steers belong to Frenchy Smith. An argument breaks out between two of the outlaws, Concho (not listed in the credits) and Elbows (Ian McDonald), and after lunch Concho sneaks up behind Elbows and shoots him in the back. Cassidy, who witnessed the killing, accuses Concho, at which point Elbows' buddy Carp (Jack Rockwell) draws on Concho and kills *him*. Hoppy proceeds to stir up even more dissension by claiming that Concho's

pal Layton (Kermit Maynard) helped murder Elbows. While the gang members are being set at each other's throats, Johnny and the Bar 20 men are following the trail signs through the Buttes that Cassidy left for them. At their night camp they are joined by Jud and June Winters and wait for the signal fire.

Back at the hideout, figuring that his men must be within striking distance, Hoppy starts a slow-burning fire in the brush. Then he joins the rustlers in a few hands of poker, but the game quickly degenerates into a two-handed grudge match between him and Layton. Cassidy uses his knowledge of the marked deck to cheat and win in such a way as to make it seem that Layton tried to cheat him. A fight breaks out and Hoppy guns Layton down.

Back at the attackers' camp, Johnny wastes time crooning and romancing June, making mincemeat of the proud boast in **Border Vigilantes** that the men of the Bar 20 don't sing. Next morning old Jud slips out of camp to tackle the rustlers alone.

159

Walter Long is cowed before William Duncan, Russell Hayden and friend in this scene from **Bar 20 Justice** (1938, Paramount).

Johnny and a hand known as Waffles (Tom London) ride after the old fool and catch him just in time for all three men to be spotted by a pair of Nevada's scouts. One outlaw rides back to warn the gang of invaders while the other bushwhacks the three riders. Johnny kills the bandit in a tame gunbattle.

Meanwhile at the hideout Nevada and his men see the signal fire blazing away and fight to put it out. The incident convinces Nevada that Cassidy has been provoking the trouble among the gang, and he sends his top henchman Gila (Weldon Heyburn) into Verde to check "Riley" out with Long Ben. Soon after Gila leaves, the second scout rides in and reports the three invaders in the Buttes. The rustlers saddle up for action, and Selander pulls off the only cliché reversal in the film by using for this sequence the footage of the Bar 20 men getting ready for a fight that was seen in the earliest Cassidys. By the time the gang reaches the spot where the three invaders were observed, the place is deserted. While all this is

going on, Gila rides into Verde and finds Long Ben drunk in the saloon. Ben blurts out the truth about Cassidy's identity. Gila rewards the gambler by shooting him in the back, then races off to warn Nevada.

In the Buttes, the gang locates the invaders' camp just as Johnny and the Bar 20 men are preparing to attack. Cassidy sabotages the outlaws' ambush plan and Johnny and company escape. Nevada and his men give chase. The Bar 20 men take refuge in a blind canyon. Nevada stampedes their horses and leaves Carp and two others to guard the canyon mouth, while he and the rest of the gang go back to the hideout and get ready to move their headquarters. At the hideout Gila is waiting with the truth about Cassidy. He draws on Hoppy the moment he sees him. Cassidy kills him and races away with California. Gila lives just long enough to tell Nevada who "Riley" is. The gang go after the two men. Hoppy and California return to the canyon mouth, trick and overpower Carp and the other guards and turn them over to

Bob Woodward watches the guard while John Beach, William Duncan, Russell Hayden and William Boyd hold a conference in this scene from **Bar 20 Justice** (1938, Paramount).

Johnny and the Bar 20 riders. Then they set an ambush for Nevada and the rest of the gang who are fast approaching. A gun battle breaks out, but all the rustlers quickly surrender except for Nevada, whom Cassidy takes on and kills in a one-on-one gun duel. With another song on their lips the men of the Bar 20 drive the stolen cattle home.

Exactly why "Pop" Sherman decided to make a relatively faithful adaptation of a Mulford novel at this time is not clear. Most likely it was a response to William Boyd's pestering for better scripts. In all probability the same motivation was responsible for Sherman's purchase, as the basis for the season's next Cassidy, of rights to a Western novel by another author entirely. When Mulford had more or less retired from writing, his place as Doubleday's ace shoot-em-up scribe was taken over by Harry Sinclair Drago (1888-1979). So prolific did Drago prove to be that Doubleday published some of his books under his own name and the rest under pseudonyms like Bliss Lomax

and Will Ermine. Like Mulford himself, Drago often fused detective and mystery elements into his Westerns, and several of his novels featured the cowboy sleuth team of Rainbow Riley and Grumpy Gibbs. (The pair bore strong resemblances to W.C. Tuttle's earlier range detective duo, Hashknife Hartley and Sleepy Stevens). Whether through Mulford's recommendation or Doubleday's or on his own, Harry Sherman became acquainted with Drago's novels and decided to buy movie rights to one of them as a basis for a Cassidy picture. He chose *Secret of the Wastelands* (Doubleday, 1940), published as by Bliss Lomax, and hired veteran Hoppy scripter Gerald Geraghty to revamp the plot for the Cassidy series. To direct the movie he settled on Derwin Abrahams, who had helmed **Border Vigilantes** the previous season. Certainly **Secrets Of The Wasteland** (1941) had one of the more offbeat storylines of any Hoppy exploit, with its lost city of Chinese gold miners in the middle of the desert dimly echoing the Shangri-La

Walter Long watches as William Boyd and Paul Sutton both reach for the assay report of Joseph De Stefani in this scene from **Bar 20 Justice** (1938, Paramount).

from the 1937 classic **Lost Horizon**. For obvious reasons most of the cast were Oriental, but Abrahams also picked Caucasians who were new to the unit: lovely Barbara Britton played an archaeologist, Douglas Fowley did well as a corrupt lawyer and Keith Richards portrayed a weak-willed government agent. Aside from Boyd, Brad King and Andy Clyde, the only familiar face in the cast was that of Jack Rockwell as the sheriff. Abrahams made effective use of some excellent desert locations, but all too much footage was shot indoors on a hideously cramped and phony-looking stage set that was supposed to represent a vast Indian ruin transformed into a Chinese city. Fred Feitshans Jr. took over as film editor under Sherman A. Rose's supervision. The other major behind-scenes personnel---Rachmil, Harlan, Talbot, Leipold---carried on as usual.

Hoppy, Johnny and California agree to take a group of archaeologists on an expedition to some Indian ruins, and arrive in the town from which the group is to depart at about the same time as the stagecoach carrying their clients. The party consists of Dr. Malcolm Birdsell (Gordon Hart), Professor Waldo Stubbs (Hal Price), and prim and bespectacled Dr. Jennifer Kendall (Barbara Britton). Accompanying them is Clay Elliott (Keith Richards), a representative of the U.S. Mint. The preparations for the expedition are spied upon by various members of the town's sizable Chinese community, one of whom throws a knife at Cassidy in the street. It's this incident which introduces Hoppy to Slade Salters (Douglas Fowley), the lawyer for the Chinese in the area.

Just before the expedition sets out, Birdsell hires a local named Doy Kee (Lee Tung Foo) to cook for the group. The result is a rather funny scene between the Oriental and California. (Doy Kee: "You like egg foo yung?" California: "Like him? I don't even know him!") For reasons unknown, Salters sends out gunmen to follow the party. The journey to the ruins passes quickly thanks to Johnny's crooning.

A day's ride from their destination, a wheel

Wen Wright, William Duncan, John Beach, Russell Hayden and Bob Woodward are ready for action in this scene from **Bar 20 Justice** (1938, Paramount).

mysteriously falls off the chuckwagon and the group camps early for the night. That evening Elliott discloses that his mission is to track down the source of some strange gold coins, not minted by the U.S. government, which have turned up in various Chinese shops. During the night Doy Kee lets the horses loose and, in an abysmally directed scene, stampedes them into the camp. Hoppy and his pals recover the animals. Investigating how the horses got free, Cassidy finds that their tie ropes were cut with a knife and realizes that there's a saboteur in the camp. At this juncture Johnny sees Jennifer with her long hair down and her glasses off and realizes for the first time what a gorgeous creature she is. Gulp and gosh!

Next morning they set out and reach the Pueblo Grande ruins at dusk. Their arrival is observed by a Chinese, Ying (Roland Got), who reports back to a powerful woman, Moy Soong (Soo Yong). The ruins are a painfully obvious indoor set with large photographs of scenery as a backdrop. Digging around, Professor Stubbs unearths a Buddha, and Birdsell, recognizing it as only about thirty years old, concludes that they've disturbed a Chinese grave. Hoppy orders everyone to stay close together in the ruins, but headstrong Jennifer goes off to climb a nearby mountain on her own and chivalrous Johnny sets out to bring her back. On the mountain Doy Kee stops both of them with a rifle but Johnny gets the drop on him and all three return to the ruins. In the far distance Johnny spots the gunmen Salters has sent to watch the explorers, and reports the newcomers to Hoppy. Having learned nothing from her last venture, Jennifer goes wandering alone in the Indian ruins. She finds a secret door and passes through it. She doesn't come back. The next morning, more problems confront the group: their water barrel has been emptied and Doy Kee is found murdered. (Abrahams never bothers to tell us who killed him or why, but presumably it was Salters' men.) The party is forced to return to the nearest town for water.

Hoppy tells Johnny and California not to report

163

Walter Long is afraid William Boyd will hit him in this scene from **Bar 20 Justice** (1938, Paramount).

Jennifer's disappearance, but they do anyway, and for unspecified reasons Sheriff Mulhall (Jack Rockwell) not only refuses to believe them but locks both of them in jail. Meanwhile a Chinese delegation has contacted Cassidy, who rides with the Orientals to Tupper's Trading Post for a secret meeting with Moy Soong. Back in town Elliott visits the sheriff and confirms Johnny's and California's story. A posse is formed to go after Hoppy, who to all intents and purposes has been kidnapped. Actually of course all the problems between the explorers and the Chinese have by now been settled, and Moy Soong has reunited Cassidy and Jennifer. But when the posse approaches the trading post, Moy Soong and her men conclude that Hoppy has betrayed them and, taking both him and Jennifer along as prisoners, race away. The posse gives chase but soon loses the Chinese.

Shortly after the Orientals have escaped the posse, they are intercepted by Salters and his gang, who want Moy Soong to go with them. A

gunfight breaks out and Cassidy proves he's the Orientals' friend by helping drive the gang away. The noise of the battle is heard by Johnny, California and Elliott, who join Cassidy for the skirmish. They all race back to the Indian ruins and take cover there with Salters' men right behind them. The gang lay siege to the ruins, resulting in long minutes of cat-and-mouse chase footage on that claustrophobic indoor set. Finally the Chinese and their white allies escape through the secret door we saw earlier in the film and along a tunnel at whose far end is nothing short of a Chinese Western Shangri-La. Unfortunately we have to imagine the lost city's splendors, for all Abrahams gives us is a couple of large photographs and some bird tweets on the soundtrack.

Hoppy and the others hear from Jennifer how she's been given the freedom of the city. Moy Soong tells Cassidy that the Chinese have been secretly working the gold mine in the lost city for years. Her people, she says, have long known that the mine property was in the public domain,

164

William Boyd seems happy in spite of the cut as Russell Hayden, Jane Clayton and Allan Garcia look on in this scene from **In Old Mexico** (1938, Paramount).

and have had the legal papers for filing on the land ready for countless months, but somehow have never gotten around to turning in the paperwork to the proper authorities. Leaping nimbly over this hole in the plot, Hoppy agrees to help the Chinese gain legal title to the mine. Meanwhile Salters and his men have found the secret tunnel, and the sheriff and his posse have reached the ruins.

Inside the lost city, Elliott, intoxicated by visions of gold, decides to slip away and file on the land for himself. Cassidy stops him and knocks him out. At this point the Salters gang, having joined forces with the posse, reach the far end of the tunnel and the entrance to the hidden city and open fire. The Chinese return their guns to Hoppy and his pals and the fight is on. When Cassidy sees that the sheriff is among the invaders he calls for a truce and, under the white flag, explains the whole situation. Suddenly Elliott makes a break for the outer world. Salters shoots him down and makes his own run, intending to file on the mine for himself. Armed with the previously drafted legal

documents, Hoppy races back through the tunnel and the ruins and then across the desert on Salters' heels, a creditable action scene complete with running inserts and good chase music. He catches up to the lawyer at the edge of town and whips him in a very strangely directed fistfight. As Hoppy and his sidekicks prepare to return to the Bar 20, Jennifer turns down the smitten Johnny's marriage proposal with a prim rejoinder---"I'm afraid, Mr. Nelson, my work comes first"---that will permanently endear Derwin Abrahams to the devotees of feminism.

It was his second Cassidy picture and his last. Abrahams moved on to other studios and a career as a director of low-budget, low-caliber action flicks: serials and Durango Kid pictures at Columbia, Johnny Mack Brown and Jimmy Wakely and Charlie Chan programmers at Monogram, not a single one of them rising above the drearily routine. In the early 1950's, when William Boyd was producing his own 30-minute Cassidy telefilms, he hired Abrahams, who by then was calling

After tying up Paul Sutton, William Boyd checks on George Hayes in this scene from **In Old Mexico** (1938, Paramount).

himself Derwin Abbe, to direct a number of them. And a couple of years later Russell Hayden, who had also turned producer in his middle years, engaged Abbe to direct on the *Judge Roy Bean* TV series. His television films were even worse than his "B" features. He died totally forgotten in 1974.

Internal evidence suggests that the outdoor scenes of **Secrets of the Wasteland** were shot simultaneously with those of another Cassidy film, **Outlaws of the Desert** (1941), with the director and cast and crew then moving indoors to ludicrous faked sets for the rest of the picture. To direct **Outlaws** Sherman again brought back the man who had made the first season of Cassidys, Howard Bretherton. The screenplay was an original by unit veteran J. Benton Cheney and a prolific scripter of B Westerns for other studios named Bernard McConville. Bretherton chose a cast made up largely of people who had never been in a Western before, a sensible procedure considering that most of the picture takes place in

Arabia. But Duncan Renaldo, recently of Republic's Three Mesquiteers series and later TV's *Cisco Kid*, was hired to play a British-educated sheik, and veteran action-film badguy George J. Lewis had a small part as a desert guide. The idea of moving Hoppy and his pals to North Africa was offbeat enough, and the spectacle of William Boyd speaking fluently in Arabic has to be seen to be believed. But the only other notable element in the film is the excellent desert locale, of which Bretherton made far too little use. In every other respect it's a deadly dull picture: flat script, weak plot, minimal and indifferently directed action, endless inane comedy skits, a host of scenes obviously shot indoors with photographs of sand dunes in the background. The usual people did the usual jobs behind the scenes, with Carrol Lewis back as film editor.

The film opens with Hoppy, Johnny and California capturing Thundercloud, a runaway black stallion whom they've been chasing for three weeks. Cassidy puts a saddle on the bucking

Jane Clayton has Paul Sutton covered as Russell Hayden tries to calm down William Boyd in this scene from **In Old Mexico** (1938, Paramount).

stallion and tames him---or rather, tames an obvious bucking barrel in tight shots while his stunt man rides the horse in long takes. They bring the stallion into the town of Gila Bend at about the same moment that Mrs. Jane Grant (Nina Guilbert) and her headstrong daughter Susan (Jean Phillips) step off a train from the east. Recognizing the horse as the property of her father, rancher Charles Grant (Forrest Stanley), Susan prevails upon some townsmen to grab Hoppy and his pals as horse thieves and take them out to the Grant ranch. There Mr. Grant makes his daughter look like an ass when he explains that he had borrowed the trio from the Bar 20 to recover Thundercloud for him. Later that day Grant invites Hoppy and his pals to accompany him and his wife and daughter to Arabia to purchase some blooded horses from Sheik Suleiman (Duncan Renaldo), an old friend of Grant's comrade Major Crawford (George Woolsley) of the Army Remount Service. Preparations for the long trip consume footage as Johnny serenades Susan,

California dreams of belly dancers, a beautiful palomino is selected as a gift for the sheik, and Johnny gets irritated at Susan's willfulness and spanks her. "I hope you paddled her good and hard," her father says, shaking the young man's hand.

Having reached Arabia, Hoppy and his pals set out with their guide Yousef (George J. Lewis) for the sheik's desert encampment. Meanwhile in the North African city, the Grants fall afoul of Marie and Nikki Karitza (Luli Deste and Albert Morin), a married confidence team who pose as brother and sister. Out on the desert Hoppy and his sidekicks rescue a camel train from a bandit raid, learn that the train is also heading for Suleiman's camp, and join forces. The sheik's encampment turns out to be an unconvincing indoor set and the ruler himself a British-educated gentleman. After a feast and a yawnful belly dancing exhibition, Suleiman refuses to sell Cassidy any horses, saying that they are his children. But as the group is about to leave next morning, he gives them two

167

An unusual camera angle gives this publicity still of Russell Hayden, Jane Clayton and William Boyd a dramatic appeal, used for the film **In Old Mexico** (1938, Paramount).

magnificent animals, Mameluke and Sheba, as presents for Grant.

Hoppy and his pals return to the city just as the Karitzas' scam reaches its climax. An apparently wounded Nikki staggers into the Grants' hotel suite, claiming that bandits waylaid him and Charles Grant on the desert and are demanding $50,000 for Grant's release. Susan orders Cassidy to use the money they brought to buy horses to pay the ransom, but Hoppy suspects a confidence game and takes matters into his own hands. As he and Johnny and California go out again into the desert, Marie Karitza sends some thugs to follow them. In the second of the film's lackluster action sequences, the three are attacked by bandits and drive them off. Back in the city Nikki and Marie persuade the anguished Susan to cable Major Crawford for another $50,000.

Hoppy and his pals return to Suleiman's camp and enlist his help. The desert ruler suspects that his arch-enemy Sheik Feran el Kadir (Jean del Val) might be involved in the Grant kidnapping.

Cassidy and his sidekicks don Arab garb and ride out with Yousef to Feran's camp. Meanwhile in the city the money has arrived, and Susan goes with the Karitzas to turn over the ransom. Naturally enough, as soon as they reach Feran's camp Susan is also taken captive so that more money can be extorted from the Grant family. Such is the situation that night as Hoppy and his party infiltrate Feran's headquarters.

They happen upon the tent where Grant and Susan are being held, and overhear the Karitzas plotting with Feran, but are then captured themselves along with the $50,000 Cassidy is carrying. The only one not taken prisoner is Yousef, who later sneaks into the tent and cuts all the captives loose. Hoppy overpowers the Karitzas and recovers the money. Then all eight of them race out of camp with Feran and his bandits in hot pursuit. The illusion of being in Arabia is ruined by Bretherton's use of all the old familiar desert trails that had been the scenes of chase sequences in earlier Cassidys. Hoppy and his

George Hayes is helped by Jane Clayton into some Mexican style clothes at William Boyd laughingly looks on in this scene from **In Old Mexico** (1938, Paramount).

party safely reach Suleiman's camp and rest for the night.

Before sunrise, Suleiman's scouts report that Feran is going to attack the encampment in the morning. Cassidy advises the sheik to make the camp appear to be unguarded so that the bandits will ride into a trap. And so it happens: at dawn the trap is sprung and the last of the film's desert action scenes unfolds, a tame battle of burnoose-clad stuntmen but no stunts, complete with pseudo-Arabian background music and the unmistakable drone of an airplane motor every so often in the sky. The climax culminates in a bland scimitar duel between Suleiman and Feran. With the desert outlaws disposed of, the Grants and Hoppy and his pals return home, and at the fade-out California is entertaining the other cowhands with his version of a belly dance while the music track performs an Orientally syncopated rendition of "Oh, Susanna"!

If nothing else, Howard Bretherton had the virtue of consistency. Whether a picture had great

potential like **Outlaws of the Desert** or none at all like his next and last Cassidy film, Bretherton directed it by the numbers, never raising it above the level of dull routine. **Twilight on the Trail** (1941) was credited to no less than three script writers---J. Benton Cheney, Ellen Corby (who turned actress and starred several decades later in *The Waltons*), and Cecile Kramer---but contained exactly one idea. Apparently it was Cheney who dreamed up the unusual method by which the film's villains made whole cattle herds vanish without trace, for he recycled the gimmick in "Rustling" (1950), an early episode of TV's *Cisco Kid* series which was directed by our old friend Derwin Abrahams. Boyd enjoys himself hugely as he impersonates a helpless dude from the East the way he did in **Sunset Trail**, and all the outdoor scenes were actually shot outdoors. Very little else can be said in praise of this exercise in boredom. Except for good old Jack Rockwell, most of the cast were newcomers to the Cassidy unit. As if Brad King's warbling weren't enough,

169

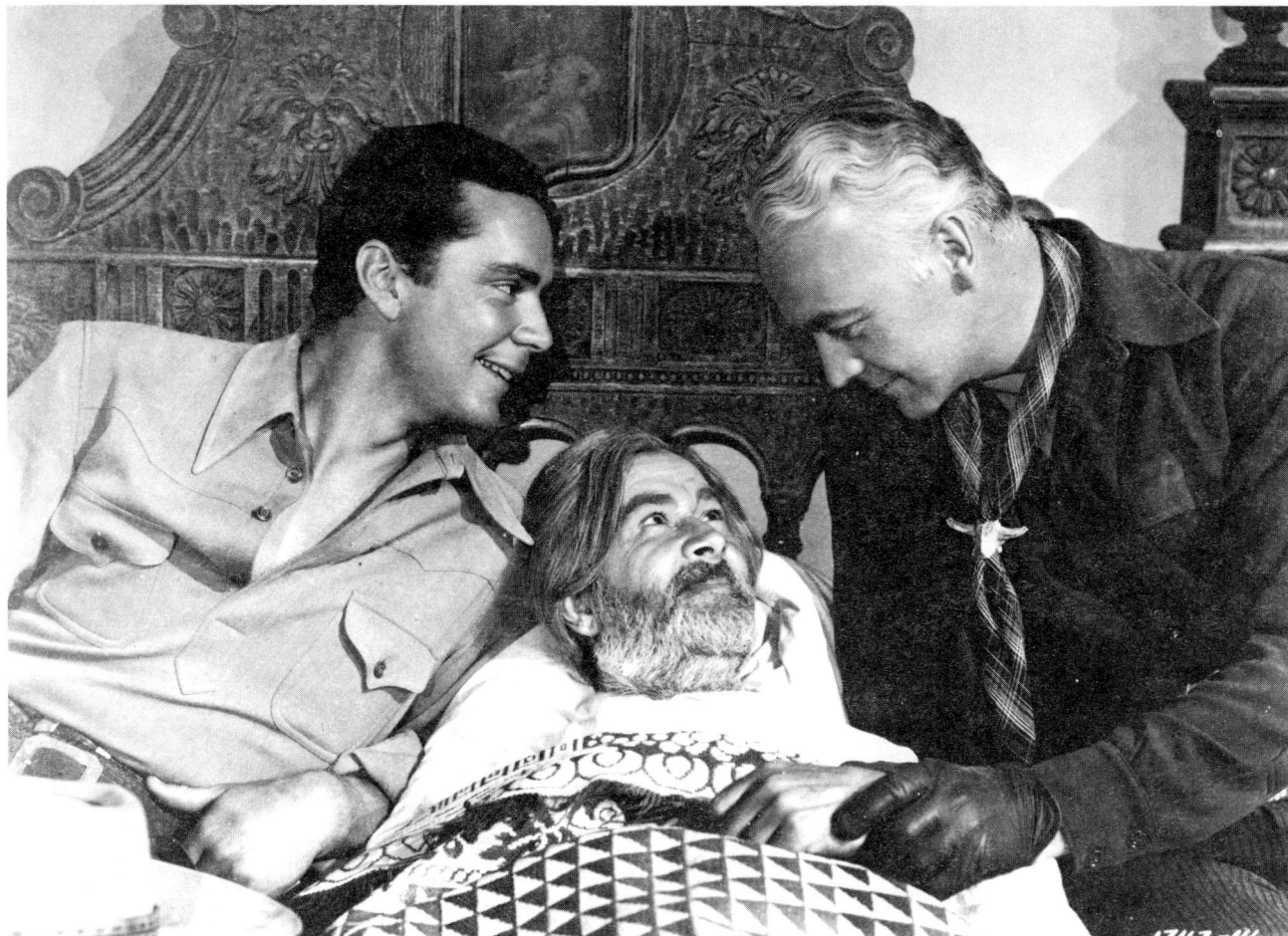

Russell Hayden and William Boyd ask George Hayes if he is going to lay in bed while they do all the work in this scene from **In Old Mexico** (1938, Paramount).

additional music is furnished by The Jimmy Wakely Trio. Fred Feitshans Jr. returned to the editing booth for this number, otherwise the technical credits were identical to those in earlier Cassidys of season seven.

The picture opens with Tim Gregg (Tom London) and his gang halting a stagecoach and demanding the detectives who are on their way to the Circle Y ranch. The driver tells the gang that the detectives hired a private coach for the last leg of their journey, and the frustrated outlaws slink away. Art Drake (Robert Kent) reports the gang's failure to the head villain, Nat Kerby (Norman Willis), who is both the foreman of the Circle Y and the man behind the rustling that has led ranch owner Jim Brent (Jack Rockwell) to send for detectives from the East. Bretherton seems to have been in love with this corrupt foreman gimmick, for **Twilight** was the third Cassidy in which he dug it out.

The private coach pulls up at the ranch and disgorges its cargo of sleuths, who are none other than Hopalong Cassidy in his dude outfit, Johnny in derby and spats, and California decked out with a fox-hunting coat, deerstalker, pipe and magnifying glass. Brent's daughter Lucy (Wanda McKay) is disappointed at the foppish trio, having no idea who they really are. In a private meeting, her father explains to the three that although the local ranchers have lost hundreds of cattle to rustlers, the trail of the stolen herds always stops at the bank of a certain river and never emerges on the far side.

Next morning, after a long comic sequence in which the three "dudes" fall all over themselves trying to mount horses, they ride out with Brent to the river. On the far side they see a shack and shed built against a cliff which Brent says belongs to Steve Farley (Frank Austin), a harmless old prospector. They question Farley, who insists he's never seen any cattle and knows nothing about the rustlers. Cassidy quickly comes to believe the man is lying.

Back at the ranch, Kerby gives Hoppy a comic

170

William Boyd loved to dress as a dude which can be seen in this publicity still for **Sunset Trail** (1939, Paramount).

shooting lesson, the Jimmy Wakely trio breaks into song, and Johnny starts romancing Lucy but blows into smithereens his cover as a dude from the East when he warbles a range ditty to the lady. Asked where he learned the cowboy song, Johnny comes up with one of the feeblest excuses imaginable: "A good detective knows everything," he says. Meanwhile, in a scene meant primarily to show Kerby's habit of bending matches in an odd way, the foreman and Drake plot to steal more Circle Y cattle.

The next day, mounted on their own horses, Hoppy and Johnny and California ride out to the Brent trail camp. In another time-wasting comic sequence, Kerby tries to teach Cassidy the game of poker and loses heavily to the meek-looking fop. Kerby learns that the herd from a neighboring ranch, the Double D, is scheduled to join the Circle Y stock for a drive, and sends word to Gregg, whose gang attacks the Double D herd on the trail. Hoppy, Johnny and California hear the shots of the gunbattle, ride to the rescue and drive off the gang, with Johnny suffering an arm wound in the process. Later Kerby slips away to the Farley shack and chews out Gregg for letting three tenderfeet defeat his gunmen. It's at this point that the foreman learns that the so-called dudes are tigers on horseback. He returns to the ranch, searches the detectives' rooms, discovers who they are and decides to set a trap.

At the trail camp, where the Jimmy Wakely Trio are making more music, Kerby arranges to go out next day with the three sleuths to hunt for the rustlers' tracks. The signs they left behind are of course quite plain, and Gregg and his gang are waiting for the three in ambush. Hoppy slips around behind the bushwhackers, killing several and chasing the rest away. With their combat skills now established beyond doubt, the three take off their monkey suits and spend the rest of the picture in their traditional outfits.

Still suspicious of Steve Farley, Hoppy and his pals pay a second visit to the riverside shack and happen to see the rustlers dismounting at the

Stagedriver Jack Rockwell climbs down as William Boyd and Maurice Cass are greeted by the townspeople (including Robert Fiske, Charlotte Wynters and George Hayes) in this scene from **Sunset Trail** (1939, Paramount). Maurice Cass plays the character who was a putdown on Mulford.

prospector's front door. The door of Farley's shed is pulled open and the outlaws and their horses disappear inside, one rustler sweeping away their tracks before entering himself. Leaving Johnny because of his wound, Hoppy and California overpower Farley, search the shed, and find a secret door opening straight into the mountain against which the shed was built. But within seconds of solving the mystery of the disappearing cattle, they are captured in the tunnel by Gregg and the gang. Johnny sees the rustlers taking their prisoners' horses into the shed and rides back to the Brent camp for help. Kerby joins the rescue party that forms but sends Drake ahead by a shortcut to alert the gang and set up an ambush that will wipe out the Brent group.

Tied up with California in a cabin on the far side of the secret mine tunnel, Hoppy notices the oddly bent matchsticks on the floor and realizes that Kerby is the boss rustler. Meanwhile the rescue party including Lucy reaches Farley's cabin, enters the shed, finds the tunnel and starts

exploring. When they emerge at the far end, the outlaws hidden in the rocks open fire. Hoppy and California kick a shelf until an empty whiskey bottle crashes to the floor and free themselves on the jagged shards of glass. Then they knock out their guard, retrieve their guns and start shooting at the gang, catching them in a crossfire. Kerby tries to escape back through the tunnel but is seen by Hoppy who follows him into the darkness. The climactic fight between the two men is not filmed at all: imitating Lesley Selander in **Hidden Gold**, Bretherton shot the sequence from the viewpoint of Lucy and California outside the tunnel, thus saving Boyd the strain of having to throw a few punches. With the rustlers caught, and after a final skit involving California seeing a gila monster under his magnifying glass, the trio head back for the Bar 20.

The closing credits of **Twilight on the Trail** signaled not only the end of this picture but the end of Howard Bretherton's connection with the Hopalong Cassidy series. After a brief stopover at

George Hayes doesn't seem to know who to cover as William Boyd has Robert Fiske covered with a derringer and Charlotte Wynters looks on in this scene from **Sunset Trail** (1939, Paramount).

Columbia to direct a Charles Starrett-Russell Hayden Western, he took over Monogram Pictures' famous Rough Riders series starring Buck Jones, Tim McCoy and Raymond Hatton. All six of the last films in which Jones appeared before his tragic death in the Cocoanut Grove fire of 1942---five Rough Riders adventures and the non-series **Dawn on the Great Divide** (Monogram, 1942)---were directed by Bretherton. For the rest of the 1940's he shuttled from Monogram to Republic to Universal to Monogram again, directing Westerns with Bill Elliott, Allan Lane, Rod Cameron, Johnny Mack Brown, Jimmy Wakely, Whip Wilson and others. Almost all of these films fell into the same rut as the majority of his Cassidys, but among his better efforts are **Ghost Town Law** (Monogram, 1942) with The Rough Riders, **Bordertown Gunfighters** (Republic, 1943) with Bill Elliott, and **Outlaws of Santa Fe** (Republic, 1944) with Don Barry. Around 1950 Bretherton moved from theatrical to television film direction, concentrating not on

Westerns but rather on situation comedies like the Stu Erwin series **Trouble With Father**. He died in April 1969. His daughter was and still is married to the man he immortalized as Hoppy's first young sidekick, Jimmy Ellison, and it's perhaps for the first Cassidy pictures that he will be most fondly remembered.

Lesley Selander rejoined the unit to direct the last of the seventh season quintet, **Riders of the Timberline** (1941), which---with its gorgeous scenery, strong action and storyline, and distinctively Selanderesque female lead---wins in a walk as the best Hoppy exploit of the group. Selander liked to use actors who had proved themselves in his own earlier Cassidy pictures and followed this policy in casting **Timberline**. He brought back Victor Jory from his classic **Wide Open Town** but gave him a role that was bizarre indeed considering Jory's slight physique: a brawny French-Canadian lumberjack. Eleanor Stewart from Selander's **Pirates On Horseback** performed nobly as the director's newest incarnation

173

Anthony Nace looks on as William Boyd and Charlotte Wynters discuss the money in their hands in this scene from **Sunset Trail** (1939, Paramount).

of the Action Woman, J. Farrell McDonald from **Stagecoach War** played her widower father, silent star Anna Q. Nilsson had a small part as the father's girlfriend, and Tom Tyler and Hal Taliaferro from Derwin Abrahams' **Border Vigilantes** led the bad guys. The screenplay was by unit regular J. Benton Cheney, and the usual people---Rachmil, Harlan, Feitshans, Rose, Talbot and Leipold---carried on in their customary functions outside camera range. Singing, which for once was not a time-wasting intrusion but a rousing and well-integrated part of the picture as a whole, was entrusted to a group called The Guardsmen.

Lumberman Jim Kerrigan (J. Farrell McDonald) has contracted to deliver 20,000,000 feet of logs to the Ajax Mills by a certain date, and will lose all his holdings if he doesn't perform. The ecology-minded Kerrigan reverently replants a tree for every one he cuts down. But his property is coveted by Eastern capitalist Preston Yates (Edward Keane), whose policy is Despoil the Land, and who has hired saloonkeeper Ed Petrie (Hal Taliaferro) to make sure Kerrigan forfeits his property under the contract so that Yates can buy it cheap. Petrie in turn has bribed Kerrigan's man Bill Slade (Tom Tyler) to orchestrate a campaign of sabotage against the workers, which convinces the timber community that Kerrigan's operation is jinxed. By this time of course it's clear to the long-memoried Hoppy fan that the film is rooted in Selander's 1938 classic **Bar 20 Justice**. When the banks cut off Kerrigan's credit he appeals for help to his old friend Buck Peters, and soon Hoppy and Johnny are headed for lumber country.

As they're approaching Kerrigan's camp, the last of the timberjacks are quitting, naturally enough since they haven't been paid in weeks. A fight breaks out between Slade and Kerrigan's loyal foreman Baptiste Deschamp (Victor Jory), and Cassidy saves Deschamp's life by shooting an axe out of Slade's hand. The loss of Kerrigan's crew is made more palatable when Cassidy gives

174

George Hayes and William Boyd are ready for action in this publicity still for **The Frontiersmen** (1938, Paramount).

the lumber boss a $15,000 loan from Buck Peters, and later that day Kerrigan's friend Donna Ryan (Anna Q. Nilsson), who owns a restaurant in town, agrees to take over as the camp cook. But because everyone is afraid of the jinx on the camp, all efforts to hire another crew fail miserably--- until a train comes to town bringing Kerrigan's lovely daughter Elaine (Eleanor Stewart) and a lusty team of timber monkeys known as The Fighting Forty, who roar through town with Elaine at their head, belting out their song: "We're the fighting forty kinkajoux, We fight we fight for the right the right to be free!" Petrie and Slade send out their goons to drive the Forty out of town, and the result is a huge and excitingly directed street brawl, in which Elaine demonstrates her Selander Woman credentials by fighting alongside the men. The goons are licked handily.

As the Forty take over the logging work, Selander gives us a montage of tree-felling shots prominently featuring Cassidy in a lumberjack's hat. The saboteurs try to shut down the camp by blowing up the flume on which the logs are floated to the mill, and Kerrigan is forced to use horses and wagons to deliver the timber. Hoppy suspects that the horses will be the saboteurs' next target, stations guards around the stables, and frustrates a night foray intended to plant poisoned oats in the animals' feed. One outlaw is killed in the skirmish and the other two escape in a wagon which Hoppy beats to town and sees pulling up in front of Petrie's saloon. He eavesdrops on the plotting in the back room, reports the saboteurs' identity to Kerrigan, but insists on not tackling the gang until he can find out who's behind them.

At Cassidy's suggestion the Forty construct a cable device so that the logs can be airlifted to the mill. When the system is tested and works, it's clear that Kerrigan will be able to fulfill his contract. This development forces Yates to come to town and hatch new plans with Petrie, and the member of the Forty who's been watching the saloon reports the financier's arrival to Hoppy.

William Boyd and George Hayes tease Russell Hayden about the lady's glove in this scene from **The Frontiersmen** (1938, Paramount).

Cassidy rigs a trap whose outlines will be familiar to all devotees of B Westerns. He and Johnny start playing poker with Kerrigan's crew and cheating them. Deschamp, who isn't in on the ruse, and Kerrigan, who of course is, catch them in the act and kick them out of camp. Hoppy and Johnny make Petrie's saloon their new base. Word spreads that they were caught cheating, and after Elaine Kerrigan slaps Johnny's face in public, Petrie is sufficiently convinced to invite them to join the gang and introduce them to Yates. Cassidy proposes that the saboteurs start a fire at the logging camp, and he and Johnny accompany Slade and several other gang members on the mission. As prearranged, they are caught by Kerrigan and the Forty while pouring oil on the logs stacked for air freight. Another brawl erupts and all the saboteurs are disposed of except Slade. Unfortunately Kerrigan, who alone knew of Cassidy's ruse, is seriously injured in the fight and so can't back up Hoppy's claim that he was a mole in the enemy camp. To make matters worse,

Slade hears Cassidy's admission while hiding in the rocks, and escapes to report back to Petrie and Yates.

Deschamp refuses to believe Hoppy's story, locks him and Johnny in a toolshed under heavy guard, and leads the Forty into town for a show-down with Petrie. Hoppy and Johnny dig their way to freedom with the shovels in the shed and flee the camp in a railroad handcar, with Deschamp and the Forty hot on their heels in a locomotive. While this hair-raising chase is going on, Kerrigan comes out of his coma and tells the truth about Cassidy to Elaine, who races off to stop the Forty.

Hoppy and Johnny reach town in the handcar, only to find that Petrie and his gang have already left for good. They catch Yates, who admits that he paid the gang a bonus to blow up the dam and flood the camp on their way out of the territory. Deschamp and the Forty storm into town but Elaine also shows up just in time to straighten matters out between Cassidy and the Forty, and

A publicity still of William Boyd, George Hayes and Jimmy Ellison used for the film **Three on the Trail** (1936, Paramount).

they all race to save the dam. There seems only one way to get there in time: Hoppy and Johnny mount a sturdy log at the lumber camp and ride the cable line through the air to the site of the dam. Petrie has just planted dynamite at the dam's base when he and his gang spot the skyriders. A gun-battle breaks out and Johnny suffers his second arm wound of the short season. He and Hoppy leap off their log to the ground and open fire on the gang. Cassidy runs out along the dam's foot-path, makes a high dive into the river, reaches the dynamite just before it explodes, and tosses it at Petrie and his men, wiping out all of them with one blow. As the film closes the Fighting Forty take their leave, singing lustily all the way.

A publicity still of William Boyd used for **Three on the Trail** (1936, Paramount).

Chapter Nine

During the first half of 1942 it would have taken no Holmes to deduce that the Hopalong Cassidy series was in deep trouble. One indication was that Paramount had released only five Hoppy pictures the prior season instead of the contractually required six, and mostly lackluster episodes at that. Another was that William Boyd, fearful of becoming permanently typecast as Cassidy, kept pressuring Harry Sherman to give him the Richard Dix-like leading roles in the producer's big-budget features and, failing that, to loan him out to competing studios. A third and subtler clue was that for the first time since he came to work for Sherman in 1937 Lesley Selander was directing elsewhere: during a temporary stint at RKO he helmed three routinely entertaining Westerns--- **Thundering Hoofs**, **The Bandit Ranger** and **Red River Robin Hood** (all 1942)---starring Tim Holt.

What saved the Cassidy series and indeed made substantial improvements in it was a crisis at another studio, one that had long prided itself as a prestige company unsullied by B pictures. United Artists had been founded in 1919 by D.W. Griffith, Mary Pickford, Douglas Fairbanks Sr. and Charlie Chaplin as a joint venture designed to give those powerhouses of the silent screen both artistic control over and more of the profits from their films. Throughout the Twenties and Thirties the company had survived and prospered as a distributor of first-rate independently produced features. But in the early Forties the supply dried up and UA suddenly found itself in desperate need of movies with which to fulfill its exhibition contracts. After frantic negotiations with several major studios, an agreement was signed whereby Paramount turned over to UA a block of 21 pictures which had already been announced in early publicity materials as Paramount releases. This block included the entire Harry Sherman package, consisting of five "action specials" plus the Cassidys. Part of the deal was that Sherman's company would make not six but seven Hoppy

exploits for the 1942-43 season so as to cover the previous shortfall. The team reassembled and everyone went back to work.

The three A features for that season, budgeted at over $350,000 apiece, were **Silver Queen** (United Artists, 1942), starring Priscilla Lane, George Brent and Bruce Cabot, and directed by Lloyd Bacon; **American Empire** (United Artists, 1942), starring Richard Dix, Preston Foster and Leo Carrillo, and directed by William McGann; and **Buckskin Frontier** (United Artists, 1943), again starring Dix, and featuring Jane Wyatt, Albert Dekker, Lee J. Cobb and Victor Jory. The last of these, which was a gem, plus five of the season's seven Cassidys were directed by Lesley Selander. Thanks to a hefty loan from the Bank of America, Sherman was able to beef up the Cassidy budgets so that they ranged from $80,000 to more than $100,000 per film, a huge amount for series Westerns. Part of the money was invested in a new outfit for William Boyd, the combination of black hat, shirt and trousers which remained his customary attire for the rest of his time with Sherman. Andy Clyde as California was scruffy and buffoonish as ever. Brad King, the singing sidekick from last season, was replaced by the non-singing and equally non-memorable Jay Kirby, who played Johnny Travers, or Breezy Travers.

Kicking off the Hoppy septet was **Leather Burners** (1942), a decently crafted adventure although it was the sole talking feature and the sole Western directed by Joseph E. Henabery (1888-1976). After playing Abraham Lincoln in D.W. Griffith's **The Birth of a Nation** (1915) and working as Griffith's assistant director on **Intolerance** (1916), Henabery had begun directing in his own right. His silent features included three starring Douglas Fairbanks, Sr.--- one of them, **His Majesty the American** (1919), was United Artists' first release---and a pair of Rudolph Valentino melodramas for Paramount. In 1930, with the coming of sound,

William Boyd protects little Dickie Jones from a beating by Emily Fitzroy in this scene from **The Frontiersmen** (1938, Paramount).

Henabery moved east and spent most of the decade directing comedy and mystery shorts at Brooklyn's Vitaphone Studios. At the time he traveled west again to helm **Leather Burners** his principal occupation was doing training films and documentaries for the U.S. Army Signal Corps. How he got the Hoppy assignment remains a puzzle: it might have been the early connections with UA or Paramount, or perhaps Sherman knew of him because of his own work in the Teens as one of **The Birth of a Nation**'s regional distributors. Before breaking into the movies Henabery had been a railroad clerk, and **Leather Burners** may have appealed to him because of its background in that industry. But he made minimal use of the railroading elements, showed no great skill as an action director and threw away the picture's few potentially exciting moments. The script by unit newcomer Jo Pagano was adapted from *The Leather Burners* (Doubleday, 1940), one of a series of novels about cowboy detectives Rainbow Riley and

Grumpy Gibbs that had been written by Harry Sinclair Drago under his Bliss Lomax byline. With Clarence E. Mulford all but finished as a writer, Sherman had decided to buy movie rights to several books by this walking word machine who was being promoted by Doubleday as Mulford's natural successor. Last season's **Secrets of the Wasteland** had been based on a Drago/Lomax opus, and for his 1942-43 productions Sherman purchased rights to three more: *The Leather Burners* and *Colt Comrades* (Doubleday, 1939) for a pair of Cassidys and *Buckskin Empire* (Doubleday, 1942), published under Drago's own name, as the source for the Richard Dix feature **Buckskin Frontier**.

Thanks in good part to its literary origin, the **Leather Burners** movie was graced by some offbeat story ingredients, including a mad giant living in a subterranean cabin and a cattle stampede through mine tunnels. But on the whole it's a slow and talky picture, with too many plotlines from the novel mentioned in passing and then

180

Evelyn Venable watches as William Boyd stares down Charles A. Hughes in this scene from **The Frontiersmen** (1938, Paramount).

unaccountably dropped. Lewis J. Rachmil, Russell Harlan, Carrol Lewis and Irvin Talbot were back in the Sherman corral respectively as associate producer, photographer, film editor and music director, with the score for the picture written by newcomer Samuel Kaylin. The subsidiary casting was especially rich, with a meaty if brief part for comedian George Givot, off-trail roles for **Gone with the Wind** veterans Victor Jory and later TV Superman George Reeves, and, in an unbilled performance as fourth-in-command of the outlaws, a weary-eyed young war plant worker named Robert Mitchum.

The film opens with stock footage of rustler raids from previous Cassidys. One of the ranches hit hardest is the Wishbone, whose youthful owner Johnny Travers (Jay Kirby) announces to his fellow cattlemen that he's sent for his old pals Hoppy and California to help out. Rancher Bart Galey (Forbes Murray), who's in league with the rustlers, brings the news of Cassidy's impending arrival to meek bespectacled Dan Slack (Victor Jory), the owner of the Buckskin Mine and apparent leader of the gang. As Hoppy and California ride into town, Slack has one of his men take a shot at him on the street and falls over as if hit. When Cassidy helps him to his feet, Slack displays his pocket watch, mashed by what he claims was the gunman's bullet, and tries to hire Hoppy to guard the Buckskin Mine against hostile cattlemen. (Why the ranchers should hate this wimp is only the first of several unsolved mysteries in the script.) Hoppy deduces at once that the murder attempt was a fake when he examines Slack's ruined watch and finds the slug in its works cold to the touch. But instead of exposing Slack he seizes the opportunity to play double agent. First he refuses to help Johnny and the ranchers unless they pay him---although it seems rather odd that they'd expect him to risk his neck for the sheer joy of it---and then, knowing that one of the cattlemen must have tipped off Slack that he was coming, he takes Slack's offer of a job so that he can learn the spy's identity from within.

William Boyd and Charles A. Hughes are about to exchange blows in this scene from **The Frontiersmen** (1938, Paramount).

Slack assigns Hoppy and California to guard the railroad owned by lovely Sharon Longstreet (Shelley Spencer), in whose ore cars the Buckskin's gold is shipped. This unaccountably enrages everybody, not only Johnny and the other ranchers but Sharon and her attorney-cum-suitor Harrison Brooke (George Reeves) and her little brother Bobby (Bobby Larson). Slack sends Hoppy and California to stay at a deserted hotel near the Buckskin. Its eccentric propri.etor Sukey Withers (not listed in the credits) tells his guests the legend of Sam Bucktoe, who discovered gold in the Buckskin many years ago but was later buried alive in a cave-in and whose ghost is rumored to walk the hills by night.

From the hotel Cassidy sends a telegram to a lawman friend, asking for information about Slack. The wire is intercepted by railroad telegrapher Lafe Bailey (Hal Taliaferro), who is also in Slack's pay. Slack prepares and Lafe transmits back to Hoppy a phony reply wire. However, the message lacks the special codeword which the lawman always uses in communicating with Cassidy, who is thus alerted that the wire is a fake and also that Bailey must be a Slack agent. That night he and California throw a scare into Lafe, lock him in a railroad shed and wait to see where he goes when he frees himself. They follow him into the mountains and straight to where the herd stolen from the Wishbone is grazing, but before they can capture Bailey a loose cinch causes him to fall off his horse and over a cliff to his death. Hoppy and California chase away the rustlers, who are led by Bart Galey, and start to drive Johnny's cattle back to the Wishbone. Galey sees his chance and rounds up Johnny and the other cattlemen, who intercept Cassidy on the trail with the steers and, prodded by Galey, accuse him of being a rustler. Johnny kicks Hoppy off his range. That night Cassidy secretly visits Sharon Longstreet, explains his double-agent gambit and asks her help in trapping Galey.

Out riding the next day, Hoppy and Sharon notice a horseman in the distance and follow him

Russell Hayden, George Hayes, William Boyd and posse members have Stanley Ridges, Roy Barcroft and their gang covered in this scene from **Silver on the Sage** (1939, Paramount).

into Coffin Canyon, where they come upon the rustlers' corral, empty at the moment. The outlaws enter the canyon and Hoppy and Sharon have to ride up the rocky face of the slope to escape. Later Cassidy returns to the canyon, accompanied this time by California. They follow cattle tracks from the corral to the foot of a mountain and into a hidden mine tunnel, which turns out to be a rear entrance to Slack's Buckskin. Young Bobby Longstreet, who's been following Hoppy from a distance, rides up at this juncture, and Cassidy uses the boy to deliver a note to the sheriff to form a posse and hit the mine from the front. Then he and California go back into the tunnels to explore.

While inside the dark passages they catch a glimpse of Slack and follow him through the labyrinth to a cabin built inside the mine itself. It's the residence of none other than Sam Bucktoe (George Givot). Eavesdropping, Hoppy and California learn that Bucktoe is a Hitleresque maniac with plans to bankrupt every rancher in the area and use the territory as powerbase to become the

president of the United States. The stolen cattle have been kept and butchered in the Buckskin tunnels and the dressed beef shipped out under the gold in the railroad's ore cars. Bucktoe is just about to kill Slack for being a bungler when Cassidy and California break into the cabin. Bucktoe starts a cave-in and escapes, chasing the terrified Slack through the tunnels and eventually strangling him.

Meanwhile the posse, augmented by the dude lawyer Harrison Brooke, sets out from town towards the front entrance of the Buckskin, and Bobby slips away from his sister and enters the mine at the rear. The boy goes wandering through the tunnels calling for Hoppy, who by this time has found Slack's body near the front of the mine and has gotten into a fierce gunbattle with Robert Mitchum and the rest of the rustlers. The gang is caught neatly in the middle when the posse arrives. The crazed Bucktoe unpens the hundreds of stolen cattle in the mine and sends them stampeding toward the front entrance. Bobby stumbles

183

Stanley Ridges, Roy Barcroft, Jack Rockwell, Edward Cassidy, George Hayes, Eddie Dew, William Boyd and Sherry Tansey are all pictured in this scene from **Silver on the Sage** (1939, Paramount).

and falls into the herd's path, only to be snatched from death at the last possible moment by Hoppy. The stampede triggers another cave-in and this one indubitably buries Bucktoe alive. With the gang rounded up and Sharon deciding that she prefers the future Superman to Johnny, that young buckaroo decides to sell his ranch and join Hoppy and California for more adventures.

Whether or not Harry Sherman realized that the strength of **Leather Burners** lay in its literary roots, the next Cassidy picture of the 1942-43 season was likewise adapted from a Western novel. Indeed its source was a book by Clarence E. Mulford himself, his then most recent yarn and the last he ever completed, *Hopalong Cassidy Serves A Writ* (1941). But the screenplay by unit veteran Gerald Geraghty touched base with Mulford's plot and characters only rarely, with so many tried-and-true shoot-em-up ingredients that few viewers could have detected what came from Mulford and what was new to the film. Behind the scenes were such old reliables as associate

producer Lewis J. Rachmil, cinematographer Russell Harlan, film editor Sherman A. Rose and music director Irvin Talbot, and no less than eight of the principal actors in the picture---Boyd, Clyde, Jay Kirby, Victor Jory, George Reeves, Hal Taliaferro, Forbes Murray and (this time with screen billing) Robert Mitchum---came straight out of **Leather Burners**. The only new names in the credits belonged to the female lead, lovely Jan Christy, and the director.

George Archainbaud (1890-1959) had been born in Paris and adopted as a son by the noted actor Emile Chautard, who launched the young man's career in the French theatrical world. After some years as an actor and assistant stage manager, Archainbaud emigrated to Hollywood and began directing movies around 1917. He racked up dozens of credits before the coming of sound and dozens more in the Thirties, working at studios like First National, Tiffany, RKO and Paramount. His titles included romantic melodramas (**Enticement**, First National, 1925, with Mary

Buzz Barton has William Boyd and Russell Hayden's attention as Ruth Rogers seems concerned about Hayden being tied up in this scene from **Silver on the Sage** (1939, Paramount).

Astor), crime pictures (**Shooting Straight**, RKO, 1930, with Richard Dix), frozen-North adventures (**The Silver Horde**, RKO, 1930, with Evelyn Brent and Joel McCrea), aviation yarns (**The Lost Squadron**, RKO, 1930, with Richard Dix and Mary Astor), courtroom tales (**State's Attorney**, RKO, 1932, with John Barrymore and featuring none other than William Boyd in one of his many character parts at RKO in the early Thirties), little-old-lady detective stories (**Murder on the Blackboard**, RKO, 1934, with Edna May Oliver and James Gleason), sarong extravaganzas (**Her Jungle Love**, Paramount, 1938, with Dorothy Lamour and Ray Milland) and musical comedies (**Some Like It Hot**, Paramount, 1938, with Bob Hope). In short, Archainbaud came out of the same mold as the first Cassidy director, Howard Bretherton, now permanently gone from the unit: a man born before the turn of the century, with long experience in low and medium budget features going far back into the silent era but few if any

prior Western credits. Perhaps this explains why "Pop" Sherman hired him to direct **Hoppy Serves A Writ** (1942). The finished film showed that, whatever Sherman's reasons, he had chosen wisely. It might not have been one of the all-time great Cassidy pictures (although such eminent Western specialists as William K. Everson and Don Miller consider it no less than that), but it was clearly among the better adventures of that mixed bag of a season.

The picture opens on a note of action as the villainous Jordan brothers and their gang hold up a stagecoach driven by that whiskered buffoon California Carlson. They steal a shipment of $500 bills, throw off a pursuing posse and cross the river that separates Texas from Oklahoma Territory where the law has no authority. A reward notice is eventually posted, listing the serial numbers of the stolen bills. California tells Hoppy, who for purposes of this film is a Texas sheriff, that one of the stage robbers had a scar on his cheek.

185

William Boyd restrains Jack Rockwell from hitting Russell Hayden. Hank Bell can be seen between Rockwell and Hayden in this scene from **Silver on the Sage** (1939, Paramount).

Some time later, Tom Colby (Roy Barcroft), owner of the TC ranch, rides in to report to Cassidy that rustlers led by a scar-cheeked man have raided his herd. He draws a map of the crime scene on the back of the flyer containing the serial numbers of the bills taken in the stage holdup. Hoppy dons his by now well-worn dude garb and enters the Oklahoma Territory.

Posing as a cattle buyer named Jones, he stops for water at a ranch owned by Ben Hollister (Forbes Murray) where he meets not only old Ben but his daughter Jean (Jan Christy) and her boyfriend Steve Jordan (George Reeves). Hoppy rides on into Mesa City, where he makes an instant enemy of scar-cheeked Tom Jordan (Victor Jory) by stopping him from beating up a clumsy bartender (Earle Hodgins). Johnny and California meanwhile have disobeyed orders by following Cassidy into Oklahoma. A runaway horse incident precipitates their meeting Steve Jordan and the third brother, Greg (Hal Taliaferro).

The next day Hoppy sits in on a poker game and manipulates Tom Jordan into flashing a $500 bill. The game leads to a brutal fistfight between the two men, excellently staged except for an abundance of careless shots revealing the face of Boyd's double Frosty Royce. Johnny and California ride into town and Hoppy pretends they are strangers to him but Greg Jordan recognizes California as the whiskered driver of the held-up coach.

Later, during a casual conversation with Hoppy, storekeeper Danvers (Byron Foulger) displays a $500 bill he was recently given by Ben Hollister. The talk is overheard by the Jordans, who had given Hollister the bill and who now race out to his ranch to shut the old man's mouth. Hoppy, Johnny and California beat the gang to the ranch. The Jordans besiege the house but are driven off after a furious gunbattle. Afterwards Hollister acknowledges that he received the $500 bill from Tom Jordan.

Hoppy leaves Johnny and California at the ranch to protect the Hollisters. When Steve Jordan next

Roy Barcroft, Edward Cassidy and William Boyd play draw poker as Eddie Dew and Sherry Tansey kibitz in this scene from **Silver on the Sage** (1939, Paramount).

comes courting Jean, she rejects him. California clumsily drops the list of serial numbers, which is retrieved by Steve. He and his gang chase and capture California. Later Hoppy and Johnny find their sidekick's hat along the trail and track him to a cabin where he's been brutally beaten by the Jordans. They rescue him and are pursued by the gang but escape.

After Hoppy demonstrates how the Jordans altered Tom Colby's TC cattle brand into their own TSJ, he and his pals hunt for the canyon where the stolen animals are being kept. They catch Steve rebranding a steer and take him back to the Jordan ranch house where they find several of the stolen $500 bills hidden in a coffee can. Steve makes a break for freedom---which is exactly what Cassidy wanted him to do---and rides to get his brothers. Hoppy, Johnny and California start herding the stolen cattle back towards the river border and the Jordans as expected chase them across the line into Texas, where they're caught up in an ambush which

Hoppy has arranged for by telegram. A rousing gunfight-and-chase scene climaxes in Hoppy roping all three Jordans off their horses just as they're escaping back across the river. In a feeble attempt to justify the title, Cassidy serves the brothers with a warrant of arrest, which is not at all the same thing as a writ.

Except for a few plot points and character names, **Hoppy Serves A Writ** had not the least connection with the Mulford novel of similar title which was the author's swan song to the old West and to his own 35-year career as a Western novelist. But it set the pattern for the best of the United Artists-released Cassidys to come. Whether directed by Archainbaud himself or by Selander, the great late Hoppy pictures of the Sherman era run on simple storylines, perfunctory characterizations, swift pace and lots of action and gorgeous outdoor scenery---and on generous budgets.

Unfortunately, even though it cost almost $104,000, the third of that season's seven

Russell Hopton, Charlotte Wynters, George Hayes and Russell Hayden watch as William Boyd bandages the leg of Sonny Bupp in this scene from **The Renegade Trail** (1939, Paramount).

Cassidys ranks not with the finest in the series but among the dullest. Lesley Selander was back at the helm for **Undercover Man** (1942), an entry woefully short on action, characterization, emotional resonance or visual splendor, with endless footage wasted on comedy shticks and plugs for President Roosevelt's "Good Neighbor" policy with Latin America. The screenplay by unit veteran J. Benton Cheney was unusual, if not complex enough for the film's running time, and featured a few good pieces of insult humor ("You don't want a man for a husband, you want a stomach with legs"). But the only signs of Selander's personality were the eerie night riding scenes and a neat reversal of expectations in the plot, plus the casting of two women from the director's previous Cassidys, Nora Lane of **Hopalong Rides Again** and **Cassidy Of Bar 20** and Esther Estrella of **Three Men From Texas**. The males in the cast included one or two old favorites like Jack Rockwell and Earle Hodgins and some newcomers like silent star

Antonio Moreno, lardbellied comic Chris-Pin Martin and rasp-voiced John Vosper. Lewis J. Rachmil carried on as associate producer, Russell Harlan behind the cameras, Carrol Lewis (supervised by Sherman A. Rose) in the editing booth, Irvin Talbot as music director.

The film might well have started as many of Selander's best do, with a burst of action, but this time he uses a static conversation between Don Tomas Gonzales (Antonio Moreno) and Ranger Captain John Hawkins (Jack Rockwell) to establish the premise: a band of American outlaws have been crossing the border to raid in Mexico while simultaneously Americans have been raided by a gang of Mexican bandits. Relations between the two countries have been strained to the breaking point, and in the meeting between Gonzales, Hawkins and chief deputy Ed Carson (John Vosper), the captain decides to send for Hopalong Cassidy.

Hoppy as usual agrees to help and heads for the Gonzales hacienda, accompanied by his pals

188

A title card for the 1939 Paramount release picturing Russell Hayden, William Boyd and Britt Wood.

Breezy and California. (Why Jay Kirby's character name was switched from Johnny to Breezy remains a mystery.) On the way the three are attacked by bandits who after a brief if loud skirmish are driven off. The trio arrive at the Gonzales place where they've been invited to stay, and where they meet not only Don Tomas but also his daughter Dolores (Esther Estrella), the American widow Louise Saunders (Nora Lane) who has raised the girl, and Louise's son Bob (Alan Baldwin). The smell of food lures California to the hacienda kitchen and into instant entanglement in a comic rivalry with the fat vaquero Miguel (Chris-Pin Martin) for the hand of the even fatter Rosita (Eva Puig), a widow with a brood of muchachos who's determined to cook her way into a second marriage. Meanwhile over a chess game Hoppy and Don Tomas decide to throw a fiesta that will introduce Cassidy to the local people.

The party is punctuated by Spanish dance sequences, more comic antics in the kitchen, and endless unsubtle lines of dialogue about the need for Anglos and Latinos to be "good neighbors." Festivities come to an end when news reaches the rancho that the American gang has pulled another raid in Mexico. Cassidy and Gonzales lead a small army of riders after the bandits, who escape as usual. Bob Saunders arouses Hoppy's suspicion by slipping away from the pursuit party for a few minutes. Several nights later, when the bandits attack a gold-laden mule train south of the border, the leader of the gang is clearly seen and described as dressed in black and riding a white stallion. When this news is reported to Don Tomas, he assigns Miguel to shadow Hoppy and his pals.

The next raid is by Mexican bandits on the U.S. side of the border, and the survivors of the attack recognize the primo bandito as none other than Don Tomas Gonzales. Hoppy learns of this development when he visits the ranger station to check in with Captain Hawkins and chief deputy Carson. Cassidy is satisfied that the border raids are the work of a single gang, dressing alternately

189

Betty Moran shows **William Boyd** the countryside in this scene from **Range War**. (1939, Paramount).

as gringos and Mexicanos, but neither he nor Gonzales knows that each is suspected by the other of being in league with the outlaws. While footage continues to be wasted on comic eating sequences and California's preparations for marriage to Rosita, the raids keep devastating both sides of the border and Hoppy and Gonzales still suspect one another.

One night Cassidy and his pals pretend to leave the hacienda but double back and keep watch on the house, hoping to catch Gonzales slipping out to meet the gang. Breezy spots what he takes to be Hoppy riding away at full speed and goes after the figure, followed by the real Cassidy and Miguel and California, who in turn are pursued by Gonzales and his men. Breezy rides into an ambush from which the others save him. Afterwards, when Hoppy and Breezy and Don Tomas exchange their stories, Cassidy finally realizes that both he and Gonzales have been the victims of an impersonator. They follow the false Hoppy's tracks back to an old winery and find a secret

room in which are kept the props for both masquerades. Cassidy decides that it's time to look more closely at the activities of young Bob Saunders.

The next day Hoppy, Breezy and California trail Saunders to a cabin where they overhear enough to realize that Bert (Pierce Lyden) is forcing Bob to help the gang. They ride to the nearest U.S. town and, for no particular reason, spend some time with Sheriff Blackburn (Earle Hodgins) sorting through old Wanted posters. Suddenly Hoppy recognizes the face on one circular, understands the whole situation and decides to bait a trap. He arranges for a mine owner to visit the Gonzales hacienda and announce loudly to Don Tomas that he's shipping a load of gold in an old water wagon along a disused trail. Hoppy, Captain Hawkins and the Rangers take cover along the trail and wait for the gang to strike. When they come into view, with the false Cassidy at their head, the posse opens fire. The outlaws race away but run smack into Don Tomas and his

Betty Moran clings to William Boyd for protection in this scene from **Range War** (1939, Paramount).

vaqueros and are caught between the two forces. The false Cassidy makes a break for it and is shot down by chief deputy Carson. Unmasked, the black-garbed rider of the white stallion proves to be Louise Saunders, who confesses with her last breath that she did what the gang leader forced her to do in order to save Bob from a false murder charge. She names as the gang leader the chief deputy ranger, Carson, and Hoppy gets the drop on the man without even a hint of resistance. A toast at the Gonzales place reaffirms the blessings of a good neighbor policy, while California's nuptial plans are aborted by the unexpected return of Rosita's first husband from the dead.

The fourth of the season's seven Cassidys was of a much higher order, thanks in part to a screenplay by a newcomer who went on like no other Hoppy scripter to fame and fortune and quite a bit of notoriety outside the Western genre. Born in McAlester, Oklahoma in 1914, Michael Wilson had been a schoolteacher and short story writer before moving to Hollywood in 1940. After doing a few Cassidy scripts he went into military service and saw combat as a Marine lieutenant. On his return to civilian life he worked on the screenplays for a number of big-budget pictures and shared an Oscar for his contribution to **A Place in the Sun** (1951), George Stevens' socially-conscious crime drama starring Montgomery Clift and Elizabeth Taylor. But the early Fifties were the grim years of Senator Joe McCarthy and the House Un-American Activities Committee, and Wilson was blacklisted when he refused to say whether he had ever belonged to the Communist Party. During the worst of the repression he collaborated with the foremost blacklisted screenwriter, Dalton Trumbo, on half a dozen scripts which were credited to pseudonyms or to politically acceptable people. Eventually Wilson moved to Paris where he could work in freedom. Although never given credit, he was responsible for much of **The Bridge on the River Kwai** (1958) and part of **Lawrence of Arabia** (1962). After the blacklist withered away he was rehabilitated in the industry and,

191

Francis McDonald and Willard Robertson gang up on William Boyd in this scene from **Range War** (1939, Paramount).

with Rod Serling, co-authored the script for **Planet of the Apes** (1968). He died in 1978.

Asking how much Communist propaganda Wilson slipped into his Hopalong Cassidy scripts would be a McCarthyist question of the dumbest sort. Three points however are clear: that Wilson's orientation was Marxist; that the Cassidys for which he is credited deal with the themes of oppression and enslavement and proletarian revolt and redistribution of wealth; and that the same themes have a long and honorable lineage in American fiction and film and appear in dozens of other Westerns including, as we've seen, a number of Cassidys. They are especially prominent in the first of Wilson's scripts for the series, **Border Patrol** (1942).

One might read the credits for this picture and expect just another routine Cassidy exploit. The usual behind-scenes names occupied the usual slots: Lewis J. Rachmil as associate producer, photography by Russell Harlan, Sherman A. Rose as film editor, Irvin Talbot as music director.

What in fact pulls this entry out of the rut is the conjunction of Michael Wilson's script and Lesley Selander's expert direction. The cast included several veterans of recent Cassidys directed by others, including George Reeves as a Mexican gentleman, Duncan Renaldo as a district commandant, and Pierce Lyden and Robert Mitchum as "dog heavies." But Selander gave the two key roles to newcomers. Dour-faced Russell Simpson, usually cast as a tyrannical backwoods patriarch, did a fine job as the king toad, and lovely Claudia Drake was excellent as the latest of Selander's fiery imperious action women. **Border Patrol** comes closer than do most of the United Artists Cassidys to "Pop" Sherman's formula for Westerns: build slowly with plot and character interplay, then ten minutes or so from the end title let all hell break loose. This time the formula works rather well.

Like Selander's much weaker **Undercover Man**, **Border Patrol** is a sort of salute to the Roosevelt Good Neighbor policies. The focus of

Russell Hayden and William Boyd are under siege in this publicity still for **Range War** (1939, Paramount).

the story is the Silver Bullet mine, which had been owned by conquistadors and worked by Indian slaves when Texas belonged to Mexico, and which is now owned by a gringo and worked by Mexican slaves. Don Enrique Perez (George Reeves) comes to the town of Silver Bullet to investigate the disappearance of twenty-five of his countrymen who were hired to work the mine at high wages. He is taken prisoner and likewise made a slave, and his servant is shot in the back while trying to escape some time later. The body is found along the trail by Texas Rangers Hoppy, Johnny and California. Fiery Inez La Barca (Claudia Drake), who is searching for the missing Don Enrique, discovers the three men beside the dead servant and accuses them of having killed him. Eventually the district commandant (Duncan Renaldo) calms her down and asks Cassidy and his pals to hunt for the vanished laborers on behalf of both the U.S. and Mexican governments. Inez demands to join the trio, then becomes outraged at a sexist remark by lovesmitten Johnny and rides

off alone. Next morning Hoppy and his companions, trailed all the way by Inez, set out for the Mountains of Missing Men.

At the outskirts of the territory which is posted as the private domain of one Orestes Krebs, the trio are shot at by Quinn (Robert Mitchum) and Barton (Cliff Parkinson), two of Krebs' gunmen. Cassidy manages to get behind Barton and suspends him over a cliff edge, while Quinn runs for his life. Cassidy makes Barton confess that he killed Don Enrique's servant, then the three take their prisoner into the town of Silver Bullet. There they encounter Krebs (Russell Simpson), who not only owns the community but is its mayor, sheriff, legislature and judge. The character is half comic buffoon and half frontier Hitler, clearly modeled on Walter Brennan's performance as Judge Roy Bean in William Wyler's **The Westerner** (1940), starring Gary Cooper. Krebs' men surround Hoppy and his pals, who surrender without a fight and submit to a hilarious trial in the saloon, with Krebs as judge and his

193

William Boyd disarms Francis McDonald and Willard Robertson in this scene from **Range War** (1939, Paramount).

hoodlums sitting on the jury. Just as Quinn is about to get up from the jury box and testify against the defendants, the trial is suspended as Inez rides into town. Krebs takes her into his office, tells her that Cassidy and his buddies murdered Don Enrique the last time they were in town, and prevails upon her to testify against them. Naturally enough they are found guilty and sentenced to hang that evening after supper. Inez then asks Krebs to show her the Silver Bullet mine, and he consents.

Krebs sends Barton ahead to tell the guards to hide the slaves in the mine shaft. Don Enrique overhears the news that a woman is coming to the mine and, believing it must be Inez, surreptitiously leaves his sombrero out in the open where she'll see it. Sure enough she does, and understanding the truth at once, she starts playing up to Krebs, offering to cook a gourmet Mexican dinner for him and, believe it or not, for the three prisoners. Back in town she slips a small pistol and some bullets into the huge tray of food she

prepares. The contributions of the dimwitted regular cook (Earle Hodgins in an unbilled bit part) are limited to remarks like: "I love beans, there isn't bones in them like in fish." As the tray is on its way to the jail cells Krebs helps himself to a tortilla---fortunately one that isn't loaded---and sets down the meal before Cassidy and his sidekicks. At the moment when their situation seems hopeless, California bites down on a bullet, and a moment later they find the pistol in the bean pot. With the hanging about to commence, the three break out of jail. After a gunfight in the street with Krebs' men in which Quinn is killed, the trio and Inez roar out of town. The slavemasters take after them in hot pursuit.

Hoppy and his comrades ride to the mine and launch a surprise attack in which Inez does her full share of the fighting. With the guards captured and the slaves freed, Don Enrique and Inez are joyously reunited. Hoppy arms the liberated workers, has them hide under tarpaulins in Krebs' ore wagons and forces the mine guards at

Another Title Card from a 1939 Paramount release pictures star William Boyd and others.

gunpoint to drive the wagons out to meet Krebs and his oncoming men. Before they know what's happening the slavemasters are surrounded by their own wagons and caught in the circle of the peons' gunfire. Krebs breaks out of the ring and tries to escape but is chased and caught by Hoppy, who appoints California the new judge of Silver Bullet and forces the deposed dictator to turn over all his money and property to the slaves as the film ends.

If the Cassidy series took one step forward with **Border Patrol**, Hoppy's next adventure went two steps back, or more precisely thirty-four steps back. The fifth film of the 1942-43 season and forty-sixth in the entire cycle of Cassidys was **Lost Canyon** (1942), an exceptionally close remake of the series' twelfth picture, **Rustlers' Valley** (1937). Harry Sherman produced, Russell Harlan photographed and William Boyd of course starred in both versions, but they were the only persons who reprised their functions in the original. Replacing Nate Watt as director was

Lesley Selander, and **Rustlers' Valley** scenarist Harry O. Hoyt was again credited with the script. (Mulford's nominal source novel, loudly acknowledged in the earlier version when Sherman was still capitalizing on the alleged literary roots of the series, isn't mentioned in the **Lost Canyon** credits at all.) Lewis J. Rachmil, Carrol Lewis and Irvin Talbot carried on respectively as associate producer, film editor and music director.

There is no need to describe the storyline, which is identical to the description of **Rustlers' Valley** in Chapter 3. A few scenes were rearranged in the new version and two sequences were added, a comedy skit where California tries to bake biscuits with plaster of Paris and a ranch-yard "detective reconstruction" scene where Cassidy convinces the sheriff that Johnny couldn't have committed the bank robbery that kicks off the picture. Except for Hoppy himself, all the **Rustlers' Valley** character names were altered. Lucky and Windy of course became Johnny and California, rancher Glenn Randall and his

Steffi Duna looks coyly at William Boyd in this publicity photo for **Law of the Pampas** (1939, Paramount).

daughter Agnes were redesignated as Tom Clark (Herbert Rawlinson) and his daughter Laura (Lola Lane), Cal Howard the crooked lawyer and Clem Crawford the shady banker became Jeff Burton (Douglas Fowley) and Zack Rogers (Guy Usher), and the treacherous foreman Taggart was in the new version called Wade Haskell (Karl Hackett).

It was the second Selander remake of a Nate Watt original, but even with an $83,000 budget, **Lost Canyon** turned out nowhere near as well as when Selander had revamped Watt's 1936 **Hopalong Cassidy Returns** into the 1941 classic **Wide Open Town**. But routine as it was, the picture provides an excellent case study in comparative directorial styles. Selander's version is better paced, its scanty action sequences somewhat more dynamic though miles from his best. His approach is cool and distanced, favoring two- and three-shots where Watt stressed emotional intensity and close-ups. (Compare for instance the key scenes where Cassidy is informed that his young sidekick is dead.) Selander pares

down the dialogue of the original to a bare minimum and, in line with then standard policy, cleans up Hoppy's grammar. But all these changes were relatively minimal and certainly didn't improve the lackluster Watt version a great deal. No one would rank **Lost Canyon** among the top ten Cassidys or even the top forty.

Both Selander and the series returned to stride with **Colt Comrades** (1943), a fine blend of action and social consciousness. Its nominal source, like that of **Secrets of the Wasteland** and **Leather Burners,** was a novel by Harry Sinclair Drago, in this case *Colt Comrades* (Doubleday, 1939), published under Drago's Bliss Lomax byline. The screenplay was by the Marxist Michael Wilson who had also scripted **Border Patrol,** and its central theme was economic exploitation by a ruthless capitalist. Lewis J. Rachmil, Russell Harlan and Irvin Talbot worked in their usual capacities, with unit newcomer Fred W. Berger credited for the first but far from the last time as film editor. For the cast Selander

196

William Boyd wonders why he is carrying Steffi Duna in this publicity photo for **Law of the Pampas** (1939, Paramount).

recruited several veterans of his earlier Cassidys: Victor Jory from **Riders of the Timberline** and **Wide Open Town** as the rapacious exploiter, George Reeves and Russell Simpson from **Border Patrol** as a nice young man in trouble and a misguided sheriff, Douglas Fowley and Herbert Rawlinson from **Lost Canyon** as a "dog heavy" and a water-starved rancher, weary-eyed Robert Mitchum as another gunman and dear old Earle Hodgins in one more variant on his snake-oil huckster character. Newcomer Lois Sherman was given the female lead, and if her relatively passive part in the picture was untypical of Selander, the siege-and-rescue sequence at the climax was squarely in his tradition, and the generous $102,000 budget and lengthy running time gave him ample opportunity for visual fireworks.

Beginning, as usual in Selander films, with a burst of action. Dirk Mason (Robert Mitchum) steals a U.S. mail pouch from a railroad station and kills the stationmaster. Pursued by deputy marshals Hoppy, Johnny and California, he desperately seeks protection from Jeb Hardin (Victor Jory), the virtual ruler of a distant town and the man who hired Mason to commit the robbery. Hardin not only refuses to help Mason but tries to shoot him to keep his mouth shut. Mason runs out of Hardin's office just as Hoppy and his pals ride into town. They corner Mason in the saloon and capture him alive but are instantly confronted by Joe Brass (Douglas Fowley), leader of the local vigilante group under Hardin's control, who demands that Mason be lynched. When Mason tries to break away Brass kills him, then boldly claims the $5000 reward on Mason's head even though it's obvious that it was Cassidy who caught the man. Hardin's intervention leads to a compromise of the dispute: Hoppy and his pals can have the reward money if they'll invest it in the community. They agree and buy from Hardin a first mortgage on the Box W ranch which Hardin was about to foreclose. What he doesn't bother to tell them is that he still controls

A duded-up William Boyd takes part in a typical saloon brawl in this scene from **Santa Fe Marshal** (1940, Paramount). Fred Graham can be seen over Boyd's shoulder.

the water rights on the ranch, and that he intends to keep Cassidy's money and have the ranch too.

Riding out to the Box W, Hoppy and his buddies find the house empty, but ever-hungry California locates a platter of fried chicken, and as the three are demolishing the bird they are surprised by Lucy Whitlock (Lois Sherman) and her brother Lin (George Reeves). The Whitlocks explain that they're trying to save their ranch from Hardin and offer Hoppy and his pals a half interest in the spread for $5000. It's only in this scene that Cassidy learns that Hardin has dammed up all the water in the region and is charging the ranchers outrageous prices with the result that the cattle of those who can't afford to pay are dying of thirst.

Hoppy gives California $500 to take into town in payment of the past-due water bill on the Box W. But at Hardin's behest a fast-talking con artist named Wildcat Willy (Earle Hodgins) tricks the whiskered old coot into using the money to buy a rig to drill for oil on the ranch. Hardin orally agrees to give the Whitlocks another thirty days to pay their water bill. When California and Willy bring the drilling equipment to the ranch, Hoppy listens to what happened and informs California that he's been swindled. California pulls his gun on Willy and keeps him a prisoner on the ranch, making him sink the oil well at the point of a .45.

Hardin orders the water to the Box W cut off. Hoppy, Johnny, Lin Whitlock and a Mr. Varney (Herbert Rawlinson), owner of the Bar V, ride to the dam to ask Hardin's men to open the spillways. Brass and his vigilantes refuse and a free-for-all breaks out. Hoppy and his allies win the brawl but then decide not to open the spillways by force because if they did Hardin could have them arrested as water thieves. Instead they decide to pay the back water bill by selling all the Box W cattle. Before they can do so however Willy's well suddenly comes in with a gigantic explosion---not of oil but of water. The well has tapped into an underground spring plenteous enough to break Hardin's power. Ideal socialist that he is, Hoppy

198

Marjorie Rambeau holds a derringer on William Boyd as Kenneth Harlan disarms him in this publicity still for **Santa Fe Marshal** (1940, Paramount). Through the door you can plainly see a movie light.

offers water free to all his neighbors.

But he still owes $500 on that unpaid bill, and Hardin refuses to take the Bar W cattle to settle the debt, demanding the entire ranch instead. Hoppy calls a meeting of his neighbors and proposes that they form a new cattlemen's association to market their herds independently of Hardin's monopolistic beef brokerage. Hardin retaliates by having Brass plant some of Varney's Bar V cattle, clumsily rebranded as Box W stock, in the Whitlock herd. Then he and the vigilantes break into the ranchers' meeting and accuse Hoppy of rustling. His neighbors stupidly believe the charge and Hoppy, Johnny and Lin Whitlock are forced to run for their lives.

They are chased across a beautiful rocky desert landscape and take cover in a spot from which they can hold off their pursuers. The vigilantes leave two men on guard, but after dark Hoppy and his pals slip away and make it back to the Box W. There Cassidy asks Wildcat Willy for anything he knows against Hardin, and Willy reveals that he

had heard that Hardin and Brass had killed Dirk Mason to shut his mouth about something. Suddenly Hoppy realizes that Mason had been hired to steal the mail pouch because it contained contracts for the sale of the ranchers' cattle. Without the contracts, Hardin could persuade the ranchers that the big cattle buyers weren't purchasing beef any more and could simultaneously tell the buyers that the ranchers' herds had been stolen and so wouldn't be shipped to market.

Suspecting that the stolen contracts are in Hardin's office, Hoppy manufactures a chance to search for them by sending California into town with a fake surrender offer from the three fugitives. When Hardin sends out all the vigilantes with orders to meet and kill the three "while resisting arrest," the coast is clear for Hoppy and his pals to slip into town. They capture Hardin in his office, tie and gag him, and hunt till they find the incriminating documents in his safe. (Don't ask what happened to the legal scruples they displayed out at the dam.) They escape with the

Marjorie Rambeau keeps them covered as William Pagan ties up one man and Kenneth Harlan ties up William Boyd in this scene from **Santa Fe Marshal** (1940, Paramount).

contracts just as the vigilantes return to town, and the climactic chase is on. Hoppy and his comrades race back to the Box W with Hardin and his gang in hot pursuit. Hardin orders an all-out attack on the ranch house. A wild bullet shatters a kerosene lantern and the house becomes an inferno. Cassidy is shot in the shoulder by Hardin while running from the well to the house with a bucket of water. Just as the gang charge towards the ranch house, the rescue party races onto the scene, led by Lucy and Willy who were able to form a posse of ranchers thanks to the evidence of the contracts Hoppy gave them in a meeting on the trail. Hardin and his men are overcome in a brief if furious fight. With the tyrant in jail, Hoppy and Johnny and California head for new adventures.

The seventh and final Cassidy adventure of that longest season was among other things an assortment of several reversals of expectation that must have delighted its director, Lesley Selander, even though he had nothing to do with many of them. **Bar 20** (1943) bore the same title as the 1907 episodic novel which launched Clarence E. Mulford as a book writer, but the volume isn't even mentioned in the film's credits and probably no one involved with the movie so much as remembered where the title had been used before. Michael Wilson was one of three men credited with the film's script---the others were newcomer Morton Grant and old hand Norman Houston---but not a trace of his personality or viewpoint appears in the picture. The budget was set at a generous $86,000 but the cast of the film was rather small and the amount of action slight. The biggest surprise in the casting was that bland Jay Kirby and his Johnny/Breezy character were gone, the role of Hoppy's young sidekick being turned over for this one film to none other than George Reeves. Supporting Boyd, Reeves and Andy Clyde were a number of veterans of recent Cassidy exploits including Victor Jory as the principal villain, Douglas Fowley and Francis McDonald as his henchmen, Earle Hodgins as another frontier idiot and---the second biggest

The tables are turned as William Boyd has Marjorie Rambeau and William Pagan covered in this scene from **Santa Fe Marshal** (1940, Paramount).

surprise in the casting---Robert Mitchum as a victimized good guy. The female lead was given to Dustine Farnum, whose father, Dustin Farnum, had starred in Sherman's 1918 production of **The Light of Western Stars** and in the Mulford-based 1920 film **The Orphan.** Betty Blythe, who had starred in exotic silent romances like **The Queen of Sheba** (1920), played Miss Farnum's mother. The key people behind the scenes were the mixture as before: associate producer Lewis J. Rachmil, Russell Harlan behind the cameras. Thematically the film echoes Selander's **Undercover Man,** with the storylines of both pictures being rooted in Cassidy and another innocent party suspecting each other of crookedness, but **Bar 20** unlike its predecessor features a few bursts of action in well-chosen locations.

Hoppy and California and their young sidekick Lin Bradley (George Reeves) have traveled far from home to inspect and, if possible, buy some purebred cattle from the Stevens ranch. Along the trail they interrupt an attack on a stagecoach by

Quirt Rankin (Francis McDonald) and his gang and drive the outlaws away, although they escape with a casket of jewels and a trunkful of wedding clothes. Cassidy and his pals are warmly thanked by the coach's passengers, Marie Stevens (Dustine Farnum) and her widowed mother (Betty Blythe) and neighboring rancher Mark Jackson (Victor Jory), who were en route to the Stevens ranch for Marie's marriage to Richard Adams (Robert Mitchum). Marie tells Hoppy that the stolen jewels were Adams family heirlooms which had been given to her by Richard as a wedding present.

During dinner at the Stevens ranch, Cassidy predicts that Rankin will demand a cash ransom in return for the jewels, and offers to furnish the money by purchasing 100 Stevens cattle. At this point Adams and Jenkins drop in and Adams announces that he's just received a note demanding $3000 for the gems. When he hears of Hoppy's prediction, Adams suspects him of being in league with Rankin. Too proud to take money

CLARENCE E. MULFORD'S HIDDEN GOLD

featuring WILLIAM BOYD · RUSSELL HAYDEN · RUTH ROGERS · MINOR WATSON · BRITT WOOD · LEE PHELPS · A HARRY SHERMAN Production

Directed by Lesley Selander · A Paramount Picture

William Boyd has the better of Roy Barcroft in this Title Card for the 1940 Paramount release.

from his fiancee, Adams decides to raise the ransom by selling some of his land.

While riding across Jackson's spread in its owner's company the next day, Hoppy and his pals are ambushed by Rankin's gang and robbed of the $4000 they brought for the cattle deal. One of the masked bandits drops a pistol bearing an RA monogram. Later back at the Stevens ranch Cassidy encounters Adams, who claims that he'd lost his pistol earlier but had forgotten to mention it. Meanwhile Jackson, the real brains behind the plot, is visiting Rankin's desert hideout and taking the $4000 Quirt stole from Cassidy so that he can use it to pay for the land he's buying from Adams. The $1000 difference between the amount lifted from Hoppy and the amount demanded for the jewels Jackson keeps for himself.

California falls into a well in the Stevens patio and becomes an inadvertent earwitness to the closing of the land deal, although he's unable to identify the buyer's voice. During the negotiations Adams accidentally drops one of the $100 bills

Jackson paid him down the well where California catches it. After Hoppy and Lin and the idiotic ranchhand Tom (Earle Hodgins) pull the old buffoon out of the well, Adams retrieves the bill, but not before Lin and Cassidy recognize it as one of the crisp new yellowbacks that Rankin had stolen from Hoppy. When Adams leaves the ranch he is trailed by Cassidy and his pals. Out on the desert near Rankin's hideout, they witness what looks to them like a conspiratorial meeting, although in reality Adams is simply paying over the ransom money. Rankin then pulls a gun on Adams and sends him away without the jewels. Hoppy and his pals prowl around the area and sneak up on the gang's hideout. A wild brawl erupts and Rankin is taken prisoner, although the rest of the bandits escape.

Cassidy and his companions start back for the ranch with their prisoner and the jewels. The rest of the gang run into Jackson and tell him what has happended. Jackson sets up an ambush along the trail and his new second-in-command Slash

202

Britt Wood, William Boyd and Russell Hayden are ready for action in this publicity still for **Hidden Gold** (1940, Paramount).

(Douglas Fowley) shoots Quirt twice with a long-range rifle. Hoppy, Lin and California escape the trap along with the mortally wounded Rankin, who clears Adams and incriminates Jackson just before he dies. At this point Adams returns with a party of his own ranchhands and captures Cassidy and his pals. Still convinced that they're thieves, he takes the three men and the dead Quirt back to the Stevens ranch where Hoppy returns the jewels to Marie. After much effort Cassidy finally convinces Adams and the Stevens women that their real enemy is Jackson, and works with them to set a trap.

The entire party starts for town with Lin and California pretending to be Adams' prisoners and Hoppy lying in a ranch wagon, disguised as Rankin. They meet Jackson along the trail and tell him that Quirt though badly wounded is alive and ready to talk. Jackson rides away on a pretext, has Slash and the gang set up yet another ambush on the road, and rejoins the party to establish his innocence as he had done during the gang's previous operations. In a gesture most untypical of Selander, Adams sends Marie out of harm's way before any action breaks out and the lady meekly assents. The gang attacks on horseback, and Lin and California throw off their shackles and lead a countercharge. In a well-directed double chase sequence full of running insert shots, Lin goes after and subdues Slash while Hoppy does likewise with Jackson, from whose pockets are recovered the last $1000 of the money stolen from Cassidy. With the wedding of Marie and Adams this acceptable but unremarkable film comes to an end, and with it the seventh, longest and next-to-last season of Harry Sherman's Cassidy series.

A general purpose publicity still of William Boyd and Topper used for the series.

Chapter Ten

The first season's worth of United Artists Cassidys had been lavishly budgeted but their financial returns were a disappointment. The abysmal **Lost Canyon** brought in about $55,000 over negative costs and the excellent **Colt Comrades** grossed only around $20,000 over its expenses, with the other five falling between these extremes. In Hollywood such numbers didn't count as profits at all. But even though the Cassidy films were fast becoming economic liabilities, Sherman not only refused to back away from them but upped the budgets for the Cassidys of the 1943-44 season to a whopping maximum of $130,000 each. The results exploded all over the screen. In terms of exciting largescale action scenes, simple uncluttered storylines, rapid pacing and visual dynamics and pulse-pounding background music, this last set of six under the Sherman logo proved to be the finest pictures in the history of the Cassidy enterprise and a rousing last hurrah for the unit.

William Boyd and Andy Clyde carried on of course as Hoppy and California, but in this sextet the young sidekick role was taken over by Jimmy Rogers (1915-   ), a son of the immortal Will Rogers and a rather low-key, unflamboyant screen personality, more like his father than like Jimmy Ellison or Russell Hayden. Three of the half-dozen were directed by Selander and three by Archainbaud, with whose work on **Hoppy Serves A Writ** Harry Sherman had been so impressed that he assigned the Frenchman to helm the last "action specials" he owed UA: **The Kansan** (United Artists, 1943), starring Richard Dix, Jane Wyatt and Albert Dekker, and **The Woman of the Town** (United Artists, 1943) with Claire Trevor, Albert Dekker and Barry Sullivan. During the time Selander wasn't busy with a Cassidy he directed War Department training films like **Disposal of Unusable Ammunition** (1943) and worked without credit as second unit director on the big-budget Western **Buffalo Bill** (20th Century-Fox, 1944), which starred Joel McCrea,

Maureen O'Hara and Linda Darnell and was produced by Sherman and directed by William Wellman.

The keynote theme for this ninth season of Cassidys was that of capitalist exploitation versus the ethic of the sharing community, and the keynote villain was Douglass Dumbrille, who had played the lead in Selander's **The Mysterious Rider** back in 1938 but was much more at home in bad-guy roles in both Westerns and Marx Brothers comedies. Lewis J. Rachmil continued as associate producer and Russell Harlan as cinematographer for the entire half-dozen, and Irvin Talbot served as music director for the first five. Screenwriting and editorial chores were parceled out among a variety of hands. For lovers of the non-stop action Western, these last "genuine" Hoppy films make up a six-course feast of the highest quality.

The season opened with **False Colors** (1943), directed by Archainbaud from a screenplay by unit newcomer Bennett Cohen, who had been writing and producing independent quickies since the golden age of the silents. Douglass Dumbrille made the first of his three appearances as chief villain in a Cassidy film, with Robert Mitchum, Glenn Strange and Roy Barcroft (in one of his last roles before signing an exclusive contract with Republic Pictures) prominent among the henchmen. Claudia Drake from **Border Patrol** was adequate in the female lead and Tom Seidel rather good in a dual role, while dear old Earle Hodgins was delightful in a small part as an inept lawyer. Fred W. Berger was credited as film editor under the supervision of Carrol Lewis.

Archainbaud's signature image was the desert panorama. He loved to set scenes in vast outcroppings of rock amid the great stretches of sand and cactus and made use of these settings in all three of his Cassidys for this season, although only in the early minutes of **False Colors**. The story begins with gunmen Sonora (Glenn Strange) and Lefty (Pierce Lyden) trailing Hoppy and his men

Dear Mike;

Thanks for the Hopalong chapter. It was very interesting and I sure liked reading it.

Since I have seen very few Hopalongs I'm sure not any kind of authority, but after seeing three or four of the ones I was in they are a lot better than I thought they were at the time we made them.

There really isn't much I can say about making them except as I think I told you Bill, Andy, every one on the pictures were really great to me and very helpful. Everyone was really professional.

Neither Bill or Andy were good riders or had any cowboy background, nor did either ever pretend that they were. Clem Fuller could double Andy, even in a closeup, but Ted Wells could never pass for Bill except at a distance so this ment Bill had to do more riding than he wanted, mounts, dismounts etc.

One time the script called for Boyd to make a fast mount. Now Topper was a good sized horse and Bill's saddle had a high cantle, so they found a place where there was a small hump, put Topper behind it, but even with the hump Topper was too tall. Next they dug out back of the hump, still not enough, so they dug out some more and then some more. Finally Les Selander said,"Let's quite messing around and we'll do it in a long shot."

Another time in a chase we were to come off this hill and at the bottom I was to stop my horse, look at the ground and say,"They went down the canyon." Comming off the hill too many of us hit a narrow place and I got crowded over a big granite boulder. My horse jumped and that boulder looked to be about a city block long. I don't know how that horse cleared it but when we hit the bottom and I pulled up and looked at the ground I couldn't remember a line, I just sat there. Les yelled cut and walked over to me and said," By God, Jim, you were doing great till you stopped that horse long enough to act." Then he laughed and said,"That sure was one hell of a jump."

Dick Dickson was always trying to get some music in the pictures but Bill did every thing he could to keep

A photocopy of part of a letter to the author.

206

them from becomming singing westerns. I know Bill
would get upset because when people like Autry and
Roy Rogers went on location the trucks all had their
names on them but when we went on location ours had
Harry Sherman's name all over them.

As long as Sherman had the Hoppy's Bill never wanted
to make a lot of appearances or do any promotion
and didn't until he got control of the pictures.

It was good to meet you and someday I hope our trails
might cross again.

Thanks

Jim

Page two of the photocopy of the letter to the author.

on a cattle drive and setting up an ambush among the rocks in an attempt to kill young cowhand Bud Lawton (Tom Seidel). Hoppy, Jimmy and California drive the bushwhackers away and save their young friend's life. When the herd reaches the railhead town, Lawton receives a letter telling him that his father is dead and that he has been left a two-thirds interest in the prosperous Diamond Hitch ranch from which Bud had run away as a boy. The young man visits absent-minded attorney Jay Griffin (Earle Hodgins) and signs an agreement making Hoppy, Jimmy and California equal partners in his share of the ranch. Immediately afterwards, Sonora and Lefty shoot Bud down on the street. Hoppy and his pals decide to visit the distant town of Poncho to claim their one-fourth apiece of Bud's two-thirds and to find his killers.

The man behind the murder is suave banker Mark Foster (Douglass Dumbrille), who wants the Diamond Hitch for its valuable water rights. Foster has located a Bud Lawton look-alike named Kit Moyer (Tom Seidel) and hired him to come to Poncho posing as the long-lost Bud and to sign over his share of the ranch. When Hoppy reaches the town he meets Lawton's sister Faith (Claudia Drake), owner of the remaining one-third interest, and the man who calls himself Bud Lawton. For the moment he decides to keep to himself the knowledge that "Lawton" is a fake.

Later Hoppy, Jimmy and California ride out to the Diamond Hitch, where Moyer is trying to persuade Faith to sell the ranch to Foster, and sign on as cowhands. Then back in town Cassidy visits Judge Stevens (Sam Flint) and tells the truth about the impersonator and about his own partnership interest in the Diamond Hitch. Meanwhile in the saloon California has gotten embroiled in a dispute with gunman Rip Austin (Robert Mitchum) and Hoppy has to rescue the old buffoon by engaging Austin in a brutal fistfight. When Austin and Moyer report Cassidy's interferences to Foster, the banker decides that Hoppy must be eliminated. At a party that night at the Diamond Hitch, the

Ruth Rogers introduces Minor Watson to Britt Wood, William Boyd and Russell Hayden in this scene from **Hidden Gold** (1940, Paramount).

fake Bud Lawton announces that he's selling the ranch and that his late father's policy of sharing water with his neighbors is terminated. Cassidy blocks the impending sale by declaring that he and his pals own 75% of Bud's two-thirds interest and accusing the young man of being an impostor. The corrupt sheriff (Roy Barcroft) charges Hoppy, Jimmy and California with the murder of the real Bud Lawton. They start to escape from the ranch at gunpoint but go back to help California, who was wounded in the scuffle. All three are caught and locked up.

Foster plots to get rid of the trio by having the sheriff release them and stationing his gunmen outside the jail to shoot them down as escaping prisoners. Hoppy anticipates the ambush and gets the drop on the sheriff and the bushwhackers. He and his pals sneak over to Foster's bank and capture Moyer, who has just entered his boss' office. Foster shoots Moyer down so that he can't talk, escapes into the main room of the bank, and he and his gang and the townspeople besiege the trio

and the badly wounded Moyer. Hoppy and his pals surrender but Moyer revives long enough to confess the entire scheme. A fine brawl between Cassidy and Foster brings the film's action to a satisfying end. Jimmy plans to stay on as Faith Lawton's foreman but at the last moment he rides off to join Hoppy and California in new adventures.

Of which the next was **Riders of the Deadline** (1943), budgeted at about $106,000 and directed by Lesley Selander with all the flair Western lovers had come to expect from him. The screenplay, again by Bennett Cohen, was actually a close rewrite of the script for an earlier B Western, **The Desert Bandit** (Republic, 1941), which had starred Don "Red" Barry and had been directed by George Sherman. Cohen had been credited both as author of the Barry picture's original story and as co-author of its screenplay. With the exception of one new name, the technical credits were as usual: Rachmil as associate producer, Harlan behind the cameras, first-timer

William Boyd, Russell Hayden and Britt Wood are ready for action in this publicity still for **Hidden Gold** (1940, Paramount).

Walter Hannemann as film editor under Lewis' supervision, Talbot as music director. The generous budget enabled Selander to hire a huge number of extras for the picture and to make full use of them in the grand-scale action sequences. The small army of outlaws was led by two actors new to the series, William Halligan and Anthony Warde, and the female lead went to another new-comer, Frances Woodward. Young Richard Crane, who had a small but significant part as a novice Texas Ranger, later transferred to the small screen and the interplanetary branch of the same service when in the early 1950s he starred in TV's incredibly bad science-fiction series *Rocky Jones, Space Ranger*. Other roles in **Riders of the Deadline** were taken by veterans of recent Cassidy pictures including Herbert Rawlinson from Selander's **Lost Canyon** as a ranger captain, Hugh Prosser from the same abysmal film as a crooked deputy, and Robert Mitchum as the gang's top gunhand. It was Mitchum's last performance in the series, and his character name

Drago may have been intended as a tip of the ten-gallon hat to the novelist Harry Sinclair Drago whose books had been adapted into four Harry Sherman-produced Westerns of the early Forties.

As the film opens, young Tim Mason (Richard Crane) is being inducted into the Texas Rangers, the ceremony being witnessed by his sister Sue (Frances Woodward) and fellow rangers Hoppy, Jimmy and California. But during Tim's first night patrolling the border with Mexico, he's approached by Gunner Madigan (Anthony Warde), owner of a trailside cantina and second-in-command of a smuggling ring. Madigan threatens to have the bank foreclose the mortgage on the Mason ranch unless Tim agrees to look the other way when the wagons full of contraband cross the border. The chief of the smugglers is banker Simon Crandall (William Halligan), and high in the chain of command is deputy sheriff Martin (Hugh Prosser).

The next day Tim intercepts a wagonload of illegal goods, refuses to let it pass, and is slugged

William Boyd wants some answers from George Anderson in this scene from **Hidden Gold** (1940, Paramount).

by gunman Nick Drago (Robert Mitchum). Further along the trail the wagon is intercepted by Hoppy, Jimmy and California, its driver is mortally wounded in a running gunbattle and Drago and the other smugglers are chased away. Before he dies, the wagon driver implicates Tim Mason---who refuses to talk, is arrested and put in jail. Hoppy agrees to help the young ranger and promises Sue that her brother will never go on trial. He rides into town to confer with Tim in his cell, and the smugglers become afraid that he'll talk and work out a murder plot similar to that of the corrupt sheriff in Cohen's earlier Cassidy script, **False Colors**. Deputy Martin unlocks Tim's cell, shoots him down in cold blood as an escaping prisoner and plants a gun in the dead boy's hand. Grieving over her brother's body, Sue remembers Hoppy's promise and accuses him of having given Tim the gun.

At a departmental hearing, Cassidy is kicked out of the Rangers. He slaps the face of Captain Jennings (Herbert Rawlinson), storms out of town,

starts hanging out at Madigan's cantina and bad-mouthing the government service. Before long Madigan invites Hoppy to join the gang. Meanwhile, banker Crandall arranges with Sue to have the bank operate the Mason ranch rather than foreclose, his aim being to use a large barn on the property as a storehouse for contraband.

Madigan assigns Cassidy and Drago to sneak into the ranger station after dark and hijack the wagonload of goods Hoppy had captured earlier in the film, but Drago slugs Cassidy in the ranger stable and escapes with the wagon, leaving Hoppy to be captured. At this point we are let in on the not terribly well kept secret that Cassidy's expulsion from the Rangers was a put-up job, designed to get him invited to join the gang. Captain Jennings lets Hoppy escape and return to Madigan's cantina, where in a slam-bang brawl he gets even with Drago for leaving him behind.

Sue Mason learns that her barn is being used as a smugglers' warehouse and is captured and locked up in an outbuilding behind the cantina.

210

Russell Hayden supports Minor Watson as William Boyd, Lee Phelps, Eddie Dean and Britt Wood are ready for trouble in this publicity still for **Hidden Gold** (1940, Paramount).

Hoppy sneaks away, releases her, and realizes from her story that Crandall must be the brains behind the smuggling. He sends Sue to bring a troop of Rangers to the ranch but is caught by Madigan and Drago before he can make his own escape. The gang take Cassidy along as their prisoner and ride to clean out the Mason barn, setting the stage for the epic chase scene that climaxes the film. Hoppy breaks away from the outlaws, joins the approaching Ranger column and a wild pursuit begins, full of running inserts and tumbling stunt riders and backed up by rousing music. Deputy Martin's wagon crashes during the chase and with his last breath he admits that his boss is Crandall. Hoppy heads into town for a confrontation with the banker, an imaginatively directed gunfight around the teller's cage. With the gang rounded up, Hoppy and Jimmy and California gallop into the sunset.

George Archainbaud took over the reins on the next Cassidy, **Texas Masquerade** (1943), from a screenplay by newcomer Jack Lait Jr. and old hand Norman Houston, a magnificent blend of slambang action, powerful story, comic skits and social consciousness. With its extreme long shots and its climax in a desert of joshua trees, the picture's visual style unmistakably belongs to Archainbaud, and even its plot betrays certain resemblances to the director's previous **False Colors**: in both films someone impersonates the part owner of a valuable ranch managed by a woman and menaced by a fancy-suited Establishment figure with the local lawman in his pocket, although in **Texas Masquerade** the impostor is not a badguy but Hoppy himself. Archainbaud divided the cast more or less evenly between familiar and unfamiliar faces: Don Costello as a saloonkeeper with a penchant for practical jokes, Mady Correll as the female lead and Nelson Leigh as the young man Hoppy impersonates were balanced by Francis McDonald as a vengeful gunman, **Border Patrol**'s Russell Simpson as a memorable "brains heavy," and J. Farrell MacDonald as a victimized rancher. Lewis J. Rachmil,

Russell Hayden is ready for Walter Long and Raphael Bennett in this scene from **Hidden Gold** (1940, Paramount).

Russell Harlan, Walter Hannemann, Carrol Lewis and Irvin Talbot performed their usual offscreen functions.

As the film opens, outlaw Sam Nolan (Francis McDonald) rolls a boulder down on the road and halts a stagecoach carrying James Corwin (Nelson Leigh), a young lawyer from Boston. Corwin jumps the bandit, who ends the excellently directed fistfight between them by shooting and wounding the young man. He's about to finish Corwin off when Cassidy comes upon the scene and saves the lawyer's life by putting a bullet in Nolan's gun hand. The captured outlaw swears to get even someday. Examining Corwin's papers, Hoppy learns that he was on his way to the small Texas town of Glenby. While Corwin recuperates at the Bar 20, Cassidy takes over his mission.

The Glenby area has been terrorized for months by a band of Night Riders whose signal call is the howl of a coyote and whose base is an eerily beautiful desert of joshua trees known as Satan's Garden. Most of the local ranchers are near bank-

rupt and heavily in debt to scheming lawyer J.K. Trimble (Russell Simpson). Jimmy and California have preceded Hoppy to the area and taken cowhands' jobs on the Lazy W, which is jointly owned by Corwin and his lovely cousin Virginia Curtis (Mady Correll). On their first visit to town Jimmy and California are treated to some rough practical joking by saloonkeeper Ace Maxson (Don Costello), who invites them to quit their jobs and leave the territory.

At this juncture Cassidy enters the saloon, sporting a snow-white suit that signals to us that once again he's posing as a bumbling dude from the East. In fruity polysyllables he proclaims he is attorney James Corwin from "Ḅahston the capital of culchah," and Maxson loses no time in humiliating the stranger by shooting at his feet and making him dance a jig. Virginia, who has never seen Corwin before but has come to town to pick him up, hears the gunfire and furiously breaks up the fandango. Hoppy motions to Jimmy and California to keep mum about his masquerade.

William Boyd and Russell Hayden lead a posse in this action scene from **Stagecoach War** (1940, Paramount).

Before he leaves for the ranch, Trimble takes him aside, offers to buy his half-interest in the Lazy W and asks him to press Virginia to sell her share as well. The road to the ranch takes Hoppy, his pals and Virginia through Satan's Garden, which is on Lazy W property. After some fine comic byplay in which Cassidy acts the useless weakling and Virginia treats him with utter contempt, Hoppy makes a date with his sidekicks to explore the Garden next morning.

During their inspection Cassidy dismounts, wanders off alone and stumbles into a quicksand-like bog, from which he emerges covered with a black gunk that he recognizes as oil. Al and Jeff (Pierce Lyden and John Merton), two gunmen skulking in the Garden, take some shots at Cassidy but he manages to get the drop on them. Virginia rides up and identifies the men as Lazy W hands, and they glibly explain that they hadn't met "Corwin" yet and mistook him for a bandit. After a delightful "bahth" back at the ranch, Hoppy has a long talk with Virginia and betrays such total

ignorance of Corwin family matters that she accuses him of being a fake. When he explains why he's impersonating her cousin, Virginia opens up to him and reveals that Trimble, who's been buying up the property of the Night Riders' victims at rock-bottom prices, must be behind the gang's raids.

The next day, wearing Western togs that had belonged to Virginia's dead father, Cassidy rides out to visit neighboring rancher John Martindale (J. Farrell MacDonald), who's been hard hit by the Night Riders. It's the same day that Trimble has picked to send out fat Marshal Rowbottom (Robert McKenzie) and vicious deputy Lew Sykes (Bill Hunter) to evict the Martindales from their spread. During the eviction Sykes knocks down Martindale's wife Emily (June Terry Pickrell), and old John draws his gun and kills the deputy in self-defense. Shortly after Rowbottom races in terror off the Martindale ranch, Hoppy and his pals arrive. While the obese marshal is reporting to Trimble and Maxson, Martindale happens to

213

William Boyd prevents a fight between Harvey Stephens and Russell Hayden in this scene from **Stagecoach War** (1940, Paramount).

mention to Cassidy the "black gumbo" all over his property, and Hoppy realizes that the whole area is rich in oil deposits. Maxson leads a mob to the ranch to lynch Martindale, but Cassidy uses his sure-fire marksmanship to chase the party away without blowing his cover. "We have shooting galleries in Bahston," he explains. Knowing that Martindale will be put on trial for Sykes' death, Hoppy offers his services as defense counsel.

Not long before the date set for trial, the town of Glenby is visited by none other than Sam Nolan, who has broken out of prison and is looking for dirty work. Maxson hires him to replace the dead Sykes on the Night Riders. Meanwhile in front of the courthouse, Trimble initiates one of the funniest sequences in any Cassidy picture when he tests the legal expertise of "Corwin" by challenging him to define a replevin. At first hemming and hawing for comic effect, Hoppy proceeds to deliver a letter-perfect longwinded definition (which he later explains to Jimmy and California by reminding them of a replevin suit that had once

been filed against the Bar 20), and caps it with a hint to Trimble that he knows there's oil on the area ranches. During this conversation Nolan steps into the street, sees "Corwin" in the distance and recognizes his archenemy.

Trimble and Maxson assemble the Night Riders in Satan's Garden and send them out with Nolan to raid the Lazy W. Hoppy is spending the night going over the evidence he's accumulated against Trimble, preparing for a showdown in the morning when the real Jim Corwin is due to arrive. When the Riders attack the ranch, Cassidy sends Virginia away with the evidence but is himself captured alive. Nolan is about to put a bullet through Hoppy's gun hand---"so that we'll be twins," he sneers---when Cassidy turns the tables and kills Nolan, then barricades himself in the house and starts a gunbattle with the gang outside. It's the classic siege climax, resolved as usual when Jimmy, California, Jim Corwin and a huge posse storm onto the scene and attack the Night Riders, a classic battle which Archainbaud directs

Britt Wood and William Boyd have the saloon covered in this publicity still for **Stagecoach War** (1940, Paramount).

superbly. Finally the outlaws retreat to Satan's Garden where Trimble and Maxson are waiting for them, and a mammoth chase sequence ensues and Hoppy and his posse ride off in pursuit. The chase climaxes in an epic battle among the joshua trees, filmed mainly in extreme long shots so that we are keenly aware of the huge cast Archainbaud is manipulating. Maxson is killed in the fighting and Hoppy shoots Trimble off his horse as the lawyer tries to escape. The wounded gang leader lurches on foot into the depths of the Garden and meets a horrible but richly deserved death in the oil bog. With Virginia and the real Corwin both reunited and fabulously wealthy, Hoppy and his pals return to the Bar 20. "With all the things you do for others," Virginia tells him, "you want nothing for yourself."

Texas Masquerade was a marvelous picture, the last Cassidy in which Boyd posed as a milquetoast from the East and one of the best in the whole series. Its successor was even better, a rousing Lesley Selander actionfest filmed in the scenic High Sierras and pitting economic exploiters against a community of share-and-share-alike timber cutters. The elements of **Lumberjack** (1944) are borrowed from earlier Selander Cassidys---the murdered man's widow whom Hoppy saves from killer capitalists is reminiscent of the 1938 classic **Bar 20 Justice**, the forest setting and sabotage-the-lumber-camp plot are recycled from 1941's **Riders of the Timberline**---but are fused together into a new and spectacular adventure. Herbert Rawlinson, who had been in **Lost Canyon, Colt Comrades** and **Riders of the Deadline**, returned this time as Buck Peters, which made him the final actor to take the part during "Pop" Sherman's nine years producing the series. Newcomer Ellen Hall portrayed the last and perhaps loveliest of the imperious boss ladies who popped up so often in Selander's Cassidy films, and Ethel Wales, who had played Buck Peters' fussy old-maid sister way back in 1935's **Bar 20 Rides Again**, came back for one more reprise. Douglass Dumbrille

215

Russell Hayden and William Boyd protect a wounded J. Farrell MacDonald in this scene from **Stagecoach War** (1940, Paramount).

and Francis McDonald made a magnificent pair of nattily attired Eisenstein capitalists, with series veteran Hal Taliaferro as their chief enforcer. Screenplay credit was shared by old hand Norman Houston and newcomer Barry Shipman. Rachmil, Harlan and Talbot carried on respectively as associate producer, cinematographer and music director, with Fred W. Berger editing under Carrol Lewis' supervision. The picture was budgeted at about $115,000, and Selander put every penny of it to work.

As the film opens, Buck Peters (Herbert Rawlinson) and Hoppy and his pals have witnessed the marriage of Buck's beautiful and iron-willed daughter Julie (Ellen Hall) to land-poor Ben Jordan (John Whitney). Right after the ceremony, Jordan is killed and Buck wounded by Taggart (Hal Taliaferro) and another gunman, who steal a satchel from Jordan's body and race off, pursued by Hoppy and Jimmy. Taggart escapes but Cassidy kills the second assassin after a wild chase and recovers the satchel---which contains an official notice that Jordan's timberland outside the High Sierras town of Pinerock is about to be auctioned off at a sheriff's sale because of delinquent taxes. It seems that Jordan had raised the money to pay the back taxes and was killed to stop him from doing so. Hoppy, Jimmy and California, along with Julie and Buck's fussbudget sister Abbie (Ethel Wales), set out for Pinerock with the cash. All the way to the distant town they are shadowed by Taggart.

They arrive just in time to pay the taxes and prevent Sheriff Miles (Jack Rockwell) from selling the timberland to Daniel Keefer (Douglass Dumbrille) and Clyde Fenwick (Francis McDonald), the suave businessmen who are behind the murder of Ben Jordan. When Julie refuses to sell them the property, they manipulate her into entering the logging business herself and contract to purchase the timber she will cut, provided she hires Taggart and his men as her work crew. The Jordan land has been occupied for years by a community of penniless squatters led by Big Joe Williams

216

Britt Wood and William Boyd listen attentively to Russell Hayden in this scene from **Stagecoach War** (1940, Paramount).

(Charles Morton), and for no compelling reason except capitalists' inborn hatred of the proletariat, Keefer and Fenwick have Taggart and his gang deputized and order them to evict the squatters. With fists, clubs and bullwhips the new deputies attack the members of the community who have come to town for the tax auction, but Big Joe and his comrades, men and women alike, fight back in a monumental brawl, assisted by Hoppy and his pals. The melee ends when Julie allows the squatters another month on the property. Although she orders Cassidy back to the Bar 20, Hoppy and California decide to stay on at the squatters' encampment and keep an eye on the situation. Jimmy meanwhile is sent to fetch Buck Peters in the hope that he'll be able to identify Taggart as Ben Jordan's killer.

In what may be a parody of union labor, the Taggart crew spend their time at the logging site drinking, playing cards, wrecking equipment, anything but cutting timber. Stymied by their failure to get the lumber moving, imperious Julie still refuses to ask Hoppy for help, although Fenwick is worried enough by Cassidy's presence that he unsuccessfully tries to shoot Hoppy on the trail. When Julie applies to Keefer and Fenwick for more time to fulfill her contract, they point out a clause in the fine print under which she forfeits the land if she doesn't deliver the logs on time. Julie rides out to the logging site for a furious confrontation with Taggart, who responds in fine Nazi fashion by flogging her with his trusty bull-whip---until Hoppy storms onto the scene and beats him senseless.

Having learned to take Cassidy's advice, Julie fires the Taggart crew and replaces them with Big Joe and the squatters, who come roaring into the campsite swinging their axes and belting out the song of the Fighting Forty from Selander's **Riders of the Timberline**. A montage of vigorous tree-felling scenes shows that with the help of these stout-hearted sons of the people the contract quota is well on the way to being met, but then comes a parallel montage of fire and

217

Britt Wood holds Rad Robinson and his gang at bay while William Boyd talks to Russell Hayden in this scene from **Stagecoach War** (1940, Paramount).

explosion scenes showing Taggart and company sabotaging the operation. Adversity only causes the squatters to redouble their efforts. In a last-ditch attempt to shut down the camp, the Taggart crew invades in full force with guns, clubs and axes, and the second of this film's fifty-stuntman mass brawls is launched. The arrival of Jimmy with Buck Peters and the men of the Bar 20 adds another dozen or so fighters to the battle. Taggart and his gang are captured, and as Keefer tries to escape Hoppy chases him along the edge of a dam and, after a spectacular one-on-one involving fisticuffs, rifles and a charge of dynamite, sends the evil capitalist to a gruesome death. Julie turns over the timberland to the squatters who own it by right of the sweat of their brows, and the Fighting Forty theme is reprised over the end titles as Cassidy and his pals head for home.

It was George Archainbaud's turn at bat for the next Cassidy, **Mystery Man** (1944), and it turned out to be another classic, full of the director's extreme long shots and desert scenery,

plus an exceptionally strong female lead and one of the best adversary figures in the series. Archainbaud and veteran scriptwriter J. Benton Cheney tried to create a master criminal who in some respects would be Cassidy's mirror image, and the effort is surprisingly successful. Most of the actors had appeared in previous Cassidys--- **Texas Masquerade**'s Don Costello as mastermind Bud Trilling, Eleanor Stewart from **Pirates on Horseback** and **Riders of the Timberline** as the take-charge woman who saves Hoppy's bacon, and such old reliables as Francis McDonald and Jack Rockwell. The simple episodic structure of the film is mainly an excuse for Archainbaud to stage several pitched battle scenes with what look like a hundred or more extras. It was almost as if the moviemakers were piling on the action as a way of apologizing for the often unexciting Cassidys of a few years before. Lewis J. Rachmil, Russell Harlan, Fred W. Berger, Carrol Lewis and Irvin Talbot did what they usually did out of camera range.

218

Russell Hayden has his arm in a sling and William Boyd has on an unusual light colored shirt in this scene from **Three Men from Texas** (1940, Paramount).

Mystery Man boils down to a series of duels between Cassidy and outlaw leader Bud Trilling (Don Costello); who is notorious as a crime strategist and master of disguise. As the film opens, Hoppy, Jimmy, California and the Bar 20 wranglers are driving a herd of cattle to the distant Circle J ranch, whose owner, Tom Hanlon (Bob Burns), is to pay cash for them on delivery. Along the route of the drive is the town of Holbrook, and the newest visitor to the town is Trilling, whose natty suit and derby and specs and meek manner echo Hoppy's own dude impersonations in Archainbaud's **Texas Masquerade** and several earlier Cassidys. After Trilling has laid the groundwork, his gang ride into town like lightning and rob the bank. It's their bad luck that Hoppy, Jimmy and California come into Holbrook for supplies just as the outlaws are leaving town. Thus breaks out the first of the film's epic battles. Cassidy cuts off the gang's escape route by throwing up a wagon barricade across the main street, and the shootout spreads all through the

town. Jimmy gets into close combat with one of the robbers, who finds a gun and is about to shoot Jimmy when he's himself gunned down by lovely Diane Newhall (Eleanor Stewart). Trilling's chief henchman Bert Ragan (Francis McDonald) and several other gang members are captured alive, and when they refuse to tell where Trilling is they are thrown into a single jail cell and denied food or water. In his dude disguise, Trilling congratulates Hoppy on a job well done, then slips a gun into the cell. Ragan and the others break jail and race out of Holbrook with a posse on their heels. After an excellent chase sequence the outlaws elude the posse in the rocky desert country that seemed to be Archainbaud's spiritual home.

The next morning, having rejoined his men, Trilling decides to get even with Cassidy by stealing the herd bound for the Circle J. The outlaws follow the drive into Texas, awaiting the right moment, and strike one evening after the Bar 20 men have made camp. While the wranglers are enjoying a song from one of their comrades (Ozie

219

Russell Hayden, **William Boyd** and Andy Clyde (who joined the series as California Carlson with this film) have Glenn Strange and friends covered in this scene from **Three Men from Texas** (1940, Paramount).

Waters), Trilling's man Red (Pierce Lyden) sneaks in and stampedes their horses. Then while the herders are chasing their mounts the thieves make off with the cattle. Hoppy leaps on the nearest horse, follows the rustlers and the herd until they stop to rest, goes back and assembles his men and leads them to the gang's camp. Archainbaud stages another large-scale battle scene among the desert rocks, and though most of Trilling's men manage to escape, Cassidy and the Bar 20 crew recover the herd.

His second defeat makes Trilling even more determined to steal the cattle. This time he and his men pose as a sheriff and posse, ride boldly up to the herders along the trail, catch Hoppy and the others off guard and make prisoners of them all. Trilling takes Cassidy's identification papers, planning to deliver the herd to the Circle J himself, keep the purchase money and then steal and resell the cattle elsewhere. Some time after Trilling and the herd have pulled out, Hoppy manages to free himself under cover of loud singing by the Bar 20

hands. He overpowers the guards, releases his men and sets out once more after the herd. Red escapes and warns Trilling, who counters by riding into the nearest town, identifying himself as Cassidy, and asking Sheriff Sam Newhall (Forrest Taylor) for help in fighting off the notorious Trilling gang. The gullible lawman rides out with a posse and captures Hoppy and the Bar 20 crew along the trail without firing a shot. Cassidy is unable to convince the sheriff of the truth. The only one of his men not captured is California, who had fallen behind when his horse picked up a stone in its hoof. Seeing what has happened, California keeps low and follows the posse and prisoners into town.

Just as Sheriff Sam is herding the small army of prisoners into a single cell, echoing the earlier treatment of Trilling's gang, his daughter Diane enters the office and identifies Cassidy and his men as the heroes who broke up the Holcomb bank robbery. The idiot sheriff refuses to believe her or to stop the sale of the herd at the Circle J.

William Boyd disarms Dick Curtis in the publicity still for **Three Men from Texas** (1940, Paramount).

California tries to break his comrades out of jail but is less adept than Trilling at this art and succeeds only in getting locked up himself.

At this point Diane takes matters into her own hands. She sends out the jail guards on a false alarm, releases Hoppy and his men and races out of town with them, pursued by her father and a huge posse. What follows is another epic chase scene. Diane shows Cassidy a short cut to the Circle J but they reach the ranch just minutes after Hanlon has paid spot cash for the cattle to Trilling. Hoppy and his crew chase the gang while Diane roars off alone to lead her father's posse on a false trail. The chase climaxes with Trilling and his men being trapped in a box canyon and having to fight their way out. The two armies clash in their final battle amid awesome desert rock formations, a combat of which Archainbaud as usual takes a God's-eye view, using such extreme long shots that it's sometimes difficult to make out individual participants. The scene culminates in a superb cliff-edge gun duel between Cassidy and Trilling,

with the expected outcome. With Trilling dead, the money recovered and the thick-witted Sheriff Sam's reputation intact, Hoppy and his men return to the Bar 20.

The series' ninth season ended on a note of triumph with **Forty Thieves** (1944), directed by Selander in nine days' time and at a negative cost of almost $130,000. The screenplay by veteran Michael Wilson and newcomer Barney Kamins was almost devoid of dialogue (although its theme of illegitimate power overcome by armed resistance might have been taken by paranoids as vaguely Marxist), but so much the better: Selander filled in the empty spaces with several epic action sequences backed up by a new and excellent music score which was credited to Republic Pictures' ace composer Mort Glickman despite much of it being recognizably the work of Raoul Kraushaar. Douglass Dumbrille was back in an exceptionally strong role as an outlaw leader and Herbert Rawlinson as Buck Peters. Subordinate no-goods included such stalwarts of previous

221

Andy Clyde, William Boyd and Thornton Edwards are served by Esther Estrella in this scene from **Three Men from Texas** (1940, Paramount).

Cassidys as Glenn Strange, Hal Taliaferro, Jack Rockwell and Bob Kortman. Lovely Louise Currie was wasted in a tiny and, for Selander, most untypical part as a judge's daughter, and Kirk Alyn, who would soon be playing super-heroes himself in low-budget Columbia serials like **Superman** (1948) and **Blackhawk** (1953), did nicely as a weak-kneed saloonkeeper. Rachmil and Harlan closed out the season as associate producer and cinematographer, and Carrol Lewis did the honors in the editing booth.

In this film Hoppy is sheriff of Buffalo Buttes and running for re-election unopposed---until the arrival in town of Tad Hammond (Douglass Dumbrille), on parole after having been caught by Cassidy and having served five years in prison. Hammond persuades saloonkeeper Jerry Doyle (Kirk Alyn) to run against Hoppy. Then, in what seems to be a conscious reflection of labor union philosophy, Hammond assembles a huge mob of outlaws and organizes the feuding factions into a single gang with himself as its head. His plan is to rig the forthcoming election by sending out gunmen to stop the ranchers from coming into town on election day. Among those who are turned back at a river crossing are Buck Peters (Herbert Rawlinson) and the men of the Bar 20. A pitched battle breaks out between the cowhands and the vicious Garms brothers (Jack Rockwell and Bob Kortman) and their gang. Buck rides to town for Hoppy, who comes back and, in a fine action sequence, helps his comrades capture the Garms bunch. But when they return to town with their prisoners, Cassidy is outraged to discover that in his absence he's lost the election, thanks to some surreptitious ballot box stuffing by Doyle's cohort Ike Simmons (Glenn Strange). The new sheriff promptly appoints the entire Hammond gang his deputies as Hoppy, Jimmy and California reluctantly turn over their symbols of office to the outlaws who have become the law.

That night, during a wild celebration in Doyle's saloon, Hammond puts a $2000 price on Cassidy's head and his men play a hand of poker to

Wen Wright has William Boyd covered in this scene from **Three Men from Texas** (1940, Paramount).

see who will get first shot at the target. The game is interrupted by Hoppy, who stalks into the lion's den alone, faces down the saloonful of killers, gives the forty thieves twelve hours to leave town, and shoots his way out of the place without suffering a scratch. It was the end of a long process of evolution for the Cassidy character, from Mulford's dust-covered, lead-slinging ranch hand to one of the ultimate frontier superheroes, and Boyd was never more incredibly heroic than in this final appearance as Hoppy in a Harry Sherman-produced film.

The next morning, while studying the election documents with Judge Reynolds (Robert Frazer), Cassidy spots a printing defect on the Doyle ballots that proves they're counterfeit. With the noon deadline at hand, Hoppy goes out alone into the town's main street to make sure Hammond and his gang are leaving. Several of the outlaws are in ambush on rooftops and in doorways, waiting to kill Cassidy, but once again with minimal outside help Hoppy beats the odds. He faces down and outfights the army of evildoers and in another fine action sequence drives them out of town, receiving only a minor arm wound in the battle.

Afterwards Hoppy sends Jimmy and Judge Reynolds' daughter Katherine (Louise Currie) to the state capital with the evidence of election fraud. But the remnants of Hammond's gang pick just the stagecoach on which the two are traveling to hold up for a last haul before they leave the territory. Hammond captures Jimmy and Katherine after a wild chase, then sends a messenger to town with a note for Cassidy: ride out to the gang's camp alone or his friends will die. Instead of following orders Hoppy pulls a gun on the terrified Sheriff Doyle and forces him to come along on the ride. What Selander conceals from us until the last moment is that each man is wearing the clothes of the other, so that when Doyle in Cassidy's black outfit is riddled with bullets by the gang, we actually believe for a few seconds as we did in Selander's **Undercover Man** that Hoppy might be dead.

223

William Boyd draws on Dick Curtis and his cronies in this scene from **Three Men from Texas** (1940, Paramount).

Hoppy sneaks behind Hammond's position and opens fire from the rear, while at the same time Jimmy frees himself and starts shooting from another spot. It's two against a mob, but once again Hammond and his army turn tail and flee--- right into the waiting gunsights of Buck Peters and the men of the Bar 20. The abundant action climaxes with a great one-on-one between Cassidy and Hammond on a rope suspension bridge hundreds of feet above a river. With Hammond fallen to his death and the forty thieves destroyed, peace returns to Buffalo Springs and a spectacular picture comes to an end.

One of the other things that ended at this time was cinematographer Russell Harlan's work for the Sherman organization. After doing 44 Cassidy films in a row plus several of the Zane Grey and Richard Dix features, Harlan was on his own. Clearly there were no hard feelings on either side, for "Pop" brought Harlan back a few years later to handle the camerawork on the last two pictures he ever produced, **Ramrod** (1947) and **Four Faces West** (1948), both starring Joel McCrea. From the late Forties through the early Sixties, Harlan served as cinematographer for producer-director Howard Hawks on films like **Red River** (1948), **The Thing** (1951), **The Big Sky** (1952), **Land of the Pharaohs** (1955), **Rio Bravo** (1959) and **Hatari!** (1962), and for other directors on such pictures as **Gun Crazy** (1949), **The Blackboard Jungle** (1955), **Witness for the Prosecution** (1958) and **Hawaii** (1966). He died in 1974.

The end of the ninth season of Cassidys was also the end of Lesley Selander's tenure with Sherman. "I was out on my own again after nearly eight years," he said. "I had to find work and I started looking around." In no time at all he signed with Republic Pictures, and for the next three years he directed one programmer after another--- shoot-em-ups, mysteries, horror flicks, vest-pocket musicals, even a serial. He helmed some fine Republic Westerns with Gene Autry, Allan Lane and Monte Hale, but perhaps his best oaters

Trevor Bardette and Raphael Bennett have William Boyd at their mercy in this scene from **Doomed Caravan** (1941, Paramount).

for the studio were **Firebrands of Arizona** (1944), with Sunset Carson and Smiley Burnette, and **Phantom of the Plains** (1945), with Bill Elliott and Bobby (later Robert) Blake. Between 1948 and 1952 Selander worked primarily at RKO, turning out first-rate Tim Holt Westerns like **Guns of Hate** (1948) and **Brothers in the Saddle** (1949). During most of the Fifties he commuted between decently-budgeted color features like **War Paint** (United Artists, 1953) and **Arrow in the Dust** (Allied Artists, 1954) and 30-minute telefilms for Western and animal series like *Cowboy G-Men*, *Fury* and *Lassie*. His work in the Sixties was almost entirely in the realm of hour-long color telefilms for network series like *Laramie*. He retired late in that decade and died in 1979.

I never met Selander, but once, near the end of his life, I came close. I was in the Los Angeles area for a few days, was given the director's phone number by a mutual friend, and one morning decided to call him. As bad luck would

have it, I woke him up. But he didn't seem to mind and we had a nice conversation. I told him how much I'd admired his pictures. "They were adequate," he said. I wanted to take him to lunch, but my business was taking me one way that day and his was taking him another. Before my next trip to the west coast, he was dead.

The movies he made are his epitaph, but one of his reflections about them makes a good farewell to him also. "I liked doing them," he said. "I was paid for it, I knew what was expected of me, and did the best I could. I didn't know then, and I don't know now, how to work any other way."

I never met the man but I miss him.

225

' William Boyd is ready for action in this publicity still for **Doomed Caravan** (1941, Paramount).

Chapter Eleven

After nine seasons of devoting most of his time to producing Hopalong Cassidy movies, Harry Sherman wanted out. Since the switch to United Artists for distribution, he'd spent more on those pictures than any other producer or studio had ever done on series Westerns, and had made some of the finest films of their kind in the history of the genre. But they had all lost money. Sherman decided it was time to drop the Cassidy films and concentrate on what had become his number one priority, making a small number of generously budgeted, full-length "A" Westerns for an exclusively adult audience. At the end of the 1943-44 season he parted company with William Boyd.

A few years earlier, Boyd had told Sherman he was afraid that if the Hoppy pictures were ever terminated he wouldn't be given any other parts to play. It was a prophecy that turned out to be true. Everyone in the business agreed that Boyd had become typecast as Cassidy, and no one would let him play anything else. For two years Boyd lived on the road, touring with various circuses at $250 a week. Every so often he'd put out a few feelers, looking for financial backers who would subsidize his return to the screen as Hoppy. Finally, around the spring of 1946, he found a money man, a Hollywood promoter with the odd name of Toby Anguish, who saw potential profit in a deal with Boyd.

Anguish had dug up some investors willing to finance a new series of Cassidy pictures, but he needed Boyd's help in more than the obvious way. Even though "Pop" Sherman had stopped producing Hoppy films, he'd continued to pay Clarence E. Mulford a modest annual sum for movie rights to the Cassidy character. The Anguish group needed to buy those rights from Sherman before it could start production, and because Sherman and Boyd had worked together so long, Anguish believed that Boyd could negotiate a better price from Sherman than an outsider could. Reluctant to spend the rest of his career as a circus performer and lacking alternative ways to

get back in the picture business, Boyd agreed to be Anguish's front man and made contact with Sherman.

The old producer was convinced that Boyd's offer to buy movie rights to the Cassidy character was a joke. According to one account of the negotiations, he laughed in Boyd's face. Eventually however he made an offer that he thought the actor would have to refuse. For $250,000 cash he'd sell Boyd not only the right to make new Hoppy pictures but also the theatrical re-release rights to the 54 Cassidys Sherman had produced (except for the first half-dozen, which he'd already sold to another releasing organization). To Sherman's astonishment, Boyd accepted the proposition, a deal was finalized, and William Boyd Productions opened its doors for business. Sherman used the money to help finance the last two films he ever produced---**Ramrod** (1947) and **Four Faces West** (1948), both starring Joel McCrea---which were critical successes and box-office losers.

Meanwhile Toby Anguish was busy raising capital for the first Hoppy pictures under the logo of William Boyd Productions. By selling off the theatrical reissue rights on the earlier Cassidys to the independent distributor Film Classics, he raised enough money to go into production. When United Artists agreed to release the new Cassidy series, Boyd and Anguish assembled their team.

Boyd billed himself as executive producer, but to actually produce the new pictures he brought back Lewis J. Rachmil, the associate producer on the last few years' worth of Sherman Cassidys. To direct the new films he engaged the genial Frenchman George Archainbaud, who had helmed **Texas Masquerade**, **Mystery Man** and several other Hoppy classics. To serve as the cinematographer he brought in Mack (formerly .Max) Stengler, a seasoned veteran of low-budget picture making. To edit the films he contracted Fred W. Berger, who had cut some of the final Cassidys under the Sherman regime. And to provide the agitato background score which was

Martin Garralaga listens as William Boyd, Jose Luis Tortosa and Russell Hayden hold a conference in this scene from **Doomed Caravan** (1941, Paramount).

an absolute necessity in a series of shoot-em-ups, Boyd commissioned the prolific Raoul Kraushaar (1908-   ), who fulfilled his contract by recycling some of the rousing themes he'd written for Republic Pictures earlier in the Forties. (It remains a mystery why, on the credits of the Boyd-produced Cassidys, the music is always credited to others like David Chudnow and Ralph Stanley, never to Kraushaar.)

When it came to recruiting actors for the parts of Hoppy's sidekicks, Boyd played in luck. Andy Clyde had found precious little work in pictures since Sherman had terminated the Cassidys, and he was happy to sign on again as that cantankerous buffoon California Carlson. Casting the role of Hoppy's younger pal took a lot more time and effort. One day while Boyd, Rachmil and Archainbaud were still searching for the right actor, a starry-eyed youth named Rand Brooks (1918-   ) came into the studio to help a friend deliver a washing machine that was going to be used as a prop. Brooks had played small juvenile

roles in pictures since 1938, and was best known of course for his part as Vivien Leigh's short-lived first husband in **Gone with the Wind** (1939), but since his return from World War II service he hadn't found any work in Hollywood. While at the studio that day he ran into J. Benton Cheney, an old friend who had written the scripts for a number of the Sherman-produced Cassidys. "Boyd needs a juvenile who can ride a horse," Cheney told Brooks, who lost no time having his agent make him an appointment to test for the part. Boyd offered him the role of Lucky almost at once.

Not long afterwards, Brooks happened to run into Russell Hayden and told him that he was about to take over the part of Hoppy's young protegé. "I wouldn't do that role again for $5,000 a week," Hayden told him, with the implication that if Hayden had found it tough to work with Boyd, Brooks was likely to find it even tougher now that Boyd was not only the star but the executive producer as well.

228

William Boyd and Georgia Hawkins in a publicity still for **Doomed Caravan** (1941, Paramount).

The shooting schedules for the new Cassidys were designed for maximum economy and for Boyd's personal convenience. The pictures were shot in six days apiece, with Boyd's scenes scheduled one right after another so that he could get away from the set as soon as possible. The other actors put in twelve-to-fourteen-hour days. The budgets were kept ultra-tight, with no time and no money for more than the barest minimum of what was supposed to be the main ingredient of Westerns: action. For example, at the climax of **Dangerous Venture** (1947), the fourth of the twelve Cassidys under William Boyd Productions, it looks as if a fine brawl might erupt between Rand Brooks and the outlaw leader played by hulking Harry Cording, but then Cording throws up his hands and surrenders before a single punch is thrown. "Why didn't you fight him?" I whispered to Brooks, who was sitting next to me watching the picture at a Western film fair. "Are you kidding?" he whispered back. "It would have cost money!"

It's no wonder that these last dozen Cassidys are not ranked in the same league with the excellent Hoppy films produced by Harry Sherman. But neither are they total disasters. When the outdoors is used at all, the desert landscapes are stunning. Boyd generates a fine camaraderie with Brooks and Clyde, and the supporting casts include a few veterans of the Sherman era like Earle Hodgins and Francis McDonald and Herbert Rawlinson as well as relative newcomers to Westerns like Elaine Riley, Don Haggerty and Leonard Penn. Although the scripts are unimpressive as Westerns, the writers made some at least halfway interesting stabs at incorporating elements from the *films noir* and series detective movies of the Forties. And one of the Boyd dozen defied all expectations and turned out to be on a par with the better Cassidys of the Sherman regime.

The first of the new Hoppy exploits wasn't quite that good, but was a crisply watchable item featuring the magnificent desert scenery that was George Archainbaud's signature image and an

Minna Gombell introduces William Boyd to Georgia Hawkins in this scene from **Doomed Caravan** (1941, Paramount).

abundance of good chase sequences. **The Devil's Playground** (1946), directed by Archainbaud from a screenplay by newcomer Ted Wilson, opens with Cassidy, Lucky and California crossing the barren wasteland of the title, on their way back to the Bar 20. Stopping for the night at a line shack, they find a horse outside and bloodstains inside. They search the area and find a wounded woman (Elaine Riley) who will give them neither her name nor any information about herself. After bandaging her arm, Hoppy leaves Lucky and California to watch over her and rides back into the Devil's Playground to investigate. In the desert he encounters a group of riders led by Judge Morton (Robert Elliott), who claims that the wounded woman is his mentally unstable daughter. Cassidy believes him and leads the group back to the line shack. One man, a dwarf known as Shorty (John George), is left behind, and stabbed in the back by the judge's henchman Roberts (Francis McDonald) just as the party sets out. But when Cassidy and the others reach the

shack they find that the wounded woman has slipped past Lucky and California and disappeared. Judge Morton's rage at this development provokes Hoppy's suspicions.

Cassidy, Lucky and California ride into the nearest town and learn that Morton never had a daughter. They also discover that one of the people Morton sent to prison was the notorious Curly Evans, the loot from whose robberies has never been found. But the fat and lazy sheriff (Joseph J. Greene) refuses to get involved in the situation, and Hoppy and his companions ride back into the desert. At what had been Morton's campsite they find Shorty's body and discover that before dying he had drawn in the sand a map which Cassidy copies on a scrap of paper. This time when they ride into town, the sheriff reluctantly agrees to form a posse and help them go after Morton and his gang. After a well-directed three-pronged chase sequence across the desert, Hoppy and the others capture all the killers. But Judge Morton concocts a ridiculous argument to

Pat J. O'Brien listens as William Boyd makes a point to Raphael Bennett in this scene from **Doomed Caravan** (1941, Paramount).

the effect that Shorty, a dwarf who was stabbed in the back, was killed in self-defense during a maniacal fit; and the lard-bellied sheriff locks up not only the Morton outfit but Hoppy and his pals too, until he can straighten out everyone's story.

From the window of his jail cell Cassidy sees the wounded woman ride into town, and guesses that she came to have a doctor treat her arm wound. He and his pals use the old fake stomach-ache trick to break jail, then take out after the young woman. Hoppy's hunch is that she's headed for the spot marked on Shorty's map, and they go back into the Devil's Playground on that assumption, cut across her trail, and catch her after a rousing chase sequence complete with running inserts. When they tell her about Shorty's murder, she explains that she and Shorty had a map showing where the bank robber Curly Evans hid his loot, and that Morton wants the money for himself.

Cassidy and his pals bring the woman back to town against her will and explain the situation to the sheriff---who waddles back to the jail, releases Judge Morton and his gang, and agrees to help him lock up the woman. The duel of words between the Morton and Cassidy groups is abruptly terminated when the judge and his men pull guns and escape out of town with the woman's map. Hoppy, Lucky and California put away the tubby sheriff in one of his own cells and, with the help of Cassidy's copy of Shorty's map, take out after the gang. Knowing the Devil's Playground better than Morton does, Hoppy and his party beat the gang to the crucial spot on the map. But on their arrival they find a stranger digging up the loot, and when they subdue him he turns out to be none other than Curly Evans (Ned Young), who had escaped from prison to return the stolen gold to the bank. Morton and his gang reach the spot, and Cassidy, Lucky, California, Evans and the woman race away with the loot. A long and exciting pursuit sequence ends up with Hoppy and his party besieged in the line shack where they'd stopped at the beginning of the film

Minna Gombell walks beside William Boyd and Topper as Georgia Hawkins ignores Russell Hayden in this scene from **Doomed Caravan** (1941, Paramount).

and almost out of bullets. It's the same situation Lesley Selander used again and again in the Cassidys he directed during the Sherman era, but this time the denouement is hopelessly tame and flat as Hoppy and his allies surrender, create a split-second diversion and get the drop on the gang in the blink of an eye. As he and his pals say their goodbyes and start back for the Bar 20, the young woman of the tale confesses to a love-smitten Lucky that she's Curly Evans' wife.

This not-half-bad effort was followed by the ridiculous **Fools' Gold** (1947), directed by Archainbaud from a screenplay by Doris Schroeder, who had been absent from the series since its first season, 1935-36, when either alone or with a collaborator she had written all the scripts for the initial half-dozen Cassidys. Her return was far from triumphant, for the plot was full of holes and featured contrivances like a mad-scientist outlaw leader and an idiot black servant on the Bar 20. The excellent outdoor locations and Kraushaar's background music helped a little, but

nothing could save this one.

Hoppy's old friend Colonel Jed Landy (Forbes Murray) visits the ranch and asks Cassidy to save his son Bruce (Stephen Barclay), who has deserted the army and joined an outlaw gang holed up in the Twin Buttes. It's typical of this picture that we're never told what was behind the young man's desertion. Hoppy dudes himself up in the Tex Riley outfit which had first come into the series in Schroeder's and Gerald Geraghty's 1935 script for **Bar 20 Rides Again**, then takes off on his mission. Again for no earthly reason, he decides not only to leave Lucky and California behind but not even to tell them where he's going. However, he does confide (though God alone knows why) in Speed (Fred "Snowflake" Toones), the Bar 20's feets-do-yo'-stuff handyman, and when his pals pry the information from this discredit to his race, they take off in Hoppy's wake.

Cassidy rides into outlaw country carrying identification as an army captain but calling

Wen Wright and Henry Wills look to William Boyd and Russell Hayden for guidance about the corpse in this scene from **Doomed Caravan** (1941, Paramount).

himself a cattle buyer. After encounters along the trail with gang members Sandler (Earle Hodgins) and Duke (Harry Cording), he stops at the Twin Buttes Inn, which is run by lovely Jessie Dixon (Jane Randolph). At this point we learn that Jessie is in love with Bruce Landy and wants him to leave the gang, but he is under the thumb of the gang leader, her father Professor Dixon (Robert Emmett Keane), a mad scientist who keeps a collection of deadly spiders in his cabin on a hill above the Inn. In order to keep watch on the so-called Captain Thompson, Dixon orders Jessie to give him a room. No sooner is Cassidy settled at the Inn than Lucky and California show up, posing as itinerant peddlers. That evening, Hoppy overhears fragments of a conversation suggesting that the next day the gang will steal $200,000 from the army. Meanwhile Jessie lets Bruce know that a Captain Thompson has followed him into the Buttes, but Dixon catches them together and forces Bruce at gunpoint to continue with the robbery plan. That night the professor plants a

tarantula in Hoppy's room, but Cassidy pulverizes the insect just as it's about to bite Lucky.

The next day Hoppy is less fortunate. Just as he's explaining who he is to Jessie and Bruce, he's caught by Dixon and his hulking henchman Blackie (William "Wee Willie" Davis). Lucky and California happen along just in time to save Cassidy from a watery grave but are themselves captured by Duke right after Hoppy's escape. Cassidy meanwhile trails Dixon to his cabin in the crags, where he finds not only the spider collection but equipment for gold-plating copper bars. In a burst of intuition he understands the outlaws' plan: dressed as cavalrymen, they're going to present fake orders, take over the escort duty when the next army gold shipment comes through, substitute gold-plated copper bars and turn these over to the real escort detail further down the trail. But then Hoppy is recaptured by the professor, who ties him and his pals in the cabin and sets loose his spiders to finish them off. Cassidy turns the tables and subdues Dixon, who

Wen Wright, Chick Hannon, Henry Wills, **William Boyd** and Russell Hayden all seem to be interested in something above in this scene from **Doomed Caravan** (1941, Paramount).

is killed off-camera by his pets a few minutes later. Hoppy, Lucky and California race to stop the robbery. They catch up with Duke and the gang after they've been given the gold but before they can make the switch, and open fire on them. Bruce Landy takes advantage of the gun battle to come over to Cassidy's side and help him win the less than pulse-pounding confrontation with which the picture's action ends. Bruce goes back to what he's been promised will be very light punishment as Cassidy and his pals return to the Bar 20.

If **Fools' Gold** had its inspiration in el cheapo horror films, the roots of the season's third Cassidy clearly lay in the B detective pictures and old-dark-house thrillers with which the Forties abounded. **Unexpected Guest** (1947), directed by Archainbaud from a screenplay by unit newcomer Ande Lamb, is no great shakes either as a mystery or a Western, but the conjunction of the two genres at least made for something out of the ordinary rut. On their way to the Box O ranch,

where California is to attend the reading of the will of his distant cousin Hiram Baxter, Hoppy and Lucky and California are ambushed by a masked and caped figure looking very much like the original pulp-magazine version of The Shadow. No one is hurt, and Hoppy and his pals continue on to the ranch, where in short order they meet a motley crew of suspects. They are: David J. Potter (John Parrish), attorney and executor of Hiram's estate; Matilda Hackett (Una O'Connor), spooky housekeeper and self-styled confidant of spirit voices; Ralph Baxter (Ned Young), Hiram's stepson, who owes a small fortune in gambling debts to saloonkeeper Matt Ogden (Robert H. Williams); Joshua Colter (Earle Hodgins), enigmatic handyman; Ruth Baxter (Patricia Tate), Hiram's niece, whose father, Tom Baxter, had owned the Box O until his apparent suicide; and Hiram's blowhard cousin Phineas Phipps (Joel Friedkin).

Hoppy, Lucky and California are installed in Hiram's bedroom, which Matilda claims is haunted by spirits. After dinner Cassidy

234

William Boyd and Russell Hayden have Pat J. O'Brien, Raphael Bennett and Trevor Bardette covered in this scene from **Doomed Caravan** (1941, Paramount).

exchanges his black monkeysuit for the light gray outfit he'll wear for the rest of the picture, and the guests at the Box O assemble in the study for the reading of the will. Potter explains that the will of Tom Baxter left his estate to seven people---his brother Hiram, California, Matilda, Ralph, Joshua, Ruth and Phineas---and that Hiram's will leaves his estate to the other six, with the proviso that any of them who dies within a certain period of time forfeits his or her share. Potter claims that Hiram's estate is almost worthless, but Hoppy begins to suspect crooked business when he learns that Hiram's account books are missing. Potter offers to buy the Box O but the legatees split 3-3 on whether to sell. Suddenly all the lights in the study go out, and when they're restored Phineas Phipps is found dead. Everyone wanders around the ranch house acting like a suspect in a Charlie Chan movie, and by the time they reassemble the corpse has vanished. During the prowling around, Hoppy overhears Matilda telling Ruth about a message from the spirits, ordering Ruth to ride out to a certain hidden canyon in the morning, and also overhears a ghostly-sounding voice speaking to Matilda in the Baxter family graveyard.

The next morning Cassidy follows Ruth to the canyon and is just in time to save her from a camouflaged pit, dug there by the Shadow figure to kill her. Later that day, Hoppy and California stumble on a secret oil well on the Box O but are driven away by Ogden and some gunmen. That evening The Shadow prowls again, spying on Hoppy from a secret passage running through the ranch house walls as Cassidy searches the study and finds the missing account books. Meanwhile Ralph Baxter is waiting in the master bedroom to confess something to Hoppy, but The Shadow murders him from a hidden peephole into the room, concealed behind the eye in a buffalo head on the wall. When this new corpse is discovered, Potter accuses Lucky of the killing, and Cassidy's pal makes a break for freedom.

Later that night, Hoppy reconstructs the

Stanley Andrews and William Boyd takes a gun away from Sarah Padden. James Seay and Eddy Waller are in the background in this scene from **In Old Colorado** (1941, Paramount).

trajectory of the bullet that killed Ralph, figures out that it came from the buffalo head, and escapes from the bedroom just in time to avoid being shot himself from the same vantage point. He goes downstairs and invites David Potter back into the master bedroom for a conference, accuses the lawyer of embezzling from the estate and manipulates the situation so that The Shadow will have to try to kill Potter too. The attorney bolts out of the room, runs into the study and through the secret passage where he confronts The Shadow and is killed. Hoppy follows through the now open passage door, finds the body of Phineas Phipps (remember him?) in the basement, corners The Shadow after a fistfight which Archainbaud directs in almost a Film Noir style, and unmasks him. The killer turns out to be none other than the supposedly long dead Hiram Baxter, who was out to murder all of his brother Tom's other legatees and keep the oil-rich Box O for himself. This doesn't make a lick of sense, but then neither do the explanations in nine out of ten of the quickie

detective pictures on which this one was modeled.

Dangerous Venture (1947), fourth in the new Cassidy series, featured the Archainbaud signature elements: panoramic sweeps of desert-and-rock scenery coupled with huge numbers of extreme long shots. Doris Schroeder's screenplay, with its beautiful archaeologist and lost city full of treasure, borrowed now and then from the 1941 Cassidy picture **Secrets of the Wasteland**, but the film was made too quickly and cheaply for Archainbaud to do any sort of justice to the unusual storyline. As the adventure begins, Hoppy and Lucky and California save an Indian boy named José (Neyle Morrow) from being chased by rancher Dan Morgan (Harry Cording) and his foreman Kane (Francis McDonald), who claim that José belongs to a tribe of "ghost Indians" that camp in the desert hills and live by rustling white men's cattle. We quickly learn however that the Indian rustlers are Morgan's men in disguise, and that José had spotted them moving a stolen herd.

William Boyd, Andy Clyde and Russell Hayden are covered by Morris Ankrum in this scene from **In Old Colorado** (1941, Paramount).

Later in town, Cassidy runs into an old friend, archaeologist Sue Harmon (Betty Alexander), who along with Dr. Atwood (Douglas Evans) is leading an expedition to locate the Tolmec Indians and prove that they're descendants of the Aztecs. The guide who is to take them to the Indians' secret city is none other than José. Morgan rides into town, warns the scientists against crossing his land, and again tries to capture José, who runs off with his sister Tolu (Patricia Tate), leaving behind a gold-handled knife which begins to tempt Dr. Atwood with dreams of native treasure ripe for the stealing. Hoppy and his sidekicks accept Sue's invitation to join the expedition. Morgan's men follow the party to their first night's camp-site, which is uncomfortably close to the canyon where Morgan has hidden the stolen cattle. That night his "ghost Indians" attack the camp.

The next day Hoppy again locates José and is taken to meet the boy's grandfather, Xeoli (Fritz Leiber), leader of the Tolmecs, who understandably doesn't believe Cassidy's assurances that the

archaeologists have not come to plunder the Indian burial caves. Meanwhile Dr. Atwood secretly visits Morgan's ranch and makes a deal with him to steal the treasures with which the Tolmec dead are buried.

That night the fake Indians again raid the scientists' camp. In the morning Atwood insists that the expedition be abandoned. Hoppy and his pals pretend to agree and ride away, but double back in time to spy on another meeting between Atwood and the Morgan gang. When the plunderers ride off towards the burial caves, Cassidy and his friends follow at a distance. On the way to the caves, the outlaws shoot and wound José, who is taken back to the secret city by his grandfather. Xeoli then goes out to retaliate for what he takes to be Cassidy's treachery by killing him, but fails. Next Tolu makes an attempt to kill Hoppy, but having never seen Cassidy, mistakenly captures California and brings him to the Tolmecs' sacrificial altar. Meanwhile Hoppy, Lucky and Sue catch Morgan and his gang at the burial caves

237

William Boyd prevents Andy Clyde from using his gun on Morris Ankrum in this publicity still for **In Old Colorado** (1941, Paramount).

and a gun battle breaks out. While trying to escape from the outlaws, Cassidy and his party discover that California is missing and follow his tracks to the sacrificial altar just in time to save the old buffoon from becoming a human offering. Morgan and his men attack the Tolmecs but are wiped out in short order, with Atwood meeting a grisly death in the Indians' fire pit. With peace restored between the Tolmecs and the honest whites the picture comes to an end.

Dangerous Venture was no gem, but it was quite good compared with its successor, **Hoppy's Holiday** (1947), an extremely leisurely film with all too little action, all too many unfunny comic skits, and, despite the services of five writers (the screenplay is credited to J. Benton Cheney, Bennett Cohen and Ande Lamb and the story to Ellen Corby and Cecile Kramer), a bare minimum of plot. Hoppy, Lucky and California visit the town of Mesa City, which is throwing a two-day festival to celebrate a coming irrigation project. Pompous mayor Frank Patton

(Andrew Tombes) tells Cassidy that the townspeople have raised more than $100,000 for the project and that the money is in the local bank. Dunning (Leonard Penn), the instigator of the project, has also brought to Mesa City the first horseless carriage the community has ever seen. Lucky and California inveigle Hoppy into staying over for the celebration, and all three purchase new clothes for the occasion, which gives William Boyd the excuse to get out and stay out of his detested black monkey suit and put on the light-colored outfit he favored.

That evening, during a square dance contest, three gunmen break into the bank and escape with the money, but not before they bump into California, who has just changed into a plaid monstrosity of a suit for the dance and is carrying his old clothes in a suitcase identical to the one in which the thieves have put the money. While Hoppy is out with the posse chasing the robbers, California goes back to his hotel room and finds the cash but is seen opening the greenback-stuffed suitcase by

238

William Boyd, Russell Hayden and Andy Clyde tie up the villains in this scene from **In Old Colorado** (1941, Paramount).

Jed (Jeff Corey), the hotel manager. When the posse returns to town, Jed tells what he saw and the sheriff (Donald Kirke) arrests California, but by this point the suitcase has vanished from the room. Hoppy figures out what must have happened---namely that California inadvertently dropped the suitcase down the room's dumbwaiter---but lets his sidekick be locked up so as to set a trap for the robbers. Meanwhile Dunning, who is behind the bank raid, has driven his horseless carriage to his men's hideout and discovered that they got away with the wrong suitcase.

Next morning in the hotel lobby, while California tries to reconstruct what he did with the suitcase, Hoppy spots Jed sneaking away to the basement and catches him retrieving the second case from beneath the dumbwaiter. But Dunning and his men kill Jed and race out of town with the suitcase in their auto. Hoppy leads a posse in pursuit. The auto runs out of gas near the gang's hideout and they take cover in their shack but Cassidy and the posse quickly and unexcitingly smoke them

out. When the second suitcase is opened and turns out not to contain the money either, Hoppy reveals that he'd found it under the dumbwaiter the night before and had removed the money for safekeeping. With which revelation the holiday and the movie end.

The season closed with **The Marauders** (1947), directed by Archainbaud from a screenplay by newcomer Charles Belden. It was a good script, featuring an offtrail plot situation and crisp dialogue (Spinster churchwoman: "You desecrator!" California: "I am not, I'm a Presbyterian"), but the picture was made on the supercheap, with two-thirds of the footage being shot on a single indoor set, and Archainbaud's direction is dull as dishwater. We open with Hoppy, Lucky and California stopping implausibly for the night at a church in the ghost town of Coltsville---a town incidentally that for budgetary reasons we never get to see. After a few false alarms when the wind blows through the organ pipes and makes the church bells ring, Cassidy and his pals are

The sheriff talks with William Boyd, Russell Hayden **and** Andy Clyde in this scene from **In Old Colorado** (1941, Paramount).

awakened by a hymn being played on the organ and discover Mrs. Crowell (Mary Newton), widow of the town minister, and her daughter Susan (Dorinda Clifton). The women tell Hoppy that four months ago everyone in Coltsville was terrorized into leaving except themselves and their friend Deacon Black (Ian Wolfe). Shortly after Susan gets up from the organ, a beam comes down that would have killed her if she'd still been playing a hymn. Hoppy observes that the beam has been sawn through.

In the morning the three friends wake to find the church about to be torn down by a gang headed by Riker (Harry Cording), who says he needs the lumber for a mining camp. Nasty words are exchanged before Hoppy nonviolently ejects the gang, who don't go far but simply surround the church and begin an unthrilling siege. After some shooting, Riker demands that Cassidy and his sidekicks surrender, and Hoppy responds by having Susan, Lucky and California pound out an organ song insulting the gang leader. The siege

resumes. Hoppy escapes by the back door, throws off pursuit, and heads for the county seat to find out what's behind the plot against the church.

Waking up the county clerk (Earle Hodgins), Cassidy learns that the entire town of Coltsville has been purchased dirt cheap by an unknown woman. The only piece of property she doesn't own is the church, which for some outlandish reason can't be bought or sold as long as it stands. Hoppy returns to Coltsville, skirmishes some more with Riker's men, and sneaks back into the church to find Lucky romancing Susan. Deacon Black comes through the gang's lines to bring the defenders a message: they can go free if they leave at once. Hoppy agrees but tells Black that he knows the truth about the plot.

In the morning, a man with Riker's gang (Dick Bailey) breaks away and tries to take refuge in the church but is shot and wounded by Black, who as we now learn is the brains behind the gang. Hoppy and his pals let the man in and try to get

240

Andy Clyde is bilked out of his money by conman Philip Van Zandt in this scene from **In Old Colorado** (1941, Paramount).

him to talk. Black climbs the church roof, hangs on by the bell in the steeple, and is about to finish off the wounded man when Cassidy notices the trembling of the bell rope, pulls on it with all his strength and sends Black plummeting through the tower to his death. The wounded man confesses that there's a huge deposit of oil beneath the church and that the mysterious woman who's been buying the town is Black's sister. A posse from the county seat rounds up the rest of the gang without even the semblance of a fight, bringing this promising but deadly dull picture to an end, and with it the first season of Cassidys under William Boyd Productions.

Russell Hayden, William Boyd and Andy Clyde are ready for action in this publicity still for **Border Vigilantes** (1941, Paramount).

Chapter Twelve

The second half-dozen Cassidys under William Boyd Productions were assembly-line products, all six being produced by Lewis J. Rachmil, photographed by Mack Stengler, edited by Fred W. Berger and directed by George Archainbaud. Despite screen credits to the contrary, most of the background music was by Raoul Kraushaar and had been heard in countless Republic Pictures B Westerns earlier in the Forties. Only in the scriptwriting department was there any diversity of personnel or ideas, with most of the story concepts being borrowed from then current mystery and suspense films. Boyd, Rand Brooks and Andy Clyde carried on of course as Hoppy, Lucky and California, supported by casts of relative newcomers to Westerns like Elaine Riley, John Parrish, Don Haggerty and Leonard Penn. Action and excitement in these pictures were minimal like their budgets, but most are mildly diverting and, by some miracle, one is actually quite good.

Silent Conflict (1948), directed by Archainbaud from a screenplay by Charles Belden, borrows its premise of a weak-willed young man hypnotized into committing a crime from one of the best of the low-budget *films noir* of the period, **Fear in the Night** (Paramount, 1947), which had been based on a story by the greatest suspense writer that ever lived, Cornell Woolrich. At the end of a cattle drive during which Hoppy has had to chew out Lucky for carelessness, Cassidy and California see their young pal talking with unsavory gambler Speed Blaney (James Harrison) and begin to worry about the company he keeps. On their way back to the Bar 20 with the cattle sale money, most of which belongs to other ranchers, the three stop for the night at the Boulder Inn. Soon Blaney too shows up at the Inn and has another enigmatic conversation with Lucky. Later in the evening, after Hoppy and California have gone to bed, Lucky is approached by crackpot inventor Doc Richards (Earle Hodgins), who is stopping at the Inn with his lovely niece Renee

(Virginia Belmont). Doc gets Lucky to talk about his troubled relationship with Cassidy and about the money from the cattle sale, then brews the young man a cup of his special herbal tea and hypnotizes him. Upstairs, California admits to Hoppy the truth behind Lucky's meetings with Blaney, namely that he owes the gambler a debt that he's trying to repay. In the morning both Lucky and the cattle sale money have disappeared. Cassidy and California go hunting for their pal, hoping against hope that he hasn't turned thief.

Along the trail, a still hypnotized Lucky intercepts Doc Richards' wagon, turns the money over to him, and is hidden in the wagon's interior. Meanwhile Randall (Forbes Murray) and some other ranchers learn at the Inn that Cassidy has gone off somewhere and, afraid that he's stolen their cattle sale money, take off after him. Hoppy and California catch up with Blaney but he claims he knows nothing about the missing money. Cassidy decides to go after Doc Richards. That night Renee, who knew nothing about her uncle's scheme, tries to help Lucky escape but is caught before she can de-hypnotize him.

The next morning, when Randall and the ranchers catch up with Hoppy, he and California have to draw their guns on their neighbors in order to escape. They continue on Doc Richards' trail and, at his last night's campsite, find Lucky's boot prints in the dirt. While they stay on the trail, Richards and Renee and Lucky stop at a shack for lunch. Seeing Hoppy and California approaching from a distance, Doc orders Lucky to go out and kill them. Zombie-like, the young man approaches his pals and starts shooting, but Hoppy is able to knock Lucky out before any harm is done, and the blow restores his mind except that he can't remember anything since he drank the first cup of Doc's herbal tea. Cassidy retraces Lucky's footprints to the shack, where he tells Doc that he had to shoot Lucky in self-defense. When Richards offers a relaxing cup of his herbal tea, Cassidy gets the drop on him actionlessly. Renee is cleared

Andy Clyde, Victor Jory, Russell Hayden, William Boyd and Hank Bell in a scene from **Border Vigilantes** (1941, Paramount).

of complicity and goes back with Hoppy and his pals to the Bar 20. It's by no means a memorable picture but it did feature some gorgeous desert-and-rocks landscapes, effectively spooky music in the hypnosis scenes, and a surprisingly good non-comic performance by that king of snake-oil peddlers, Earle Hodgins.

The old-dark-house detective thrillers which had inspired the previous season's **Unexpected Guest** also gave birth to the next Cassidy exploit, **The Dead Don't Dream** (1948): if you gave Hoppy a paunch and a Fu Manchu mustache and a book of quotations from Confucius, and turned Lucky and California into Number One and Two sons, *voila*! you'd have a Charlie Chan picture. Archainbaud directed from a screenplay by Francis Rosenwald. As the film opens, Hoppy and Lucky and California are on their way to the Last Chance Inn, a hotel in the middle of the desert, where Lucky is to be married to lovely Mary Benton (Mary Tucker). On their arrival, wheelchair-bound innkeeper Jeff Potter (John

Parrish) tells them that the wedding will have to be postponed, for Mary's uncle, well-to-do prospector Jim Benton, has vanished from his room at the Inn during the night. While investigating the room, Cassidy and his pals are spied on by the Inn's hulking handyman Duke (Richard Alexander). Then Hoppy is taken to Benton's mine by the missing man's neighbor Earl Wesson (Leonard Penn) and the two men find Benton's body in one of the tunnels. While Wesson goes to inform his partner Bart Lansing (Francis McDonald), a gunman shoots at Cassidy and vanishes in the maze of mine shafts. Later back at the Inn, Hoppy and his pals meet Jeff Potter's visiting younger brother Larry (Bob Gabriel), who acts more than a bit suspiciously.

That evening an old friend of Hoppy's named Jesse Williams (Stanley Andrews) checks in at the Last Chance and is given what had been Benton's room. Before going to bed, Williams tells Hoppy that others before Jim Benton have disappeared from the Inn. That night, old Jesse joins the van-

Jack Rockwell, William Boyd, Russell Hayden, Andy Clyde and Chick Hannon in a scene from **Border Vigilantes** (1941, Paramount).

ished. Larry Potter claims that Williams left at dawn, but Cassidy and his pals find the burned remnants of Jesse's saddlebag in the Inn's courtyard. Sheriff Thompson (Forbes Murray) shows up to investigate, but by the time he and Hoppy visit Benton's mine, the body has vanished again. Meanwhile everyone in the cast gets a chance to look guilty. Mary admits that she inherits everything under her uncle's will, the sheriff recognizes Larry as a man wanted for murder elsewhere, and there are hints that Jeff Potter may be only pretending to be crippled. That night the sheriff, who has been given the room Benton and Williams disappeared from, also vanishes. Cassidy surprises Larry Potter in the missing men's room but he escapes and is shot by an unknown gunman before Hoppy can catch him.

The next evening at dinner, Hoppy announces that he knows the killer's identity and asks to move into the room of vanished men. This of course is the old bait-a-trap gimmick used in dozens of cheap detective flicks, and as usual the murderers fall into it. At 3:00 A.M. the overhead canopy of the bed mechanically descends to smother Hoppy as he sleeps. Luckily Cassidy was sitting up in a chair for the night. He gets the drop on the villains---Wesson and Lansing, if anyone needs to be told---and polishes them off in a mildly exciting fistfight. All the unanswered questions, like how the killers managed to rig that deadly bed, and why they wanted to murder so many people, and what Larry had to do with the plot, remain unanswered as Mary Benton decides not to marry Lucky after all, leaving the trio intact for further and perhaps more comprehensible adventures.

Sinister Journey (1948) was scripted by Doris Schroeder, who had written many of the earliest screenplays for the Cassidy series, but its roots were in contemporary *film noir*. Archainbaud's direction made use of some magnificent scenery and took full advantage of the several trains that figured in the plot, but he couldn't lick the meandering and actionless storyline. On their

Victor Jory looks unhappy at what Russell Hayden, William Boyd and Andy Clyde have found in this scene from **Border Vigilantes** (1941, Paramount).

way to the railroad town of Wheeler at the request of the line's vice-president Tom Smith (Stanley Andrews), Hoppy and Lucky and California watch a train steaming majestically by. Later the three separate, and Cassidy is alone when a young man rushes out of a cabin and asks for help. He is Lee Garvin (John Kellogg), a brakeman for the railroad, and his wife Jessie (Elaine Riley) has just been poisoned by water from their well. Hoppy administers a baking-soda cure and is invited--- along with Lucky and California, who have rejoined him---for supper. Lee claims that he's being persecuted by his father-in-law, Tom Smith, who is violently opposed to his daughter's marrying a brakeman. Just why the well water was poisoned is never explained, nor even mentioned again.

Cassidy and his pals reach Wheeler and meet Smith and his secretary Harmon Roberts (Don Haggerty), whom Hoppy dislikes at once because he's a man holding down a woman's job. Smith describes a series of "accidents" that have recently

befallen him and insists that his hot-tempered proletarian son-in-law Lee Garvin is trying to kill him so that Jessie and he will inherit the family fortune. In order to keep watch on Garvin, Hoppy and his companions take jobs with the railroad. When Lee comes to work the next day, he finds the three on the payroll, instantly concludes that they're spying on him for Smith, and picks a fight with Lucky which Cassidy has to break up. It's clear as day that Garvin is hiding something in his past, and in the next few minutes we learn what it is.

Lee discovers a hobo in the freight yard who happens to be Ben Watts (Will Orlean), a former cellmate of his. Watts demands money to keep Garvin's prison record a secret, and that night Lee gives the drunken Watts some cash, but has the stupidity to do it on the main street of town where the payoff is observed by Hoppy, Lucky, California, Harmon Roberts, and freight yard foreman Banks (Harry Strang). After Watts reels off, Garvin spots Cassidy and Jessie apparently spying on

Andy Clyde, Russell Hayden and William Boyd talks with Frances Gifford in this scene from **Border Vigilantes** (1941, Paramount).

him and picks another fight with Hoppy. Disgusted with her husband's bad temper, Jessie decides to go back to her father.

Meanwhile Roberts and Banks have overtaken Watts and are trying to learn Garvin's secret from him, but the man is too drunk to talk so they lock him in a storage shack. Then Roberts shoots and wounds Tom Smith through the window of his house and plants Watts' distinctive polka-dot scarf near the scene so that both the hobo and Lee Garvin, who was publicly seen giving him money, will be incriminated respectively as hit man and employer. Hoppy and his pals ride to the Garvin house to hear Lee's side of the story. The young man confesses his secret and Cassidy suspects that someone is trying to frame both him and Watts. When the marshal comes out to arrest Garvin for the attack on Smith, Hoppy and his pals hide Lee under the bed.

The next morning Roberts and Banks convince Watts that he shot Smith in a drunken stupor and tell him to hop a freight out of the territory.

Prowling around the yards, Cassidy spots and captures Watts, but before the man can incriminate them, Roberts and Banks shoot him down and then plant a gun on him so that it looks as if the hobo was about to kill Hoppy. To make matters worse, they both swear that they heard Watts confess with his dying breath that Lee Garvin had paid him to shoot Smith.

That night Hoppy again visits Garvin's cabin, brings him up to date on plot developments and persuades him to go to Smith and admit his crooked past and make up with the old man. Lee agrees, but his reconciliation with Smith is overheard by Roberts, who takes instant action. He knocks out Lee, murders Smith and rigs the evidence so that Garvin looks like the murderer. But Garvin escapes before Roberts can summon the marshal. A reward is offered for his capture and a posse scours the countryside.

While the manhunt is going on, Hoppy visits the Garvin house, finds Jessie packing her belongings, and learns that she's going back east in a

247

Andy Clyde, William Boyd, Morris Ankrum, Bernice Kay (later Cara Williams) and Russell Hayden are seen in this publicity still for **Wide Open Town** (1941, Paramount).

special train with Roberts. A clue in a farewell note Lee left for his wife enables Cassidy and his pals to find him that afternoon, hiding in an abandoned silver mine. The train carrying Jessie, Roberts and (luckily for the plot) the marshal is due to pass by the mine shortly. Cassidy diverts the train to a siding, gets the drop on Roberts, pretends to read a confession by his partner Banks and in a split second bluffs Roberts into making a full confession. With the Garvins reunited and Lee about to become vice-president of the railroad, Hoppy and his pals pass another train on their way home.

Borrowed Trouble (1948), directed by Archainbaud from a Charles Belden screenplay, is perhaps the dullest of the final half-dozen Cassidys. Its only connection with detective movies is the attempt to keep the villain's identity hidden until the climax, but like everything else in the picture, the surprise is a big dud. At the close of a Bar 20 cattle drive, California decides to guzzle some sarsaparilla at the Golden Mill saloon before hitting the trail for home. But the saloon happens to be next door to the town schoolhouse, and the spinster teacher Lucy Abbott (Anne O'Neal) is carrying on a vendetta against the Golden Mill's owner, Steve Mawson (John Parrish). Hoppy and Lucky join California at the bar just before Miss Abbott lets loose a barrage of apples and breaks most of the Golden Mill's windows. Mawson blames the episode on his business rival Dink Davis (Cliff Clark), cigar-chomping proprietor of the Big Dome saloon, and threatens retaliation. The only person who saw that the apple-thrower was Miss Abbott is Hoppy, who visits her at the schoolhouse and tries to persuade her that peaceful methods are better. Meanwhile Mawson's men have broken all the Big Dome's windows and Davis and his cronies are about to shoot up the Golden Mill. Cassidy breaks up the altercation and Miss Abbott admits her responsibility.

In the morning, dance hall girl Lola Blair (Helen Chapman), who has taken a liking to Lucky, tells

248

Andy Clyde and William Boyd hold Kermit Maynard, Jack Rockwell and friends at gunpoint in this scene from **Stick to Your Guns** (1941, Paramount).

Hoppy that she overheard Mawson and his men plotting against Miss Abbott the night before. Cassidy discovers that the teacher is not in school and that her house is a mess. He accuses Mawson of kidnaping her, shoots a gun out of his hand, then goes next door and takes over Miss Abbott's class, allowing us to watch him "heartwarmingly" interact with children. During this scene one of the students happens to mention a cabin Mawson owns in the desert. Leaving California in charge of the class---which turns out to be a huge mistake---Cassidy goes off with Lucky to investigate the cabin. Mawson sees them riding off and sends out his henchman Lippy (Don Haggerty) to follow, but they catch him, leave him tied up along the trail and go on to their destination. They find Miss Abbott imprisoned in the cabin, release her, shoot it out unexcitingly with the three gunmen who were guarding her, and make their getaway.

Back in town, Dink Davis has dropped in at the Golden Mill to gloat over the fact that the town blames Mawson for the schoolmarm's disappear-

ance. Hoppy and his pals arrive and accuse Davis of being behind the kidnaping himself. Their evidence? Well, it seems that, unseen by us in the audience, Cassidy had found a band from one of Davis' distinctive cigars amid the mess at Miss Abbott's house. Hoppy kills Davis in a quickie shootout, and Mawson settles his dispute with the schoolteacher by agreeing to buy the Big Dome from Davis' estate and donate it to the town as an education center. On this unlikely note Cassidy and his buddies head back for the Bar 20.

By far the best of the dozen Hoppy pictures produced by Boyd's company was **False Paradise** (1948), written by old reliable Harrison Jacobs, with "additional dialogue" credited to William Conselman Jr. and Doris Schroeder. For the first and only time in his career as executive producer of the series, Boyd adopted Harry Sherman's old principle that a Cassidy picture should build to and end with an all-out action climax. The storyline owes nothing to detective and suspense films and would have served just as well during the

William Boyd looks dubious at what Jean Phillips is telling him. Forrest Stanley, Nina Guilbert and Andy Clyde (in right background) look on in this scene from **Outlaws of the Desert** (1941, Paramount).

Sherman era when the Cassidys were budgeted at over $100,000 apiece.

Hoppy, wearing the light gray outfit he preferred over the traditional black monkeysuit, stops a runaway buckboard and rescues Anne Larson (Elaine Riley), who with her father, retired entomology professor Alonzo Larson (Joel Friedkin), are on their way to the ranch the professor has bought with his life's savings. Cassidy, Lucky and California accompany the Larsons to their new home but find that the Paradise Ranch is nothing but a ramshackle cabin surrounded by rocks. The professor shamefacedly admits that he bought the property sight unseen from Bentley (Kenneth MacDonald), a local realtor. Hoppy, however, suddenly remembers that he had once come across traces of silver ore in a box canyon on the ranch, so it seems that the Larsons have lucked out.

Cassidy goes to town and arranges with banker Waite (Cliff Clark) for a $15,000 loan so that a silver mine can be started. But Waite happens to be in league with Bentley, and sends out both the realtor and gunman Deal Marden (Don Haggerty) to make the professor sell back the property. Hoppy returns from town just in time to kick the two off the ranch.

Waite now launches another plan. His loan agreement requires that the professor will forfeit his ranch if the first $5,000 of the money is not repaid within thirty days. Waite has gunmen Sam (Richard Alexander) and Buck (Zon Murray) join the mining crew and sabotage the operation. The work goes on despite a series of "accidents," and smelter owner Radley (George Eldredge) deposits the needed $5,000 in Waite's bank, to be applied to the loan upon delivery of the first ore shipment. As the deadline nears, Sam and Buck plant dynamite to blow up the mine, but are interrupted by Professor Larson. They knock him out and leave him to be blown up in the shaft, but Cassidy steps into the scene, saves the professor and kills both saboteurs, although he's unable to stop the explosion.

But once again luck plays his way: the dynamite

250

Luli Deste looks to William Boyd as he and Albert Morin are concerned about something off camera in this scene from **Outlaws of the Desert** (1941, Paramount).

opens up a whole new ledge of silver. Hoppy tells the good news to Waite, who counters by having Deal Marden join the new crew of miners Cassidy is hiring. The work continues and three wagon-loads of silver are readied for shipment to the smelter. When Marden fakes a toothache and rides into town for treatment, Hoppy follows and eavesdrops on a meeting Marden has with Bentley and Waite.

The ore wagons set out in the morning, with Bentley and his gang in ambush along the trail. The attack begins and the chase is on, and it turns out to be a startlingly well directed and exciting action scene, one that wouldn't be out of place in the best Cassidy pictures of the Harry Sherman era. The wagons of course are filled with extra fighting men as well as silver, and the outlaws are beaten back, but instead of giving up they go on at once to prepare a second ambush. This time Hoppy and Lucky get the drop on them from behind and capture all of them except Bentley, whom Cassidy chases back to town. At the bank

he catches Bentley and Waite together and makes them accompany him and Radley's $5,000 to the smelter so that the payment is handed over in the nick of time. With the professor and his daughter securely in possession of their mine, Hoppy and his pals ride out of this well above average picture and back to the Bar 20.

The sixty-sixth and last of the Cassidy features was one of the most disappointing in the series' history, a sad comedown from the standards of the Harry Sherman classics and even from **False Paradise. Strange Gamble** (1948) was directed by Archainbaud from a screenplay by the first Cassidy scriptwriter, Doris Schroeder, but it was even duller than her previous effort, **Sinister Journey**. At least the picture used a few old veterans of the series like Herbert Rawlinson and Francis McDonald, and Elaine Riley in her fourth female lead for William Boyd Productions looked lovely as ever.

Government agents Hoppy, Lucky and California are on their way to Silver City after receiving a

251

George J. Lewis and William Boyd protect their fallen comrade in this scene from **Outlaws of the Desert** (1941, Paramount).

letter from an anonymous informant who signs himself with the drawing of a comet and claims that the town is headquarters for a gang counterfeiting both U.S. and Mexican currency. On the trail they encounter three unusual stagecoach passengers: Nora Murray (Elaine Riley), her dipsomaniac brother Sid (William Leicester), and Sid's gravely ill wife Mary (Joan Barton). When the coach reaches Silver City, town boss Ora Mordigan (James Craven) refuses the Murrays space in his hotel, but Doc White (Joel Friedkin) gives them his room. While the doctor is treating Mary, Sid gets drunk in Mordigan's saloon and claims that he and Nora are co-owners of the lost Silver Belle mine which had belonged to their father, John Murray, long missing and presumed dead. Mordigan has Sid shot in the saloon and---just like Big Henry in Doris Schroeder's script for the second Cassidy film, **The Eagle's Brood**--- claims that the death was suicide. Hoppy insists Sid was murdered, but everyone in the saloon at the time of the shooting sides with Mordigan.

Longhorn (Francis McDonald), Mordigan's henchman, rides into town and has a conversation with his boss about a secret mine. Their talk is overheard by DeLara (Albert Morin), Mordigan's Mexican card dealer. Around this time Mary Murray dies of her illness, leaving Nora stranded in Silver City and friendless except for Hoppy and his pals, who make camp outside of town.

That night, in perhaps the clumsiest action scene in any Cassidy film, Longhorn and his men stampede a herd of stock-footage cattle into a blatantly indoors set meant to represent Hoppy's campsite. Unhurt, Cassidy rides into town and forces Mordigan at gunpoint to pay $50 in gold for his and his friends' ruined equipment. By now he has a strong suspicion that the counterfeit money is being produced in the lost Silver Belle mine and that Mordigan killed Sid Murray to keep the mine for his own use. He rides out next day to hunt for the mine and is ambushed by Mordigan's gunman Pete (Robert B. Williams), who bungles the job. Meanwhile, to avoid being kicked out of town,

William Boyd introduces Jean Phillips and Forrest Stanley to Duncan Renaldo in this scene from **Outlaws of the Desert** (1941, Paramount).

Nora claims that she and Cassidy are engaged, and with help from Lucky and California she buys the town's Chinese restaurant and renames it The Comet Cafe.

Still out in the desert searching for the mine, Hoppy stumbles on an old man (Herbert Rawlinson) who turns out to be John Murray, Nora's father. Murray says he's been held in the Silver Belle for years and forced to print counterfeit U.S. and Mexican money for Mordigan. Hoppy slips away and lets the Silver Belle guards recapture Murray so that they'll lead him back to the mine.

Back in town, Doc White visits the Comet Cafe and, by displaying a comet-shaped pin to Lucky and California, reveals himself as the author of the letter that brought them and Hoppy to Silver City. Mordigan's men open fire on the cafe, killing the doctor. The siege is lifted when Cassidy rides back into town and gets the drop on the gang. But instead of turning them in, he demands a 50% cut of Mordigan's counterfeiting profits, and the town boss agrees, planning of course to kill Hoppy

later. That night Cassidy happens to overhear Mordigan and Pete expose DeLara as an agent of the Mexican government, sent to Silver City by a Comet letter like the one sent to Hoppy himself. Cassidy intervenes and saves DeLara's life by persuading Mordigan that it would be safer to take him out to the Silver Belle the next day and rig an accident. In the morning they all ride out to the mine for the murder, but when they get there, in an almost completely actionless and boring finale, Hoppy and his pals capture the gang, free John Murray, reunite him with his daughter and bring both this film and the entire long-running Cassidy series to a sad and lackluster end.

William Boyd is ready for action in this scene from **Lost Canyon** (1943, United Artists).

Chapter Thirteen

Routine as most of these last twelve Cassidys had been, Boyd was apparently satisfied with them, for no sooner had he completed the dozen than he began preparations for a third set of six. It was only after his company had contracted with a number of key actors and technical people that Boyd was told that United Artists was unhappy with the box-office returns to date and uninterested in distributing any more Hoppy pictures. The dozen produced by Boyd had been competing head-to-head in theaters with the Cassidys of the Sherman era which Boyd had re-released in order to finance his new productions, and audiences clearly preferred the earlier vintage. When no other distributor could be found to take over for UA, Boyd had no choice but to throw up his hands and suspend operations. Rand Brooks quixotically tore up his contract and released William Boyd Productions from its financial commitment to him.

For a while it seemed that Hopalong Cassidy the movie hero was dead as a doornail. But Boyd still had faith in the character and in himself. He and Toby Anguish decided to shoot the works on one last gamble, selling off everything they owned and going deeply in debt in order to establish Hoppy and his first 54 screen exploits in a new medium struggling for survival: television.

In the late 1940s, all the major Hollywood studios saw TV as the enemy, as the dinky little box that offered free of charge the same sorts of visual entertainment for which people had been paying since the beginning of the century. The majors were refusing to let any of their contract actors and actresses appear on the small screen or even to let any of their old pictures be broadcast. With very few exceptions, the only features seen on TV were independent releases (usually of Grade Triple Z quality) and imports from England. Boyd's 1946 deal with Harry Sherman gave him the right to exhibit the earlier Cassidys on television as well as in theaters, and Toby Anguish managed to raise the $50,000 needed to strike new 16mm prints of the films for TV distribution. Then, just when Boyd's desperate gamble seemed to be paying off, the time bomb exploded that had been ticking away in a New York file cabinet for the past thirteen years.

Harry Sherman had already paid Clarence E. Mulford for the right to make the first 54 Cassidys just as Boyd and Anguish had paid for the right to make the final dozen. But now, in 1947, the lawyers for Doubleday & Co., Mulford's publisher, reminded Boyd of the clause they had inserted in the original 1935 option agreement to the effect that Mulford retained "All television...rights...." At the time the option had been signed, the parties seem to have assumed without discussion that the clause meant merely that Mulford was keeping control of the right to license live TV dramas based on his books and stories in the event television, which was in its fetal stage during the Thirties, ever developed into an economically viable medium. Now, thirteen years later, Doubleday on Mulford's behalf claimed that the works to which Mulford owned the TV rights included not just Mulford's own novels and stories but also the movies which had been made under the agreement. In other words, Doubleday was arguing that neither Harry Sherman nor anyone else could license the first 54 Cassidys for television without going back and purchasing the right to do so from Mulford. Rather than risk a long, costly and chancy lawsuit, Boyd decided to settle with Mulford, and then, just to make sure that no one else came forward with a surprise claim to own the TV rights, he also purchased a quitclaim from Paramount Pictures, which had released the Cassidys theatrically during most of the years Sherman was in production.

Finally the way was clear for putting the films on television. Stations around the country, desperate for feature material, bought exhibition rights. The Cassidys began running in New York as a regular weekly series in November of 1948. In order to fit the pictures into the 60-minute time

William Boyd tries to convince the Arab that Andy Clyde is harmless as Brad King looks on in this scene from **Outlaws of the Desert** (1941, Paramount).

slots that were becoming the norm in the new medium, Boyd went back to the negatives and casually destroyed as many minutes of footage at the beginning of each film as was necessary to reduce it to 54-minute length. If the butchery made the film's story incomprehensible, as it often did, Boyd couldn't have cared less.

And apparently neither did the home viewing audience. With precious little else of the same quality available, the Sherman Cassidys scored high in the ratings almost from their first exposure on the small screen, and before long the NBC network made a deal to put the features on its prime time schedule. The big gamble had paid off. Hopalong Cassidy became one of the first television superstars and a hero to millions of children who hadn't been born when the films were first shown in theaters. Boyd found himself a millionaire and a tycoon overnight.

Hoppymania swept the country. Hundreds of manufacturers with eyes on the juvenile market paid millions of dollars for the right to use Boyd's image and the Cassidy name on bedcovers, bicycles, blankets, breakfast foods, candy bars, clip-on ties, cookies, lamps, lunch boxes, penknives, soap, spur skates, towels, wallets, wallpaper, wastebaskets and wristwatches. Boyd's national popularity was so immense that he made the cover of Life, whose June 12, 1950 issue featured a long story on the Hoppy phenomenon. But perhaps the most lucrative of all the items of tie-in merchandise was clothing. Rare and fortunate indeed were the parents of the early 1950s who weren't pestered to death by their kids for Hopalong Cassidy cowboy duds. The basic ensemble with denim shirt and trousers cost slightly over $20, and assorted extras could boost the price close to the $30 mark. Throw in a Hoppy leather jacket and the bill climbed above $45. Department stores all over the country set up Hopalong Cassidy hitching posts where these togs could be purchased, and the kids kept coming in waves. Time reported that demand for the outfit had caused a national shortage of black dye.

256

William Boyd and Brad King are ready for action in this scene from **Riders of the Timberline** (1941, Paramount).

Boyd's income from merchandising rights in 1951 alone was estimated at $25,000,000. He spent some of the money buying out Toby Anguish's share in William Boyd Productions.

During the years of the Hoppy craze, Boyd divided his time among overseeing his business empire, making hundreds of live personal appearances, and starring in the *Hopalong Cassidy* radio series, which was a sort of Western mystery program, co-starring Andy Clyde as California, and heard weekly between 1950 and 1952, first on the Mutual network and later over CBS. He also made a cameo appearance in his Hoppy monkey suit in Cecil B. De Mille's circus spectacular **The Greatest Show on Earth** (1952), as if to say thanks once again to the director who'd started him on his Hollywood career a third of a century before.

Shrewd businessman that he was, Boyd sensed that it was time to go back into production. After a few years of nonstop TV exposure, the 54 Sherman Cassidys were becoming stale and overfamiliar, even when augmented by Boyd's release to TV of the dozen later pictures his own company had produced. The New York Times for May 7, 1952 reported on his announcement of plans to make a series of 52 half-hour films expressly for television. And make those films he did, except that, as usual, he cut corners.

Twenty-six episodes of the *Hopalong Cassidy* teleseries were broadcast on the NBC network during the 1952-53 season and another 26 during 1953-54. But the first dozen telefilms turned out to be Boyd's own twelve Cassidy features of 1946-48, each cut down to 30 minutes and supplemented with his voice-over narration to bridge the gaps in the storylines. As a result, he needed to crank out only fourteen truly new episodes for the 1952-53 season, and these were plainly shot in an awful hurry and with almost nothing in the way of production value.

Boyd himself starred as Hoppy of course, and even in his middle fifties he still looked good in the saddle. But for budget reasons he eliminated

257

William Boyd, J. Farrell MacDonald, Eleanor Stewart and Brad King seem shocked at something off camera in this scene from **Riders of the Timberline** (1941, Paramount).

the traditional role of Cassidy's romantic young sidekick, and in the part of the older, comic-relief sidekick he refused to rehire Andy Clyde and turned instead to pudgy, gravel-voiced Edgar Buchanan (1903-1979), whose asking price was cheaper. A problem, however, quickly became apparent, namely that Buchanan was no comedian. After a while Boyd tried to persuade Andy Clyde to come aboard and replace Buchanan, but Clyde was still miffed by Boyd's earlier rejection and this time turned *him* down. Buchanan grouched and grumped his way through the role of Red Connors in all forty of the Cassidy telefilms.

Of all the Western series that proliferated on the small screen during the early Fifties, *Hopalong Cassidy* was just about the worst. Scripts were standard issue, outdoor locations dreary-looking, action sequences minimal or non-existent. The only saving grace of the series was that all exterior scenes were actually shot outdoors, not on the cheap and phony-looking stage sets that had

become a staple of rival TV shows like *The Lone Ranger*. Each episode featured a huge amount of Boyd's voice-over narration and was capped by a mini-sermon in which Hoppy counseled the kids to drink their milk, obey their mommies or cross at the green light. The theme song by Nacio Herb Brown and L. Wolfe Gilbert---"Here he comes, Here he comes, Man the trumpets, Man the drums, Here he comes, Hopalong Cassidy, Here he comes"---was the absolute pits.

Boyd made it a policy to hire as many directors, writers, actors and technicians as possible who had worked on the classic Cassidy features. An even dozen of Hoppy's 40 small-screen exploits were scripted by Harrison Jacobs, who'd contributed to Cassidy screenplays since 1935 when the series began. Other episodes were written by veterans of Cassidy features such as J. Benton Cheney, Ande Lamb and Joseph O'Donnell. Mack Stengler, cinematographer on the dozen features of 1946-48 which in condensed form made up twelve of the first season's TV

258

William Boyd and Andy Clyde are ready for action in this scene from **Leather Burners** (1942, United Artists).

output, was also hired to photograph all fourteen of that season's new episodes. Editing or supervising the editorial work on all forty TV Cassidys was the man who'd done the same job on most of the Hoppy features since 1943, Fred W. Berger. The background score for Hoppy's 30-minute exploits was once again by Raoul Kraushaar, who this time got screen credit as well as cash, and even though the themes were recycled to death in the Fifties---in Allied Artists' Bill Elliott Westerns and literally dozens of Revue Studios' TV series like *Soldiers of Fortune*, *Crusader* and *Mike Hammer*---Kraushaar's score is still one of the high spots of the small screen Cassidys.

Even more impressive are the cast lists on Hoppy's forty telequests. Popping up in various character roles are at least ten well-known veterans of the Cassidy features: Morris Ankrum, Roy Barcroft, Harry Cording, Richard Crane, Earle Hodgins, Frank Lackteen, Nelson Leigh, Pierce Lyden, John Merton and Glenn Strange. Three past or future Western stars---Raymond Hatton,

Richard Powers (Tom Keene) and Clayton Moore---have prominent parts in one episode apiece. Of the fine Fifties actors who appeared in the vast majority of episodes, a few such as Paul Richards, Hugh Beaumont and Marjorie Lord went on to TV stardom outside the Western genre.

When it came to directors, Boyd ran true to form and tended to hire men he'd worked with in the Cassidy features. Of the 14 first-season episodes, six were directed by Thomas Carr (1907-   ), who lacked previous experience with Boyd but had helmed many B Westerns (including a six-picture Lippert series co-starring two of Boyd's former young sidekicks, Jimmy Ellison and Russell Hayden) and segments of early TV series like *Wild Bill Hickok* and *Superman*. The remaining eight of the first season's 14 were directed by Derwin Abrahams, who had recently changed his name to Derwin Abbe. Abrahams had gotten his start in the business as an assistant director on the Sherman Cassidys and had made his directorial debut with the adequate if not

William Boyd, Andy Clyde, Bobby Larson and Jay Kirby in a publicity still for **Leather Burners** (1942, United Artists).

outstanding **Border Vigilantes** and **Secrets Of The Wasteland** back in 1941. Afterwards he had helmed low-budget serials and Westerns for Columbia, Monogram and smaller studios, and had moved into TV in 1950 as the first director of *The Cisco Kid*. His hallmark was drab competence without the least visual distinction, and he worked fast and cheap. Boyd hired him back for the 1953-54 season of TV Cassidys and let him direct twelve of that season's quota of 26. The other fourteen he assigned to the director of all the Boyd-produced Cassidy features, George Archainbaud. Archainbaud's episodes are perhaps a bare notch above those of Abrahams, and Thomas Carr's perhaps a bare notch above Archainbaud's. But what fatally compromises all forty of the TV Cassidys is Boyd's near-complete disinterest in the one element Harry Sherman had put into all his Cassidy features: production value.

Many of those Sherman classics had been a bit light on stunts and action sequences, but when Boyd became his own producer in 1946 he'd adopted a deliberate policy of minimal action. The Cassidy TV series has even less action than those last dozen Hoppy features. In one episode, "Copper Hills," there's a hilarious exchange of dialogue that puts Boyd's el cheapo policy in its place. This comes right after one of those blink-and-you-missed-it brawls.

Red Connors: It always makes me hungry to fight.

Cassidy: Do you call *that* a fight?

Connors: Sure!

Cassidy: Then all you need is a cup of coffee.

Even after viewing all forty episodes, it's hard to recommend any as head and shoulders above the others. The best directed are the early Thomas Carr entries like "Guns Across the Border" and "Alien Range." The sharpest dialogue and the most unusual plots are in the episodes written by the team of Robert Schaefer and Eric Freiwald. B Western historians will be curious about the telefilms that were unacknowledged remakes of theatrical shoot-em-ups. *Lone Ranger* fans will

Andy Clyde reads the telegram which has just been delivered to William Boyd in this scene from **Leather Burners** (1942, United Artists).

want to watch Boyd fight Clayton Moore in "Lawless Legacy" even though director Derwin Abbe keeps the brawl on a routine level. Those who love the Cassidys of the Sherman era will enjoy hunting for episodes of the TV series which recycle characters or incidents from those 54 pictures: for example, the villain in "Illegal Entry," scripted by Harrison Jacobs, is an intellectual posing as an alcoholic bum, very much like the unforgettable Loco in the Jacobs script for **Borderland** (1937). Even though *Hopalong Cassidy* was one of the weakest of all the weekly Westerns seen during TV's dawn years, at least it offers incidental pleasures like these. A detailed log of the series, with cast, credits and a brief summary for each episode, will be found in this book after the feature filmography.

What Harry Sherman might have thought of the telefilms will never be known. By 1952 he was living well as far as superficial appearances went, but in fact he was near bankruptcy, thanks to his penchant for backing the wrong movies, and

surviving on the generosity of neighbors and colleagues like Louis B. Mayer. On September 25 of that year, almost simultaneously with the debut of the Cassidy teleseries, Sherman died after abdominal surgery at Cedars of Lebanon Hospital.

Over the next few years the Hopalong Cassidy phenomenon ran its course and died away. The 66 Hoppy theatrical films left network prime time and were relegated to weekday afternoon and Saturday morning slots on local independent stations. The radio series ended in 1952 and the TV series in 1954. In the fall of 1955 CBS launched a new TV series called *Gunsmoke* which ushered in the era of the "adult Western" and swept away the kid-oriented shoot-em-ups like *The Lone Ranger, Roy Rogers, Gene Autry, Wild Bill Hickok* and *The Range Rider* that had dominated the small screen in the early 1950s. One entertainment era was fading away as another was being born.

On May 8, 1956, 73-year-old Clarence Mulford packed a tattered suitcase and an old shawl and

261

William Boyd has Forbes Murray covered as Andy Clyde and Bob Burns look on in this scene from **Leather Burners** (1942, United Artists).

checked into Maine General Hospital, complaining of a lung condition. The doctors examined him and said his only hope was major chest surgery. They were wrong. Two days later he was dead. When reporters called William Boyd at his California desert home and broke the news, he responded with a canned statement of sorrow that held more than a little truth. "I am deeply grieved at the loss of my dear friend Clarence. I shall always be grateful to him for letting me live so much of my life in the character of his dream. Clarence set down his vast knowledge of the West better than any other writer ever has. He left his mark in the happiness of millions throughout the world."

In the world of movies and television there is nothing deader than last year's craze, but the sudden change in the nature of the small-screen Western had little or no financial impact on Boyd. He sold his business interests for a reported capital gain of $8,000,000 and retired with his fifth and final wife, former actress Grace Bradley,

to whom he'd been married since 1937, to a luxurious home in Palm Desert, California, where he amused himself by dabbling in real estate. By 1963, when the copyrights on the first Cassidy features were due for renewal, no one bothered to file the necessary forms with the Copyright Office, with the result that between then and 1972 all 54 of the Sherman-produced Cassidys fell one by one into the public domain.

The year the last of those films died, their star died too. In 1968 Boyd had undergone surgery for removal of a cancerous tumor from a lymph gland. The operation failed and his face continued to be eaten away by the cancer. In his devastated final years he refused all requests for interviews or photographs. He died of Parkinson's Disease and congestive heart failure on September 13, 1972.

Did you think he'd live forever?

Of those who worked with Boyd on the last dozen Cassidys, all but one have joined him in death. The producer, Lewis J. Rachmil, went on to serve as a vice president at several major

William Boyd explains some evidence to Victor Jory and Andy Clyde in this scene from **Leather Burners** (1942, United Artists).

studios, culminating in a ten-year term as executive manager of the motion picture division of MGM. He retired from that post in 1982 and died of a heart attack less than a year later. The director, George Archainbaud, became the first established man in his field to make 30-minute Western telefilms, helming fourteen of the earliest TV adventures (1949-50) of *The Lone Ranger*. During the Fifties he worked primarily for Gene Autry's Flying A Productions, directing countless episodes of Autry's own TV series, plus other Flying A series like *The Range Rider* and *Annie Oakley*, plus the last dozen Autry theatrical features, plus, as we've seen, fourteen units of the Cassidy TV series. He died (of overwork?) in 1959. The last of Boyd's great comic sidekicks, Andy Clyde, played a California-like buffoon in Monogram's B Western series starring Whip Wilson, then migrated to television and had at least three continuing roles---as Homer Tubbs on *Rin Tin Tin*, as old Cully on *Lassie*, and as a comic grandpa on *No Time for Sergeants*---

before his death on May 18, 1967 at age 75.

Rand Brooks, the last man to play Hoppy's young protegé, is alive and well in his late sixties. He too kept busy in Fifties TV---most memorably as Corporal Boone on *Rin Tin Tin*---but gave up acting when that series folded and eventually founded his own business. Today his company, Professional Ambulance Service, handles the paramedic needs of several southern California cities. At least two of Boyd's earlier sidekicks, Jimmy Ellison and Jimmy Rogers, are still healthy in their seventies. No one seems to know what happened to Brad King after his time in the protegé slot. Rand Brooks tells me that Jay Kirby was killed in an auto accident years ago. The most durable of the Johnny-Lucky-Jimmy brigade was Russell Hayden, who played opposite Boyd in 27 Cassidys, then commuted from studio to studio, starring in Westerns, serials and B action features at Columbia, Universal, Screen Guild, and finally in 1950 at Lippert in a quickie six-picture series that co-starred his predecessor as Hoppy's juvenile

William Boyd has made a hit with Bobby Larson and Shelley Spencer in this publicity still for **Leather Burners** (1942, United Artists).

sidekick, Jimmy Ellison. Hayden then went into television, first as the star of the syndicated *Cowboy G-Men* series which gave Lesley Selander his first telefilm director credits, then as producer of low-budget Western series like *Judge Roy Bean* (starring the last Cassidy sidekick of all, Edgar Buchanan) and *26 Men*. Hayden's health failed relatively early, and he died in 1981.

When you write about old movies, whether Westerns or any other sort, you can't help writing about death.

And yet the films live. As of this writing, the Cassidys that Boyd produced can be seen weekly on cable TV, thanks to The Disney Channel. The Hoppy TV series still pops up on an occasional independent station. The much better Cassidy features of the Harry Sherman regime are almost never seen on the small screen, thanks to an incredibly stupid and inconclusive lawsuit over rights in the late 1970s. But when they are shown at film fairs, the best of those pictures can turn an audience on like very little else in the Western genre. Perhaps someday a new generation will discover them as I did when I was a boy.

Right, Hoppy?

264

Filmography

HOP-A-LONG CASSIDY
(aka Hopalong Cassidy Enters)

Distributor . . . . .Paramount
Copyrighted . . . . August 22, 1935
Released . . . . July 30, 1935
Director . . . . Howard Bretherton
Producer . . . . Harry Sherman
Associate Producer . . . . .George Green
Photographer . . . . Archie Stout
Film Editor . . . . .Edward Schroeder
Assistant Director . . . . none credited
Screenplay . . . . .Doris Schroeder
Additional Dialogue . . . . . . Harrison Jacobs
Source Novel . . . . Clarence E. Mulford,
Hopalong Cassidy (1910)

Cast

William Boyd . . . . Hopalong Cassidy
Jimmy Ellison . . . . .Johnny Nelson
Paula Stone . . . . Mary Meeker
George Hayes . . . . Uncle Ben
Kenneth Thomson . . . . . Pecos Jack Anthony
Frank McGlynn, Jr. . . . . Red Connors
Charles Middleton . . . . .Buck Peters
Robert Warwick . . . . .Jim Meeker
Willie Fung . . . . Salem
Frank Campeau . . . . .Frisco
James Mason . . . . Tom Shaw
Ted Adams . . . . .Hall
Franklyn Farnum . . . . Doc Riley
John Merton . . . . Party Guest
Wally West . . . . Uncredited Bit Part

THE EAGLE'S BROOD

Distributor . . . . Paramount
Copyrighted . . . . .October 25, 1935
Released . . . . .October 10, 1935
Director . . . . Howard Bretherton
Producer . . . . Harry Sherman
Associate Producer . . . . .George Green
Photographer . . . . Archie Stout
Film Editor . . . . .Edward Schroeder
Assistant Director . . . . Ray Flynn
Screenplay . . . . Doris Schroeder,
Harrison Jacobs
Source Novel . . . . Clarence E. Mulford,
Hopalong Cassidy and the Eagle's Brood (1931)

Cast

William Boyd . . . . .Hopalong Cassidy
Jimmy Ellison . . . . .Johnny Nelson
William Farnum . . . . .El Toro
George Hayes . . . . Spike
Addison Richards . . . . Big Henry
Nana Martinez (Joan Woodbury). . Dolores
Frank Shannon . . . . Mike
Dorothy Revier . . . . Dolly
Paul Fix . . . . Steve
Al Lydell . . . . Pop
John Merton . . . . .Ed
George Mari . . . . .Pablo
Juan Torena . . . . .Esteban
Henry Sylvester . . . . .Sheriff

BAR 20 RIDES AGAIN

Distributor . . . . .Paramount
Copyrighted . . . . December 20, 1935
Released . . . . .November 20, 1935
Director . . . . .Howard Bretherton
Producer . . . . Harry Sherman
Associate Producer . . . . .George Green
Photographer . . . . Archie Stout
Film Editor . . . . .Edward Schroeder
Assistant Director . . . . Ray Flynn
Screenplay . . . . Doris Schroeder,
Gerald Geraghty
Source Novel . . . . Clarence E. Mulford,
The Bar-20 Rides Again (1926)

William Boyd and Andy Clyde study the ink pen and well in this scene from **Leather Burners** (1942, United Artists).

Cast

William Boyd	Hopalong Cassidy
Jimmy Ellison	Johnny Nelson
Jean Rouverol	Margaret Arnold
George Hayes	Windy
Harry Worth	George Perdue/Nevada
Frank McGlynn, Jr.	Red Connors
Howard Lang	Jim Arnold
Ethel Wales	Clarissa Peters
Paul Fix	Gila
J.P. McGowan	Buck Peters
Joe Rickson	Herb Layton
Al St. John	Cinco
John Merton	Carp
Frank Layton	Elbows
Chill Wills and his Avalon Boys	Bar 20 Hands

CALL OF THE PRAIRIE

Distributor	Paramount
Copyrighted/Released	March 6, 1936
Director	Howard Bretherton
Producer	Harry Sherman
Associate Producer	George Green
Photographer	Archie Stout
Film Editor	Edward Schroeder
Assistant Director	none credited
Screenplay	Doris Schroeder, Vernon Smith
Source Novel	Clarence E. Mulford, *Hopalong Cassidy's Protegé*, (1926)

Cast

William Boyd	Hopalong Cassidy
Jimmy Ellison	Johnny Nelson
Muriel Evans	Linda McHenry
Chester Conklin	Sheriff Sandy McQueen
George Hayes	Shanghai McHenry

William Boyd and Andy Clyde listen at the window in this scene from **Leather Burners** (1942, United Artists).

Al Bridge . . . . Sam Porter
Willie Fung . . . . Wong
Howard Lang . . . . .Buck Peters
Hank Mann . . . . Tom
Al Hill . . . . Slade
James Mason . . . . Hoskins
John Merton . . . . Arizona
Chill Wills And His Avalon Boys . . .
. . . Bar 20 Hands

THREE ON THE TRAIL

Distributor . . . . .Paramount
Copyrighted . . . . April 24, 1936
Released . . . . .April 14, 1936
Director . . . . .Howard Bretherton
Producer . . . . .Harry Sherman
Associate Producer . . . . .George Green
Photographer . . . . Archie Stout
Film Editor . . . . .Edward Schroeder
Assistant Directors . . . . .Theodore Joos,
D.M. (Derwin) Abrahams

Screenplay . . . . Doris Schroeder,
Vernon Smith
Source Novel . . . . Clarence E. Mulford,
The Bar-20 Three (1921)

Cast

William Boyd . . . . Hopalong Cassidy
Jimmy Ellison . . . . .Johnny Nelson
Onslow Stevens . . . . Pecos Kane
Muriel Evans . . . . .Mary Stevens
George Hayes . . . . .Windy
Claude King . . . . .J.P. Ridley
William Duncan . . . . .Buck Peters
Clara Kimball Young . . . . Rose Peters
John St. Polis . . . . Sheriff Sam Corwin
Ernie Adams . . . . .Idaho
Al Hill . . . . .Kit Thorpe
Ted Adams . . . . Jim Trask
John Rutherford . . . . Lewis
Lita Cortez . . . . .Conchita
Hank Bell . . . . .Rancher

267

William Boyd protects Bobby Larson in this scene from **Leather Burners** (1942, United Artists).

Lew Meehan . . . . .Uncredited Bit Parts
Artie Ortego
Franklyn Farnum

HEART OF THE WEST

Distributor . . . . .Paramount
Copyrighted . . . . July 10, 1936
Released . . . . July 24, 1936
Director . . . . Howard Bretherton
Producer . . . . .Harry Sherman
Associate Producer . . . . .George Green
Photographer . . . . Archie Stout
Film Editor . . . . .Edward Schroeder
Assistant Directors . . . . Phil Ford,
Theodore Joos
Screenplay . . . . .Doris Schroeder
Source Novel . . . . Clarence E. Mulford,
Mesquite Jenkins, Tumbleweed (1932)

Cast

William Boyd . . . . Hopalong Cassidy
Jimmy Ellison . . . . .Johnny Nelson
George Hayes . . . . .Windy
Sidney Blackmer . . . . Big John Trumbull
Lynn Gabriel . . . . .Sally Jordan
Fred Kohler . . . . Barton
Warner Richmond . . . . Johnson
John Rutherford . . . . Tom Paterson
Walter Miller . . . . Whitey
Charles Martin . . . . Jim Jordan
Ted Adams . . . . Saxon
Robert McKenzie . . . . Tim Grady
John Elliott . . . . Judge

HOPALONG CASSIDY RETURNS

Distributor . . . . .Paramount
Copyrighted . . . . .October 16, 1936
Released . . . . .October 12, 1936

William Boyd and Andy Clyde listen to Shelley Spencer in this scene from **Leather Burners** (1942, United Artists).

Director . . . . Nate Watt	
Producer . . . . .Harry Sherman	
Associate Producer . . . . Eugene Strong	
Photographer . . . . Archie Stout	
Film Editor . . . . Robert Warwick	
Assistant Directors . . . . .V.O. Smith,	
D.M. (Derwin) Abrahams	
Screenplay . . . . .Harrison Jacobs	
Source Novel . . . . Clarence E. Mulford,	
Hopalong Cassidy Returns (1924)	

Cast

William Boyd . . . . Hopalong Cassidy	
George Hayes . . . . .Windy Halliday	
Gail Sheridan . . . . Mary Saunders	
Evelyn Brent . . . . .Lilli Marsh	
Stephen Morris (Morris Ankrum) . . .	
. . . Blackie Felton	
William Janney . . . . .Buddy Cassidy	
Irving Bacon . . . . Peg Leg Holden	
Grant Richards . . . . .Bob Claiborne	

John Beck . . . . Robert Saunders
Al St. John .Luke
Ernie Adams . . . . Benson
Joe Rickson . . . . Buck
Ray Whitley . . . . .Davis
Claude Smith . . . . Dugan

TRAIL DUST

Distributor . . . . Paramount
Copyrighted . . . . December 11, 1936
Released . . . . December 19, 1936
Director . . . . Nate Watt
Producer . . . . .Harry Sherman
Associate Producer . . . . . . .Eugene Strong
Photographer . . . . Archie Stout
Film Editor . . . . Robert Warwick
Assistant Directors . . . . Harry Knight,
D.M. (Derwin) Abrahams
Screenplay . . . . Al Martin
Source Novel . . . . Clarence E. Mulford,
Trail Dust (1934)

William Boyd disarms a player as Andy Clyde watches in this scene from **Leather Burners** (1942, United Artists).

Cast

William Boyd . . . . Hopalong Cassidy
Jimmy Ellison . . . . .Johnny Nelson
George Hayes . . . . .Windy Halliday
Stephen Morris (Morris Ankrum) . . .
. . . Tex Anderson
Gwynne Shipman . . . . Beth Clark
Britt Wood . . . . Lanky
Dick Dickinson . . . . Waggoner
Earl Askam . . . . .Red
Al Bridge . . . . .Babson
John Beach . . . . .Hank
Ted Adams . . . . Joe Wilson
Tom Halligan . . . . .Skinny
Dan Wolkeim . . . . .Borden
Harold Daniels . . . . Lewis
Emmett Daly . . . . George
Al St. John . . . . .Al
Kenneth Harlan . . . . .Bowman
George Chesebro . . . . Saunders
Robert Drew . . . . Bob

John Elliott . . . . .John Clark

BORDERLAND

Distributor . . . . .Paramount
Copyrighted/Released. . . .February 26, 1937
Director . . . . Nate Watt
Producer . . . . Harry Sherman
Associate Producer . . . . Eugene Strong
Photographer . . . . Archie Stout
Film Editor . . . . Robert Warwick
Assistant Directors . . . . Harry Knight,
D. M. (Derwin) Abrahams
Screenplay . . . . .Harrison Jacobs
Source Novel . . . . Clarence E. Mulford,
Bring Me His Ears (1922)

Cast

William Boyd . . . . Hopalong Cassidy
Jimmy Ellison . . . . .Johnny Nelson

William Boyd gleefully ties up a villain in this scene from **Hoppy Serves a Writ** (1942, United Artists).

George Hayes . . . . .Windy Halliday
Stephen Morris (Morris Ankrum) . . .
. . . Loco/The Fox
John Beach . . . . Ranger Bailey
Nora Lane . . . . Grace Rand
Charlene Wyatt . . . . Molly Rand
Trevor Bardette . . . . Colonel Gonzales
Earle Hodgins . . . . .Major Stafford
Al Bridge . . . . .Dandy Morgan
George Chesebro . . . . .Tom Parker
John St. Polis . . . . Doctor
Slim Whittaker . . . . .Rancher
Karl Hackett . . . . .American Visitor
Robert Walker . . . . American Visitor
Frank Ellis . . . . Frank
J.P. McGowan . . . . .El Rio Sheriff
Cliff Parkinson . . . . Gunman
Edward Cassidy . . . . .Gunman
Jack Evans . . . . .Gunman

HILLS OF OLD WYOMING

Distributor . . . . .Paramount
Copyrighted/Released . . . . . . April 16, 1937
Director . . . . Nate Watt
Producer . . . . .Harry Sherman
Associate Producer . . . . none credited
Photographer . . . . Archie Stout
Film Editor . . . . Robert Warwick
Assistant Director . .D.M. (Derwin) Abrahams
Screenplay . . . . .Maurice Geraghty
Source Novel . . . . Clarence E. Mulford,
The Round-Up (1933)

Cast

William Boyd . . . . Hopalong Cassidy
George Hayes . . . . .Windy Halliday
Russell Hayden . . . . Lucky Jenkins
Stephen Morris (Morris Ankrum) . . .
. . . Andrews
Gail Sheridan . . . . Alice Hutchins

271

William Boyd, Andy Clyde, Jay Kirby and friends are ready for action in this scene for **Hoppy Serves a Writ** (1942, United Artists).

John Beach . . . . Saunders
Clara Kimball Young . . . . Ma Hutchins
Earle Hodgins . . . . Thompson
Steve Clemente . . . . Lone Eagle
Chief John Big Tree . . . . Chief Big Tree
George Chesebro . . . . Peterson
Paul Gustine . . . . Daniels
Leo McMahon . . . . Steve
John Powers . . . . Smiley
James Mason . . . . Deputy

NORTH OF THE RIO GRANDE

Distributor . . . . Paramount
Copyrighted . . . . June 18, 1937
Released . . . . June 28, 1937
Director . . . . Nate Watt
Producer . . . . Harry Sherman
Associate Producer . . . . none credited
Photographer . . . . Russell Harlan
Film Editor . . . . Robert Warwick

Assistant Directors . . . . D. M. (Derwin)
Abrahams, V.O. Smith
Screenplay . . . . Jack (Joseph) O'Donnell
Source Novel . . . . Clarence E. Mulford,
Cottonwood Gulch (1924)

Cast

William Boyd . . . . Hopalong Cassidy
George Hayes . . . . Windy Halliday
Russell Hayden . . . . Lucky Jenkins
Stephen Morris (Morris Ankrum) . . .
. . . Henry Stoneham/The Lone Wolf
Bernadene Hayes . . . . Faro Annie
John Rutherford . . . . Ace Crowder
Lorraine Randall . . . . Mary Cassidy
Walter Long . . . . Bull O'Hara
Lee Colt (Lee J. Cobb) . . . . . . Mr. Wooden
Al Ferguson . . . . Deputy Jim Plunkett
John Beach . . . . Clark
Lafe McKee . . . . Joe

George Reeves and Jan Christy listen as William Boyd tries to convince Forbes Murray not to use the rifle in this scene from **Hoppy Serves a Writ** (1942, United Artists).

RUSTLERS' VALLEY

Distributor . . . . .Paramount
Copyrighted/Released . . . . . . July 23, 1937
Director . . . . Nate Watt
Producer . . . . Harry Sherman
Associate Producer . . . . none credited
Photographer . . . . .Russell Harlan
Film Editor . . . . Sherman A. Rose
Supervising Film Editor . . .
. . . . .Robert Warwick
Assistant Directors . . . . D. M. (Derwin)
Abrahams, V.O. Smith
Screenplay . . . . .Harry O. Hoyt
Source Novel . . . . Clarence E. Mulford,
Rustlers' Valley (1924)

Cast

William Boyd . . . . Hopalong Cassidy
George Hayes . . . . .Windy Halliday
Russell Hayden . . . . Lucky Jenkins

Stephen Morris (Morris Ankrum) . . .
. . . Glenn Randall
Muriel Evans . . . . Agnes Randall
Lee Colt (Lee J. Cobb) . . . . . . .Cal Howard
Ted Adams . . . . Taggart
Al Ferguson . . . . .Joe
John Beach . . . . .Sheriff Boulton
Oscar Apfel . . . . Clem Crawford
Horace B. Carpenter . . . . .Party Guest
John Powers . . . . Stuttering Man
Bernadene Hayes . . . . . .Uncredited Bit Parts
John St. Polis

HOPALONG RIDES AGAIN

Distributor . . . . .Paramount
Copyrighted/Released . . September 30, 1937
Director . . . . Lesley Selander
Producer . . . . Harry Sherman
Associate Producer . . . . none credited
Photographer . . . . .Russell Harlan

273

William Boyd and Andy Clyde seem to be looking off camera for an explanation of the money they have just found in this scene from **Hoppy Serves a Writ** (1942, United Artists).

Film Editor	Robert Warwick
Assistant Directors	.D.M. (Derwin)
	Abrahams, Theodore Joos
Screenplay	Norman Houston
Source Novel	Clarence E. Mulford,
	Black Buttes (1923)

Cast

William Boyd	Hopalong Cassidy
George Hayes	Windy Halliday
Russell Hayden	Lucky Jenkins
Nora Lane	Nora Blake
Harry Worth	Prof. Horace Hepburn
Lois Wilde	Laura Peters
Billy King	Artie Peters
William Duncan	Buck Peters
John Rutherford	Blackie
Ernie Adams	Keno
John Beach	Pete
Black Jack Ward	Slim
Frank Ellis	Rustler

Ben Corbett	.Rustler
Artie Ortego	Uncredited Bit Part

TEXAS TRAIL

Distributor	Paramount
Copyrighted/Released . .	November 26, 1937
Director	.David Selman
Producer	.Harry Sherman
Associate Producer	none credited
Photographer	.Russell Harlan
Film Editor	Sherman A. Rose
Assistant Directors	D.M. (Derwin)
	Abrahams, Theodore Joos
Screenplay	Jack (Joseph) O'Donnell
Additional Dialogue	Jack Mersereau
Source Novel	Clarence E. Mulford,
	Tex (1922)

Cast

William Boyd	Hopalong Cassidy

William Boyd motions for Forbes Murray to hand it over as Jay Kirby and Jan Christy look on in this scene from **Hoppy Serves a Writ** (1942, United Artists).

Russell Hayden	Lucky Jenkins	Released	January 14, 1938
George Hayes	Windy Halliday	Director	Lesley Selander
Judith Allen	Barbara Allen	Producer	Harry Sherman
Billy King	Boots McCreedy	Associate Producer	none credited
Alexander Cross	Black Jack Carson	Photographer	Russell Harlan
Karl Hackett	Major McCreedy	Film Editor	Robert Warwick
Bob Kortman	Hawks	Assistant Directors	D.M. (Derwin)
Jack Rockwell	Shorty		Abrahams, Theodore Joos
John Beach	Smokey	Screenplay	Harrison Jacobs
Raphael Bennett	Brad	Source Novel	Clarence E. Mulford,
Philo McCullough	Jordan		*The Man From Bar-20* (1918)
Earle Hodgins	General		
Ben Corbett	Stockade Guard		
John Judd	Lieutenant		
Clyde Kinney	Courier		
Leo McMahon	Corporal		

Cast

William Boyd	Hopalong Cassidy
Russell Hayden	Lucky Jenkins
Harvey Clark	Baldy Morton
Gwen Gaze	Lorna Drake
Hilda Plowright	Aunt Martha
John Warburton	Ronald Harwood
Al Bridge	Scar Lewis
Al Hill	Doc Galer

PARTNERS OF THE PLAINS

Distributor . . . . .Paramount
Copyrighted . . . . .January 28, 1938

275

William Boyd hands Andy Clyde and Jay Kirby some money and explains his plan in this scene from **Hoppy Serves a Writ** (1942, United Artists).

Earle Hodgins . . . . Sheriff
John Beach . . . . Mr. Benson
Jim Corey . . . . Uncredited Bit Part

CASSIDY OF BAR 20

Distributor . . . . .Paramount
Copyrighted/Released . . . February 25, 1938
Director . . . . Lesley Selander
Producer . . . . .Harry Sherman
Associate Producer . . . . none credited
Photographer . . . . .Russell Harlan
Film Editor . . . . Sherman A. Rose
Assistant Directors . . . . .D. M. (Derwin) Abrahams, Theodore Joos
Screenplay . . . . .Norman Houston
Source Novel . . . . Clarence E. Mulford, *Me An' Shorty* (1929)
Cast

William Boyd . . . . Hopalong Cassidy

Russell Hayden . . . . Lucky Jenkins
Frank Darien . . . . .Pappy
Nora Lane . . . . Nora Blake
Robert Fiske . . . . .Clay Allison
John Elliott . . . . .Tom Dillon
Margaret Marquis . . . . Mary Dillon
Gertrude Hoffmann . . . . Ma Caffrey
Carleton Young . . . . .Jeff Caffrey
Gordon Hart . . . . .Judge Belcher
Edward Cassidy . . . . .Sheriff Hawley
Jim Toney . . . . Uncredited Bit Part

HEART OF ARIZONA

Distributor . . . . .Paramount
Copyrighted/Released . . . . . April 22, 1938
Director . . . . Lesley Selander
Producer . . . . Harry Sherman
Associate Producer . . . . J.D. Trop
Photographer . . . . .Russell Harlan
Film Editor . . . . Sherman A. Rose

276

William Boyd and Forbes Murray seem to finally be on friendly terms as Jan Christy tends to Jay Kirby's wound in this scene from **Hoppy Serves a Writ** (1942, United Artists).

Assistant Directors . . . . .D.M. (Derwin)
Abrahams, Theodore Joos
Screenplay . . . . .Norman Houston

Cast

William Boyd . . . . .Hopalong Cassidy
George Hayes . . . . .Windy Halliday
Russell Hayden . . . . .Lucky Jenkins
John Elliott . . . . .Buck Peters
Billy King . . . . Artie Peters
Natalie Moorhead . . . . Belle Starr
Dorothy Short . . . . Jacqueline Starr
Alden (Stephen) Chase . . . . . . .Dan Ringo
John Beach . . . . .Sheriff Hawley
Lane Chandler . . . . Trimmer Winkler
Leo McMahon . . . . Twister
Lee Phelps . . . . Uncredited Bit Parts
Robert McKenzie

BAR 20 JUSTICE

Distributor . . . . .Paramount
Copyrighted/Released . . . . . . June 24, 1938
Director . . . . Lesley Selander
Producer . . . . Harry Sherman
Associate Producer . . . . J.D. Trop
Photographer . . . . .Russell Harlan
Film Editor . . . . Robert Warwick
Assistant Directors . . . . . . D.M. (Derwin)
Abrahams, Theodore Joos
Screenplay . . . . Arnold Belgard
Additional Dialogue . . . . . . Harrison Jacobs

Cast

William Boyd . . . . Hopalong Cassidy
George Hayes . . . . .Windy Halliday
Russell Hayden . . . . Lucky Jenkins
Gwen Gaze . . . . Ann Dennis
William Duncan . . . . .Buck Peters
Pat (J.) O'Brien . . . . .Frazier

William Boyd tries to beat a confession out of Victor Jory in this scene from **Hoppy Serves a Writ** (1942, United Artists).

Paul Sutton . . . . .Slade
John Beach . . . . .Denny Dennis
Joseph De Stefani . . . . .Perkins
Walter Long .Pierce
H. Bruce Mitchell . . . . .Ross
Frosty Royce . . . . Uncredited Bit Parts
Jim Toney

PRIDE OF THE WEST

Distributor . . . . .Paramount
Copyrighted/Released . . . . July 8, 1938
Director . . . . Lesley Selander
Producer . . . . .Harry Sherman
Associate Producer . . . . none credited
Photographer . . . . .Russell Harlan
Film Editor . . . . Sherman A. Rose
Music Director . . . . Boris Morros
Assistant Directors . . . . .D.M. (Derwin)
Abrahams, Theodore Joos
Screenplay . . . . Nate Watt

Cast

William Boyd . . . . Hopalong Cassidy
George Hayes . . . . .Windy Halliday
Russell Hayden . . . . Lucky Jenkins
Earle Hodgins . . . . Sheriff Tom Martin
Charlotte Field . . . . Mary Martin
Billy King . . . . Dick Martin
Kenneth Harlan . . . . .Caldwell
Glenn Strange . . . . .Saunders
James Craig . . . . .Nixon
H. Bruce Mitchell . . . . .Detective
Willie Fung . . . . .Sing Loo
George Morrell . . . . Townsman
Earl Askam . . . . .Uncredited Bit Parts
Jim Toney
Horace B. Carpenter
Henry Otho

Benny Corbett and Bob Burns (in background) watch as William Boyd and Victor Jory engage in a brawl in this scene from **Hoppy Serves a Writ** (1942, United Artists).

IN OLD MEXICO

Distributor . . . . Paramount
Copyrighted/Released . . .September 9, 1938
Director . . . . Edward D. Venturini
Producer . . . . .Harry Sherman
Associate Producer . . . . none credited
Photographer . . . . .Russell Harlan
Film Editor . . . . Robert Warwick
Music Score . . . . .Gregory Stone
Music Director . . . . Boris Morros
Assistant Directors . . . . D.M. (Derwin)
Abrahams, Theodore Joos
Screenplay . . . . .Harrison Jacobs

Cast

William Boyd . . . . Hopalong Cassidy
George Hayes . . . . .Windy Halliday
Russell Hayden . . . . Lucky Jenkins
Paul Sutton . . . . .The Fox
Allan Garcia . . . . Don Carlos Gonzales
Jane (Jan) Clayton . . . . Anita Gonzales
Trevor Bardette . . . . Colonel Gonzales
Betty Amann . . . . Janet Leeds
Anna Demetrio . . . . .Elena
Glenn Strange . . . . .Burke
Tony Roux .Pancho
Fred Burns . . . . .Uncredited Bit Parts
Cliff Parkinson

THE FRONTIERSMEN

Distributor . . . . Paramount
Copyrighted/Released . . .December 16, 1938
Director . . . . Lesley Selander
Producer . . . . Harry Sherman
Associate Producer . . . . none credited
Photographer . . . . .Russell Harlan
Film Editor . . . . Sherman A. Rose
Music Director . . . . Boris Morros
Assistant Directors . . . . .D. M. (Derwin)
Abrahams, Theodore Joos

Jay Kirby has George Reeves covered as William Boyd and Andy Clyde look on in this scene from **Hoppy Serves a Writ** (1942, United Artists).

Screenplay . . . . Norman Houston
Additional Dialogue . . . . . . Harrison Jacobs

Cast

William Boyd . . . . .Hopalong Cassidy
George Hayes . . . . .Windy Halliday
Russell Hayden . . . . Lucky Jenkins
Evelyn Venable . . . . June Lake
Charles A. Hughes . . .
. . .Mayor Judson Thorpe/Dan Rawley
William Duncan . . . . .Buck Peters
Clara Kimball Young . . . . . . Amanda Peters
Emily Fitzroy . . . . Miss Snook
Dickie Jones . . . . Artie Peters
John Beach . . . . .Quirt
Roy Barcroft . . . . .Buster Sutton
St. Brendan Boys Choir . . . . . School Boys
Black Jack Ward . . . . . . Uncredited Bit Parts
George Morrell
Jim Corey

SUNSET TRAIL

Distributor . . . . .Paramount
Copyrighted/Released . . . February 24, 1939
Director . . . . Lesley Selander
Producer . . . . .Harry Sherman
Associate Producer . . . . none credited
Photographer . . . . .Russell Harlan
Film Editor . . . . Robert Warwick
Music Director . . . . Ed Paul
Assistant Directors . . . . D.M. (Derwin)
Abrahams, Theodore Joos
Screenplay . . . . .Norman Houston

Cast

William Boyd . . . . Hopalong Cassidy
George Hayes . . . . .Windy Halliday
Russell Hayden . . . . Lucky Jenkins
Charlotte Wynters . . . . Ann Marsh
Jane (Jan) Clayton . . . . Dorrie Marsh
Robert Fiske . . . . Monte Keller

Andy Clyde seems amazed at William Boyd and Jay Kirby's comment about his chicken in this scene from **Colt Comrades** (1943, United Artists).

Kenneth Harlan . . . . .John Marsh
Anthony Nace . . . . .Steve Dorman
Kathryn Sheldon . . . . .Abigail Snodgrass
Maurice Cass . . . . E. Prescott Furbush
Alphonse Ethier . . . . Superintendent
Glenn Strange . . . . Bouncer
Claudia Smith . . . . Mary Rogers
Jack Rockwell . . . . Stage Driver
Tom London . . . . Patrol Captain
Jim Toney . . . . Uncredited Bit Parts
Fred Burns
Jerry Jerome
Jim Corey
Frank Ellis
Horace B. Carpenter

Producer . . . . Harry Sherman
Associate Producer . . . . .J.D. Trop
Photographer . . . . .Russell Harlan
Film Editor . . . . Robert Warwick
Music Director . . . . Boris Morros
Assistant Directors . . . . .D.M. (Derwin)
Abrahams, Theodore Joos
Screenplay . . . . .Maurice Geraghty

Cast

William Boyd . . . . Hopalong Cassidy
Russell Hayden . . . . Lucky Jenkins
George Hayes . . . . .Windy Halliday
Ruth Rogers . . . . .Barbara Hamilton
Stanley Ridges . . . . Earl Brennan/Dave Talbot
Frederick Burton . . . . Tom Hamilton
Jack Rockwell . . . . City Marshal
Roy Barcroft . . . . .Ewing
Edward Cassidy . . . . Pierce
Wen Wright (Sherry Tansey) . . . . . .Lane
H. Bruce Mitchell . . . . Bartender

SILVER ON THE SAGE

Distributor . . . . .Paramount
Copyrighted/Released . . . . March 31, 1939
Director . . . . Lesley Selander

William Boyd disturbs Andy Clyde's reading in this scene from **Colt Comrades** (1943, United Artists).

Hank Bell . . . . .Uncredited Bit Parts
Jim Corey
George Morrell
Frank O'Connor
Buzz Barton
Herman Hack
Dick Dickinson

THE RENEGADE TRAIL

Distributor . . . . .Paramount
Copyrighted . . . . August 18, 1939
Released . . . . .July 25, 1939
Director . . . . Lesley Selander
Producer . . . . .Harry Sherman
Associate Producer . . . . none credited
Photographer . . . . .Russell Harlan
Film Editor . . . . Sherman A. Rose
Music Director . . . . Boris Morros
Assistant Directors . . . . .D.M. (Derwin)
Abrahams, Theodore Joos

Screenplay . . . . John Rathmell
Additional Dialogue . . . . . . Harrison Jacobs

Cast

William Boyd . . . . Hopalong Cassidy
Russell Hayden . . . . Lucky Jenkins
George Hayes . . . . Windy Halliday
Charlotte Wynters . . . . Mary Joyce
Russell Hopton . . . . Bob "Smoky" Joslin
Roy Barcroft . . . . Stiff Hat Bailey
John Merton . . . . .Tex Traynor
Sonny Bupp . . . . Joey Joyce
Eddie Dean .Red
Jack Rockwell . . . . Slim Baker
Bob Kortman . . . . Haskins
The King's Men (Ken Darby, Rad Robinson, John Dobson, Bud Linn) . . .
. . . Musicians

William Boyd, George Reeves and Jay Kirby are ready for action in this scene from **Colt Comrades** (1943, United Artists).

RANGE WAR

Distributor . . . . .Paramount
Copyrighted/Released . . . September 8, 1939
Director . . . . Lesley Selander
Producer . . . . Harry Sherman
Associate Producer . . . . none credited
Photographer . . . . .Russell Harlan
Film Editor . . . . Sherman A. Rose
Music Score . . . . Victor Young
Assistant Director . D.M. (Derwin) Abrahams
Screenplay . . . . Sam Robins
Additional Dialogue . . . . Walter Roberts
Story . . . . Josef Montiague

Cast

William Boyd . . . . Hopalong Cassidy
Russell Hayden . . . . Lucky Jenkins
Britt Wood . . . . Speedy McGinnis
Pedro de Cordoba . . . . .Padre Jose
Willard Robertson . . . . .Buck Collins

Matt Moore . . . . Jim Marlow
Betty Moran . . . . Ellen Marlow
Kenneth Harlan . . . . Charles Higgins
Francis McDonald . . . . .Dave Morgan
Eddie Dean . . . . .Pete
Earle Hodgins . . . . Deputy
Jason Robards, Sr. . . . . Rancher
Stanley Price . . . . Agitator
Raphael Bennett . . . . Staley
Glenn Strange . . . . Sheriff
Don Latorre . . . . .Felipe
George Chesebro . . . . . . .Uncredited Bit Part

LAW OF THE PAMPAS

Distributor . . . . .Paramount
Copyrighted/Released . . . November 3, 1939
Director . . . . Nate Watt
Producer . . . . Harry Sherman
Associate Producer . . . . . .Joseph W. Engel
Photographer . . . . .Russell Harlan

283

William Boyd and Andy Clyde are gleefully tying up Victor Jory in this scene from **Colt Comrades** (1943, United Artists).

Film Editor . . . . Carrol Lewis	
Music Score . . . . Victor Young	
Assistant Director . D.M. (Derwin) Abrahams	
Screenplay . . . . Harrison Jacobs	

Cast

William Boyd . . . . Hopalong Cassidy	
Russell Hayden . . . . .Lucky Jenkins	
Sidney Toler . . . . .Fernando Ramirez	
Steffi Duna . . . . .Chiquita	
Sidney Blackmer . . . . .Ralph Merritt	
Pedro de Cordoba . . . . .Don Jose Valdez	
William Duncan . . . . .Buck Peters	
Anna Demetrio . . . . Dolores Ramirez	
Eddie Dean . . . . .Curly Naples	
Glenn Strange . . . . Slim Schultz	
Jojo La Sadio . . . . Ernesto Valdez	
The King's Men . . . . .Musicians	
Tony Roux . . . . Gaucho	
Martin Garralaga . . . . Bolo Carrier	

SANTA FE MARSHAL

Distributor . . . . .Paramount	
Copyrighted/Released . . . . January 26, 1940	
Director . . . . Lesley Selander	
Producer . . . . .Harry Sherman	
Associate Producer . . . . . . Joseph W. Engel	
Photographer . . . . .Russell Harlan	
Film Editor . . . . Sherman A. Rose	
Music Score . . . . .John Leipold	
Assistant Director . .D.M. (Derwin) Abrahams	
Screenplay . . . . .Harrison Jacobs	

Cast

William Boyd . . . . .Hopalong Cassidy	
Russell Hayden . . . . Lucky Jenkins	
Marjorie Rambeau . . . . .Ma Burton	
Bernadene Hayes . . . . .Paula Bates	
Earle Hodgins . . . . Doc Bates	
Britt Wood . . . . .Axel	
Kenneth Harlan . . . . Blake	

Jay Kirby smiles as William Boyd seems upset with Andy Clyde in this scene from **Colt Comrades** (1943, United Artists).

William Pagan . . . . .Flint
George Anderson . . . . .Tex Barnes
Jack Rockwell . . . . .John Gardner
Eddie Dean . . . . .Town Marshal
Fred Graham . . . . Uncredited Bit Parts
Matt Moore
Duke Green
Billy Jones
Tex Phelps
Cliff Parkinson

THE SHOWDOWN

Distributor . . . . .Paramount
Copyrighted/Released . . . . . March 8, 1940
Director . . . . .Howard Bretherton
Producer . . . . Harry Sherman
Associate Producer . . . . none credited
Photographer . . . . .Russell Harlan
Film Editor . . . . Carrol Lewis
Music Score . . . . .John Leipold

Assistant Director . D.M. (Derwin) Abrahams
Screenplay . . . . .Harold and Daniel Kusell
Story . . . . Jack Jungmeyer

Cast

William Boyd . . . . Hopalong Cassidy
Russell Hayden . . . . Lucky Jenkins
Britt Wood . . . . .Speedy McGinnis
Morris Ankrum . . . . .Baron Rendor
Jane (Jan) Clayton . . . . Sue Williard
Wright Kramer . . . . Col. Rufus White
Donald Kirke . . . . Harry Cole
Roy Barcroft . . . . .Bowman
Eddie Dean . . . . .Marshal
Kermit Maynard . . . . .Johnson
Walter Shumway . . . . Snell
The King's Men . . . . .Musicians

William Boyd, Jay Kirby, George Reeves and Gayle Lord plan strategy in this scene from **Colt Comrades** (1943, United Artists).

HIDDEN GOLD

Distributor . . . . .Paramount
Copyrighted/Released . . . . June 7, 1940
Director . . . . Lesley Selander
Producer . . . . Harry Sherman
Associate Producer . . . . . .Joseph W. Engel
Photographer . . . . .Russell Harlan
Film Editor . . . . Carrol Lewis
Music Director . . . . .Irvin Talbot
Assistant Director . .D.M. (Derwin) Abrahams
Screenplay . .Gerald Geraghty, Jack Mersereau

Cast

William Boyd . . . . Hopalong Cassidy
Russell Hayden . . . . .Lucky Jenkins
Britt Wood . . . . .Speedy McGinnis
Minor Watson . . . . .Ed Colby
Ruth Rogers . . . . Jane Colby
Ethel Wales . . . . Matilda Purdy
Lee Phelps . . . . Sheriff Cameron

Roy Barcroft . . . . Hendricks
George Anderson . . . . Ward Ackerman
Eddie Dean . . . . Logan
Raphael Bennett . . . . .Fleming
Jack Rockwell . . . . Stage Driver
Walter Long . . . . .Uncredited Bit Parts
Bob Kortman
Merrill McCormack

STAGECOACH WAR

Distributor . . . . .Paramount
Copyrighted/Released . . . . . . July 12, 1940
Director . . . . Lesley Selander
Producer . . . . .Harry Sherman
Associate Producer . . . . . . Joseph W. Engel
Photographer . . . . .Russell Harlan
Film Editor . . . . Sherman A. Rose
Music Score . . . . .John Leipold
Music Director . . . . Irvin Talbot
Assistant Director . D.M. (Derwin) Abrahams

286

William Boyd makes a point to Earle Hodgins as Gayle Lord serves more chicken in this scene from **Colt Comrades** (1943, United Artists).

Screenplay . . . . .Norman Houston,
Harry F. Olmstead

Cast

William Boyd . . . . .Hopalong Cassidy
Russell Hayden . . . . Lucky Jenkins
Britt Wood . . . . .Speedy McGinnis
Julie Carter . . . . Shirley Chapman
Harvey Stephens . . . . Neal Holt
J. Farrell MacDonald . . . . . . .Jeff Chapman
Rad Robinson . . . . Smiley
Eddy Waller . . . . Quince Cobalt
Frank Lackteen . . . . .Twister Maxwell
Jack Rockwell . . . . .Mart Gunther
Eddie Dean . . . . Tom
The King's Men . . . . .Musicians
Bob Kortman . . . . Uncredited Bit Parts
Hank Bell

THREE MEN FROM TEXAS

Distributor . . . . .Paramount
Copyrighted/Released . . November 15, 1940
Director . . . . Lesley Selander
Producer . . . . .Harry Sherman
Associate Producer . . . . . . .Joseph W. Engel
Photographer . . . . .Russell Harlan
Film Editor . . . . Carrol Lewis
Supervising Editor . . . . . . Sherman A. Rose
Music Score . . . . Victor Young
Assistant Director . .D.M. (Derwin) Abrahams
Screenplay . . . . Norton S. Parker

Cast

William Boyd . . . . .Hopalong Cassidy
Russell Hayden . . . . Lucky Jenkins
Andy Clyde . . . . .California Carlson
Morris Ankrum . . . . .Bruce Morgan
Morgan Wallace . . . . Capt. Andrews
Thornton Edwards . . . . Pico Serrano

287

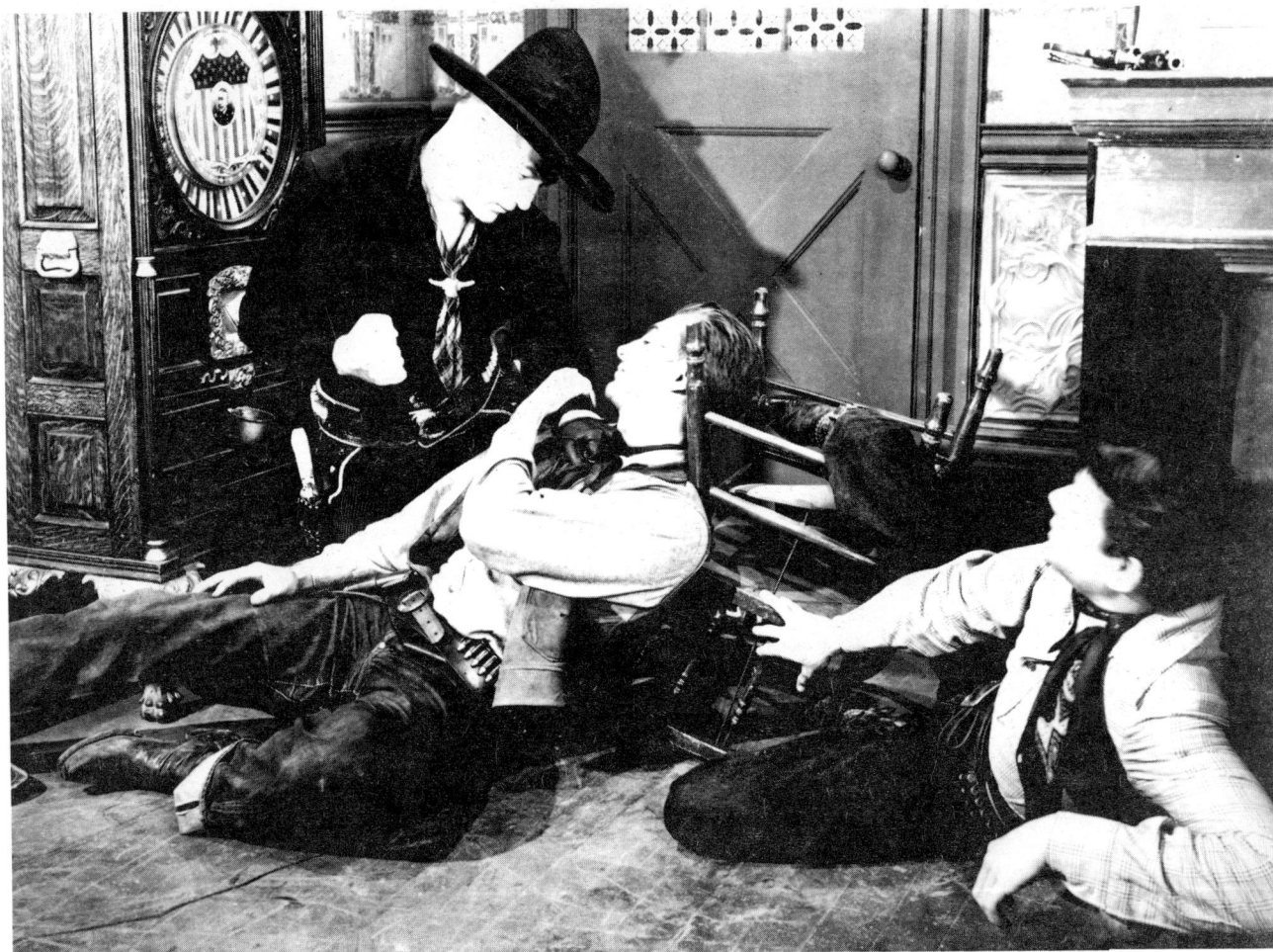

William Boyd has the best of Robert Mitchum as Jay Kirby untangles himself from a chair in this scene from **Colt Comrades** (1943, United Artists).

Esther Estrella . . . . .Paquita	**Film Editor** . . . . Carrol Lewis
Davidson Clark . . . . .Thompson	**Supervising Editor** . . . . . . Sherman A. Rose
Dick Curtis . . . . .Gardner	**Music Directors** . . Irvin Talbot, John Leipold
George Lollier . . . . Dave	**Assistant Director** . D.M. (Derwin) Abrahams
Glenn Strange . . . . Ben Stokes	**Screenplay** . . . . .Johnston McCulley,
Neyl Marx . . . . .Juanito	J. Benton Cheney
Bob Burns . . . . Uncredited Bit Parts	
Jim Corey	

Cast

George Morrell	
Frank McCarroll	**William Boyd** . . . . Hopalong Cassidy
Lucio Villegas	**Russell Hayden** . . . . Lucky Jenkins
Win Wright	**Andy Clyde** . . . . .California Jack
	Minna Gombell . . . . .Jane Travers
	Morris Ankrum . . . . .Stephen Westcott
THE DOOMED CARAVAN	**Georgia Hawkins** . . . . Diana Westcott
	Trevor Bardette . . . . Ed Martin
	Pat J. O'Brien . . . . .Jim Ferber
Distributor . . . . .Paramount	**Raphael Bennett** . . . . Pete Gregg
Copyrighted/Released . . . January 10, 1941	**Jose Luis Tortosa** . . . . Don Pedro
Director . . . . Lesley Selander	**Henry Wills** . . . . Uncredited Bit Parts
Producer . . . . Harry Sherman	**Edward Cassidy**
Associate Producer . . . . . . Joseph W. Engel	**Martin Garralaga**
Photographer . . . . .Russell Harlan	**Chick Hannon**

Robert Mitchum pulls back from William Boyd's punch in this scene from **Colt Comrades** (1943, United Artists).

IN OLD COLORADO

Distributor . . . . .Paramount
Copyrighted/Released . . . . . March 14, 1941
Director . . . . .Howard Bretherton
Producer . . . . Harry Sherman
Associate Producer . . . . . . Joseph W. Engel
Photographer . . . . .Russell Harlan
Film Editor . . . . Carrol Lewis
Supervising Editor . . . . . . Sherman A. Rose
Music Directors . . Irvin Talbot, John Leipold
Assistant Director . . . . . . Derwin Abrahams
Screenplay . . . . .Norton S. Parker,
J. Benton Cheney

Cast

William Boyd . . . . Hopalong Cassidy
Russell Hayden . . . . Lucky Jenkins
Andy Clyde . . . . California
Margaret Hayes . . . . Myra Woods
Morris Ankrum . . . . Joe Weiler
Sarah Padden . . . . Ma Woods

Cliff Nazarro . . . . Nosey Haskins
Stanley Andrews . . . . George Davidson
James Seay . . . . .Hank Merritt
Morgan Wallace . . . . Jack Collins
Weldon Heyburn . . . . Blackie Reed
Eddy Waller . . . . Jim Stark
Philip Van Zandt . . . . Confidence Man
Glenn Strange . . . . Uncredited Bit Parts
Henry Wills
Curley Dresden

BORDER VIGILANTES

Distributor . . . . .Paramount
Copyrighted/Released . . . . . . April 18, 1941
Director . . . . .Derwin Abrahams
Producer . . . . .Harry Sherman
Associate Producer . . . . . . Joseph W. Engel
Photographer . . . . .Russell Harlan
Film Editor . . . . Robert Warwick
Supervising Editor . . . . . . Sherman A. Rose

William Boyd is about ready to draw but Gayle Lord looks bored in this scene from **Colt Comrades** (1943, United Artists).

Music Directors . . .Irvin Talbot, John Leipold
Assistant Director . . . . . . .Frederick Spencer
Screenplay . . . . J. Benton Cheney

Chuck Morrison
Ted Wells
Chick Hannon

Cast

William Boyd . . . . .Hopalong Cassidy
Russell Hayden . . . . .Lucky Jenkins
Andy Clyde . . . . .California Carlson
Frances Gifford . . . . Helen Forbes
Victor Jory . . . . .Henry Logan
Ethel Wales . . . . .Aunt Jennifer
Morris Ankrum . . . . Dan Forbes
Tom Tyler . . . . Jim Yager
Hal Taliaferro . . . . Ed Stone
Jack Rockwell . . . . .Hank Weaver
Britt Wood . . . . Lafe Willis
Hank Worden . . . . Wagon Driver
Edward Earle . . . . Banker Stevens
Hank Bell . . . . Liveryman
Al Haskell . . . . Uncredited Bit Parts
Curley Dresden

PIRATES ON HORSEBACK

Distributor . . . . Paramount
Copyrighted . . . . May 23, 1941
Released . . . . May 31, 1941
Director . . . . Lesley Selander
Producer . . . . Harry Sherman
Associate Producer . . . . . . Joseph W. Engel
Photographer . . . . .Russell Harlan
Film Editor . . . . .Fred Feitshans, Jr.
Supervising Editor . . . . . . Sherman A. Rose
Music Directors . . . . John Leipold,
Maurice Lawrence
Assistant Director . . . . . . .Frederick Spencer
Screenplay . . . . .Ethel La Blanche,
J. Benton Cheney

Jay Kirby, Gayle Lord, George Reeves, William Boyd and Forbes Murray in a publicity still for **Colt Comrades** (1943, United Artists).

Cast

William Boyd . . . . Hopalong Cassidy
Russell Hayden . . . . Lucky Jenkins
Andy Clyde . . . . .California Carlson
Eleanor Stewart . . . . Trudy Pendleton
Morris Ankrum . . . . Ace Gibson
William Haade . . . . .Bill Watson
Dennis Moore . . . . Jud Carter
Henry Hall . . . . .Sheriff John Blake
Britt Wood . . . . .Ben Pendleton
Jack Rockwell . . . . .Stable Owner
Silver Tip Baker . . . . Uncredited Bit Part

WIDE OPEN TOWN

Distributor . . . . Paramount
Copyrighted . . . . August 15, 1941
Released . . . . August 8, 1941
Director . . . . Lesley Selander
Producer . . . . Harry Sherman

Associate Producer . . . . . . Lewis J. Rachmil
Photographer . . . . .Russell Harlan
Film Editor . . . . Carrol Lewis
Supervising Editor . . . . . . Sherman A. Rose
Music Directors . . .Irvin Talbot, John Leipold
Assistant Director . . . . . . .Frederick Spencer
Screenplay . . . . J. Benton Cheney,
                                    Harrison Jacobs
Uncredited Source . . . .**Hopalong**
        Cassidy Returns (Paramount, 1936)

Cast

William Boyd . . . . Hopalong Cassidy
Russell Hayden . . . . Lucky Jenkins
Andy Clyde . . . . .California Carlson
Evelyn Brent . . . . .Belle Langtry
Victor Jory . . . . .Steve Fraser
Morris Ankrum . . . . Jim Stuart
Bernice Kay (Cara Williams) . . Joan Stuart
Kenneth Harlan . . . . .Tom Wilson
Roy Barcroft . . . . Red

William Boyd disarms Victor Jory in this scene from **Colt Comrades** (1943, United Artists).

Glenn Strange . . . . Ed Stark
Edward Cassidy . . . . Brad Jackson
Jack Rockwell . . . . Rancher
Bob Kortman . . . . .Blackie
George Cleveland . . . . .Pete Carter

STICK TO YOUR GUNS

Distributor . . . . .Paramount
Copyrighted . . . . .September 19, 1941
Released . . . . .September 27, 1941
Director . . . . Lesley Selander
Producer . . . . Harry Sherman
Associate Producer . . . . . Lewis J. Rachmil
Photographer . . . . .Russell Harlan
Film Editor . . . . Carrol Lewis
Supervising Editor . . . . . . Sherman A. Rose
Music Score . . . . .John Leipold
Music Director . . . . .Irvin Talbot
Assistant Director . . . . .Glenn Cook
Uncredited Source . . . . . . .Bar 20 Rides
Again (Paramount, 1935)

Cast

William Boyd . . . . Hopalong Cassidy
Andy Clyde . . . . .Calfiornia Carlson
Brad King . . . . Johnny Nelson
Jacqueline (Jennifer) Holt . . . June Winters
Dick Curtis . . . . Nevada
Weldon Heyburn . . . . Gila
Henry Hall . . . . Jud Winters
Jack Rockwell . . . . .Carp
Ian McDonald . . . . Elbows
Kermit Maynard . . . . Layton
Charles Middleton . . . . Long Ben
Homer Holcomb . . . . Frenchy Smith
Tom London . . . . Waffles
The Jimmy Wakely Trio (Jimmy Wakely,
Johnny Bond, Dick Rinehart) . . . . Singers
Joe Whitehead . . . . Buck
Jack Smith . . . . Tex
Jack Trent . . . . Red
Mickey Eissa . . . . Ed

292

It takes a lot of people behind the camera in addition to the movie stars as can be seen from this publicity still for **Bar 20** (1943, United Artists). Sorry, we couldn't identify them for you.

Robert Card . . . . Uncredited Bit Parts
Herman Hack
Frank Ellis

SECRETS OF THE WASTELAND

Distributor . . . . .Paramount
Copyrighted . . . . November 1, 1941
Released . . . . .November 15, 1941
Director . . . . .Derwin Abrahams
Producer . . . . Harry Sherman
Associate Producer . . . . . . Lewis J. Rachmil
Photographer . . . . .Russell Harlan
Film Editor . . . . .Fred Feitshans, Jr.
Supervising Editor . . . . . . Sherman A. Rose
Music Score . . . . .John Leipold
Music Director . . . . .Irvin Talbot
Assistant Director . . . . John Sherwood
Screenplay . . . . Gerald Geraghty
Source Novel . . . .Bliss Lomax (Harry Sinclair
        Drago), *Secret of the Wastelands* (1940)

Cast

William Boyd . . . . Hopalong Cassidy
Andy Clyde . . . . .California Carlson
Brad King . . . . Johnny Nelson
Soo Yong . . . . .Moy Soong
Barbara Britton . . . . .Jennifer Kendall
Douglas Fowley . . . . .Slade Salters
Keith Richards . . . . .Clay Elliott
Richard Loo . . . . Quon
Lee Tung Foo . . . . Doy Kee
Gordon Hart . . . . Dr. Malcolm Birdsell
Earl Gunn . . . . Clanton
Ian McDonald . . . . Hollister
John Rawlins . . . . .Williams
Roland Got . . . . Ying
Hal Price . . . . Prof. Waldo Stubbs
Jack Rockwell . . . . Sheriff Mulhall

293

William Boyd, Andy Clyde and George Reeves minister to a unconscious Francis McDonald in this scene from **Bar 20** (1943, United Artists).

OUTLAWS OF THE DESERT

Distributor . . . . .Paramount
Copyrighted . . . . December 3, 1941
Released . . . . .November 1, 1941
Director . . . . .Howard Bretherton
Producer . . . . Harry Sherman
Associate Producer . . . . . . Lewis J. Rachmil
Photographer . . . . .Russell Harlan
Film Editor . . . . Carrol Lewis
Supervising Editor . . . . . . Sherman A. Rose
Music Score . . . . .John Leipold
Music Director . . . . Irvin Talbot
Assistant Director . . . . .Glenn Cook
Screenplay . . . . J. Benton Cheney,
Bernard McConville

Cast

William Boyd . . . . Hopalong Cassidy
Andy Clyde . . . . .California Carlson
Brad King . . . . Johnny Nelson
Duncan Renaldo . . . . Sheik Suleiman
Jean Phillips . . . . .Susan Grant
Forrest Stanley . . . . .Charles Grant
Nina Guilbert . . . . .Mrs. Jane Grant
Luli Deste . . . . Marie Karitza
Albert Morin . . . . Nikki Karitza
George J. Lewis . . . . Yussef
Jean del Val . . . . .Sheik Feran el Kadir
George Woolsley . . . . .Major Crawford
Mickey Eissa . . . . Salim
Jamiel Hassan . . . . .Ali

TWILIGHT ON THE TRAIL

Distributor . . . . .Paramount
Copyrighted . . . . December 3, 1941
Released . . . . .September 27, 1941
Director . . . . Howard Bretherton
Producer . . . . .Harry Sherman
Associate Producer . . . . . . Lewis J. Rachmil
Photographer . . . . .Russell Harlan
Film Editor . . . . .Fred Feitshans, Jr.

William Boyd welcomes Dustine Farnum, Victor Jory and Betty Blythe in this scene from **Bar 20** (1943, United Artists).

Supervising Editor . . . . . . Sherman A. Rose
Music Score . . . . .John Leipold
Music Director . . . . .Irvin Talbot
Assistant Director . . . . .Glenn Cook
Screenplay . . . . J. Benton Cheney,
    Ellen Corby, Cecile Kramer

Cast

William Boyd . . . . Hopalong Cassidy
Andy Clyde . . . . .California Carlson
Brad King . . . . Johnny Nelson
Wanda McKay . . . . Lucy Brent
Jack Rockwell . . . . Jim Brent
Norman Willis . . . . .Nat Kerby
Robert Kent . . . . Art Drake
Tom London . . . . Tim Gregg
Frank Austin . . . . .Steve Farley
The Jimmy Wakely Trio (Jimmy Wakely, Johnny Bond, Dick Rinehart) . . . . Singers
Clem Fuller . . . . .Stage Driver
Johnny Powers . . . . .Drummer

Bob Kortman . . . . Uncredited Bit Parts
Frank Ellis
Bud Osborne

RIDERS OF THE TIMBERLINE

Distributor . . . . .Paramount
Copyrighted . . . . December 3, 1941
Released . . . . .September 17, 1941
Director . . . . Lesley Selander
Producer . . . . .Harry Sherman
Associate Producer . . . . . . Lewis J. Rachmil
Photographer . . . . .Russell Harlan
Film Editor . . . . .Fred Feitshans, Jr.
Supervising Editor . . . . . . Sherman A. Rose
Music Score . . . . .John Leipold
Music Director . . . . Irvin Talbot
Assistant Director . . . . .Glenn Cook
Screenplay . . . . .J. Benton Cheney

William Boyd congratulates Dustine Farnum and Robert Mitchum as Bob Burns, Betty Blythe and George Reeves look on in this scene from **Bar 20** (1943, United Artists).

Cast

William Boyd	Hopalong Cassidy
Andy Clyde	California Carlson
Brad King	Johnny Nelson
Victor Jory	Baptiste Deschamp
Eleanor Stewart	Elaine Kerrigan
J. Farrell McDonald	Jim Kerrigan
Anna Q. Nilsson	Donna Ryan
Tom Tyler	Bill Slade
Edward Keane	Preston Yates
Hal Taliaferro	Ed Petrie
Mickey Eissa	Larry
The Guardsmen	Singers
Hank Bell	Uncredited Bit Part

LEATHER BURNERS

Distributor	United Artists
Copyrighted	October 26, 1942
Released	May 28, 1942

Director	Joseph A. Henabery
Producer	Harry Sherman
Associate Producer	Lewis J. Rachmil
Photographer	Russell Harlan
Film Editor	Carrol Lewis
Music Score	Samuel Kaylin
Music Director	Irvin Talbot
Assistant Director	Glenn Cook
Screenplay	Jo Pagano
Source Novel	Bliss Lomax (Harry Sinclair Drago), *The Leather Burners* (1940)

Cast

William Boyd	Hopalong Cassidy
Andy Clyde	California Carlson
Jay Kirby	Johnny Travers
Victor Jory	Dan Slack
George Givot	Sam Bucktoe
Shelley Spencer	Sharon Longstreet
Bobby Larson	Bobby Longstreet
George Reeves	Harrison Brooke

William Boyd grasps the lapels of Victor Jory in this publicity still for **Bar 20** (1943, United Artists).

Hal Taliaferro . . . . .Lafe Bailey
Forbes Murray . . . . Bart Galey
Robert Mitchum . . . . . . .Uncredited Bit Parts
Bob Kortman
Herman Hack

HOPPY SERVES A WRIT

Distributor . . . . United Artists
Copyrighted . . . . .November 25, 1942
Released . . . . .March 12, 1942
Director . . . . George Archainbaud
Producer . . . . Harry Sherman
Associate Producer . . . . . Lewis J. Rachmil
Photographer . . . . .Russell Harlan
Film Editor . . . . Sherman A. Rose
Music Director . . . . .Irvin Talbot
Assistant Director . . . . .Glenn Cook
Screenplay . . . . Gerald Geraghty
Source Novel . . . . Clarence E. Mulford,
Hopalong Cassidy Serves A Writ (1941)

Cast

William Boyd . . . . Hopalong Cassidy
Andy Clyde . . . . .California Carlson
Jay Kirby . . . . Johnny Travers
Victor Jory . . . . Tom Jordan
George Reeves . . . . .Steve Jordan
Jan Christy . . . . .Jean Hollister
Hal Taliaferro . . . . .Greg Jordan
Forbes Murray . . . . Ben Hollister
Robert Mitchum . . . . .Rigney
Byron Foulger . . . . Danvers
Earle Hodgins . . . . .Jim Belson
Roy Barcroft . . . . Tom Colby
Ben Corbett . . . . .Card Player
Art Mix . . . . Uncredited Bit Part

UNDERCOVER MAN

Distributor . . . . United Artists
Copyrighted . . . . December 10, 1942

William Boyd and Francis McDonald have a fight in this scene from **Bar 20** (1943, United Artists).

Released . . . . .October 23, 1942
Director . . . . Lesley Selander
Producer . . . . Harry Sherman
Associate Producer . . . . . Lewis J. Rachmil
Photographer . . . . .Russell Harlan
Film Editor . . . . Carrol Lewis
Supervising Editor . . . . . Sherman A. Rose
Music Director . . . . .Irvin Talbot
Assistant Director . . . . .Glenn Cook
Screenplay . . . . .J. Benton Cheney

Alan Baldwin . . . . Bob Saunders
Jack Rockwell . . . . Capt. John Hawkins
Pierce Lyden . . . . Bert
Tony Roux . . . . .Chavez
Ted Wells . . . . .Jim
Martin Garralaga . . . . Cortez
Joe Dominguez . . . . Caballero
Earle Hodgins . . . . Sheriff Blackburn
Bennett George . . . . Uncredited Bit Parts
Frank Ellis

Cast

William Boyd . . . . Hopalong Cassidy
Andy Clyde . . . . .California Carlson
Jay Kirby . . . . Breezy Travers
Antonio Moreno . . . . . . Don Tomas Gonzales
Nora Lane . . . . Louise Saunders
Chris-Pin Martin . . . . Miguel
Esther Estrella . . . . .Dolores Gonzales
John Vosper . . .Ed Carson/Idaho Pete Jackson
Eva Puig . . . . Rosita Lopez

BORDER PATROL

Distributor . . . . United Artists
Copyrighted . . . . .December 11, 1942
Released . . . . April 2, 1943
Director . . . . Lesley Selander
Producer . . . . Harry Sherman
Associate Producer . . . . . . Lewis J. Rachmil
Photographer . . . . .Russell Harlan
Film Editor . . . . Sherman A. Rose

William Boyd and Andy Clyde are ready for action in this scene from **Bar 20** (1943, United Artists).

Music Director . . . . .Irvin Talbot
Assistant Director . . . . .Glenn Cook
Screenplay . . . . Michael Wilson

Cast

William Boyd . . . . Hopalong Cassidy
Andy Clyde . . . . California Carlson
Jay Kirby . . . . Johnny Travers
Russell Simpson . . . . Orestes Krebs
Claudia Drake . . . . Inez La Barca
George Reeves . . . . .Don Enrique Perez
Duncan Renaldo . . . . .Commandant
Pierce Lyden . . . . Loren
Robert Mitchum . . . . .Quinn
Cliff Parkinson . . . . Barton
Earle Hodgins . . . . Cook
Merrill McCormack . . . . .Uncredited Bit Part

LOST CANYON

Distributor . . . . United Artists
Copyrighted . . . . December 11, 1942
Released . . . . December 18, 1943
Director . . . . Lesley Selander
Producer . . . . .Harry Sherman
Associate Producer . . . . . Lewis J. Rachmil
Photographer . . . . .Russell Harlan
Film Editor . . . . Carrol Lewis
Music Director . . . . Irvin Talbot
Assistant Director . . . . .Glenn Cook
Screenplay . . . . .Harry O. Hoyt
Uncredited Source . . . . **Rustlers'**
Valley (Paramount, 1937)

Cast

William Boyd . . . . Hopalong Cassidy
Andy Clyde . . . . .California Carlson
Jay Kirby . . . . Johnny Travers
Lola Lane . . . . .Laura Clark

William Boyd is thoughtful about his talk with Betty Blythe in this scene from **Bar 20** (1943, United Artists).

Douglas Fowley . . . . .Jeff Burton
Herbert Rawlinson . . . . Tom Clark
Guy Usher . . . . Zack Rogers
Karl Hackett . . . . .Wade Haskell
Hugh Prosser . . . . .Jim Stanton
Bob Kortman .Joe
The Sportsmen Quartette . . . . Singers
Keith Richards . . . . . . .Uncredited Bit Parts
Herman Hack
Merrill McCormack
George Morrell
Spade Cooley
John Cason
Henry Wills

COLT COMRADES

Distributor . . . . United Artists
Copyrighted . . . . .February 1, 1943
Released . . . . .June 18, 1943
Director . . . . Lesley Selander

Producer . . . . .Harry Sherman
Associate Producer . . . . . Lewis J. Rachmil
Photographer . . . . .Russell Harlan
Film Editor . . . . .Fred W. Berger
Music Director . . . . .Irvin Talbot
Assistant Director . . . . .Glenn Cook
Screenplay . . . . Michael Wilson
Source Novel . . . . Bliss Lomax (Harry
Sinclair Drago), *Colt Comrades* (1939)

Cast

William Boyd . . . . Hopalong Cassidy
Andy Clyde . . . . .California Carlson
Jay Kirby . . . . Johnny Travers
Lois Sherman . . . . .Lucy Whitlock
Victor Jory . . . . Jeb Hardin
George Reeves . . . . .Lin Whitlock
Douglas Fowley . . . . Joe Brass
Herbert Rawlinson . . . . .Varney
Earle Hodgins . . . . .Wildcat Willy
Robert Mitchum . . . . .Dirk Mason

300

William Boyd and George Reeves tease Andy Clyde in this scene from **Bar 20** (1943, United Artists).

Russell Simpson . . . . Sheriff
Jack Mulhall . . . . .Postmaster
Fred Kohler, Jr. . . . . Uncredited Bit Part

BAR 20

Distributor . . . . United Artists
Copyrighted . . . . .June 1, 1943
Released . . . . .October 1, 1943
Director . . . . Lesley Selander
Producer . . . . .Harry Sherman
Associate Producer . . . . . . Lewis J. Rachmil
Photographer . . . . .Russell Harlan
Film Editor . . . . Carrol Lewis
Music Director . . . . Irvin Talbot
Assistant Director . . . . .Glenn Cook
Screenplay . . Morton Grant, Norman Houston,
Michael Wilson
Cast

William Boyd . . . . Hopalong Cassidy

Andy Clyde . . . . .California Carlson
George Reeves . . . . .Lin Bradley
Dustine Farnum . . . . Marie Stevens
Victor Jory . . . . Mark Jackson
Douglas Fowley . . . . .Slash
Betty Blythe . . . . .Mrs. Stevens
Robert Mitchum . . . . Richard Adams
Francis McDonald . . . . Quirt Rankin
Earle Hodgins . . . . .Tom
Buck Bucko . . . . .Uncredited Bit Part

FALSE COLORS

Distibutor . . . . United Artists
Copyrighted . . . . .September 27, 1943
Released . . . . .November 5, 1943
Director . . . . George Archainbaud
Producer . . . . Harry Sherman
Associate Producer . . . . . . Lewis J. Rachmil
Photographer . . . . .Russell Harlan
Film Editor . . . . .Fred W. Berger

301

William Boyd and Claudia Drake in a publicity still for **False Colors** (1943, United Artists).

Supervising Editor . . . . Carrol Lewis
Music Director . . . . Irvin Talbot
Assistant Director . . . . .Glenn Cook
Screenplay . . . . .Bennett Cohen

Elmer Jerome
Ray Jones
Bob Burns
Tom Smith

Cast

William Boyd . . . . Hopalong Cassidy
Andy Clyde . . . . .California Carlson
Jimmy Rogers . . . . Jimmy Rogers
Douglass Dumbrille . . . . Mark Foster
Tom Seidel . . . . .Bud Lawton/Kit Moyer
Claudia Drake . . . . Faith Lawton
Robert Mitchum . . . . Rip Austin
Glenn Strange . . . . Sonora
Pierce Lyden . . . . Lefty
Roy Barcroft . . . . Sheriff Clem Martin
Earle Hodgins . . . . .Jay Griffin
Sam Flint . . . . Judge Stevens
Tom London . . . . .Uncredited Bit Parts
George Morrell
Dan White

RIDERS OF THE DEADLINE

Distributor . . . . United Artists
Copyrighted . . . . .September 27, 1943
Released . . . . December 3, 1943
Director . . . . Lesley Selander
Producer . . . . .Harry Sherman
Associate Producer . . . . . . Lewis J. Rachmil
Photographer . . . . .Russell Harlan
Film Editor . . . . Walter Hannemann
Supervising Editor . . . . .Carrol Lewis
Music Director . . . . .Irvin Talbot
Assistant Director . . . . .Glenn Cook
Screenplay . . . . .Bennett Cohen
Uncredited Source . . . . **The Desert Bandit**
(Republic, 1941)

Jimmy Rogers, William Boyd and Andy Clyde in a publicity still for **False Colors** (1943, United Artists).

Cast

William Boyd . . . . Hopalong Cassidy
Andy Clyde . . . . .California Carlson
Jimmy Rogers . . . . Jimmy Rogers
Frances Woodward . . . . Sue Mason
William Halligan . . . . Simon Crandall
Robert Mitchum . . . . .Nick Drago
Richard Crane . . . . Tim Mason
Anthony Warde . . . . .Gunner Madigan
Hugh Prosser . . . . . . .Deputy Sheriff Martin
Herbert Rawlinson . . . . . . .Captain Jennings
Jack Rockwell . . . . Tex
Earle Hodgins . . . . Sourdough
Montie Montana . . . . .Private Calhoun
Jim Bannon . . . . Uncredited Bit Parts
Bill Beckford
Pierce Lyden
Art Felix
Roy Bucko
Cliff Parkinson

TEXAS MASQUERADE

Distributor . . . . United Artists
Copyrighted . . . . December 8, 1943
Released . . . . .February 8, 1943
Director . . . . George Archainbaud
Producer . . . . .Harry Sherman
Associate Producer . . . . . . Lewis J. Rachmil
Photographer . . . . .Russell Harlan
Film Editor . . . . Walter Hannemann
Supervising Editor . . . . .Carrol Lewis
Music Director . . . . .Irvin Talbot
Assistant Director . . . . .Glenn Cook
Screenplay . . .Jack Lait Jr., Norman Houston

Cast

William Boyd . . . . Hopalong Cassidy
Andy Clyde . . . . .California Carlson
Jimmy Rogers . . . . Jimmy Rogers
Don Costello . . . . .Ace Maxson
Mady Correll . . . . .Virginia Curtis

303

Robert Mitchum and William Boyd have a fight in this scene from **False Colors** (1943, United Artists).

Francis McDonald . . . . Sam Nolan
Russell Simpson . . . . J.K. Trimble
J. Farrell MacDonald . . . . .John Martindale
Nelson Leigh . . . . James Corwin
Robert McKenzie . . . . Constable Rowbottom
June Terry Pickrell . . . . Mrs. Martindale
Pierce Lyden . . . . .Al
Bill Hunter . . . . .Lew Sykes
John Merton .Jeff
Keith Richards . . . . . . .Uncredited Bit Parts
George Morrell

LUMBERJACK

Distributor . . . . United Artists
Copyrighted . . . . .March 24, 1944
Released . . . . .April 28, 1944
Director . . . . Lesley Selander
Producer . . . . .Harry Sherman
Associate Producer . . . . . Lewis J. Rachmil
Photographer . . . . .Russell Harlan

Film Editor . . . . Fred W. Berger
Supervising Editor . . . . .Carrol Lewis
Music Director . . . . Irvin Talbot
Assistant Director . . . . .Glenn Cook
Screenplay . . . . Norman Houston,
Barry Shipman

Cast

William Boyd . . . . .Hopalong Cassidy
Andy Clyde . . . . .California Carlson
Jimmy Rogers . . . . Jimmy Rogers
Douglass Dumbrille . . . . . .Daniel J. Keefer
Ellen Hall . . . . .Julie Peters Jordan
Francis McDonald . . . . .Clyde Fenwick
Ethel Wales . . . . .Aunt Abbie Peters
Hal Taliaferro . . . . .Taggart
Charles Morton . . . . .Big Joe Williams
Herbert Rawlinson . . . . Buck Peters
Frances Morris . . . . Mrs.Williams
John Whitney . . . . .Benton C. Jordan
Jack Rockwell . . . . Sheriff Miles

William Boyd, Jimmy Rogers and Andy Clyde have Roy Barcroft covered in this scene from **False Colors** (1943, United Artists).

Henry Wills . . . . Uncredited Bit Parts
Bob Burns
Hank Worden
Earle Hodgins
Pierce Lyden

MYSTERY MAN

Distributor . . . . United Artists
Copyrighted/Released . . . . . . May 31, 1944
Director . . . . George Archainbaud
Producer . . . . Harry Sherman
Associate Producer . . . . . . Lewis J. Rachmil
Photographer . . . . .Russell Harlan
Film Editor . . . . .Fred W. Berger
Supervising Editor . . . . .Carrol Lewis
Music Director . . . . Irvin Talbot
Assistant Director . . . . .Glenn Cook
Screenplay . . . . .J. Benton Cheney

Cast

William Boyd . . . . Hopalong Cassidy
Andy Clyde . . . . .California Carlson
Jimmy Rogers . . . . Jimmy Rogers
Don Costello . . . . .Bud Trilling
Eleanor Stewart . . . . .Diane Newhall
Francis McDonald . . . . Bert Ragan
Forrest Taylor . . . . .Sheriff Sam Newhall
Jack Rockwell . . . . .Tod Blane
John Merton . . . . .Bill
Pierce Lyden . . . . Red
Bob Burns . . . . Tom Hanlon
Ozie Waters . . . . Singing Ranch Hand
Bill Hunter. . . . . Uncredited Bit Parts
Art Mix
Hank Bell
Bob Baker
George Morrell

305

William Boyd, Andy Clyde and friend in a publicity still for **False Colors** (1943, United Artists).

FORTY THIEVES

Distributor . . . . United Artists
Copyrighted/Released . . . . . . June 23, 1944
Director . . . . Lesley Selander
Producer . . . . .Harry Sherman
Associate Producer . . . . . . Lewis J. Rachmil
Photographer . . . . .Russell Harlan
Film Editor . . . . Carrol Lewis
Music Score . . . . Mort Glickman
Music Supervisor . . . . David Chudnow
Assistant Director . . . . .George Tobin
Screenplay . . . Michael Wilson, Bernie Kamins

Cast

William Boyd . . . . Hopalong Cassidy
Andy Clyde . . . . .California Carlson
Jimmy Rogers . . . . Jimmy Rogers
Douglass Dumbrille . . . . .Tad Hammond
Louise Currie . . . . Katherine Reynolds
Kirk Alyn . . . . .Jerry Doyle

Herbert Rawlinson . . . . Buck Peters
Robert Frazer . . . . .Judge Reynolds
Glenn Strange . . . . Ike Simmons
Hal Taliaferro . . . . .Clanton
Jack Rockwell . . . . .Sam Garms
Bob Kortman . . . . .Joe Garms
Earle Hodgins . . . . Uncredited Bit Part

THE DEVIL'S PLAYGROUND

Distributor . . . . United Artists
Copyrighted/Released . . November 15, 1946
Director . . . . George Archainbaud
Producer . . . . Lewis J. Rachmil
Executive Producer . . . . William Boyd
Photographer . . . . .Mack Stengler
Film Editor . . . . .Fred W. Berger
Music . . . . .David Chudnow
Assistant Director . . . . .George Tobin
Screenplay . . . . .Ted Wilson

William Boyd and Andy Clyde comfort Jimmy Rogers about being in jail in this scene from **False Colors** (1943, United Artists).

Cast

William Boyd . . . . Hopalong Cassidy
Andy Clyde . . . . .California Carlson
Rand Brooks . . . . Lucky Jenkins
Elaine Riley . . . . .Mrs. Evans
Robert Elliott . . . . Judge Morton
Joseph J. Greene . . . . .Sheriff
Francis McDonald . . . . .Roberts
Ned Young . . . . Curly Evans
Earle Hodgins . . . . Dan'l
George Eldredge . . . . .U.S. Marshal
Everett Shields . . . . Wolfe
John George . . . . .Shorty
Glenn Strange . . . . Uncredited Bit Part

FOOLS' GOLD

Distributor . . . . United Artists
Copyrighted . . . . .January 31, 1947
Director . . . . George Archainbaud

Producer . . . . Lewis J. Rachmil
Executive Producer . . . . William Boyd
Photographer . . . . .Mack Stengler
Film Editor . . . . .Fred W. Berger
Music . . . . .David Chudnow
Assistant Director . . . . .George Tobin
Screenplay . . . . .Doris Schroeder

Cast

William Boyd . . . . Hopalong Cassidy
Andy Clyde . . . . .California Carlson
Rand Brooks . . . . Lucky Jenkins
Robert Emmett Keane . . . . Professor Dixon
Jane Randolph . . . . Jessie Dixon
Stephen Barclay . . . . .Bruce Landy
Harry Cording . . . . Duke
Earle Hodgins . . . . .Sandler
Bob Bentley . . . . Barton
William "Wee Willie" Davis . . . . . Blackie
Forbes Murray . . . . Col. Jed Landy
Glen B. Gallagher . . . . .Lieutenant Anderson

307

William Boyd hides something in Andy Clyde's boot in this scene from **False Colors** (1943, United Artists).

Ben Corbett . . . . Sergeant
Fred "Snowflake" Toones . . . . Speed

UNEXPECTED GUEST

Distributor . . . . United Artists
Copyrighted/Released . . . . . March 28, 1947
Director . . . . George Archainbaud
Producer . . . . Lewis J. Rachmil
Executive Producer . . . . William Boyd
Photographer . . . . Mack Stengler
Film Editor . . . . .Fred W. Berger
Music . . . . .David Chudnow
Assistant Director . . . . .George Tobin
Screenplay . . . . Ande Lamb

Cast

William Boyd . . . . Hopalong Cassidy
Andy Clyde . . . . .California Carlson
Rand Brooks . . . . Lucky Jenkins

Una O'Connor . . . . Matilda Hackett
John Parrish . . . . David J. Potter
Patricia Tate . . . . Ruth Baxter
Ned Young . . . . .Ralph Baxter
Earle Hodgins . . . . .Joshua Colter
Joel Friedkin . . . . Phineas Phipps
Robert B. Williams . . . . Matt Ogden
William Ruhl . . . . Sheriff

DANGEROUS VENTURE

Distributor . . . . United Artists
Copyrighted/Released . . . . . . May 23, 1947
Director . . . . George Archainbaud
Producer . . . . .Lewis J. Rachmil
Executive Producer . . . . William Boyd
Photographer . . . . Mack Stengler
Film Editor . . . . .Fred W. Berger
Music . . . . .David Chudnow
Assistant Director . . . . .George Tobin
Screenplay . . . . Doris Schroeder

William Boyd, Claudia Drake, Jimmy Rogers and Andy Clyde look at something off camera in this scene from **False Colors** (1943, United Artists).

Cast

William Boyd . . . . Hopalong Cassidy
Andy Clyde . . . . .California Carlson
Rand Brooks . . . . Lucky Jenkins
Fritz Leiber . . . . Xeoli
Douglas Evans . . . . Dr. Atwood
Harry Cording . . . . Dan Morgan
Betty Alexander . . . . Dr. Sue Harmon
Francis McDonald . . . . Kane
Neyle Morrow . . . . .Jose
Patricia Tate . . . . Tolu
Bob Faust .Stark
Ken Tobey . . . . Red
Jack Quinn . . . . Marshal
Bill Nestell . . . . Pete

HOPPY'S HOLIDAY

Distributor . . . . United Artists
Copyrighted . . . . July 19, 1947

Released . . . . July 18, 1947
Director . . . . George Archainbaud
Producer . . . . .Lewis J. Rachmil
Executive Producer . . . . William Boyd
Photographer . . . . Mack Stengler
Film Editor . . . . .Fred W. Berger
Music . . . . .David Chudnow
Assistant Director . . . . George Tobin
Screenplay . . . . J. Benton Cheney,
Bennett Cohen, Ande Lamb
Story . . . . Ellen Corby, Cecile Kramer

Cast

William Boyd . . . . Hopalong Cassidy
Andy Clyde . . . . .California Carlson
Rand Brooks . . . . Lucky Jenkins
Andrew Tombes . . . . Mayor Frank Patton
Leonard Penn . . . . .Dunning
Jeff Corey . . . . .Jed
Mary Ware . . . . .Gloria Patton
Donald Kirke . . . . Sheriff

309

William Boyd, Jimmy Rogers and Andy Clyde offer Tom Seidel their help in this scene from **False Colors** (1943, United Artists).

Hollis Bane (Mike Ragan) . . . . Ace
Gil Patric . . . . Jay
Frank Henry . . . . Bart

THE MARAUDERS

Distributor . . . . United Artists
Copyrighted . . . . .September 12, 1947
Released . . . . .July 1, 1947
Director . . . . George Archainbaud
Producer . . . . Lewis J. Rachmil
Executive Producer . . . . William Boyd
Photographer . . . . Mack Stengler
Film Editor . . . . Fred W. Berger
Music . . . . Ralph Stanley
Assistant Director . . . . . . George Templeton
Screenplay . . . . .Charles Belden

Cast

William Boyd . . . . .Hopalong Cassidy

Andy Clyde . . . . California Carlson
Rand Brooks . . . . Lucky Jenkins
Ian Wolfe . . . . .Deacon Edwin Black
Dorinda Clifton . . . . .Susan Crowell
Mary Newton . . . . Mrs. Crowell
Harry Cording . . . . Riker
Earle Hodgins . . . . County Clerk
Dick Bailey . . . . Oil Driller
Richard Alexander . . . . .Uncredited Bit Parts
Herman Hack

SILENT CONFLICT

Distributor . . . . United Artists
Copyrighted/Released . . . . . March 19, 1948
Director . . . . George Archainbaud
Producer . . . . Lewis J. Rachmil
Executive Producer . . . . William Boyd
Photographer . . . . Mack Stengler
Film Editor . . . . .Fred W. Berger
Music . . . . Darrell Calker

Tom Seidel and William Boyd take cover in the rocks in this scene from **False Colors** (1943, United Artists).

Assistant Director .... William Dario Faralla
Screenplay ....Charles Belden

Cast

William Boyd .... Hopalong Cassidy
Andy Clyde ....California Carlson
Rand Brooks .... Lucky Jenkins
Virginia Belmont .... Renee Richards
Earle Hodgins ....Doc Richards
James Harrison ....Speed Blaney
Forbes Murray .... Randall
John Butler ....Clerk
Herbert Rawlinson ....Jake
Richard Alexander ....Rancher
Don Haggerty ....Rancher

THE DEAD DON'T DREAM

Distributor .... United Artists
Copyrighted/Released ......April 30, 1948
Director .... George Archainbaud

Producer .... Lewis J. Rachmil
Executive Producer .... William Boyd
Photographer ....Mack Stengler
Film Editor ....Fred W. Berger
Music .... Darrell Calker
Assistant Director ....William Dario Faralla
Screenplay ....Francis Rosenwald

Cast

William Boyd .... Hopalong Cassidy
Andy Clyde ....California Carlson
Rand Brooks .... Lucky Jenkins
John Parrish .... Jeff Potter
Leonard Penn ....Earl Wesson
Mary Tucker .... Mary Benton
Francis McDonald .... Bart Lansing
Richard Alexander ....Duke
Bob Gabriel .... Larry Potter
Stanley Andrews .... Jesse Williams
Forbes Murray .... Sheriff Thompson
Don Haggerty .... Deputy

311

Tom Seidel, Claudia Drake, William Boyd, Jimmy Rogers and Andy Clyde in a publicity still for **False Colors** (1943, United Artists).

SINISTER JOURNEY

Distributor . . . . United Artists
Copyrighted/Released . . . . . . June 11, 1948
Director . . . . George Archainbaud
Producer . . . . Lewis J. Rachmil
Executive Producer . . . . William Boyd
Photographer . . . . .Mack Stengler
Film Editor . . . . .Fred W. Berger
Music . . . . Darrell Calker
Assistant Director . . . . William Dario Faralla
Screenplay . . . . .Doris Schroeder

Cast

William Boyd . . . . Hopalong Cassidy
Andy Clyde . . . . .California Carlson
Rand Brooks . . . . Lucky Jenkins
Elaine Riley . . . . .Jessie Garvin
John Kellogg . . . . Lee Garvin
Don Haggerty . . . . Harmon Roberts
Stanley Andrews . . . . Tom Smith

Harry Strang . . . . .Banks
Herbert Rawlinson . . . . Storekeeper
John Butler . . . . Constable Reardon
Will Orlean . . . . Ben Watts
Wayne C. Tredway . . . . Engineer

BORROWED TROUBLE

Distributor . . . . United Artists
Copyrighted/Released . . . . July 1, 1948
Director . . . . George Archainbaud
Producer . . . . .Lewis J. Rachmil
Executive Producer . . . . William Boyd
Photographer . . . . Mack Stengler
Film Editor . . . . .Fred W. Berger
Music . . . . Darrell Calker
Assistant Director . . . . .William Dario Faralla
Screenplay . . . . .Charles Belden

312

Andy Clyde, Jimmy Rogers and William Boyd are let out of jail by Roy Barcroft in this scene from **False Colors** (1943, United Artists).

Cast

William Boyd	Hopalong Cassidy
Andy Clyde	California Carlson
Rand Brooks	Lucky Jenkins
Anne O'Neal	Lucy Abbott
John Parrish	Steve Mawson
Cliff Clark	Dink Davis
Helen Chapman	Lola Blair
Earle Hodgins	Sheriff
Herbert Rawlinson	Groves
Don Haggerty	Lippy
James Harrison	Rocky
Clarke Stevens	Henchman
George Sowards	Henchman
Eileen Janssen	Children
Nancy Stone	
Jimmy Crane	
Billy O'Leary	
Norman Ollestad Jr.	

FALSE PARADISE

Distributor	United Artists
Copyrighted	July 15, 1948
Released	September 10, 1948
Director	George Archainbaud
Producer	Lewis J. Rachmil
Executive Producer	William Boyd
Photographer	Mack Stengler
Film Editor	Fred W. Berger
Music	Ralph Stanley
Assistant Director	William Dario Faralla
Screenplay	Harrison Jacobs
Aditional Dialogue . .	William Conselman Jr., Doris Schroeder

Cast

William Boyd	Hopalong Cassidy
Andy Clyde	California Carlson
Rand Brooks	Lucky Jenkins
Elaine Riley	Anne Larson
Cliff Clark	Waite

William Boyd has a talk with a hurt Tom Seidel in this scene from **False Colors** (1943, United Artists).

Joel Friedkin . . . . Prof. Alonzo Larson
Kenneth MacDonald . . . . Bentley
Don Haggerty . . . . .Deal Marden
George Eldredge . . . . Radley
Richard Alexander . . . . .Sam
Zon Murray . . . . Buck
William Norton Bailey . . Uncredited Bit Part

STRANGE GAMBLE

Distributor . . . . United Artists
Copyrighted . . . . August 1, 1948
Released . . . . .October 8, 1948
Director . . . . George Archainbaud
Producer . . . . Lewis J. Rachmil
Executive Producer . . . . William Boyd
Photographer . . . . Mack Stengler
Film Editor . . . . .Fred W. Berger
Music . . . . Ralph Stanley
Assistant Director . . . . William Dario Faralla
Screenplay . . . . .Doris Schroeder

Cast

William Boyd . . . . .Hopalong Cassidy
Andy Clyde . . . . California Carlson
Rand Brooks . . . . Lucky Jenkins
Elaine Riley . . . . .Nora Murray
James Craven . . . . .Ora Mordigan
Robert B. Williams . . . . Pete
Albert Morin . . . . DeLara
Joel Friedkin . . . . .Doc White
Herbert Rawlinson . . . . .John Murray
Francis McDonald . . . . Longhorn
William Leicester . . . . .Sid Murray
Joan Barton . . . . .Mary Murray
Lee Tung Foo . . . . Wong

RUNNING TIMES

My filmography does not give the running time
of any Hopalong Cassidy picture. The standard
sources disagree about these movies' running

William Boyd, Andy Clyde and Jimmy Rogers in a publicity still for **Riders of the Deadline** (1943, United Artists).

times more often than they agree. Instead of arbitrarily deciding which of the sources is right, I've prepared a chart showing the running times as given by the four most often used reference works in this field: the reviews of the Cassidy films in Variety, the Cassidy filmographies in James Robert Parish's *The Great Movie Series* (1971) and David Zinman's *Saturday Afternoon at the Bijou* (1973), and the listings in Les Adams' and Buck Rainey's monumental *Shoot-em-Ups* (1978).

Where all four agree, the running time given is probably correct. Where they disagree, the longest time given is probably the most reliable. As the chart shows, at least five Cassidy pictures were reviewed in Variety twice, with a different running time given with each review. Occasionally Variety didn't bother to review a Hoppy picture at all, and one entry in the series was missed even by *Shoot-em-Ups*! Omissions of this sort are indicated by an xx symbol.

Title	Variety	Parish	Zinman	Shoot-Em-Ups
Hop-A-Long Cassidy	60	62	63	63
The Eagle's Brood	61	59	65	59
Bar 20 Rides Again	63	62	65	65
Call of the Prairie	65	65	65	65
Three on the Trail	66	67	67	67
Heart of the West	63	60	63	60
Hopalong Cassidy Returns	75	71	71	71
Trail Dust	70	77	77	77
Borderland	82	82	82	82
Hills of Old Wyoming	78	79	78	75
North of The Rio Grande	xx	65	70	70
Rustlers' Valley	58	60	60	60
Hopalong Rides Again	63 or 65	65	65	65
Texas Trail	58	58	58	60

315

Title	Variety	Parish	Zinman	Shoot-Em-Ups
Partners of the Plains	70	70	70	68
Cassidy of Bar 20	60	56	56	56
Heart of Arizona	68	68	68	68
Bar 20 Justice	63	70	70	70
Pride of the West	55	56	56	56
In Old Mexico	67	62	62	62
The Frontiersmen	71	74	74	74
Sunset Trail	67	60	60	60
Silver on the Sage	xx	66	68	66
The Renegade Trail	57	61	58	61
Range War	64	64	64	66
Law of the Pampas	74	72	72	74
Santa Fe Marshal	66	65	68	65
The Showdown	63	65	65	65
Hidden Gold	60	61	61	61
Stagecoach War	61	63	63	63
Three Men from Texas	75	70	76	70
The Doomed Caravan	60	62	62	62
In Old Colorado	67	66	66	66
Border Vigilantes	61	62	63	62
Pirates on Horseback	69	69	69	69
Wide Open Town	77	78	79	78
Stick to Your Guns	61	63	63	63
Secrets of the Wastelands	66	66	66	66
Outlaws of the Desert	66	66	66	66
Twilight on the Trail	66	58	58	58
Riders of the Timberline	66 or 67	59	59	59
Leather Burners	66	66	58	58
Hoppy Serves a Writ	66 or 67	67	67	67
Undercover Man	58 or 68	68	68	68
Border Patrol	65	64	65	60
Lost Canyon	61	61	61	61
Colt Comrades	67	67	67	67
Bar 20	54	54	54	54
False Colors	64	65	65	65
Riders of the Deadline	68 or 70	68	70	60
Texas Masquerade	59	59	58	59
Lumberjack	65	65	65	65
Mystery Man	58	58	58	58
Forty Thieves	60	60	60	60
The Devil's Playground	62	62	65	62
Fools' Gold	63	65	63	63
Unexpected Guest	61	59	61	61
Dangerous Venture	59	59	59	59
Hoppy's Holiday	70	60	60	60
The Marauders	63	63	63	63
Silent Conflict	61	61	61	61
The Dead Don't Dream	68	62	62	68
Sinister Journey	59	60	72	59
Borrowed Trouble	61	60	58	xx
False Paradise	xx	66	59	60
Strange Gamble	xx	61	61	62

Hopalong Cassidy TV Series

starring William Boyd

with Edgar Buchanan

First Season, 1952-53

GUNS ACROSS THE BORDER

Copyrighted . . . . .September 19, 1952
Director . . . . Thomas Carr
Teleplay . . . . .Harrison Jacobs
Cast
William Boyd . . . . Hopalong Cassidy
Edgar Buchanan . . . . .Red Connors
Myra Marsh . . . . .Mamie Taylor
Keith Richards . . . . Capt. Lee Sterling
Henry Rowland . . . . .Daly

Story: A fast-shooting woman marshal interferes with the efforts of Hopalong Cassidy and his sidekick Red Connors to track down the bandits who stole a shipment of Army rifles.

THE KNIFE OF CARLOS VALERO

Copyrighted . . . . September 25, 1952
Director . . . . Derwin Abbe
Teleplay . . . . .Harrison Jacobs
Cast
William Boyd . . . . .Hopalong Cassidy
Edgar Buchanan . . . . .Red Connors
Harry Cording . . . . Bailey/Blake
John Crawford . . . . Ross
Olin Howlin . . . . Sheriff
Victor Millan . . . . .Carlos Valero
Lillian Moliere . . . . Trini
Byron Foulger . . . . Hotel Clerk

Story: Hoppy and Red hide an innocent young Mexican from a lynch mob and then go after the murderer who framed the boy.

THE TRAP

Copyrighted . . . . .September 26, 1952
Director . . . . Derwin Abbe
Teleplay . . . . .Sherman L. Lowe
Cast
William Boyd . . . . Hopalong Cassidy
Edgar Buchanan . . . . .Red Connors
Howard Negley . . . . .Lou Forler
Lane Bradford . . . . .Tom Stacy
Bill Henry . . . . .Norman Blaine
Cajan Lee . . . . Christine Russell
Maudie Prickett . . . . Maudie

Story: Hoppy tries to help an ex-convict, hoping to go straight, who is being blackmailed into joining a plot to rob the Cattlemen's Association.

Note: This episode is a remake of "Wedding Blackmail," a 1950 episode of *The Cisco Kid* TV series.

ALIEN RANGE

Copyrighted . . . . .October 1, 1952
Director . . . . Thomas Carr
Teleplay . . . . .Sherman L. Lowe
Cast
William Boyd . . . . Hopalong Cassidy
Edgar Buchanan . . . . Red Connors
Otto Waldis . . . . Vandermeer
Maria Palmer . . . . .Lilli Vandermeer
Glenn Strange . . . . .Simon Cosgrove
James Griffith . . . . Roscoe Hicks

Story: Hoppy and Red combat a rancher and a crooked lawyer who are trying to drive immigrant settlers off their land.

THE FEUD

Copyrighted . . . . October 28, 1952
Director . . . . Thomas Carr
Teleplay . . . . Sherman L. Lowe
Cast
William Boyd . . . . Hopalong Cassidy
Edgar Buchanan . . . . Red Connors
Hugh Beaumont . . . . .Frank Scofield
Lucia Carroll . . . . Nancy Croft
Steve Darrell . . . . Neil Croft
Harold Goodwin . . . . .John Emery
Herbert Lytton . . . . Doc

Story: Hoppy saves an innocent man from hanging and tracks down a murderer who's manipulating the feud between two rival ranchers.

GHOST TRAILS

Copyrighted . . . . .October 28, 1952
Director . . . . Thomas Carr
Teleplay . . . . .Harrison Jacobs
Cast
William Boyd . . . . Hopalong Cassidy
Edgar Buchanan . . . . .Red Connors
Frank Ferguson . . . . Deacon Denby
Edward Clark . . . . .Boyle
Jack Harden . . . . Gil
Ted Mapes . . . . Steve
John Cason . . . . Henchman
Charles F. Seel
Frank Jaquet
Tom London . . . . Morgan

Story: Hoppy tries to prove that a traveling preacher is behind a series of robberies by three men who have a habit of vanishing into thin air.

MARKED CARDS

Copyrighted . . . . .October 28, 1952
Director . . . . Derwin Abbe
Teleplay . . . . .Harrison Jacobs
Cast
William Boyd . . . . Hopalong Cassidy
Edgar Buchanan . . . . Red Connors
Tommy Ivo . . . . Tommy Lewis
George Wallace . . . . .Brad Mason
Crane Whitley . . . . Sam Coates
James Diehl . . . . .Jack Gardner
Emmett Vogan . . . . Judge Graham
John Deering . . . . Dick Lewis

Story: Hoppy uses an incriminating letter and a crooked card deck to hunt down the murderers of a small boy's parents.

DON COLORADO

Copyrighted . . . . December 1, 1952
Director . . . . .Derwin Abbe
Teleplay . . . . Sherman L. Lowe
Cast
William Boyd . . . . Hopalong Cassidy
Edgar Buchanan . . . . .Red Connors
Nelson Leigh . . . . Hobart
George Wallace . . . . .Roger Endicott
Noreen Nash . . . . Noreen Thomas
Stanley Blystone . . . . Doc
Bud Osborne . . . . .Stage Driver
John Frank . . . . .Manager

Story: Hoppy's efforts to save a young woman's mine from swindlers are complicated when Red Connors develops amnesia and claims to be a Spanish nobleman.

BLACK WATERS

Copyrighted . . . . December 1, 1952
Director . . . . Thomas Carr
Teleplay . . . . .Harrison Jacobs
Cast
William Boyd . . . . Hopalong Cassidy
Edgar Buchanan . . . . .Red Connors
Rick Vallin . . . . Johnny Tall Horse
Marilyn Nash . . . . Betty Turner
Walter Reed . . . . Blaine Turner
Morris Ankrum . . . . .Chief Tall Horse
Clarence Straight . . . . .Sheriff
Malcolm Beggs . . . . Brandon

Story: Hoppy uses an intricately carved bracelet to trap some swindlers who are trying to cheat the Indians out of their oil-rich reservation lands.

BLIND ENCOUNTER

Copyrighted . . . . December 1, 1952
Director . . . . Thomas Carr
Teleplay . . . . Sherman L. Lowe
Cast
William Boyd . . . . Hopalong Cassidy
Edgar Buchanan . . . . Red Connors
Pepe Hern . . . . Manuel Soledad
Denver Pyle . . . . .Poynter
Robert Bice . . . . .Andrews
Donna Martell . . . . .Carmencita Escobar
John Halloran . . . . Corporal Gonzales
Philip Van Zandt . . . . .Blackie
Argentina Brunetti . . . . Senora Soledad

Story: A blind Mexican woman asks Hoppy to help her fugitive son, who's been falsely accused of murder.

THE PROMISED LAND

Copyrighted . . . . December 10, 1952
Director . . . . Derwin Abbe
Teleplay . . . . Sherman L. Lowe
Cast
William Boyd . . . . Hopalong Cassidy
Edgar Buchanan . . . . .Red Connors
John Crawford . . . . Frank Dale
Maura Murphy . . . . Irene Mayo
Thurston Hall . . . . .Arnold Rivers
Edwin Parker . . . . Slim
Sandy Sanders . . . . Henchman
William Fawcett . . . . .Mr. Todd
Story: When Red Connors buys some arid land on the strength of a promised irrigation project, Hoppy investigates and learns that the promoters of the scheme are guilty of forgery, embezzlement and murder.

THE VANISHING HERD

Copyrighted . . . . December 12, 1952
Director . . . . Derwin Abbe
Teleplay . . . . .Harrison Jacobs
Cast
William Boyd . . . . Hopalong Cassidy
Edgar Buchanan . . . . Red Connors
Betty Ball . . . . Nelson Whitley
Edward Colmans . . . . Col. Chavez
Keith Richards . . . . .Ramon Gardena
Lee Roberts . . . . .Dillon
Pierce Lyden . . . . Burke
Edgar Carpenter . . . . Bascomb
Story: Hoppy helps government agents search for a herd of 625 stolen horses intended for the Spanish-American War, but when he finds the animals, he has to save them from a grass fire.

BLACK SHEEP

Copyrighted . . . . December 26, 1952
Director . . . . Derwin Abbe
Teleplay . . . . .Harrison Jacobs
Cast
William Boyd . . . . .Hopalong Cassidy
Edgar Buchanan . . . . Red Connors
Richard Crane . . . . Bob Norman
Richard Travis . . . . Rance Barlow
Claire Carleton . . . . Lucy Barlow
Antoinette Gerry . . . . Mary Warner
Edwin Parker . . . . .Biggs
Ted Mapes . . . . .Morse
Sam Flint . . . . .Sam Burger
Wheaton Chambers . . . . Doc
Story: Hoppy and Red try to settle a dispute between cattle ranchers and sheep grazers.

LAWLESS LEGACY

Copyrighted . . . . December 31, 1952
Director . . . . Derwin Abbe
Teleplay . . . . Royal Cole
Cast
William Boyd . . . . .Hopalong Cassidy
Edgar Buchanan . . . . .Red Connors
Claudia Barrett . . . . Judy Marlow
Stephen Rowland . . . . .Tom Marlow
Clayton Moore . . . . .Trimmer Lane
Marshall Reed . . . . Bob Hayes
Tim Graham . . . . .Judd Marlow
Edgar Dearing . . . . Sheriff
Story: Hoppy helps a young man and woman who are framed as counterfeiters just before they are to claim their uncle's estate.

Second Season, 1953-54

THE DEVIL'S IDOL

Copyrighted . . . . .October 9, 1953
Director . . . . George Archainbaud
Teleplay . . . . . . Robert Schaefer/Eric Freiwald
Cast
William Boyd . . . . .Hopalong Cassidy
Edgar Buchanan . . . . Red Connors
Ron Hagerthy . . . . Johnny Bolton
Nolan Leary . . . . .Rev. Edward Adams
Don C. Harvey . . . . Burke Ramsey
Harry Harvey . . . . Ed Garver
Danny Mummert . . . . Ralph Higgins
Story: Hoppy and a young minister try to convince a boy who's just committed his first holdup that his gunman idol has feet of clay.

THE SOLE SURVIVOR

Copyrighted . . . . .October 16, 1953
Director . . . . George Archainbaud
Teleplay . . . . .Ande Lamb
Cast
William Boyd . . . . Hopalong Cassidy
Edgar Buchanan . . . . Red Connors
Richard Reeves . . . . Fred Loomis
Kenneth MacDonald . . . . . . .Sheriff Gordon
Dorothy Green . . . . .Carol Madden
David Bruce . . . . Dick Madden
Harry Hines . . . . John Henderson
Story: As they ride into an apparently deserted town, Hoppy and Red are shot at, and then discover the town's only resident, also shot and left for dead.

THE VALLEY RAIDERS

Copyrighted . . . . .October 23, 1953
Director . . . . George Archainbaud
Teleplay . . . . .George W. Sayre
Cast
William Boyd . . . . .Hopalong Cassidy
Edgar Buchanan . . . . .Red Connors
Lyle Talbot . . . . Stephen Roberts
Henry Rowland . . . . .Morgan
Harte Wayne . . . . .Doctor

Story: Hoppy and Red discover that two out-laws have ambushed the sheriff of Stone Valley and determine to help the local ranchers against an exploiter who wants to take over the valley and sell it to the cavalry.

TWISTED TRAILS

Copyrighted . . . . .October 30, 1953
Director . . . . Derwin Abbe
Teleplay . . . . .Joseph O'Donnell
Cast
William Boyd . . . . Hopalong Cassidy
Edgar Buchanan . . . . .Red Connors
Herbert Lytton . . . . Frank Walton
Richard Farmer . . . . Gale
Gloria Talbott . . . . Pat Dougherty
Lane Bradford . . . . Buckley
George Spaulding . . . . Herb Dougherty
Wheaton Chambers . . . . .Cashier
Rusty Wescoatt . . . . Bart

Story: Hoppy fakes amnesia in an attempt to save the cattlemen's bank and the local ranchers from ruin springing from an embezzlement.

Note: This episode is a remake of the B Western feature Wolves of the Range (PRC, 1943), starring Bob Livingston and also written by Joseph O'Donnell.

THE LAST LAUGH

Copyrighted . . . . .November 6, 1953
Director . . . . Derwin Abbe
Teleplay . . . . Ande Lamb
Cast
William Boyd . . . . Hopalong Cassidy
Edgar Buchanan . . . . .Red Connors
Edward Clark . . . . .Mayor Hiram Tilden
Edgar Dearing . . . . .Richard Wald
Alan Wells . . . . .Don Moore
John Crawford . . . . Sid Michael
Jeanne Dean . . . . .Betty Black

Story: Hoppy poses as a cattle buyer in order to break up a ring of thieves who are stealing gold from a smelter.

THE JINX WAGON

Copyrighted . . . . .November 13, 1953
Director . . . . George Archainbaud
Teleplay . . . . . Robert Schaefer/Eric Freiwald
Cast
William Boyd . . . . Hopalong Cassidy
Edgar Buchanan . . . . Red Connors
Thurston Hall . . . . Dan Clemens
Steve Conte . . . . Lait
Myron Healey . . . . Rick Bayless
Paul Burns . . . . .Sandy Morgan
Kathleen Case . . . . .Ginny Clemens
Michael Thomas . . . . .Jeff Clemens

Story: Hoppy encounters bank robbers who are trying to recover the loot they hid in an old wagon inside the Twin Rivers livery stable.

ILLEGAL ENTRY

Copyrighted . . . . .November 20, 1953
Director . . . . George Archainbaud
Teleplay . . . . .Harrison Jacobs
Cast
William Boyd . . . . Hopalong Cassidy
Edgar Buchanan . . . . .Red Connors
Emerson Treacy . . . Wilberforce Lawrence Edgemont/The Professor
Harry Lauter . . . . Cal Foster
Frank Hagney . . . . Grimes
Spencer Chan . . . . .Sing Lee
Paul Marion . . . . Capt. Moreno
Larry Hudson . . . . Jim Morgan

Story: Hoppy and Red help the U.S. Immigration Service investigate the deaths of smuggled Chinese aliens.

GYPSY DESTINY

Copyrighted . . . . .November 27, 1953
Director . . . . Derwin Abbe
Teleplay . . . . Ande Lamb
Cast
William Boyd . . . . Hopalong Cassidy
Edgar Buchanan . . . . .Red Connors
Robert Cabal . . . . .Artaro
Pilar del Rey . . . . .Marella
Belle Mitchell . . . . .Mother Kiomi
Paul Richards . . . . .Jeff
John Merton . . . . Charley Mitchell
Frank Lackteen . . . . King Lasho

Story: Hoppy tries to prove that a gypsy boy's dead father was not a thief so that the boy can marry his sweetheart.

ARIZONA TROUBLESHOOTERS

Copyrighted . . . . December 4, 1953
Director . . . . George Archainbaud
Teleplay . . . . .William Lively
Cast
William Boyd . . . . Hopalong Cassidy
Edgar Buchanan . . . . .Red Connors
Richard Avonde . . . . Turk Shanns
Mort Mills . . . . George Byers
Howard Negley . . . . Big John Bragg
Gregg Barton . . . . .Jack Lawson
Nan Leslie . . . . Jane Sawyer
Ned Davenport . . . . Frank Sawyer

Story: Assigned to guard the workers building Arizona's first telegraph line, Hoppy learns that a supposedly retired man who owns several stores will lose a fortune if the line is completed, and uses wiretapping to foil a sabotage scheme.

DEATH BY PROXY

Copyrighted . . . . December 11, 1953
Director . . . . Derwin Abbe
Teleplay . . . . Cecile Kramer
Cast
William Boyd . . . . Hopalong Cassidy
Edgar Buchanan . . . . Red Connors
Paul Richards . . . . .Jim Adams
Fred Sherman . . . . Doc Weston
Duane Thorsen . . . . .Slade
Pierce Lyden . . . . Burke
Charles Cane . . . . .Frank Samuels
John Deering . . . . Bank Clerk

Story: Hoppy uses a health tonic to prove the innocence of a convicted murderer and the guilt of the real killer.

FRONTIER LAW

Copyrighted . . . . December 18, 1953
Director . . . . Derwin Abbe
Teleplay . . . . .William Lively
Cast
William Boyd . . . . Hopalong Cassidy
Edgar Buchanan . . . . Red Connors
Bill Henry . . . . Clay Morgan
Robert Griffin . . . . .Buck Staley
Barbara Knudson . . . . Jenny Warren
Pierre Watkin . . . . .Henry Warren
Marshall Reed . . . . .Rawhide Carney
Dan White . . . . .Bearcat Smith

Story: When Hoppy and Red try to conduct an honest election in outlaw territory, the outlaws retaliate by getting Hoppy's nephew into trouble.

Note: This episode is a remake of the B Western feature Marshal of Gunsmoke (Universal, 1944), starring Tex Ritter, and also written by William Lively.

DON'T BELIEVE IN GHOSTS

Copyrighted . . . . December 25, 1953
Director . . . . George Archainbaud
Teleplay . . . . Ande'Lamb
Cast
William Boyd . . . . Hopalong Cassidy
Edgar Buchanan . . . . .Red Connors
Anthony Sydes . . . . Billy Murdock
Aline Towne . . . . Dorothy Murdock
Carleton Young . . . . Henry Grant
Steve Pendleton . . . . Frank Ellis
Almira Sessions . . . . Miss Kerner
Stanley Blystone . . . . Sheriff Lane

Story: Hoppy risks death to convince the family and friends of vanished rancher Tom Murdock that his ghost has not returned from the dead to haunt them.

THE RENEGADE PRESS

Copyrighted . . . . .January 1, 1954
Director . . . . George Archainbaud
Teleplay . . . . . . Robert Schaefer/Eric Freiwald
Cast
William Boyd . . . . Hopalong Cassidy
Edgar Buchanan . . . . .Red Connors
Rick Vallin . . . . .Ramon Torres
William Fawcett . . . . .Tom McLean
Terry Frost . . . . .Steve
William Phillips . . . . Frank Harrison
Lou Nova . . . . .Jim Woods
I. Stanford Jolley . . . . Wade

Story: In his search for a gang counterfeiting Mexican currency, Hoppy learns that the Twin Rivers newspaper is printing more than news.

DOUBLE TROUBLE

Copyrighted . . . . .January 8, 1954
Director . . . . Derwin Abbe
Teleplay . . . . Joe Richardson
Cast
William Boyd . . . . Hopalong Cassidy
Edgar Buchanan . . . . Red Connors
Victor Millan . . . . Jose Martinez
Charlita Roeder . . . . .Maria Martinez
Sam Flint . . . . .Ollie Gray
Robert Knapp . . . . .Ted Gray
John Pickard . . . . Trig Dawson
Donald Novis . . . . Monte Kane

Story: Hoppy tries to help a young Mexican laborer whose knife was found in a banker's back.

COPPER HILLS

Copyrighted . . . . January 15, 1954
Director . . . . Derwin Abbe
Teleplay . . . . Harrison Jacobs
Cast
William Boyd . . . . Hopalong Cassidy
Edgar Buchanan . . . . Red Connors
Joseph Waring . . . . Tommy Red Arrow
George Wallace . . . . Judson Rush
Edwin Rand . . . . Constable Martin
Lee Roberts . . . . Leeds
Earle Hodgins . . . . Picture Pete
Paul Birch . . . . Nat Burnham
Story: While investigating raids by white men dressed as Indians, Hoppy and Red find valuable copper on the Indians' land.

NEW MEXICO MANHUNT

Copyrighted . . . . January 22, 1954
Director . . . . George Archainbaud
Teleplay . . . . William Lively
Cast
William Boyd . . . . Hopalong Cassidy
Edgar Buchanan . . . . Red Connors
Raymond Hatton . . . . Soakie
Russ Conway . . . . Frank Bent
Leslie O'Pace . . . . Sam Hardin
Douglas Kennedy . . . . Stacy Keller
Dolores Mann . . . . Marian
House Peters, Jr. . . . . Dakota
Story: Hoppy tries to clear an old prospector who's been found in possession of the gold stolen in a train robbery.

THE OUTLAW'S REWARD

Copyrighted . . . . January 29, 1954
Director . . . . George Archainbaud
Teleplay . . . . . Robert Schaefer/Eric Freiwald
Cast
William Boyd . . . . Hopalong Cassidy
Edgar Buchanan . . . . Red Connors
Harlan Warde . . . . Dr. Glenn Scott
John Alvin . . . . Frank Prescott
Griff Barnett . . . . Charles Scott
Elaine Riley . . . . Nancy Mathews
Denver Pyle . . . . Vic James
William Haade . . . . Al
Story: Hoppy steps in when a notorious outlaw tries to force his honest father and brother to help him collect the reward for his own capture.

GRUBSTAKE

Copyrighted . . . . February 2, 1954
Director . . . . Derwin Abbe
Teleplay . . . . Ande Lamb
Cast
William Boyd . . . . Hopalong Cassidy
Edgar Buchanan . . . . Red Connors
Christopher Dark . . . . Dr. Sheldon Lowe
Percy Helton . . . . Bummer Lowe
Gladys George . . . . Mrs. Turner
Robert Paquin . . . . Trem Hardy
Timothy Carey . . . . Dan Warner
Michael Fox . . . . Brock Fane
Story: Hoppy helps an old prospector whose discovery of gold has earned him several new friends and enemies.

STEEL TRAILS WEST

Copyrighted . . . . February 12, 1954
Director . . . . Derwin Abbe
Teleplay . . . . Harrison Jacobs
Cast
William Boyd . . . . Hopalong Cassidy
Edgar Buchanan . . . . Red Connors
Richard Powers . . . . Bill Bricker
Robert Bice . . . . Sam Murdock
Lewis Martin . . . . Jim Taggart
Donald Kennedy . . . . Bob Murdock
Story: Hoppy steps in when the nephew of a contractor building a railroad is killed and all the construction plans stolen.

SILENT TESTIMONY

Copyrighted . . . . February 19, 1954
Director . . . . George Archainbaud
Teleplay . . . . Ande Lamb
Cast
William Boyd . . . . Hopalong Cassidy
Edgar Buchanan . . . . Red Connors
Hank Patterson . . . . Pop Ashton
James Best . . . . Rick Ashton
Vici Raaf . . . . Trixie Brown
Richard Cutting . . . . Jason Rand
Keith Richards . . . . Pike Jenning
Steve Clark . . . . Marshal
Story: Hoppy helps an old settler and his son fight a land grabber who's determined to take over their ranch.

3-7-77

Copyrighted . . . . .February 26, 1954
Director . . . . George Archainbaud
Teleplay . . . . Ande Lamb
Cast
William Boyd . . . . Hopalong Cassidy
Edgar Buchanan . . . . .Red Connors
James Anderson . . . . Sheriff Ray Barnett
James Seay . . . . David Barnett
Ted Stanhope . . . . Chad Young
Leonard Penn . . . . Sam Wade
Dick Rich . . . . .Earl Fox
Bud Osborne . . . . .Stage Driver

Story: Hoppy frightens an outlaw gang by writing in prominent places the code numbers 3-7-77, the symbol of a band of vigilante terrorists.

MASQUERADE FOR MATILDA

Copyrighted . . . . .March 5, 1954
Director . . . . Derwin Abbe
Teleplay . . . . Joe Richardson
Cast
William Boyd . . . . Hopalong Cassidy
Edgar Buchanan . . . . .Red Connors
Hazel Keener . . . . Matilda Harron
Phil Tead . . . . Samuel Harron
George Keymas . . . . .Nail
Zon Murray . . . . .Jeb
Roy Barcroft . . . . . . .Constable Tom Gorham
Frank Marlowe . . . . Breck

Story: Hoppy tries to trick an elderly woman's kidnappers by inducing Red Connors to wear her clothes.

FRAME-UP FOR MURDER

Copyrighted . . . . .March 12, 1954
Director . . . . Derwin Abbe
Teleplay . . . . .Harrison Jacobs
Cast
William Boyd . . . . Hopalong Cassidy
Edgar Buchanan . . . . .Red Connors
Bill Henry . . . . Lt. Rex Melton
Ray Walker . . . . Morse
Robert Knapp . . . . Brenner
Harry Hayden . . . . Doctor

Story: Hoppy and Red arrest a young man whom they find wounded near the body of his uncle, but they soon learn that he's suffering from amnesia and try to clear him.

THE BLACK SOMBRERO

Copyrighted . . . . .March 19, 1954
Director . . . . Derwin Abbe
Teleplay . . . . George W. Sayre
Cast
William Boyd . . . . Hopalong Cassidy
Edgar Buchanan . . . . .Red Connors
Rick Vallin . . . . Marco Rodriquez
Cajan Lee . . . . .Dorothy Preston
Morris Ankrum . John Preston/Jose Hernandez
Duane Thorsen . . . . Belker
Larry Hudson . . . . Carter
Edward Colmans . . . . Felix Sanchez
Forrest Taylor . . . . .Judge
Tony Roux . . . . Servant

Story: When a Mexican rancher accuses an innocent man of murder, Hoppy uses a black sombrero to clear the frame-up victim and save a wealthy young heiress.

THE EMERALD SAINT

Copyrighted . . . . .March 26, 1954
Director . . . . George Archainbaud
Teleplay . . . . .J. Benton Cheney
Cast
William Boyd . . . . Hopalong Cassidy
Edgar Buchanan . . . . .Red Connors
George Wallace . .Sam Chapman/Jim Forrester
Don Alvarado . . . . Don Miguel Alvarez
Anna Navarro . . . . .Lola Alvarez
Jack Ingram . . . . .Frazer
Salvador Baguez . . . . Jose
Ted Bliss . . . . Wilks
Julia Montoya . . . . .Mexican Woman

Story: While chasing a murderer, Hoppy and Red are locked in a shrine with an emerald religious statue during a Mexican festival.

TRICKY FINGERS

Copyrighted . . . . April 2, 1954
Director . . . . George Archainbaud
Teleplay . . . . .Harrison Jacobs
Cast
William Boyd . . . . Hopalong Cassidy
Edgar Buchanan . . . . .Red Connors
Marjorie Lord . . . . Adele Keller
Mark Dana . . . . Harry Keller
Stanley Andrews . . . . Albert Biggs

Story: Hoppy and Red are trapped in a burning house by a lovely young woman who has robbed a bank while posing as an old lady.

One of the last publicity photos of William Boyd shot in the 1950s.

Top: Rand Brooks, William Boyd and Andy Clyde seem unhappy at the message Glenn Gallagher has just delivered in this scene from **Fool's Gold** (1947, United Artists). **Bottom:** Glenn Gallagher takes care of William Boyd and Andy Clyde while Stephen Barclay watches Rand Brooks and the army men in this scene from **Fool's Gold** (1947, United Artists).

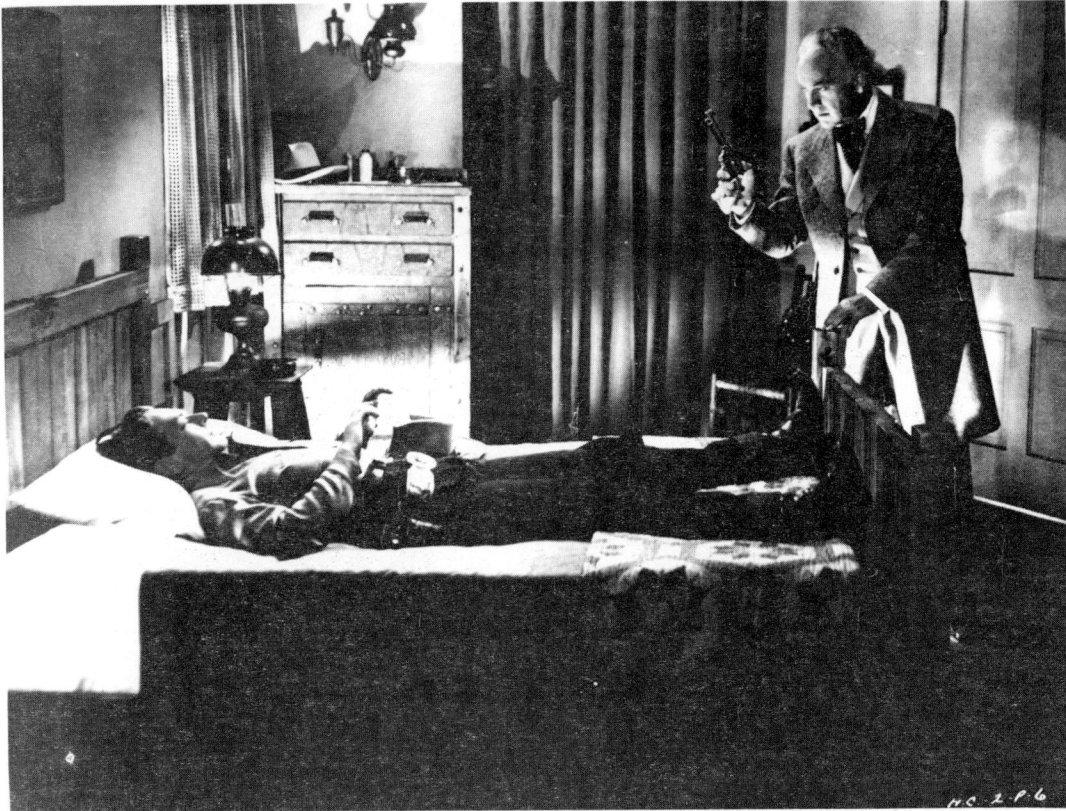

Top: Rand Brooks protests unknowingly as William Boyd gets ready to shoot the tarantula off the head board in this tense scene from **Fool's Gold** (1947, United Artists). **Bottom:** Andy Clyde, Rand Brooks and William Boyd don't seem pleased with villain Robert Emmett Keane's plan to let loose his tarantula friends while he makes his getaway in this climactic scene from **Fool's Gold** (1947, United Artists).

Top: A standard publicity pose for **Fool's Gold** (1947, United Artists) of Rand Brooks, Andy Clyde and William Boyd. **Bottom:** Another publicity photo from **Fool's Gold** (1947, United Artists) shows William Boyd pointing something out to saddle pals Andy Clyde and Rand Brooks.

Top: Another publicity photo of Rand Brooks, William Boyd and Andy Clyde but this time from **The Marauders** (1947, United Artists). **Bottom:** Something off camera concerns Rand Brooks, William Boyd, Andy Clyde and Elaine Riley in this scene from **False Paradise** (1948, United Artists).